STUDY GUIDE
Volume II

A History of Western Society

STUDY GUIDE
Volume II

James Schmiechen
Central Michigan University

A History of Western Society

Fourth Edition

John P. McKay
University of Illinois at Urbana-Champaign

Bennett D. Hill
Georgetown University

John Buckler
University of Illinois at Urbana-Champaign

HOUGHTON MIFFLIN COMPANY   BOSTON
DALLAS   GENEVA, ILLINOIS   PALO ALTO   PRINCETON, NEW JERSEY

Printed in the U.S.A.

ISBN: 0-395-55874-3

BCDEFGHIJ-WC-965432

Contents

To the Student   vii

Chapter 12   The Crisis of the Later Middle Ages   195

Chapter 13   European Society in the Age of the Renaissance   209

Studying Effectively—Exercise 3: Learning How to Identify Main Points That Are Effects, Results, Consequences   225

Chapter 14   Reform and Renewal in the Christian Church   227

Primary Sources: Two Sixteenth-Century Thinkers   245

Chapter 15   The Age of European Expansion and Religious Wars   249

Chapter 16   Absolutism and Constitutionalism in Western Europe (ca 1589–1715)   266

Chapter 17   Absolutism in Eastern Europe to 1740   284

Chapter 18   Toward a New World-View   299

Studying Effectively—Exercise 4: Learning to Classify Information According to Sequence   315

Chapter 19   The Expansion of Europe in the Eighteenth Century   318

Chapter 20   The Life of the People   332

Chapter 21   The Revolution in Politics, 1775–1815   344

Primary Sources: The Rights of Man and of Woman   361

Chapter 22   The Revolution in Energy and Industry   365

Studying Effectively—Exercise 5: Learning to Identify Main Points That Are Causes or Reasons   381

Primary Sources: Industrialization and Urban Life for the Working Classes   385

Chapter 23   Ideologies and Upheavals, 1815–1850   397

Chapter 24   Life in Urban Society   415

Chapter 25   The Age of Nationalism, 1850–1914   429

Primary Sources: Varieties of Socialism   447

Chapter 26   The West and the World   452

Chapter 27   The Great Break: War and Revolution   468

Studying Effectively—Learning to Make Historical Comparisons   485

Chapter 28   The Age of Anxiety   487

Chapter 29   Dictatorships and the Second World War   503

Chapter 30   The Recovery of Europe and the Americas   520

Chapter 31   Life in the Postwar Era   537

Chapter 32   The Recent Past, 1968 to the Present   548

Primary Sources: The Vietnam War   563

Appendixes   A-1

Answers to Objective Questions   A-1

Outline Maps   A-13

To the Student

How to Study History and Prepare for Exams

The study of history can be rewarding but also perplexing. Most history courses require you to read and understand large bodies of detailed information. The history student is expected to perform many tasks—memorize information, study the reasons for change, analyze the accomplishments and failures of various societies, understand new ideas, identify historical periods, pick out broad themes and generalizations in history, and so forth. These jobs often present difficulties. This guide will make your study easier and increase your efficiency. It has been developed to help you read, study, and review *A History of Western Society*, and regular and systematic use of it will improve your grade in this course. You may use the guide in a variety of ways, but for best results you might choose the following approach:

1. *Preview the entire chapter* by reading the "Chapter Questions" and "Chapter Summary"; then quickly read through the study outline, noting the reading with understanding exercises. All of this will take only a few minutes but is an important first step in reading. It is called *previewing*. By pointing out what the chapter is about and what to look for, previewing will make your reading easier and improve your reading comprehension.

2. *Now read your assignment in the textbook*. Pay attention to features that reveal the scope and major emphasis of a chapter or section, such as the chapter title, chapter and section introductions, questions, headings, conclusions, and illustrative material (e.g., maps and photographs). Note study hint 3 on page ix about underlining.

3. After reading, *review what you have read* and check your comprehension by going over the chapter outline once again—but this time make sure that you understand all the points and subpoints. If you do not fully understand a particular point or subpoint, then you need to return to the text and reread. It is not at all uncommon to need to read the text at least twice.

4. Continue your review. *Answer the review questions* that follow the study outline. It is best to write out or outline your answer on a sheet of paper or a note card. Be sure to include the supporting facts. Reread your answers periodically. This process will help you build a storehouse of information and understanding to use at the time of the exam.

5. Now work on the definitions, identifications, and explanations in the study-review exercises provided in each chapter of the *Study Guide*. This will help you to understand and recall both concepts and specific facts. Know not just who or what, but also why the term is significant. Does it illustrate or represent some fundamental change or process? Note that if a particular term appears in the text *and* in your lecture notes, it is of special importance. Do the geography exercises found in all appropriate chapters. This is important because they will enable you to visualize the subject matter and thus remember it better. It will take a few minutes, but the payoff is considerable. (Duplicate copies of all outline maps in the *Study Guide* can be found at the end of the book.)

6. Next, *complete the multiple-choice and fill-in exercises* for each *Study Guide* chapter. Some of these questions look for basic facts, while others test your understanding and ability to synthesize material. *The answers are at the end of the Guide*. If you miss more than two or three, you need to restudy the text or spend more time working on the *Guide*.

7. The section "Major Political Ideas" will help you understand some of the political concepts that are raised in the text. Keep a special section in your notebook where you write out the answers to these questions. By the time you take your exam you will have a good understanding of what these political concepts are and how and why they developed.

8. "Issues For Essay and Discussion" sets out one or two broad questions of the type you may be asked to answer in an essay exam or discuss in a classroom discussion. Answer these by writing a one to two page essay in which you address each part of the question with a well-organized answer based on material from the text. Remember, your instructor is looking for your ability to back up your argument with historical evidence.

9. Last, "Interpretation of Visual Primary Sources" is a way for you to expand your understanding of the chapter and to help you learn how to use prints, photographs, architectural artifacts and the like in assessing historical change. Keep a section in your notebook where you answer these questions—but also use your new skills in this area when you study the other visuals in the chapter. Don't be reluctant to make reference to these visual sources when you write your examination essays.

Additional Study Hints*

1. *Organize your study time effectively*. Many students fail to do well in courses because they do not organize their time effectively. In college, students are expected to read the material before class, review, and do the homework on their own. Many history teachers give only two or three tests during the semester; therefore, assuming personal responsibility for learning the material is vital. Mark up a semester calendar to show scheduled test dates, when term projects are due, and blocks of time to be set aside for exam study and paper writing. Then, at the beginning of each week, check the calendar and your course outlines

---

*For a complete text and workbook written to meet the needs of students who want to do their best in college, see James F. Shepherd, *RSVP, The Houghton Mifflin Reading, Study, and Vocabulary Program*, Third Edition (1988).

and notes to see what specific preparation is necessary for the coming week, and plan your time accordingly. Look at all the reading with understanding exercises in this *Study Guide* and try to estimate how much time you will need to master study skills. Set aside a block of time each day or once every several days for reading your text or studying your lecture notes and working in the *Study Guide*. Despite what one observes on college campuses, studying is not done most effectively late at night or with background music. Find a quiet place to study alone, one where you can tune out the world and tune into the past.

2. *Take good lecture notes*. Good notes are readable, clear, and above all reviewable. Write down as much of the lecture as you can without letting your pen get too far behind the lecturer. Use abbreviations and jot down key words. Leave spaces where appropriate and then go back and add to your notes as soon after the lecture as possible. You may find it helpful to leave a wide margin on the left side for writing in subject headings, important points, and questions, as well as for adding information and cross-references to the text and other readings. One way to use your notes effectively is by *reciting*. Reciting is the act of asking a question and then repeating the answer silently or aloud until you can recall it easily. Above all, do not wait until the night before an exam to use lecture notes you have not looked at for weeks or months. Review your lecture notes often and see how they complement and help you interpret your reading.

3. *Underline*. Too often students mark almost everything they read and end up with little else than an entire book highlighted in yellow. Underlining can be extremely helpful or simply a waste of time in preparing for exams; the key is to be selective in what you underline. Here are some suggestions:

   a. Underline major concepts, ideas, and conclusions. You will be expected to interpret and analyze the material you have read. In many cases the textbook authors themselves have done this, so you need to pinpoint their comments as you read. Is the author making a point of interpretation or coming to a conclusion? If so, underline the key part. Remember, learning to generalize is very important, for it is the process of making history make sense. The author does it and you must learn to identify his or her interpretation as well as conflicting interpretations; then to make your own. Here is where your study of history can pay big rewards. The historian, like a good detective, not only gathers facts but also analyzes, synthesizes, and generalizes from that basic information. This is the process of historical interpretation, which you must seek to master.

   b. Underline basic facts. You will be expected to know basic facts (names, events, dates, places) so that you can reconstruct the larger picture and back up your analysis and interpretations. Each chapter of this guide includes several lists of important items. Look over these lists before you begin to read, and then underline these words as you read.

   c. Look at the review questions in the *Study Guide*—they will point to the major themes and questions to be answered. Then, as you read, underline the material that answers these questions. Making marginal notations can often complement your underlining.

4. *Work on your vocabulary*. The course lectures and each chapter in the text will probably include words that you do not know. Some of these will be historical terms or special

concepts, such as *polis, feudalism,* or *bourgeoisie*—words that are not often used in ordinary American speech. Others are simply new to you but important for understanding readings and discussion. If you cannot determine the meaning of the word from the context in which it appears or from its word structure, then you will need to use a dictionary. *Keep a list of words* in your lecture notebook or use the pages in the back of this guide. Improving your historical and general vocabulary is an important part of reading history as well as furthering your college career. Most graduate-school entrance exams and many job applications, for instance, have sections to test vocabulary and reading comprehension.

5. *Benefit from taking essay exams.* Here is your chance to practice your skills in historical interpretation and synthesis. Essay exams demand that you express yourself through ideas, concepts, and generalizations as well as by reciting the bare facts. The key to taking an essay exam is preparation. Follow these suggestions:

    a. *Try to anticipate the questions on the exam.* As you read the text, your notes, and this guide, jot down what seem to be logical essay questions. This will become easier as the course continues, partly because you will be familiar with the type of question your instructor asks. Some questions are fairly broad, such as the chapter questions at the beginning of each chapter in this guide; others have a more specific focus, such as the review questions. Take a good look at your lecture notes. Most professors organize their daily lectures around a particular theme or stage in history. You should be able to invent a question or two from each lecture. Then answer the question. Do the same with the textbook, using the *Study Guide* for direction. Remember, professors are often impressed when students include in their essay textbook material not covered in class.

    b. *Aim for good content and organization.* Be prepared to answer questions that require historical interpretation and analysis of a particular event, series of events, movement, process, person's life, and so forth. You must also be prepared to provide specific information to back up and support your analysis. In some cases you will be expected to give either a chronological narrative of events or a topical narrative (for example, explaining a historical movement in terms of its social, political, and economic features). Historians often approach problems in terms of cause and effect, so spend some time thinking about events in these terms. Remember, not all causes are of equal importance, so you must be ready to make distinctions—and to back up these distinctions with evidence. This is all part of showing your skill at historical interpretation.

    When organizing your essay, you will usually want to sketch out your general thesis (argument) or point of interpretation first, in an introductory sentence or two. Next move to the substance. Here you will illustrate and develop your argument by weighing the evidence and marshaling reasons and factual data. After you have completed this stage (writing the body of your essay), go on to your conclusion, which most likely will be a restatement of your original thesis. It is often helpful to outline your major points before you begin to write. Be sure you answer all parts of the question. Write clearly and directly. All of this is hard to do, but you will get better at it as the course moves along.

6. *Enhance your understanding* of important historical questions by undertaking additional reading and/or a research project as suggested in the "Understanding History Through the Arts" and "Problems for Further Investigation" sections in the *Study Guide*. Note also that

each textbook chapter has an excellent bibliography. Many of the books suggested are available in paperback editions, and all of the music suggested is available in most record-lending libraries and record stores. If your instructor requires a term paper, these sections are a good starting point.

7. *Know why you are studying history.* Nothing is worse than having to study a subject that appears to have no practical value. And indeed, it is unlikely that by itself this history course will land you a job. What, then, is its value, and how can it enrich your life? Although many students like history simply because it is interesting, there are a number of solid, old-fashioned reasons for studying it. It is often said that we need to understand our past in order to live in the present and build the future. This is true on a number of levels. On the psychological level, identification with the past gives us a badly needed sense of continuity and order in the face of ever more rapid change. We see how change has occurred in the past and are therefore better prepared to deal with it in our own lives. On another level, it is important for us to know how differing political, economic, and social systems work and what benefits and disadvantages accrue from them. As the good craftsperson uses a lifetime of experience to make a masterpiece, so an understanding of the accumulated experiences of the past enables us to construct a better society. Further, we need to understand how the historical experiences of peoples and nations have differed, and how these differences have shaped their respective visions. Only then can we come to understand how others view the world differently from the ways in which we do. Thus, history breaks down the barriers erected by provincialism and ignorance.

The strongest argument for the study of history, though, is that it re-creates the big picture at a time when it is fashionable and seemingly prudent to be highly specialized and narrowly focused. We live in the Age of Specialization. Even our universities often appear as giant trade schools, where we are asked to learn a lot about a little. As a result, it is easy to miss what is happening to the forest because we have become obsessed with a few of the trees. While specialization has undeniable benefits, both societies and individuals also need the generalist perspective and the ability to see how the entire system works. History is the queen of the generalist disciplines. Looking at change over time, history shows us how to take all the parts of the puzzle—politics, war, science, economics, architecture, sex, demography, music, philosophy, and much more—and put them together so that we can understand the whole. It is through a study of the interrelationships of the parts over a long expanse of time that we can develop a vision of society. By promoting the generalist perspective, history plays an important part on today's college campus.

Finally, the study of history has a personal and practical application. It is becoming increasingly apparent to many employers and educators that neglect of the liberal arts and humanities by well-meaning students has left them unable to think and reason analytically and to write and speak effectively. Overspecialized, narrowly focused education has left these students seriously deficient in basic skills, and an understanding of the meaning of Western culture, placing them at a serious disadvantage in the job market. Here is where this course can help. The study of the past enables us to solve today's problems. It is universally recognized that studying history is an excellent way to develop the ability to reason and write. And the moving pageant of centuries of human experience you are about to witness will surely spark your interest and develop your aptitude if you give it the chance.

Chapter 12
The Crisis of the Later Middle Ages

Chapter Questions

After reading and studying this chapter you should be able to answer the following questions:

What economic difficulties did Europe experience in the later Middle Ages? What were the causes and the effects of the repeated attacks of plague and disease? Was war a catalyst for change? What political and social developments do new national literatures express? What provoked the division in the church in the fourteenth century? What impact did the schism have on the common people? What were the dominant features of life for ordinary people during this era?

Chapter Summary

The fourteenth century was a time of disease, war, crime, and violence. The art and literature of the period are full of the portrayal of death, just as the historical accounts are full of tales of conflict and violence. There were several major causes for this century of human suffering. Natural disaster—including changes in climate and horrible new diseases—attacked Europe. A long series of wars between France and England not only brought death and economic ruin but increased personal violence and crime as well. In addition, a serious shortage of labor, created by the bubonic plague, resulted in intense social conflict among landlords. Economic crisis during the century also resulted in a bitter struggle between urban workers and their guild masters.

Amid such violence the church lost power and prestige, partly because of the religious disillusionment that accompanied the plague. In short, the institutional church failed to fill the spiritual vacuum left by the series of disasters. A more immediate reason for the decline of the church's influence and prestige was the Babylonian Captivity and the Great Schism. The call for reform, often in the form of the conciliar movement, by people such as Marsiglio of Padua and John Wyclif, was a signal of things to come in the sixteenth century.

But the century of disaster was also a century of change, some of it for the good of ordinary people. It is in this light that the chapter examines some important changes in marriage practices, family relations, and the life of the people. The decline in population meant that those who survived had better food and higher wages. Peasants in western Europe used the labor-shortage problem to demand higher wages and freedom from serfdom. These demands often resulted in conflict with their lords. The disillusionment with the organized church also led to greater lay independence and, ultimately, ideas of social and political equality. The wars actually fostered the development of constitutionalism in England. All in all, it was a period of important changes.

Study Outline

Use this outline to preview the chapter before you read a particular section in your textbook and then as a self-check to test your reading comprehension after you have read the chapter section.

I. Death and disease in the fourteenth century
   A. Prelude to disaster
      1. Poor harvests led to famines in the years 1315–1317 and 1321.
      2. Diseases killed many people and animals.
      3. Economies slowed down and population growth came to a halt.
      4. Weak governments were unable to deal with these problems.
   B. The Black Death
      1. Genoese ships brought the bubonic plague—the Black Death—to Europe in 1347.
         a. The bacillus lived in fleas that infested black rats.
         b. The bubonic form of the disease was transmitted by rats; the pneumonic form was transmitted by people.
         c. Unsanitary and overcrowded cities were ideal breeding grounds for the black rats.
      2. Most people had no rational explanation for the disease, and out of ignorance and fear many blamed it on Jews, causing thousands of Jews to be murdered.
      3. The disease, which killed millions, recurred often and as late as 1700.
   C. The social and psychological consequences of the Black Death
      1. The plague hit the poor harder than the rich, but all classes suffered; the clergy was particularly affected.
      2. Labor shortages meant that wages went up and social mobility increased, as did per capita wealth.
      3. The psychological consequences of the plague were enormous: pessimism, gross sensuality, religious fervor, flagellantism, and obsession with death.
II. The Hundred Years' War (ca 1337–1453)
   A. The causes of the war
      1. Edward III of England, the grandson of the French king Philip the Fair, claimed the French crown by seizing the duchy of Aquitaine in 1337.
      2. French barons backed Edward's claim as a way to thwart the centralizing goals of their king.
      3. Flemish wool merchants supported the English claim to the crown.
      4. Both the French and the English saw military adventure as an excuse to avoid domestic problems.

    B. The popular response to the war
       1. Royal propaganda for war and plunder was strong on both sides.
       2. The war meant opportunity for economic or social mobility for poor knights, criminals, and great nobles.
    C. The Indian summer of medieval chivalry
       1. Chivalry, a code of conduct for the knightly class, enjoyed its final days of glory during the war.
       2. Chivalry and feudal society glorified war.
    D. The course of the war to 1419
       1. The battles took place in France and the Low Countries.
       2. At the Battle of Crécy (1346), the English disregarded the chivalric code and used new military tactics: the longbow and the cannon.
       3. The English won major battles at Poitiers (1356) and Agincourt (1415) and had advanced to Paris by 1419.
    E. Joan of Arc and France's victory
       1. Joan of Arc participated in the lifting of the British siege of Orleans in 1429.
       2. She was turned over to the English and burned as a heretic in 1431.
    F. Costs and consequences
       1. The war meant economic and population decline for both France and England.
       2. Taxes on wool to finance the war caused a slump in the English wool trade.
       3. In England, returning soldiers caused social problems.
       4. The war encouraged the growth of parliamentary government, particularly in England.
          a. The "Commons" (knights and burgesses) acquired the right to approve all taxes and developed its own organization.
          b. In France, neither the king nor the provincial assemblies wanted a national assembly.
       5. The war generated feelings of nationalism in England and France.
III. Vernacular literature
    A. The emergence of national consciousness is seen in the rise of literature written in national languages—the vernacular.
    B. Three literary masterpieces manifest this new national pride.
       1. Dante's *Divine Comedy*, a symbolic pilgrimage through Hell, Purgatory, and Paradise to God, embodies the psychological tensions of the age and contains bitter criticism of some church authorities.
       2. Chaucer, in the *Canterbury Tales*, depicts the materialistic, worldly interests of a variety of English people in the fourteenth century.
       3. Villon used the language of the lower classes to portray the reality, beauty, and hardships of life here on earth.
IV. The decline of the church's prestige
    A. The Babylonian Captivity (1309–1377)
       1. The pope had lived at Avignon since the reign of King Philip the Fair of France and thus was subject to French control.
          a. The Babylonian Captivity badly damaged papal prestige.
          b. It left Rome poverty-stricken.
       2. Pope Gregory XI brought the papacy back to Rome in 1377, but then Urban VI alienated the church hierarchy in his zeal to reform the church.

        3. A new pope, Clement VII, was elected, and the two popes both claimed to be legitimate.

   B. The Great Schism (1378–1417)

        1. England and Germany recognized Pope Urban VI, while France and others recognized the antipope, Clement VII.

        2. The schism brought the church into disrepute and wakened the religious faith of many.

   C. The conciliar movement was based on the idea of reform through a council of church leaders.

        1. Marsiglio of Padua had claimed in 1324, in *Defensor Pacis*, that authority within the church should rest with a church council and not the pope and that the church was subordinate to the state.

        2. John Wyclif attacked papal authority and called for even more radical reform of the church.

           a. He believed that Christians should read the Bible for themselves, prompting the first English translation of the Bible.

           b. His followers, called Lollards, disseminated his ideas widely.

        3. Wyclif's ideas were spread to Bohemia by John Hus.

        4. An attempt in 1409 to depose both popes and select another led to a threefold schism.

        5. Finally, the council at Constance (1414–1418) ended the schism with the election of Pope Martin V.

  V. The life of the people in the fourteenth and fifteenth centuries

   A. Marriage and the family

        1. Marriage usually came at 16 to 18 years for women and later for men.

        2. Legalized prostitution existed in urban areas and was the source of wealth for some women.

        3. Economic factors, rather than romantic love, usually governed the decision to marry.

        4. Divorce did not exist.

        5. Many people did not observe church regulations and married without a church ceremony.

   B. Life in the parish

        1. The land and the parish were the centers of life.

        2. Opportunities to join guilds declined in the fourteenth century, and strikes and riots became frequent.

        3. Cruel sports, such as bullbaiting, and bearbaiting, as well as drunkenness, reflect the violence and frustrations of the age.

        4. Lay people increasingly participated in church management.

   C. Fur-collar crime

        1. In England, nobles returning from war had little to do and were in need of income; thus they resorted to crime.

        2. Kidnaping, extortion, and terrorism by the upper classes were widespread.

        3. Because governments were not able to stop abuses, outlaws such as Robin Hood sought to protect the people.

    D. Peasant revolts
       1. Peasants revolted against the nobility in France in 1358 (the *Jacquerie*), 1363, 1380, and 1420, and in England in 1381.
          a. One cause of the Peasant's Revolt of 1381 was the lords' attempt to freeze wages.
          b. In general, peasants were better off; the revolts were due to rising expectations.
          c. The 1381 revolt in England was due to economic grievances, antiaristocratic sentiment, and protest against taxes.
       2. Workers in Italy (the *ciompi*), Germany, and Spain also revolted.

Review Questions

Check your understanding of this chapter by answering the following questions.

1. What were the causes of the population decline that began in the early fourteenth century?
2. What was the source of the bubonic plague and why did it spread so rapidly in Europe?
3. What impact did the plague have on wages and the demand for labor? What happened to land values?
4. Describe the psychological effects of the plague. How did people explain this disaster?
5. What were the immediate and other causes of the Hundred Years' War?
6. Why did the people support their kings in war?
7. Did feudalism tend to encourage or prevent war? Explain.
8. What were the results of the Hundred Years' War? Who were the winners and losers within both countries?
9. How did the Babylonian Captivity greatly weaken the power and prestige of the church?
10. Why were there three popes in 1409? Who were they and how did this situation occur?
11. What was the conciliar movement and who were its advocates? Was this a revolutionary idea?
12. Why was Wyclif a threat to the institutional church?
13. What was fur-collar crime and why did it become a central feature of European life in the fourteenth and fifteenth centuries?
14. Did peasants' lives improve or deteriorate in the fourteenth and fifteenth centuries? In what ways?
15. What were the reasons for the French Jacquerie of 1358 and the English Peasants' Revolt of 1381?
16. Why did a great amount of conflict and frustration among guild members develop in the fourteenth century?

Study-Review Exercises

Define the following key concepts and terms.
Pasteurella pestis

fur-collar crime

English Statute of Labourers

conciliar movement

vernacular literature

craft guild

Identify and explain the significance of the following people and terms.
Queen Isabella of England

Hundred Years' War

Robin Hood

Marsiglio of Padua

Battle of Crécy (1346)

Martin V

Joan of Arc

Babylonian Captivity

Margaret Paston

Lollards

House of Commons

Edward III

John Hus

John Wyclif

Jacquerie

Explain the importance of each of the following concepts in late medieval life and describe what changes it was subject to in this period.

marriage

feudal chivalry

individual Christian faith

leisure time

nationalism

Test your understanding of the chapter by providing the correct answers.

1. In reaction to the calls for reform in the fourteenth century, the church *did/did not* enter into a period of reform and rejuvenation.

2. Prior to the plague in 1348, Europe experienced a period of unusually *good/bad* harvests.

3. The Hundred Years' War was between the kings of _____ and

   _____ .

4. The followers of the English theologian Wyclif. _____

5. Up to the nineteenth century, *economic/romantic* factors usually determined whom and when a person married.

6. For the most part, job mobility within the late medieval guilds tended to *increase/decrease*.

Place the following events in correct chronological order.

First instance of the bubonic plague in Europe
Babylonian Captivity
Start of the Hundred Years' war
Council of Constance
Battle of Crécy
Jacquerie
Dante's *Divine Comedy*
Great Schism

1.

2.

3.

4.

5.

6.

7.

8.

Multiple-Choice Questions

1. The conciliar movement was
   a. an effort to give the pope the power to use councils to wipe out heresy.
   b. the effort by the French lords to establish a parliament.
   c. a new monastic order vowing poverty.
   d. an attempt to place ultimate church authority in a general council.

2. The plague was probably brought into Europe by
   a. Chinese soldiers.
   b. Spanish warriors returning from South America.
   c. English soldiers pushing into France.
   d. Genoese ships from the Crimea.

3. In general, farm laborers who survived the bubonic plague faced
   a. higher wages.
   b. food shortages.
   c. the need to migrate.
   d. excommunication from the church.

4. Generally, the major new source of criminals after the Hundred Years' War was
   a. the urban mobs.
   b. the rural peasants.
   c. the nobility.
   d. the bourgeoisie.

5. Which of the following statements about the fourteenth century is *false?*
   a. The population declined.
   b. The standard of living fell drastically.
   c. The power of the church declined.
   d. War between England and France was frequent.

6. Most people in the fourteenth century believed that the Black Death was caused by
   a. bad air.
   b. poor sanitation and housing.
   c. a bacillus living in fleas.
   d. black rats.

7. Generally, the plague disaster of the fourteenth century resulted in all but which of the following for European society?
   a. Higher wages for most workers
   b. A severe decline in the number of German clergymen
   c. A decline in flagellantism
   d. An obsession with death

8. Which of the following did *not* participant in the Hundred Years' War?
   a. Edward III of England
   b. King Philip the Fair
   c. Joan of Arc
   d. The Dauphin Charles of France

9. One reason for peasant-landlord conflict in the fourteenth century was
   a. peasants' opposition to declining wages and inflation.
   b. landlords' attempts to legislate wages.
   c. land scarcity.
   d. peasants' refusal to be drafted for war service.

10. The author of *Defensor Pacis* and proponent of the idea that authority in the Christian church rested in a general council rather than in the papacy was
   a. Cardinal Robert of Geneva.
   b. Pope Urban V.
   c. John Wyclif.
   d. Marsiglio of Padua.

11. Which of the following statements about the Hundred Years' War is true?
   a. It discouraged representative government.
   b. It depressed the English wool trade.
   c. It increased the amount of arable land in England.
   d. It created a surplus of manpower.

12. The followers of the English theologian-reformer Wyclif were called
   a. Protestants.
   b. outlaws.
   c. Lollards.
   d. flagellants.

13. *Fur-collar crime* is a term used to describe
   a. the robbery and extortion inflicted on the poor by the rich.
   b. the criminal activity carried out by bandits such as Robin Hood.
   c. crimes committed by churchmen.
   d. the illegal activities of noblewomen.

14. After 1347, the Black Death generally moved
   a. from north to south.
   b. from west to east.
   c. from south to north.
   d. from east to west.

15. Initially the Hundred Years' War was fought over
   a. Aquitaine.
   b. King Edward III's claim to the French crown.
   c. the control of the Flemish wool trade.
   d. religion.

16. English military innovation(s) during the Hundred Years' War included
    a. the crossbow.
    b. the cannon and the longbow.
    c. cavalry.
    d. the pike.

17. Which of the following statements about marriage during the Middle Ages is true?
    a. Most marriages were based on romantic love.
    b. Most marriages were arranged.
    c. Divorce was common.
    d. Marriage without the church's sanction was unheard of.

18. Which of the following was a writer of vernacular literature?
    a. Dante
    b. Jacques de Vitry
    c. Clement VII
    d. Marsiglio of Padua

19. Which of the following statements about Joan of Arc is *false?*
    a. She dressed like a man.
    b. The English king was her greatest supporter.
    c. She was accused of being a heretic and was burned.
    d. She was from a peasant family.

20. For the French, the turning point of the Hundred Years' War was
    a. the relief of Paris.
    b. the defeat of the English fleet in the English Channel.
    c. the relief of Orléans.
    d. the Battle of Poitiers.

21. Prostitution in late medieval society
    a. did not exist.
    b. existed only among the lower classes.
    c. was not respected but was legalized.
    d. existed in the countryside but not the city.

22. In the fourteenth century craft guilds began to change in that
    a. master and journeyman distinctions began to disappear.
    b. the guilds lost control over the production process.
    c. apprenticeship was abandoned.
    d. membership became more restrictive and master-journeyman relations deteriorated.

23. Chaucer's *Canterbury Tales* is important because
    a. it depicts the impact of the plague on Italian life.
    b. it reflects the cultural tensions of the times.
    c. it illustrates the highly religious interests of most people.
    d. it show how people were obsessed with the next world.

24. The effect of the Hundred Years' War on England was that it
    a. brought great wealth in the form of cash reserves to England.
    b. caused a great increase in wool exports.
    c. allowed many English knights to become very rich.
    d. resulted in a great net loss in cash.

25. The English Peasants' Revolt most probably
    a. was the largest single uprising of the entire Middle Ages.
    b. was an event of little significance at the time.
    c. affected only a very small number of people.
    d. was engineered by the landowners.

Major Political Ideas

1. Define nationalism. How did the Hundred Years' War encourage nationalism? What is the purpose and function of a national assembly? Why did a national representative assembly emerge in England but not in France?

2. What were the ideas set forth by Marsiglio of Padua in his *Defensor Pacis*? What were the political implications of these ideas?

Issues for Essays and Discussion

Some historians have argued that war is the engine of change. Does this theory have any validity for the fourteenth century? Discuss this in terms of the political, economic, and social experience of the fourteenth century.

Interpretation of Visual Sources

Study the reproduction of the painting *The Plague-Stricken* on page 358 of the textbook. How did people respond to this mysterious disease? Look carefully at the figures in this painting. Who seems to be in control of the situation? Does the group of figures in the upper left-hand corner provide any information as to what was thought to be the origins of the disease?

Geography

Use maps 12.2 and 12.3 in the textbook to complete the following:

1. Locate the extent of the English possessions in France. What were the origins of English claims to French land?
2. Why was it unlikely that England could have held these territories permanently?
3. Locate the main centers of popular revolt in France and England.
4. Why were so many of the English revolts in the highly populated and advanced areas of the country?

Understanding History Through the Arts

1. What was the music of this period like? An excellent introduction is a recording, *Instruments of the Middle Ages and Renaissance*, with an accompanying illustrated book by David Munro (Angel recording number SB2-3810 [1976]). For the French chansons and the English madrigals, listen to the recording titled *The King's Singers Sing of Courtly Pleasures*, which includes text and translations (Angel recording number s-37025 [1974]).

2. How did the Black Death affect art? While some members of society responded to the plague with religious fervor, others merely looked to enjoy life as best they could. The fourteenth-century Italian writer Boccaccio wrote the *Decameron*, a series of bawdy tales told by a group of Florentine men and women who fled to the countryside to escape the plague.

Problems for Further Investigation

1. How can a single disease affect the course of history? Students interested in the plague should begin with G. C. Coulton, *The Black Death* (1929); P. Zeigler, *The Black Death: A Study of the Plague in Fourteenth Century Europe* (1969); and W. McNeill, *Plagues and Peoples* (1976).

2. What was the cause of the Hundred Years' War? What effect did it have on English and French society? E. Perroy, *The Hundred Years' War** (1951), is a good start for anyone interested in that subject.

3. Why did the peasant revolts start? Those interested in popular protest during this age should consult M. Mullett, *Popular Culture and Popular Protest in Medieval and Early Modern Europe* (1987). The fourteenth century is analyzed in the interesting book, *A Distant Mirror: The Calamitous Fourteenth Century* (1978) by B. W. Tuchman.

---

*Available in paperback.

4. What was the cause of the conflict between Philip the Fair of France and the pope? Was the French king out to destroy the power of the papacy? These and other questions are debated by a number of historians in C. T. Wood, ed., *Philip the Fair and Boniface VIII** (1967).

5. How did the plague affect religion? One of the results of the Black Death was a revival of Christian mysticism—a search for meaning in life through a personal relationship with God. One of the most popular books of this movement was *The Imitation of Christ** by Thomas à Kempis.

6. What was medieval chivalry and how did it reflect changes in medieval society? Begin your study with R. Barber, *The Knight and Chivalry** (1990). You may want to supplement this with M. W. Thompson, *The Decline of the Castle* (1988).

---

*Available in paperback.

Chapter 13
European Society in the Age of the Renaissance

Chapter Questions

After reading and studying this chapter you should be able to answer the following questions:

What does the term *Renaissance* mean? How did the Renaissance influence politics, government, and social organization? What were the intellectual and artistic hallmarks of the Renaissance? Did the Renaissance cause shifts in religious attitudes? What developments occurred in the evolution of the nation-state?

Chapter Summary

The Renaissance was an era of intellectual and artistic brilliance unsurpassed in European history. It is clear that some thinking people in this era, largely a mercantile elite, saw themselves living in an age more akin to that of the bright and creative ancient world than that of the recent dark and gloomy Middle Ages. Although many of the supposedly "new" Renaissance ideas are actually found in the Middle Ages, scholars generally agree that the Renaissance was characterized by a number of distinctive ideas about life and humanity—individualism, secularism, humanism, materialism, and hedonism.

The Renaissance began in Florence, Italy, in the late thirteenth century. It subsequently spread to the rest of Italy—particularly Rome—and then to northern Europe, where it developed somewhat differently. The best-known expressions of the bold new Renaissance spirit can be seen in the painting, sculpture, and architecture of the period. New attitudes were also found in education, politics, and philosophy; in Northern Europe new ideas of social reform developed. Although the Renaissance brought some benefits to the masses of people, such as the printing press, it was basically an elitist movement. A negative development of the age was a deterioration in the power and position of women in society.

In politics, the Renaissance produced an approach to power and the state that historians often call "new monarchies." The best known and most popular theoretician of this school was the Florentine Niccolò Machiavelli. Its most able practitioners are the fifteenth- and sixteenth-century monarchs of France, England, and Spain. In Italy, the city-state system led to wealthy and independent cities that were marvelously creative but also vulnerable to invasion and control from the outside by powerful Spanish and French kings.

Study Outline

Use this outline to preview the chapter before you read a particular section in your textbook and then as a self-check to test your reading comprehension after you have read the chapter section.

I. The evolution of the Italian Renaissance
  A. Beginnings
    1. The Renaissance was a period of commercial, financial, political, and cultural achievement in two phases, from 1050 to 1300 and from 1300 to about 1600.
    2. The northern Italian cities led the commercial revival, especially Venice, Genoa, and Milan.
    3. The first artistic and literary flowerings of the Renaissance appeared in Florence.
      a. Florentine mercantile families dominated European banking.
      b. The wool industry was the major factor in the city's financial expansion and population increase.
  B. Communes and republics
    1. Northern Italian cities were communes—associations of free men seeking independence from the local lords.
      a. The nobles, attracted by the opportunities in the cities, often settled there and married members of the mercantile class, forming an urban nobility.
      b. The *popolo*, or middle class, was excluded from power.
      c. Popolo-led republican governments failed, which led to the rule of despots (*signori*) or oligarchies.
      d. In the fifteenth century, the princely courts of the rulers were centers of wealth and art.
  C. The balance of power among the Italian city-states
    1. Italy had no political unity; it was divided into city-states such as Milan, Venice, and Florence, the Papal States, and a kingdom of Naples in the south.
    2. The political and economic competition among the city-states prevented centralization of power.
    3. Shifting alliances among the city-states led to the creation of permanent ambassadors.
    4. After 1494 a divided Italy became a European battleground.
II. Intellectual hallmarks of the Renaissance
  A. Many, like the poet and humanist Petrarch, saw the fourteenth century as a new golden age and a revival of ancient Roman culture.
  B. Individualism
    1. Literature specifically concerned with the nature of individuality emerged.
    2. Renaissance people believed in individual will and genius.
  C. The revival of antiquity
    1. Italians copied the ancient Roman lifestyle.
    2. The study of the classics led to humanism, an emphasis on human beings.
      a. Humanists sought to understand human nature through a study of pagan and classical authors *and* Christian thought.
      b. The humanist writer Pico della Mirandola believed that there were no limits to what human beings could accomplish.
    3. Ancient Latin style was considered superior to medieval Latin.

D. Secular spirit
1. *Secularism* means a concern with materialism rather than religion.
2. Unlike medieval people, Renaissance people were concerned with money and pleasure.
    a. In *On Pleasure,* Lorenzo Valla defended the pleasure of the senses as the highest good.
    b. In the *Decameron,* Boccaccio portrayed an acquisitive and worldly society.
3. The church did little to combat secularism; in fact, many popes were Renaissance patrons and participants.
E. Art and the artist
1. The *quattrocento* (1400s) and the *cinquecento* (1500s) saw dazzling artistic achievements, led by Florence and Rome.
2. Art and power
    a. In the early Renaissance, powerful urban groups commissioned works of art, which remained overwhelmingly religious.
    b. In the later fifteenth century, individuals and oligarchs began to sponsor works of art as a means of self-glorification.
    c. As the century advanced, art became more and more secular, and classical subjects became popular.
3. The style of art changed in the fifteenth century.
    a. The individual portrait emerged as a distinct genre.
    b. Painting and sculpture became more naturalistic and realistic, and the human body was glorified, as in the work of the sculptors Donatello and Michelangelo.
    c. A new "international style" emphasized color, decorative detail, and curvilinear rhythms.
    d. In painting, the use of perspective was pioneered by Brunelleschi and della Francesca.
4. The status of the artist
    a. The status of the artist improved during the Renaissance; most work was done by commission from a prince.
    b. The creative genius of the artist was recognized and rewarded.
    c. The Renaissance was largely an elitist movement; Renaissance culture did not directly affect the middle classes.
III. Social change during the Renaissance
A. Education and political thought
1. Vergerio wrote a treatise on education that stressed the teaching of history, ethics, and rhetoric (public speaking).
2. Castiglione's *The Courtier,* which was widely read, describes the model Renaissance gentleman as a man of many talents, including intellectual and artistic skills.
3. Machiavelli's *The Prince* describes how to acquire, maintain, and increase political power.
    a. Machiavelli believed that the politician should manipulate people and use any means to gain power.
    b. Machiavelli did not advocate amoral behavior but believed that political action cannot be governed by moral considerations.

    B. The printed word
1. The invention in 1455 of movable type by Gutenberg, Fust, and Schöffer made possible the printing of a wide variety of texts.
2. Printing transformed the lives of Europeans by making propaganda possible, encouraging a wider common identity, and improving literacy.

    C. Women in Renaissance society
1. Compared to women in the previous age, the status of upper-class women declined during the Renaissance.
2. Although the Renaissance brought improved educational opportunities for women, they were expected to use their education solely to run a household.
3. Women's status declined with regard to sex and love.
    a. Renaissance humanists laid the foundations for the bourgeois double standard.
    b. The rape of women by upper-class men was frequent and not considered serious.
4. Because of poverty, infanticide and abandonment of children were frequent and eventually led to the establishment of foundling hospitals.

    D. Blacks in Renaissance society
1. Beginning in the fifteenth century, black slaves were brought into Europe in large numbers.
2. Blacks as slaves and freemen filled a variety of positions, from laborers to dancers and actors and musicians.
3. The European attitude toward blacks was ambivalent—blackness symbolized both evil and humility.
4. In the Renaissance, blacks were displayed as signs of wealth.

IV. The Renaissance in the north began in the last quarter of the fifteenth century
    A. It was more Christian than the Renaissance in Italy, and it stressed social reform based on Christian ideals.
    B. Christian humanists sought to create a more perfect world by combining the best elements of classical and Christian cultures.
1. Humanists like Lefèvre believed in the use of the Bible by common people.
2. Thomas More, the author of *Utopia*, believed that society, not people, needed improving.
3. The Dutch monk Erasmus best represents Christian humanism in his emphasis on education as the key to a moral and intellectual improvement and inner Christianity.

    C. The stories of the French humanist Rabelais were distinctly secular but still had a serious purpose.
1. Like More, Rabelais believed that institutions molded individuals and education was the key to moral life.
2. He combined a Renaissance zest for life with a classical insistence on the cultivation of body and mind.

    D. Northern art and architecture were more religious than in Italy and less influenced by classical themes and motifs.
1. Van Eyck painted realistic, incredibly detailed works.
2. Bosch used religion and folk legends as themes.

V. Politics and the state in the Renaissance (ca 1450–1521)
   A. The "new" monarchs
      1. The fifteenth century saw the rise of many powerful and ruthless rulers interested in the centralization of power and the elimination of disorder and violence.
      2. Many of them, such as Louis XI of France, Henry VII of England, and Ferdinand and Isabella of Spain, seemed to be acting according to Machiavelli's principles.
      3. These monarchs invested kingship with a strong sense of royal authority and national purpose.
      4. The ideas of the new monarchs were not entirely original—some of them had their roots in the Middle Ages.
   B. France after the Hundred Years' War
      1. Charles VII ushered in an age of recovery and ended civil war.
         a. He expelled the English, reorganized the royal council, strengthened royal finances, reformed the justice system, and remodeled the army.
         b. He made the church subject to the state.
      2. Louis XI expanded the French state and laid the foundations of later French absolutism.
   C. England
      1. Feudal lords controlled the royal council and Parliament in the fifteenth century.
      2. Between 1455 and 1471, the houses of York and Lancaster fought a civil war called the Wars of the Roses that hurt trade, agriculture, and domestic industry.
      3. Edward IV and his followers began to restore royal power.
      4. The English Parliament had become a power center for the aristocracy but was manipulated by Henry VII into becoming a tool of the king.
      5. Henry VII used the royal council and the court of Star Chamber to check aristocratic power.
      6. Henry and his successors won the support of the upper middle class by linking government policy with their interests.
   D. Spain
      1. The *reconquista* was the centuries-long attempt to unite Spain and expel Arabs and Jews.
      2. The marriage of Ferdinand and Isabella was the last major step in the unification and Christianization of Spain.
         a. Under their reign, however, Spain remained a loose confederation of separate states.
         b. They used the *hermandades*, or local police forces, to administer royal justice.
      3. They restructured the royal council to curb aristocratic power.
      4. The church was also used to strengthen royal authority.
      5. Ferdinand and Isabella completed the *reconquista* in 1492, but many Jews remained.
         a. Jews were often financiers and professionals; many (called *conversos*) had converted but were still disliked and distrusted.
         b. Ferdinand and Isabella revived the Inquisition and used its cruel methods to unify Spain and expel the Jews.

Review Questions

Check your understanding of this chapter by answering the following questions.

1. What new social class developed in twelfth-century Italy? How did this social class affect the movement toward republican government?
2. What five powers dominated the Italian peninsula in the fifteenth century? How did the Italian city-states contribute to modern diplomacy?
3. How does the concept of individualism help explain the Renaissance?
4. How do Valla and Boccaccio illustrate and represent what Renaissance people were like?
5. What is humanism? What do humanists emphasize?
6. According to Vergerio, what is the purpose of education? Was he a humanist?
7. How does Castiglione's *The Courtier* define the "perfect Renaissance man"? How does this book serve as an example of humanism?
8. How did the invention of movable type revolutionize European life?
9. How did the Renaissance in northern Europe differ from that of Italy?
10. Discuss Christian humanism by describing the works and ideas of Thomas More and Desiderius Erasmus.
11. Why did Italy became a battleground for the European superpowers after 1494?
12. What were the obstacles to royal authority faced by the kings of France in the fifteenth century? How did Charles VII and his successors strengthen the French monarchy?
13. What devices did Henry VII of England use to check the power of the aristocracy and strengthen the monarchy?
14. Why is the reign of Ferdinand and Isabella one of the most important in Spanish history? What were their achievements in the areas of national power and national expansion?
15. Why were blacks valued in Renaissance society? What roles did they play in the economic and social life of the times?
16. In what ways did life for upper-class women change during the Renaissance?
17. How was Renaissance art different from medieval art? How did the status of the artist change?

Study-Review Exercises

Define the following key concepts and terms.

Renaissance

oligarchy

signori

communes

popolo

reconquista

humanism

secularism

individualism

materialism

hermandades

Machiavellian

Identify and explain the significance of the following people and terms.
English Royal Council and Court of Star Chamber

conquest of Granada

Habsburg-Valois wars

Brunelleschi's Founding Hospital in Florence

Pico della Mirandola

Desiderius Erasmus

Jan van Eyck

Thomas More

Donatello

Baldassare Castiglione

Niccolò Machiavelli

Johan Gutenberg

Lefèvre d'Etaples

Saint John Chrysostom

Lorenzo Valla

Savonarola

Jerome Bosch

François Rabelais

Explain why each of the following is considered a "new monarch."
Louis XI of France

Henry VII of England

Ferdinand and Isabella of Spain

Charles VII of France

Cesare Borgia

Test your understanding of the chapter by providing the correct answers.

1. The author of a best-selling political critique called *The Prince*. _____

2. Renaissance humanists tended to be *more/less* concerned about religion than about people.

3. In the fifteenth century, infanticide *increased/decreased*.

4. An important English humanist and the author of *Utopia*. _____

5. Generally, the legal status of upper-class women *improved/declined* during the Renaissance.

6. It *is/is not* clear that the economic growth and the material wealth of the Italian cities were direct causes of the Renaissance.

Multiple-Choice Questions

1. Which of the following statements about the earliest printed books is *false?*
    a. They dealt mainly with economic and business subjects.
    b. They encouraged literacy.
    c. Movable type was first developed in Mainz, Germany.
    d. They had an effect on the process of learning.

2. The Renaissance began in
    a. the Low Countries.
    b. Rome.
    c. France.
    d. Florence

3. The patrons of the Renaissance were mostly
    a. churchmen.
    b. the popes.
    c. the common people.
    d. merchants and bankers.

4. The frail and ugly king who began French economic and political recovery in the early fifteenth century was
    a. Henry Tudor.
    b. Charles VII.
    c. Philip the Fair.
    d. Louis XI.

5. It appears that in Renaissance society blacks were
   a. valued as soldiers.
   b. valued as servants and entertainers.
   c. considered undesirable and not allowed in society.
   d. not much in demand.

6. A major difference between northern and Italian humanism is that northern humanism stressed
   a. economic gain and materialism.
   b. social reform based on Christian ideals.
   c. pagan virtues.
   d. scholastic dogma over reason.

7. Local groups in Spain that were given royal authority to administer justice were the
   a. *conversos.*
   b. liberals.
   c. *hermandades.*
   d. royal tribunal.

8. The court of Star Chamber in England was
   a. a common-law court.
   b. under the control of the barons in the House of Lords.
   c. done away with by the powerful Tudors.
   d. used to check aristocratic power.

9. The superiority of the French monarch over the church was the object of the
   a. Pragmatic Sanction of Bourges.
   b. Habsburg-Valois wars.
   c. Declaration of Calais.
   d. Hundred Years' War.

10. Most of the northern Renaissance thinkers agreed that
    a. democracy, not monarchy, was the only workable political system.
    b. humanity is basically sinful.
    c. Christianity is unacceptable.
    d. society is perfectible.

11. The late-fifteenth-century ruler of England who ended the civil war and strengthened the crown was
    a. John I.
    b. William III.
    c. Henry II.
    d. Henry VII.

12. Which of the following statements about Florence at the time of the Renaissance is *false?*
    a. Its major industry was wool production.
    b. It lost probably half its population to the Black Death.
    c. It was a major banking center.
    d. It was an important Mediterranean port city.

13. The dome of St. Peter's in Rome is considered to be the greatest work of
    a. Brunelleschi.
    b. Donatello.
    c. Michelangelo.
    d. Ghiberti.

14. The term *Renaissance* means
    a. a rise in the average standard of living among the masses.
    b. a resurgence of art and culture in the fourteenth through sixteenth centuries.
    c. an increase in the population after the ravaging effects of the "Four Horsemen of the Apocalypse."
    d. the recovery of the church from economic and moral decline.

15. The financial and military strength of the towns of northern Italy was directly related to
    a. their wealth, which enabled them to hire mercenary soldiers to protect their commercial interests.
    b. their contractual and marital alliances with the rural nobility.
    c. protections provided them by the Holy Roman Emperor.
    d. their alliance with the papacy.

16. The northern Renaissance differed from the Italian Renaissance in that the former was characterized by all of the following *except*
    a. interest in biblical scholarship.
    b. an emphasis on secular and pagan themes in art.
    c. the combination of the best aspects of antiquity and Christianity.
    d. an emphasis on the use of reason.

17. Erasmus advocated
    a. paganism.
    b. Christian education for moral and intellectual improvement.
    c. a monastic life of contemplation and divorce from the material world.
    d. obedience to church doctrine and ritual.

18. The Renaissance artist of talent and ability often lived a life
    a. of economic desperation.
    b. of economic security through patronage.
    c. of luxury, but without social status.
    d. like that of the masses.

19. The most influential book on Renaissance court life and behavior was
    a. Castiglione's *The Courtier*.
    b. Machiavelli's *The Prince*.
    c. Augustine's *City of God*.
    d. Boccaccio's *Decameron*.

20. The best description of Machiavelli's *The Prince* is that it is
    a. a description of how government should be organized and implemented.
    b. a satire on sixteenth-century politics.
    c. a call for Italian nationalism.
    d. an accurate description of politics as practiced in Renaissance Italy.

21. The Wars of the Roses were
    a. civil wars between the English ducal houses of York and Lancaster.
    b. between England and France.
    c. civil wars between the English king, Henry VI, and the aristocracy.
    d. minor disputes among English gentry.

22. Just before the advent of Ferdinand and Isabella, the Iberian Peninsula could best be
    described as
    a. a homogeneous region sharing a common language and cultural tradition.
    b. a heterogeneous region consisting of several ethnic groups with a diversity of linguistic
       and cultural characteristics.
    c. tolerant of religious and ethnic traditions different from Christianity.
    d. a region dominated equally by Arabs and Jews.

23. Thomas More's ideas, as best expressed in his book *Utopia*, centered on the belief that
    a. evil exists because men and women are basically corrupt.
    b. political leaders must learn how to manipulate their subjects.
    c. social order is only an unattainable ideal.
    d. corruption and war are due to acquisitiveness and private property.

24. Renaissance men's view of educated women was that they should
    a. be encouraged and given an equal place in society.
    b. have a voice in the affairs of the city.
    c. not be encouraged in any manner.
    d. be allowed to add a social touch to the household, but otherwise remain subservient to
       men.

25. The culture of the Renaissance
    a. was largely limited to a small mercantile elite.
    b. was widely spread and practiced by a broad middle class.
    c. was confined to the church.
    d. affected all classes, including the peasants.

Major Political Ideas

1. What were the political ideas behind the concept of the "new monarch"?

2. In what ways does Machiavelli represent a change in political thought? What were his suggestions for and philosophy of the acquisition and meaning of political power?

Issues for Essays and Discussion

The Renaissance was a period during which many people began to think and act in different ways. Sometimes this is referred to as a "self-conscious awareness," a stress on "humanism," and a "secular spirit. " What do these terms mean? Answer by making specific reference to developments in literature, political thought, and art.

Interpretation of Visual Sources

1. Study the reproduction of the painting entitled *Death and the Miser* by Jerome Bosch on page 409 of your textbook. Describe how this painting reflects the religious orientation of the Renaissance in the north of Europe. What is happening in this scene? Account for as many symbolic references as you can. What do you believe to be Bosch's message?

2. Study the reproduction of the painting *Journey of the Magi* on page 397 of your textbook. How does this painting reflect corporate patronage of the arts? Is it a religious or a secular painting?

Geography

On Outline Map 13.1 provided, and using Map 13.1 in the textbook as a reference, mark the following: the names of the Italian city-states and their principal cities, underlining the five major powers of Venice, Milan, Florence, the Papal States, and the kingdom of Naples.

Outline Map 13.1

Understanding History Through the Arts

1. What does the music of the Renaissance tell us about the period? The music of the Renaissance is introduced in two recordings, *From the Renaissance* (STL-150) and *From the Renaissance-Concert* (STL-160), in the Time-Life series *The Story of Great Music* (1967), which also includes a book with a good introduction to the period and its musical styles, art, and history. Good written introductions to Renaissance music are H. Brown, *Music in the Renaissance** (1976), and G. Reese, *Music in the Renaissance* (1954).

2. What impact did Renaissance thinking have on the arts? Fine illustrations and a discussion of new directions in the arts are woven into a number of interesting essays on the age in D. Hay, *The Renaissance* (1967).

3. What were the interests and motives of Renaissance artists? A good introduction to Renaissance art and the life of the artist and writer is J. H. Plumb, *The Renaissance* (1961), which includes biographies of Michelangelo, Petrarch, da Vinci, and others and includes hundreds of color plates and a comprehensive history of Renaissance art.

4. How did the art of Rome and Florence differ? What characteristics did they share? Begin your study with R. Goldthwaite, *The Building of Renaissance Florence** (1983); M. Andres et al., *The Art of Florence*, 2 vols. (1989); and J. Andreae, *The Art of Rome* (1989). For the northern Renaissance see O. Benesch, *The Art of the Renaissance in Northern Europe* (1965). Two of the finest Renaissance artists are the subjects of M. Kemp and J. Roberts, *Leonardo Da Vinci, Artist, Scientist, Inventor* (1989), and M. Levey, *Giambattista Tiepolo* (1987).

Problems for Further Investigation

1. Was the Renaissance an age of progress and advancement? Urban and rural life, court life, war, and witchcraft are among the many aspects of Renaissance life covered in E. R. Chamberlin, *Everyday Life in Renaissance Times** (1967).

2. What did popular Renaissance writers believe to be important about the age in which they lived? One of the best ways to understand the Renaissance is to read the works of its participants. Three works dealt with in this chapter are Niccolò Machiavelli, *The Prince** (a number of paperback translations are available); Baldassare Castiglione, *The Courtier,** Charles Singleton, trans. (1959); and Thomas More, *Utopia.**

3. How did the Renaissance alter the status of women? Begin your study by reading J. Kelly-Gadol, "Did Women Have a Renaissance?" in R. Bridenthal and C. Koontz, eds., *Becoming Visible: Women in European History* (1977), and M. Rose et al., *Women in the Middle Ages and the Renaissance: Literary and Historical Perspectives* (1986).

---

*Available in paperback.

4. The Swiss historian Jacob Burckhardt called the Renaissance the "mother" of our modern world. Was the Renaissance as important as Burckhardt and others have claimed? Did it dramatically change the way people acted and the direction history was to take? These and other questions are considered in several historical debates on the Renaissance: D. Hay, ed., *The Renaissance Debate** (1965); B. Tierney et al., *Renaissance Man—Medieval or Modern?** (1967); and K. H. Dannenfeldt, ed., *The Renaissance—Medieval or Modern?** (1959).

---

*Available in paperback.

Studying Effectively—Exercise 3

Learning How to Identify Main Points That Are Effects, Results, Consequences

In the introduction to this *Study Guide* and in the "Studying Effectively" exercises 1 and 2, we noted that learning to underline properly plays an important part in college work. Underlining (or highlighting with a felt-tipped pen) provides a permanent record of what you study and learn. It helps you review, synthesize, and do your best on exams.

We suggested three simple guidelines for effective underlining or highlighting:*

1. Be selective; do not underline or highlight too much.
2. Underline or highlight the main points.
3. Consider numbering the main points.

These guidelines will help you in courses in many different subjects.

Cause and Effect in History

The study of history also requires learning to recognize special kinds of main points. These points are *explanatory* in nature. *They answer why and how questions,* thereby helping you to interpret and make sense of the historical record.

Two particularly important types of why and how questions focus on *cause* and *effect* in history. You are already familiar with questions of this nature, questions that provide much of history's fascination and excitement. "Why did the Roman Empire decline and fall?" That is, what *causes* explain the decline and fall of the Roman Empire? "What were the *effects* of the Black Death?" You should pay particular attention to questions of cause and effect. They give history meaning. They help you increase your ability to think and reason in historical terms.

Two other insights will help you greatly in identifying main points involving cause and effect. First, historians use a number of different words and verbal constructions to express these concepts. Thus "causes" often become "reasons" or "factors," or things that "account for," "contribute to," or "play a role in" a given development. "Effects" often become "results" or

---

*The guidelines for underlining are from *RSVP: The Houghton Mifflin Reading, Study, & Vocabulary Program*, third edition, by James F. Shepherd (Houghton Mifflin, 1988). We urge students to consult this very valuable book for additional help in improving their reading and study skills.

"consequences," or are "the product of an impact." In most cases students can consider such expressions as substitutes for cause and effect, although they should be aware this historians are not of one mind on these matters.

Second, cause and effect are constantly interrelated in the historical process. Yesterday's results become today's causes, which will in turn help bring tomorrow's results. To take examples you have studied, the *causes* of the fall of the Roman Empire (such as increasing economic difficulties) brought *results* (such as the self-sufficient agrarian economy) that contributed to—helped *cause*—the rise of Benedictine monasticism. In short, *a historical development can usually be viewed as a cause or an effect, depending on what question is being answered.*

Exercise A

Read the following passage once as a whole. Read it a second time to underline or highlight it in terms of main points identified as effects or results. Consider numbering the effects in the margin. Then do Exercise B at the end of the passage.

The effects of the invention of movable-type printing were not felt overnight. Nevertheless, within a half-century of the publication of Gutenberg's Bible of 1456, movable type brought about radical changes. Printing transformed both the private and the public lives of Europeans. Governments that "had employed the cumbersome methods of manuscripts to communicate with their subjects switched quickly to print to announce declarations of war, publish battle accounts, promulgate treaties or argue disputed points in pamphlet form. Theirs was an effort 'to win the psychological war.' " Printing made propaganda possible, emphasizing differences between various groups, such as Crown and nobility, church and state. These differences laid the basis for the formation of distinct political parties. Printed materials reached an invisible public, allowing silent individuals to join causes and groups of individuals widely separated by geography to form a common identity; this new group consciousness could compete with older, localized loyalties.

Printing also stimulated the literacy of lay people and eventually came to have a deep effect on their private lives. Although most of the earliest books and pamphlets dealt with religious subjects, students, housewives, businessmen, and upper- and middle-class people sought books on all subjects. Printers responded with moralizing, medical, practical, and travel manuals. Pornography as well as piety assumed new forms. Broadsides and flysheets allowed great public festivals, religious ceremonies, and political events to be experienced vicariously by the stay-at-home. Since books and printed materials were read aloud to the illiterate, print bridged the gap between written and oral cultures.

Exercise B

Study the last paragraph again. Can you see how it is a good example of the historical interaction of cause and effect? Do you see how a given development is an effect or a cause *depending on what historical question is being asked?* Be prepared for such "reversals" in the text, in lecture and class discussion, and on exams.

Hint: In the last paragraph, what is an *effect* of the invention of the printing press? (Ideas could be spread more rapidly.) What "stimulated"—helped *cause*—the spread of literacy? (The invention of the printing press. The authors develop this point further in Chapter 14.)

Chapter 14
Reform and Renewal in the Christian Church

Chapter Questions

After reading and studying this chapter you should be able to answer the following questions:

What late medieval religious developments paved the way for the adoption and spread of Protestant thought? What role did social and political factors play in the several reformations? What were the consequences of religious division? Why did Luther's ideas trigger political, social, and economic reactions and how did the Catholic church respond?

Chapter Summary

A great religious upheaval called the Protestant Reformation ended the centuries-long religious unity of Europe and resulted in a number of important political changes. In the sixteenth century, cries for reform were nothing new, but this time they resulted in revolution. There were a number of signs of disorder within the church, pointing to the need for moral and administrative reform. For example, it was the granting of indulgences that propelled Martin Luther into the movement for doctrinal change in the church. Luther had come to the conclusion that salvation could not come by good works or indulgences, but only through faith. This was to be one of the fundamental tenets of Protestantism and one of the ideas that pushed Luther and the German nobility to revolt against not only Rome but Rome's secular ally, the Holy Roman Emperor.

It is important to recognize that Luther's challenge to the authority of the church and to Catholic unity in Europe invited and supported an attack on the emperor by the German nobility. The pope and the emperor, as separate powers and allies, represented religious and political unity and conformity in Germany. Thus, the victory of Luther and the nobility was a victory for decentralized authority. It meant the collapse of Germany as a unified power in Europe. This is one reason Catholic France usually supported the German Protestants in their quarrel with Rome.

Outside of Germany the Protestant reformer Calvin had a greater impact on Europe than Luther. Calvin's harsh and dogmatic religion spread from Geneva into northern Europe, England, and Scotland. It was England, in fact, that eventually became the political center of Protestantism. Initiated by Henry VIII, the English Protestant Reformation was at first motivated by the personal and political interests of the king himself. The type of Protestantism eventually adopted by the Church of England was much more moderate—and closer to Catholicism—than that of Scotland.

With the Council of Trent of 1545–1563, the Catholic church, finding the Habsburgs unable to destroy the heretical Protestantism, launched a massive and partly successful Counter-Reformation to convince dissidents to return to the church.

All in all, Protestantism developed and spread for economic and political reasons as well as religious ones. In the end, Protestantism meant greater spiritual freedom for some individuals, but spiritual disunity and disorganization for Europe as a whole. In England, Scotland, the Scandinavian countries, and elsewhere, it contributed to the power of the nation and thus meant a further political division of Europe, while in Germany it slowed down the movement toward nationhood.

Study Outline

Use this outline to preview the chapter before you read a particular section in your textbook and then as a self-check to test your reading comprehension after you have read the chapter section.

I. The condition of the church (ca 1400–1517)
   A. The declining prestige of the church
      1. The Babylonian Captivity and the Great Schism damaged the church's prestige.
      2. Secular humanists satirized and denounced moral corruption within the church.
   B. Signs of disorder in the early sixteenth century
      1. The parish clergy, largely poor peasants, brought spiritual help to the people.
      2. Critics of the church wanted moral and administrative reform in three areas.
         a. Clerical immorality (neglect of celibacy, drunkenness, gambling) created a scandal among the faithful.
         b. The lack of education of the clergy and law standards of ordination were condemned by Christian humanists.
         c. The absenteeism, pluralism (holding of several benefices, or offices), and wealth of the greater clergy bore little resemblance to Christian gospel.
      2. The prelates and popes of the period, often members of the nobility, lived in splendor and moral corruption.
   C. Signs of vitality in the late fifteenth and early sixteenth centuries
      1. Sixteenth-century Europe remained deeply religious, and calls for reform testify to the spiritual vitality of the church.
      2. New organizations were formed to educate and minister to the poor.
         a. The Brethren of the Common Life in Holland lived simply and sought to make religion a personal, inner experience based on following the scriptures.
         b. *The Imitation of Christ* by Thomas à Kempis urged Christians to seek perfection in a simple way of life.
         c. The Oratories of Dive Love in Italy were groups of priests who worked to revive the church through prayer and preaching.
      3. Pope Julius II summoned an ecumenical council on reform in the church called the Lateran Council (1512–1527).

II. Martin Luther and the birth of Protestantism
- A. Luther's early years
  1. Luther was a German monk and professor of religion whose search for salvation led him to the letters of St. Paul.
  2. He concluded that faith was central to Christianity and the only means of salvation.
- B. Luther's Ninety-five Theses (October 1517)
  1. Luther's opposition to the sale of indulgences (remissions of penalties for sin) prompted his fight with Rome.
  2. His Ninety-five Theses, or propositions on indulgences, raised many theological issues and initiated a long period of debate in Europe.
     a. Luther rejected the idea that salvation could be achieved by good works, such as indulgences.
     b. He also criticized papal wealth.
  3. Luther later denied the authority of the pope and was excommunicated and declared an outlaw by Charles V at Worms in 1521.
- C. Basic theological tenets of Protestantism
  1. Protestant thought was set forth in the Confession of Augsburg, in which Luther provided new answers to four basic theological issues.
     a. He believed that salvation derived through faith alone, not faith and good works.
     b. He stated that religious authority rests with the Bible, not the pope.
     c. He believed that the church consists of the entire community of Christian believers.
     d. And he believed that all work is sacred and everyone should serve God in his or her individual vocation.
  2. Protestantism, therefore, was a reformulation of Christian beliefs and practices

III. The social impact of Luther's beliefs
- A. By 1521 Luther's religious ideas had a vast following among all social classes.
  1. Luther's ideas were popular because of widespread resentment of clerical privileges and wealth.
  2. Luther's ideas attracted many preachers, and they became Protestant leaders.
  3. Peasants cited Luther's theology as part of their demands for economic reforms.
     a. Luther did not support the peasants' revolts; he believed in obedience to civil authority.
     b. Widespread peasant revolts in 1525 were brutally crushed, but some land was returned to common use.
  4. Luther's greatest weapon was his mastery of the language, and his words were spread by the advent of printing.
     a. Zwingli and Calvin were greatly influenced by his writings.
     b. The publication of Luther's German translation of the New Testament in 1523 democratized religion.
     c. Catechisms and hymns enabled people, especially the young, to remember central points of doctrine.
- B. Luther's impact on women
  1. Luther gave dignity to domestic work, stressed the idea of marriage and the Christian home, ended confession, and encouraged education for girls.

2. Luther held enlightened views on sex and marriage, although he claimed that women should be no more than efficient wives.

IV. Germany and the Protestant Reformation
  A. The Holy Roman Empire in the fourteenth and fifteenth centuries
    1. The Golden Bull of 1356 gave each of the seven electors virtual sovereignty.
    2. Localism and chronic disorder allowed the nobility to strengthen their territories and reduced the authority of the emperor.
  B. The rise of the Habsburg dynasty
    1. The Habsburgs gave unity to much of Europe, especially with the marriage of Maximilian I of Austria and Mary of Burgundy in 1477.
    2. Charles V, their grandson, inherited much of Europe and was committed to the idea of its religious and political unity.
  C. The political impact of Luther's beliefs
    1. The Protestant Reformation stirred nationalistic feelings in Germany against the wealthy Italian papacy.
    2. Luther's appeal to patriotism earned him the support of the princes, who used religion as a means of gaining more political independence and preventing the flow of German money to Rome.
    3. The Protestant movement proved to be a political disaster for Germany.
      a. The dynastic Habsburg-Valois wars advanced the cause of Protestantism and promoted the political fragmentation of Germany.
      b. By the Peace of Augsburg of 1555, Charles recognized Lutheranism as a legal religion and each prince was permitted to determine the religion of his territory.

V. The Growth of the Protestant Reformation
  A. Calvinism
    1. Calvin believed that God selects certain people to do his work and that he was selected to reform the church.
    2. Under Calvin, Geneva became a theocracy, in which the state was subordinate to the church.
    3. Calvin's central ideas, expressed in *The Institutes of Christian Religion*, were his belief in the omnipotence of God, the insignificance of humanity, and predestination.
    4. Austere living and intolerance of dissenters characterized Calvin's Geneva.
      a. The Genevan Consistory monitored the private morals of citizens.
      b. Michael Servetus was burned at the stake for denying the Christian dogma of the Trinity and rejecting child baptism.
    5. The city of Geneva was the model for international Protestantism, and Calvinism, with its emphasis on the work ethic, became the most dynamic and influential form of Protestantism.
  B. The Anabaptists
    1. This Protestant sect believed in adult baptism, revelation, religious tolerance, pacifism, and the separation of church and state.
    2. Their beliefs and practices were too radical for the times, and they were bitterly persecuted.

C. The English Reformation
1. The Lollards, although driven underground in the fifteenth century, survived and stressed the idea of a direct relationship between the individual and God.
2. The English humanist William Tyndale began printing an English translation of the New Testament in 1525.
3. The wealth and corruption of the clergy, as exemplified by Thomas Wolsey, stirred much resentment.
4. Henry VIII desired a divorce from his queen, Catherine, daughter of Ferdinand and Isabella of Spain, so he could marry Anne Boleyn.
5. Pope Clement VII (who did not wish to admit papal error) refused to annul Henry's marriage to Catherine.
6. Archbishop Cranmer, however, engineered the divorce.
7. The result was the nationalization of the English church and a break with Rome as Henry used Parliament to legalize the Reformation.
    a. Henry needed money so he dissolved the monasteries and confiscated their lands, but this did not lead to more equal land distribution.
    b. Some traditional Catholic practices, such as confession and the doctrine of transubstantiation, were maintained.
    c. Nationalization of the church led to changes in governmental administration, resulting in greater efficiency and economy.
8. Under Edward VI, Henry's heir, England shifted closer to Protestantism.
9. Mary Tudor attempted to bring Catholicism back to England.
10. Under Elizabeth I a religious settlement requiring outward conformity to the Church of England was made.

D. The establishment of the Church of Scotland
1. Scotland was an extreme case of clerical abuse and corruption.
2. John Knox brought Calvinism to Scotland from Geneva.
3. The Presbyterian church became the national church of Scotland.

E. Protestantism in Ireland
1. The English ruling class in Ireland adopted the new faith.
2. Most of the Irish people defiantly remained Catholic.

F. Lutheranism in Scandinavia
1. In Sweden, Norway, and Denmark the monarchy led the religious reformation.
2. The result was Lutheran state churches.

VI. The Catholic and the Counter-Reformations
A. There were two types of reform within the Catholic church in the sixteenth and seventeenth centuries.
1. The Catholic Reformation sought to stimulate a new religious fervor.
2. The Counter-Reformation started in the 1540s as a reaction to Protestantism and progressed simultaneously with the Catholic Reformation.

B. The slowness of institutional reform
1. Too often the popes were preoccupied with politics or sensual pleasures.
2. Popes resisted calls for the formation of a general council because it would limit their authority.

C. The Council of Trent
1. Pope Paul III called the Council of Trent (1545–1563).
    a. An attempt to reconcile with the Protestants failed.

b. International politics hindered the theological debates.
2. Nonetheless, the principle of papal authority was maintained, considerable reform was undertaken, and the spiritual renewal of the church was begun.
    a. Tridentine decrees forbade the sale of indulgences and outlawed pluralism and simony.
    b. Attempts were made to curb clerical immorality and to encourage education.
    c. Great emphasis was placed on preaching.
D. New religious orders
1. The Ursuline order of nuns gained enormous prestige for the education of women.
    a. The Ursulines sought to re-Christianize society by training future wives and mothers.
    b. The Ursulines spread to France and North America.
2. The Society of Jesus played a strong international role in resisting Protestantism.
    a. Obedience was the foundation of the Jesuit tradition.
    b. With their schools, political influence, and missionary work, they brought many people into the Catholic fold.
E. The Sacred Congregation of the Holy Office
1. This group, established by Pope Paul III in 1542, carried out the Roman Inquisition as a way to combat heresy.
2. It had the power to arrest, imprison, and execute, but its influence was confined to papal territories.

Review Questions

Check your understanding of this chapter by answering the following questions.

1. What was the condition of the church in 1517? Were the village clergy useless and corrupt?
2. What were some of the signs of disorder within the early sixteenth-century church? What impact did church wealth have on the condition of the church?
3. What were some of the signs of religious vitality in fifteenth- and early sixteenth-century society?
4. What circumstances prompted Luther to post his Ninety-five Theses?
5. Describe the practice of indulgence selling. What authority did Luther question and on what argument did he base his position?
6. What were Luther's answers, as delineated in the Confession of Augsburg, to the four basic theological issues?
7. What effect did Luther's concept of state authority over church authority have on German society and German history?
8. Why was the condemnation of Luther in 1521 at Worms not enforced by the German nobility? What was the result?
9. Why was Calvin's Geneva called "the city that was a church"? What is a theocracy?
10. In what ways were the Anabaptists radical for their time? Why did many of their beliefs cause them to be bitterly persecuted?
11. What were the causes and results of the English Reformation?
12. What was the Elizabethan Settlement?

13. What were the repercussions of the marriage of Maximilian and Mary? What impact did this marriage have on France?
14. Charles V has been considered a medieval emperor. In what respects is this true? What were the origins of his empire?
15. What were the goals and methods of the Ursuline order and the Society of Jesus?
16. Why was reform within the Catholic church often unwelcome and slow in coming?
17. What were the achievements of the Council of Trent?
18. What was the Inquisition? How extensive was its power?

Study-Review Exercises

Identify and explain the significance of the following people and terms.

Brethren of the Common Life

John Knox

Pope Paul III

Archbishop Cranmer

John Tetzel

Martin Luther

Angela Merici

Henry VIII

Charles V

Mary Tudor

Pope Alexander VI

Council of Trent

Counter-Reformation

Elizabethan Settlement

Act of Restraint of Appeals

pluralism

benefices

Peace of Augsburg

Ninety-five Theses

preacherships

Explain the subject matter and historical significance of the following works.
The Imitation of Christ

Appeal to the Christian Nobility of the German Nation

The Institutes of the Christian Religion

Define the basic beliefs of the following Christian religions and churches.
Roman Catholicism

Lutheranism

Calvinism

Anabaptism

Church of England

Presbyterian Church of Scotland

Test your understanding of the chapter by providing the correct answers.

1. The Council of Trent *did/did not* reaffirm the seven sacraments, the validity of tradition, and transubstantiation.

2. The English Supremacy Act of 1534 declared the _____ to be the Supreme Head of the Church of England.

3. For the most part, the English Reformation under Henry VIII dealt with *political/theological* issues.

4. He wrote: "How comes it that we Germans must put up with such robbery and such

    extortion of our property at the hands of the pope?" _____

5. This pope's name became a synonym for moral corruption. _____

6. Mary Tudor, the English queen and daughter of Henry VIII, *was/was not* interested in the restoration of Catholicism in England.

7. In general, Protestantism tended to *strengthen/weaken* Germany as a political unit.

8. During the reign of Elizabeth, the English church moved in a moderately *Protestant/Catholic* direction.

Multiple-Choice Questions

1. Under the Presbyterian form of church government, the church is governed by
    a. bishops.
    b. the king of Scotland.
    c. ministers.
    d. the people.

2. Which one of the following did *not* come from the Anabaptist tradition?
   a. Congregationalists
   b. Puritans
   c. Quakers
   d. Jesuits

3. According to Luther, salvation comes through
   a. good works.
   b. faith.
   c. indulgences.
   d. a saintly life.

4. The cornerstone of Calvin's theology was his belief in
   a. predestination.
   b. indulgences.
   c. the basic goodness of man.
   d. religious tolerance and freedom.

5. John Knox and the Reformation movement in Scotland were most influenced by which of the following?
   a. Catholicism
   b. Calvinism
   c. Lutheranism
   d. The Church of England

6. Which of the following is *not* identified with corrupt practices in the early sixteenth-century church?
   a. Pluralism
   b. The Brethren of the Common Life
   c. Pope Alexander VI
   d. Absenteeism

7. Which of the following clearly did *not* support Luther?
   a. The German peasants
   b. The German nobility
   c. Charles V
   d. Ulrich Zwingli

8. Overall, Henry VIII's religious reformation in England occurred
   a. strictly for economic reasons.
   b. for religious reasons.
   c. mostly for political reasons.
   d. mostly for diplomatic reasons.

9. The Reformation in Germany resulted in
   a. a politically weaker Germany.
   b. a politically stronger Germany.
   c. no political changes of importance.
   d. a victory for imperial centralization.

10. The great Christian humanists of the fifteenth and sixteenth centuries believed that reform could be achieved through
    a. the use of violent revolution.
    b. education and social change.
    c. mass support of the church hierarchy.
    d. the election of a new pope.

11. Luther tacked his Ninety-five Theses to the door in Wittenberg as a response to
    a. the sale of indulgences and papal wealth.
    b. a revelation he experienced instructing him to start a new church.
    c. the illiteracy of the clergy.
    d. the oppressive rule of Frederick of Saxony.

12. The peasants who revolted in 1525 wanted all of the following *except*
    a. the abolition of serfdom.
    b. the reform of the clergy.
    c. the suppression of Luther's movement.
    d. an end to taxes and tithes.

13. Luther's success was a result of all of the following *except*
    a. his appointment by the pope to a church position.
    b. the development of the printing press.
    c. his appeal to the nobility and the middle classes.
    d. a strong command of language.

14. The Holy Roman Emperor who tried to suppress the Lutheran revolt was
    a. Christian III.
    b. Charles V.
    c. Adrian VI.
    d. Henry VII.

15. By 1555 the Protestant Reformation had spread to all but
    a. England.
    b. Scandinavia.
    c. Spain.
    d. Scotland.

16. The chief center of the Protestant reformers in the sixteenth century was
    a. Paris.
    b. Geneva.
    c. Zurich.
    d. Cologne.

17. The Anabaptists appealed to
    a. the nobility.
    b. the poor, uneducated, and unemployed.
    c. the intellectuals.
    d. the merchant classes.

18. Henry VIII dissolved the monasteries largely because
    a. he wanted to distribute the land more equitably.
    b. they were symbolic of papal authority.
    c. he needed the wealth they would bring.
    d. they were a burden on the state.

19. The Scandinavian countries were most influenced by the religious beliefs of
    a. Martin Luther.
    b. John Knox.
    c. Olaus Petri.
    d. the Jesuits.

20. A vow of the Jesuit order making it uniquely different from others was
    a. poverty.
    b. chastity.
    c. obedience to the pope.
    d. pacifism.

21. Luther's German translation of the New Testament
    a. proved that the state was supreme over the church.
    b. convinced women that they had no constructive role in life.
    c. democratized religion.
    d. turned the common people away from the church.

22. The marriage of Maxmilian of Habsburg and Mary of Burgandy in 1477 was a decisive event in early modern history in that
    a. Austria became an international power.
    b. France emerged as the leading continental power.
    c. England became tied to Spain.
    d. German principalities became tied to Austria.

23. The man who wrote *The Institutes of the Christian Religion* and did the most to internationalize Protestantism was
    a. John Knox
    b. Martin Luther
    c. Ulrich Zwingli
    d. John Calvin

24. Henry VIII of England's divorce from his wife Catherine was complicated by the fact that Catherine's nephew was
    a. the pope.
    b. the emperor, Charles V.
    c. the king of France.
    d. the leader of the English Parliament.

25. The *Index of Prohibited Books* was published by
    a. the Calvinist government of Geneva.
    b. the princes who supported Luther.
    c. the Sacred Congregation of the Holy Office of the pope.
    d. the Anabaptists.

Major Political Ideas

1. In what ways was Protestantism a political idea? Did it help or hinder the development of the nation-state? Compare and contrast the religious settlements made in the German states, England, Scotland, and Ireland. Why was Protestantism on the one hand a source of national strength and on the other a source of national weakness?

2. What was the political message behind Luther's 1520 book *Appeal to the Christian Nobility of the German Nation*?

Issues for Essays and Discussion

Was the Reformation a blessing or a disaster for the people of Europe? Support your argument by making specific reference to Germany, England, and Scotland. What impact did the Reformation have on the power of the monarchs, the well-being of the common man and woman, and the overall balance of European power?

Interpretation of Visual Sources

Study the sixteenth-century woodcut titled *The Folly of Indulgences* on page 429 of your textbook. Describe the participants and the event. What is the message? What image of the church does this woodcut present to the popular mind? How important do you believe such prints were in forming public opinion?

Geography

On Outline Map 14.2 provided, and using maps 14.1 and 14.2 in the textbook as a reference, mark the following: the boundary of the Holy Roman Empire, the territory under the control of Charles V, the approximate areas of Lutheran influence, the approximate areas of Calvinist influence.

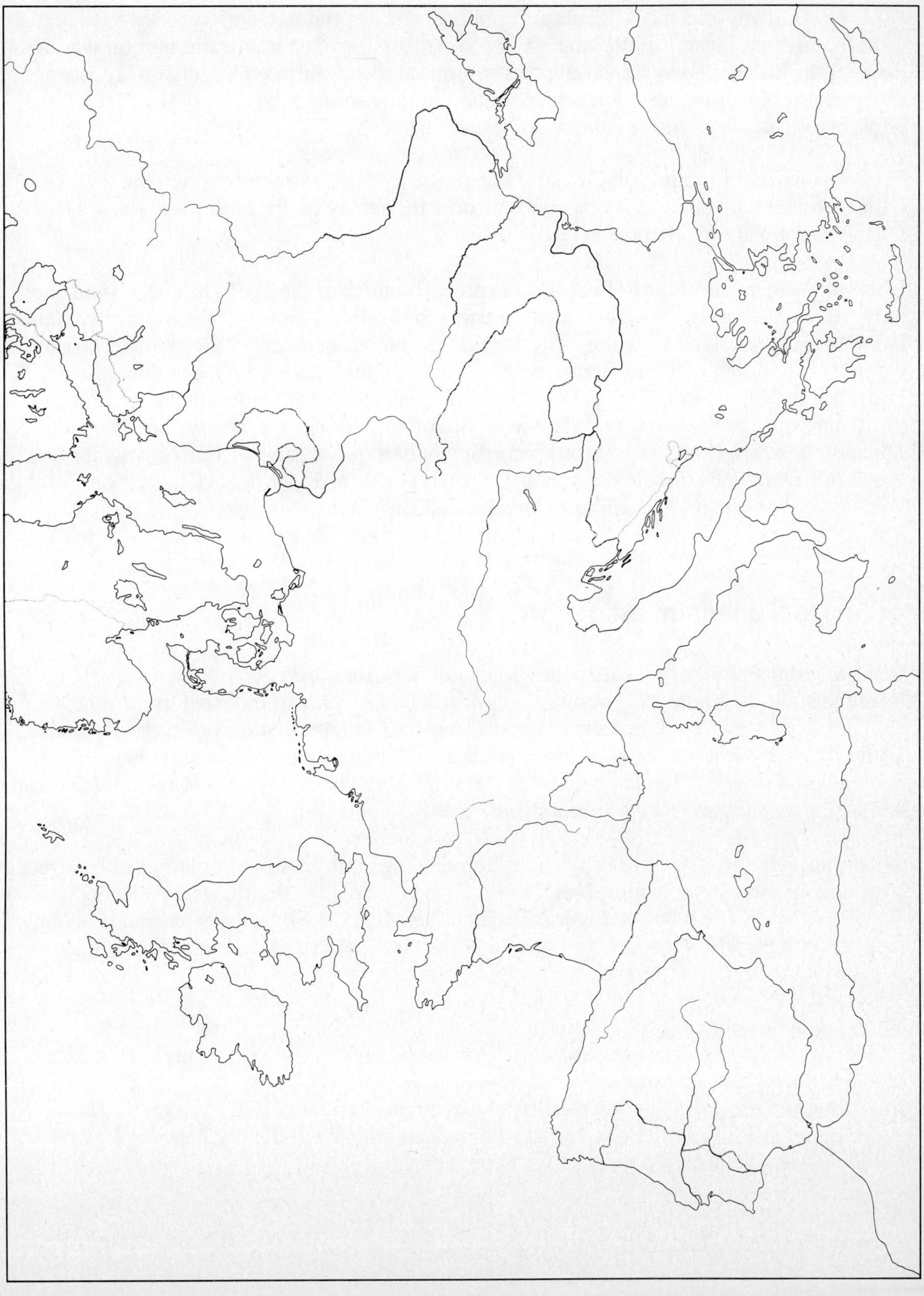

Outline Map 14.1

Understanding History Through the Arts

1. What effect, if any, did the religious and political strife of the sixteenth century have on the arts? In northern Europe in the later sixteenth century the most important painter was Pieter Bruegel the Elder, who avoided religious subjects and concentrated largely on landscapes and peasant life. Bruegel's work can be found in many sources, but one of the best is F. Grossmann, ed., *Bruegel, The Paintings: Complete Edition* (1956).

2. How was baroque architecture, in part, a response by the Catholic church to the threat of heresy and loss of believers? For a good introductory essay on the baroque style, see H. W. Janson, *History of Art*, Chapter 6 (1963).

3. How does the music of the Reformation express the spirit of the age? The church was the only place where music was regularly available to the public. Some of the most important baroque music evolved from the Protestant cities of north and central Germany. The leading composers of organ music in Germany were Dietrich Buxtehude in Lübeck, Johann Pachebell in Nuremberg, George Bohm in Luneburg, and Johann Sebastian Bach. For a written account of the baroque style, see M. Bukofzer, *Music in the Baroque Era: From Monteverdi to Bach* (1947). Numerous recording of baroque organ music are available; one of the best is *Dietrich Buxtehude, Organ Works*, vol. 1, performed by Michel Chapuis on Das Alte Werke, Telefunken. 6.42001.AF., and vol. 2. as 6.35307.EK.

Problems for Further Investigation

1. What led Martin Luther to launch the Protestant Reformation? Few men in history have been the subject of more biographies than Martin Luther. One of the most important is a psychological study by E. Erikson entitled *Young Man Luther: A Study in Psychoanalysis and History** (1962). Other books about Luther include R. Bainton, *Here I Stand** (1950); E. Schwiebert, *Luther and His Times* (1952); G. Forel, *Faith Active in Love* (1954); and J. Atkinson, *Martin Luther and the Birth of Protestantism** (1968).

2. What motivated Henry VIII's break with Rome? King Henry VIII of England is the subject of a number of interesting biographies. Three of the best are L. B. Smith, *Henry VIII* (1971); A. F. Pollard, *Henry VIII** (1905); and J. Scarisbrick, *Henry VIII* (1968). Henry's marital problems, as seen from his wife's side, are the subject of the fascinating and exciting *Catherine Of Aragon** (1941) by G. Mattingly.

3. What were the political implications of Calvinism? Start your investigation with R. Kingdom, *Calvin and Calvinism: Sources of Democracy** (1970). Students interested in further study of the religious revolution of the sixteenth century will find some of the problems of interpretation and investigation relative to that subject set out in L. W. Spitz, ed., *The Reformation** (1972), and K. Sessions, ed., *Reformation and Authority: The Meaning of the Peasant's Revolt** (1968).

---

*Available in paperback.

4. What is the relationship between the Protestant religion and economic growth? This historical problem is defined in R. Green, ed., *Protestantism, Capitalism, and Social Science* (1973).

5. How successful was the Counter-Reformation? Students interested in the Counter-Reformation should begin with E. M. Bums, *The Counter Reformation** (1964).

---

*Available in paperback.

Primary Sources
Two Sixteenth-Century Thinkers

Niccolò Machiavelli and Martin Luther were both mirrors of the sixteenth century, and both contributed to a new view of the relationship between man, God, and the state. However, Machiavelli is viewed as a man of the Renaissance, while Luther is largely associated with the Reformation. The following selections illustrate some of the similarities and some of the differences in their thought.

Niccolò Machiavelli, *The Prince**

Machiavelli was a political analyist, not a theoretician. He based his observations on politics and government and on practical reality, not an ideal state. What does he say here about effective political leadership? How could this be misconstrued to support authoritarian rule?

Here the question arises: is it better to be loved than feared, or vice versa? I don't doubt that every prince would like to have both; but since it is hard to accommodate these qualities, if you have to make a choice, to be feared is much safer than to be loved. For it is a good general rule about men, that they are ungrateful, fickle, liars, and deceivers, fearful of danger and greedy for gain. While you serve their welfare, they are all yours, offering their blood, their belongings, their lives, and their children's lives, as we noted above—so long as the danger is remote. But when the danger is close at hand, they turn against you. Then, any prince who has relied on their words and has made no other preparations will come to grief; because friendships that are bought at a price, and not with greatness and nobility of soul, may be paid for but they are not acquired, and they cannot be used in time of need. People are less concerned with offending a man who makes himself loved than one who makes himself feared: the reason is that love is a link of obligation which men, because they are rotten, will break any time they think doing so serves their advantage; but fear involves dread of punishment, from which they can never escape.

Still, a prince should make himself feared in such a way that, even if he gets no love, he gets no hate either; because it is perfectly possible to be feared and not hated, and this will be the

*Source: Reprinted from *The Prince* by Niccolò Machiavelli, Translated and Edited by Robert M. Adams. A Norton Critical Edition. With the permission of W. W. Norton & Company, Inc. Copyright © 1977 by W. W. Norton & Company, Inc.

result if only the prince will keep his hands off the property of his subjects or citizens, and off their women. When he does have to shed blood, he should be sure to have a strong justification and manifest cause; but above all, he should not confiscate people's property, because men are quicker to forget the death of a father than the loss of a patrimony. Besides, pretexts for confiscation are always plentiful; it never fails that a prince who starts living by plunder can find reasons to rob someone else. Excuses for proceeding against someone's life are much rarer and more quickly exhausted.

But a prince at the head of his armies and commanding a multitude of soldiers should not care a bit if he is considered cruel; without such a reputation, he could never hold his army together and ready for action. Among the marvelous deeds of Hannibal, this was prime: that, having an immense army, which included men of many different races and nations, and which he led to battle in distant countries, he never allowed them to fight among themselves or to rise against him, whether his fortune was good or bad. The reason for this could only be his inhuman cruelty, which, along with his countless other talents, [virtù], made him an object of awe and terror to his soldiers; and without the cruelty, his other qualities [le altre sua virtù] would never have sufficed. The historians who pass snap judgements on these matters admire his accomplishments and at the same time condemn the cruelty which was their main cause.

When I say, "His other qualities would never have sufficed," we can see that this is true from the example of Scipio, an outstanding man not only among those of his own time, but in all recorded history; yet his armies revolted in Spain, for no other reason than his excessive leniency in allowing his soldiers more freedom than military discipline permits. Fabius Maximus rebuked him in the senate for his failing, calling him the corrupter of the Roman armies. When a lieutenant of Scipio's plundered the Locrians, he took no action in behalf of the people; and did nothing to discipline that insolent lieutenant; again, this was the result of his easygoing nature. Indeed, when someone in the senate wanted to excuse him on this occasion, he said there are many men who knew better how to avoid error themselves than how to correct error in others. Such a soft temper would in time have tarnished the fame and glory of Scipio, had he brought it to the office of emperor; but as he lived under the control of the senate, this harmful quality of his not only remained hidden but was considered creditable.

Returning to the question of being feared or loved, I conclude that since men love at their own inclination but can be made to fear at the inclination of the prince, a shrewd prince will lay his foundations so what is under his own control, not on what is controlled by others. He should simply take pains not to be hated, as I said.

Sermon Preached by Martin Luther in Erfurt, Germany, 1521*

On his way to the Diet of Worms in 1521, Martin Luther preached this sermon to the citizens of Erfurt. What teachings of the Roman church did he criticize? What ideas of his own did he emphasize? And how did Luther think salvation was to be achieved? If you did not know who had written this sermon, how would you describe its author's mind and education?

Source: From *Luther's Works: Sermons I, Vol. 51*, edited by Helmut T. Lehmann and John W. Doberstein, translated by John W. Doberstein, copyright © 1959 Fortress Press. Used by permission of Augsburg Fortress.

Now it is clear and manifest that every person likes to think that he will be saved and attain to eternal salvation. This is what I propose to discuss now.

You also know that all philosophers, doctors and writers have studiously endeavored to teach and write what attitude man should take to piety. They have gone to great trouble, but, as is evident, to little avail. Now genuine and true piety consists of two kinds of work: those done for others, which are the right kind, and those done for ourselves, which are unimportant. In order to find a foundation, one man builds churches; another goes on a pilgrimage to St. James' or St. Peter's; a third fasts or prays, wears a cowl, goes barefoot, or does something else of the kind. Such works are nothing whatever and must be completely destroyed. Mark these words: none of our works have any power whatsoever. For God has chosen a man, the Lord Christ Jesus, to crush death, destroy sin, and shatter hell, since there was no one before he came who did not inevitably belong to the devil. The devil therefore thought he would get a hold upon the Lord when he hung between the two thieves and was suffering the most contemptible and disgraceful of deaths, which was cursed both by God and by men [cf. Deut. 21:23; Gal. 3:13]. But the Godhead was so strong that death, sin, and even hell were destroyed.

Therefore you should note well the words which Paul writes to the Romans [Rom. 5:12–21]. Our sins have their sources in Adam, and because Adam ate the apple, we have inherited sin from him. But Christ has shattered death for our sake, in order that we might be saved by his works, which are alien to us, and not by our works.

But the papal dominion treats us altogether differently. It makes rules about fasting, praying, and butter-eating, so that whoever keeps the commandments of the pope will be saved and whoever does not keep them belongs to the devil. It thus seduces the people with the delusion that goodness and salvation lies in their own works. But I say that none of the saints, no matter how holy they were, attained salvation by their works. Even the holy mother of God did not become good, was not saved, by her virginity or her motherhood, but rather by the will of faith and the works of God, and not by her purity, or her own works. Therefore, mark me well: this is the reason why salvation does not lie in our own works, no matter what they are; it cannot and will not be effected without faith.

Now, someone may say: Look, my friend, you are saying a lot about faith, and claiming that our salvation depends solely upon it; now, I ask you, how does one come to faith? I will tell you. Our Lord Christ said, "Peace be with you. Behold my hands, etc." [John 20:26–27]. [In other words, he is saying:] Look, man, I am the only one who has taken away your sins and redeemed you, etc.; now be at peace. Just as you inherited sin from Adam—not that you committed it, for I did not eat the apple, any more than you did, and yet this is how we came to be in sin—so we have not suffered [as Christ did], and therefore we were made free from death and sin by God's work, not by our works. Therefore God says: Behold, man, I am your redemption [cf. Isa. 43:3]; just as Paul said to the Corinthians: Christ is our justification and redemption, etc. [I Cor. 1:30]. Christ is our justification and redemption, as Paul says in this passage. And here our [Roman] masters say: Yes, Redemptor, Redeemer; this is true, but it is not enough.

Therefore, I say again: Alien works, these made us good! Our Lord Christ says: I am your justification. I have destroyed the sins you have upon you. Therefore only believe in me; believe that I am he who has done this; then you will be justified. For it is written, Justicia est fides, righteousness is identical with faith and comes through faith. Therefore, if we want to have faith, we should believe the gospel, Paul, etc., and not the papal breves, or the decretals, but rather guard ourselves against them as against fire. For everything that comes from the pope cries out: Give, give; and if you refuse, you are of the devil. It would be a small matter if they

248 / *Primary Sources*

were only exploiting the people. But, unfortunately, it is the greatest evil in the world to lead the people to believe that outward works can save or make a man good.

In conclusion, then, every single person should reflect and remember that we cannot help ourselves, but only God, and also that our works are utterly worthless. So shall we have the peace of God. And every person should so perform his work that it benefits not only himself alone, but also another, his neighbor. If he is rich, his wealth should benefit the poor. If he is poor, his service should benefit the rich. When persons are servants or maidservants, their work should benefit their master. Thus no one's work should benefit him alone; for when you note that you are serving only your own advantage, then your service is false. I am not troubled; I know very well what man-made laws are. Let the pope issue as many laws as he likes, I will keep them all so far as I please.

Therefore, dear friends, remember that God has risen up for our sakes. Therefore let us also arise to be helpful to the weak in faith, and so direct our work that God may be pleased with it. So shall we receive the peace he has given to us today. May God grant us this every day. Amen.

Chapter 15
The Age of European Expansion and Religious Wars

Chapter Questions

After reading and studying this chapter you should be able to answer the following questions:

Why and how did Europeans gain control over distant continents? What effect did overseas expansion have on Europe and on conquered societies? What were the causes of religious wars in France, the Netherlands, and Germany? How did the religious wars affect the status of women? How and why did African slave labor become the dominant form of labor organization in the New World? What religious and intellectual developments led to the growth of skepticism? What literary masterpieces did this period produce?

Chapter Summary

In this chapter we see how the trends in the High Middle Ages toward centralized nations ruled by powerful kings and toward European territorial expansion were revitalized. The growth of royal power and the consolidation of the state in Spain, France, and England accompanied and supported world exploration and a long period of European war.

The Portuguese were the first to push out into the Atlantic, but it was Spain, following close behind, that built a New World empire that provided the economic basis for a period of Spanish supremacy in European affairs. In the short run, Spanish gold and silver from the New World made the Spanish Netherlands the financial and manufacturing center of Europe, and Spain became Europe's greatest military power. In the long run, however, overseas expansion ruined the Spanish economy, created massive European inflation, and brought the end of Spain's empire in Europe.

The attempts by Catholic monarchs to re-establish European religious unity and by both Catholic and Protestant monarchs to establish strong centralized states led to many wars among the European states. Spain's attempt to keep religious and political unity within her empire led to a long war in the Netherlands—a war that pulled England over to the side of the Protestant Dutch. There was bitter civil war in France, which finally came to an end with the reign of

Henry of Navarre and the Edict of Nantes in 1598. The Thirty Years' War in Germany from 1618 to 1648 left that area a political and economic shambles.

The sixteenth century also saw a vast increase in witch-hunting and the emergence of modern racism, sexism, and skepticism. Generally, the power and status of women in this period did not change. Protestantism meant a more positive attitude toward marriage, but the revival of the idea that women were the source of evil and the end of the religious orders for women caused them to become increasingly powerless in society. North American slavery and racism had their origins in the labor problems in America and in Christian and Muslim racial attitudes. Skepticism was an intellectual reaction to the fanaticism of both Protestants and Catholics and a sign of things to come, while the Renaissance tradition was carried on by Shakespeare's work in early sixteenth-century England.

Study Outline

Use this outline to preview the chapter before you read a particular section in your textbook and then as a self-check to test your reading comprehension after you have read the chapter section.

I. Discovery, reconnaissance, and expansion (1450–1650)
   A. Overseas exploration and conquest
      1. The outward expansion of Europe began with the Viking voyages, then the Crusades, but the presence of the Ottoman Turks in the East frightened the Europeans and forced their attention westward.
      2. Political centralization in Spain, France, and England prepared the way for expansion.
      3. The Portuguese, under the leadership of Prince Henry the Navigator, pushed south from North Africa.
         a. By 1500 Portugal controlled the flow of gold to Europe.
         b. Diaz, da Gama, and Cabral established trading routes to India.
         c. The Portuguese gained control of the Indian trade by overpowering Muslim forts in India.
      4. Spain began to play a leading role in exploration and exploitation.
         a. Columbus sailed under the Spanish flag and opened the Caribbean for trade and conversion of the Indians.
         b. Spanish exploitation in the Caribbean led to the destruction of the Indian population.
         c. In 1519 Magellan sailed southwest across the Atlantic for Charles V of Spain; his expedition circumnavigated the earth.
         d. Cortez conquered the Aztec Empire and founded Mexico City as the capital of New Spain.
         e. Pizarro crushed the Inca empire in Peru and opened the Potosí mines, which became the richest silver mines in the New World.
      5. The Low Countries, particularly the cities of Antwerp and Amsterdam, had been since medieval times the center of European trade.
         a. The Dutch East India Company became the major organ of Dutch imperialism.
         b. The Dutch West India Company gained control of much of the African and American trade.

      6. France and England made sporadic efforts at exploration and settlement.
- B. The explorers' motives
  1. The desire to Christianize the Muslims and pagan peoples played a central role in European expansion.
  2. Limited economic and political opportunity for upper-class men in Spain led to emigration.
  3. Government encouragement was also important.
  4. Renaissance curiosity caused people to seek out new worlds.
  5. Spices were another important incentive.
  6. The economic motive—the quest for material profit—was the basic reason for European exploration and expansion.
- C. Technological stimuli to exploration
  1. The development of the cannon aided European expansion.
  2. New sailing and navigational developments, such as the caravel ship, the magnetic compass, and the astrolabe, also aided the expansion.
- D. The economic effects of Spain's discoveries in the New World
  1. Enormous amounts of American gold and silver poured into Spain in the sixteenth century.
  2. It is probable that population growth and not the flood of American bullion caused inflation in Spain.
  3. European inflation hurt the poor the most.
- E. Colonial administration
  1. The Spanish monarch divided his new world into four viceroyalties, each with a viceroy and *audiencia*, or board of judges that served as an advisory council and judicial body.
  2. The intendants were royal officials responsible directly to the monarch.
  3. The Spanish acted on the mercantilist principle that the colonies existed for the financial benefit of the mother country.
     a. The Crown claimed the *quinto*, one-fifth of all precious metals mined in South America.
     b. The development of native industries were discouraged.
  4. Portuguese administration in Brazil was similar to Spain's, although one unique feature was the thorough mixture of the races.

II. Politics, religion, and war
- A. The Spanish-French wars ended in 1559 with a Spanish victory, leading to a variety of wars centering on religious and national issues.
  1. These wars used bigger armies and gunpowder, and led to the need for administrative reorganization.
  2. Governments had to use various propaganda devices, including the printing press, to arouse public opinion.
  3. The Peace of Westphalia (1648) ended religious wars but also ended the idea of a unified Christian society.
- B. The origins of difficulties in France (1515–1559)
  1. By 1500, France was recovering from plague and disorder, and the nobility began to lose power.

2. The French kings, such as Francis I and Henry II, continued the policies of centralization and were great patrons of Renaissance art but spent more money than they raised.

3. The wars between France and Emperor Charles V—the Habsburg-Valois wars—were also costly.

4. To raise money, Francis sold public offices and signed the Concordat of Bologna (1516), in which he recognized the supremacy of the papacy in return for the right to appoint French bishops.
   a. This settlement established Catholicism as the state religion in France.
   b. It also perpetuated corruption within the French church.
   c. The corruption made Calvinism attractive to Christians eager for reform: some clergy and members of the middle and artisan classes.

C. Religious riots and civil war in France (1559–1589)

1. The French nobility, many of them Calvinist, attempted to regain power over a series of weak monarchs.

2. Frequent religious riots symbolized the struggle for power in the upper classes and serious religious concerns among the lower classes.

3. The Saint Bartholomew's Day massacre of Calvinists in 1572 led to the War of the Three Henrys, a damaging conflict for secular power.

4. King Henry IV's Edict of Nantes (1598) saved France from further civil war by allowing Protestants to worship.

D. The Netherlands under Charles V

1. The Low Countries were part of the Habsburg empire and enjoyed commercial success and relative autonomy.

2. In 1556 Charles V abdicated and divided his empire between his brother, Ferdinand, and his son, King Philip of Spain.

E. The revolt of the Netherlands (1556–1587)

1. Calvinism took deep root among the merchants and financiers.

2. Regent Margaret attempted to destroy Protestantism by establishing the Inquisition in the Netherlands.

3. She also raised taxes, causing those who opposed the repression of Calvinism to unite with those who opposed the taxes.

4. Popular support for Protestantism led to the destruction of many Catholic churches.

5. The duke of Alva and his Spanish troops were sent by Philip II to crush the disturbances in the Low Countries.

6. Alva's brutal actions only inflamed the religious war, which raged from 1568 to 1578.

7. The Low Countries were finally split into the Spanish Netherlands in the south, under the control of the Spanish Habsburgs, and the independent United Provinces of the Netherlands in the north.
   a. The north was Protestant and ruled by the commercial aristocracy.
   b. The south was Catholic and ruled by the landed nobility.

8. Elizabeth I of England supported the northern, or Protestant, cause as a safeguard against Spain attacking England.
   a. The wars in the Low Countries had badly hurt the Enlish economy.
   b. She had her rival Mary, Queen of Scots, beheaded.

F. Philip II and the Spanish Armada
1. Philip II planned war on England for several reasons.
   a. He wanted to keep England in the Catholic fold.
   b. He believed he would never conquer the Dutch unless he defeated England first.
2. The destruction of the Spanish Armada of 1588 did not mean the end of the war, but it did prevent Philip from forcibly unifying western Europe.
3. In 1609, Philip III agreed to a truce, recognizing the independence of the United Provinces.
G. The Thirty Years' War (1618–1648)
1. Protestant Bohemian revolt over religious freedom led to war in Germany.
2. The Bohemian phase (1618–1625) was characterized by civil war in Bohemia between the Catholic League and the Protestant Union.
   a. The Bohemians fought for religious liberty and independence from Habsburg rule.
   b. Ferdinand II wiped out Protestantism in Bohemia.
3. The Danish phase of the war (1625–1629) led to further Catholic victory.
4. The Swedish phase of the war (1630–1635) ended the Habsburg plan to unite Germany.
5. The French phase (1635–1648) ended with a destroyed Germany and an independent Netherlands.
   a. The "Peace of Westphalia" recognized the independent authority of the German princes.
   b. The treaties allowed France to intervene at will in German affairs.
   c. They also denied the pope the right to participate in German religious affairs.
H. Germany after the Thirty Years' War
1. The war was economically disastrous for Germany.
2. The war led to agricultural depression in Germany, which in turn encouraged a return to serfdom for many peasants.
III. Changing attitudes
A. The status of women
1. Literature on women and marriage called for a subservient wife, whose household was her first priority, and a protective, firm-ruling, and loyal husband.
   a. Catholic marriages could not be dissolved, while Protestants held that divorce and remarriage were possible.
   b. Women did not lose their identity or meaningful work, but their subordinate status did not change.
2. Prostitution was common, and brothels were licensed.
3. Protestant reformers believed that convents were antifeminist and that women would find freedom in marriage.
4. With the closing of convents, marriage became virtually the only occupation for upper-class Protestant women.
B. The great European witch hunt
1. Growth in religion and the advent of religious struggle led to a rise in the belief in the evil power of witches.
2. The thousands of people executed as witches represent society's drift toward social and intellectual conformity.

       3. Witch-hunting reflects widespread misogyny and a misunderstanding of women.

  C. European slavery and the origins of American racism

       1. Black slavery originated with the end of white slavery (1453) and the widespread need for labor, particularly in the new sugar-producing settlements.

       2. Africans were brought to America to replace the Indians beginning in 1518.

       3. Settlers brought to the Americas the racial attitudes they had absorbed in Europe from Christianity and Islam, which by and large depicted blacks as primitive and inferior.

IV. Literature and art

  A. The origins of modern skepticism in the essays of Montaigne

       1. Skeptics doubt whether definitive knowledge is ever attainable.

       2. Montaigne is the best representative of early modern skepticism and a forerunner of modern attitudes.

          a. In the *Essays* he advocated open-mindedness, tolerance, and rejection of dogmatism.

          b. He rejected the claim that one culture may be superior over another, and he inaugurated an era of doubt.

  B. Elizabethan and Jacobean literature

       1. Shakespeare reflects the Renaissance appreciation of classical culture, individualism, and humanism.

       2. The *Authorized Bible* of King James I (*King James Bible*) is a masterpiece of English vernacular writing.

  C. Baroque art and music

       1. In the late sixteenth century, the papacy and the Jesuits encouraged the growth of an emotional, exuberant art intended to appeal to the senses and kindle the faith of ordinary churchgoers.

       2. The baroque style took definite shape in Italy after 1600 and developed with exceptional vigor in Catholic countries.

          a. Rubens developed a sensuous, colorful style of painting characterized by animated figures and monumental size.

          b. In music the baroque style reached its culmination with Bach.

Review Questions

Check your understanding of this chapter by answering the following questions.

1. Describe the Portuguese explorations. Who were the participants and what were their motives?
2. What role did Antwerp and Amsterdam play in international commerce?
3. Why was there such severe inflation in the sixteenth century?
4. What role did technology play in European expansion?
5. What were the major reasons for European expansion in the fifteenth and sixteenth centuries?
6. What were the causes and consequences of the French civil war of 1559 to 1589? Was the war chiefly a religious or a political event?

7. What were the origins and the outcome of the war between the Netherlands and Spain in the late sixteenth and early seventeenth centuries?
8. What were the circumstances surrounding Elizabeth's decision to aid the United Provinces in their war against Spain? What was the Spanish reaction?
9. Why did Catholic France side with the Protestants in the Thirty Years' War?
10. What were the political, religious, and economic consequences of the Thirty Years' War in Europe?
11. What was the social status of women between 1560 and 1648?
12. What do the witch hunts tell us about social attitudes toward women?
13. What were the origins of North American racism?
14. What is skepticism? Why did faith and religious certainty begin to come to an end in the first part of the seventeenth century?
15. What were the major literary masterpieces of this age? In what ways can Shakespeare be regarded as a true Renaissance man?
16. What was the baroque style?

Study-Review Questions

Define the following key concepts and terms.

mercantilism

inflation

sexism

racism

skepticism

misogyny

baroque

Identify and explain the significance of the following people and terms.

politiques

Elizabeth I of England

Huguenots

Philip II of Spain

Prince Henry the Navigator

Michel de Montaigne

Christopher Columbus

Bartholomew Diaz

Hernando Cortez

Habsburg-Valois wars

quinto

audiencia

corregidores

Thirty Years' War

defeat of the Spanish Armada

Concordat of Bologna

Peace of Westphalia

Saint Bartholomew's Day massacre

War of the Three Henrys

Edict of Nantes

Test your understanding of the chapter by providing the correct answers.

1. The war that brought destruction and political fragmentation to Germany.

   _____

2. The Spanish explorer who conquered the Aztecs. _____

3. The law of 1598 that granted religious freedom to French Protestants.

   _____

4. Spain's golden century. _____

5. The king of Sweden who intervened in the Thirty Years' War. _____

6. After 1551, the seven northern provinces of the Netherlands were called

   _____.

7. The city that became the financial capital of Europe by 1600. _____

8. The monarch of Britain at the time of the Spanish Armada. _____

9. The idea that nothing is completely knowable. _____

10. The emperor who divided the Habsburg empire into two parts. _____

11. The 1516 compromise between church and state in France. _____

12. The first European country to establish sea routes to the east. _____

Multiple-Choice Questions

1. Which of the following was a motive for Portuguese exploration in the late fifteenth and sixteenth centuries?
   a. The search for gold
   b. The conversion of peoples to the Islamic religion
   c. The discovery of sea routes to North America
   d. The conquest of Constantinople

2. Beginning in 1581, the northern Netherlands revolted against their political overlord, which was
   a. France.
   b. Spain.
   c. Elizabeth I of England.
   d. Florence.

3. North American racist attitudes toward African blacks originated in
   a. South America.
   b. Spain.
   c. France.
   d. England.

4. In the Thirty Years' War, France supported
   a. the German Catholics.
   b. the Holy Roman Emperor.
   c. Spain.
   d. the German Protestants.

5. Which of the following statements about the Spanish Armada of 1588 is *false?*
   a. It was the beginning of a long war with England.
   b. It failed in its objective.
   c. It prevented Phillip II from reimposing unity on western Europe by force.
   d. It made possible Spanish conquest of the Netherlands.

6. The nation that considered itself the international defender of Catholicism was
   a. France.
   b. Spain.
   c. Italy.
   d. England.

7. Columbus, like many of his fellow explorers, was principally motivated by
   a. a desire to discover India.
   b. a desire to Christianize the Americans.
   c. the desire of Spain to control the New World.
   d. the Spanish need to control the Mediterranean.

8. The earliest known explorers of North America were
   a. the Spanish.
   b. the Vikings.
   c. the Italians.
   d. the English.

9. Which of the following statements describes a feature of Spanish colonial policy?
   a. The New World was divided into four vice-royalties.
   b. Native industries were established.
   c. Each territory had local officials, or *corregidores*, who held judicial and military powers.
   d. The Spanish crown had only indirect and limited control over colonies.

10. To gain control of the spice trade of the Indian Ocean, the Portuguese had to defeat
    a. Spain.
    b. England.
    c. the Muslims.
    d. France.

11. The main contribution of Cortez and Pizarro to Spain was
    a. the tapping of the rich silver resources of Mexico and Peru.
    b. the Christianizing of the New World peoples.
    c. the further exploration of the Pacific Ocean.
    d. the discovery of South Africa.

12. The flow of huge amounts of gold and silver from the New World caused
    a. serious inflation in Spain and the rest of Europe.
    b. the Spanish economy to become dependent on New World gold and silver.
    c. the suffering of the poor because of the dramatic rise in food prices.
    d. Spain's economic strength and dominance in Europe.

13. By which treaty did the king of France, Francis I, recognize the supremacy of the papacy?
    a. The Treaty of Westphalia
    b. The treaty of Cateau-Cambrésis
    c. The Concordat of Bologna
    d. The Edict of Nantes

14. France was saved from religious anarchy when religious principles were set aside for political necessity by King
    a. Henry III.
    b. Francis I.
    c. Henry IV of Navarre.
    d. Charles IX.

15. Calvinism was appealing to the middle classes for each of the following reasons *except*
    a. its heavy moral emphasis.
    b. its stress on leisure and ostentatious living.
    c. its intellectual emphasis.
    d. its approval of any job well done, hard work, and success.

16. The vast palace of the Spanish monarchs, built under the direction of Philip II, was called
    a. Versailles.
    b. the Escorial.
    c. Tournai.
    d. Hampton Court.

17. The Treaty of Westphalia, which ended the Thirty Years' War
    a. further strengthened the Holy Roman Empire.
    b. completely undermined the Holy Roman Empire as a viable state.
    c. maintained that only Catholicism and Lutheranism were legitimate religions.
    d. refused to recognize the independence of the United Provinces of the Netherlands.

18. Who among the following best represents early modern skepticism?
    a. Las Casas
    b. James I
    c. Calvin
    d. Montaigne

19. The Spanish missionary Las Casas convinced Charles V to import Africans to Brazil because of all the following *except*
    a. the enslavement of Africans seemed more acceptable to the church.
    b. he believed they could endure better than the Indians.
    c. the native Indians were not durable enough under such harsh conditions.
    d. the native Indians revolted and refused to work as slave labor.

20. The Portuguese explorer who first reached India was
    a. Bartholomew Diaz.
    b. Prince Henry the Navigator.
    c. Vasco da Gama.
    d. Hernando Cortez.

21. The style of art popular in late-eighteenth-century Europe was called
    a. Elizabethan.
    b. Jacobean.
    c. skepticism.
    d. baroque.

22. The appearance of gunpowder in Europe
    a. made the common soldier inferior to the gentleman soldier.
    b. changed the popular belief that warfare bettered the individual.
    c. eliminated the need for governments to use propaganda to convince their people to support war.
    d. had little effect on the nature of war

23. The ten southern provinces of the Netherlands, known as the Spanish Netherlands, became the future
    a. Netherlands.
    b. Bohemia.
    c. Belgium.
    d. Schleswig.

24. The Thirty Years' war was fought primarily
    a. on German soil.
    b. in France.
    c. in eastern Europe.
    d. in Spain.

25. The Ottoman capture of Constantinople in 1453 was significant in the history of slavery and racism in that it
    a. introduced the concept of slavery to the Christian European world.
    b. ended the transport of black slaves to Europe.
    c. caused Europeans to turn to sub-Saharan Africa for their slaves.
    d. ushered in a flow of slaves from the Indies.

Major Political Ideas

1. This chapter emphasizes how the medieval concept of a unified Christian society under one political ruler and one church began to break down. What was the cause of this breakdown?

2. *Misogyny* and *racism* are "political" terms in that they help to explain the distribution of power within society. Discuss each of these terms in the context of the sixteenth and seventeenth centuries.

3. It is suggested in this chapter (see pages 473–474) that Calvinism contributed to Dutch ideas of national independence. Explain the connection. Do you agree?

Issues for Essays and Discussion

The age of European expansion and religious wars was a period of both the breakdown and reconstruction of society. Describe this process of breakdown and reconstruction by discussing civil war, international war, and overseas expansion from about 1450 to about 1560. What were the causes of these events? What country (or countries) emerged from this era as the most powerful?

Interpretation of Visual Sources

Study the sixteenth-century print that has been reproduced on page 473 of your textbook. Describe the scene by identifying the precise actions of the participants. What specific types of offensive references are being destroyed? What are the ideas behind this "purification"?

Geography

1. On Outline Map 15.1 provided, and using maps 15.1 and 15.2 in the textbook as a reference, mark the following: the exploration routes of da Gama, Columbus, and Magellan, Cueta, the Cape of Good Hope, Amsterdam, Guinea, Calicut, Cape Horn, London, Lisbon, Goa, Antwerp, Mexico City, Moluccas.

2. Using Map 15.4 in the textbook as a reference, identify the areas that were the main sources of African slaves and the main areas of slave importation into the New World. Do the latter areas illustrate the economic origins of the slave trade?

3. On Outline Map 15.3 provided, and using Map 15.3 in the textbook as a reference, mark the following: the areas under Spanish Habsburg control, the areas under Austrian Habsburg control, Prussian lands, the United Netherlands, the German states, the boundary of the old Holy Roman Empire, Swedish possessions, Madrid, Lisbon, Vienna, Amsterdam.

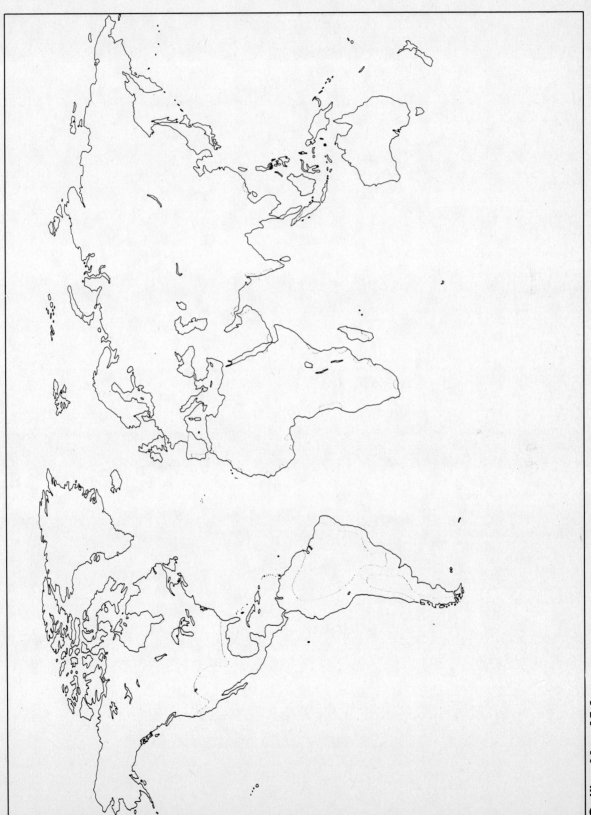

Outline Map 15.1

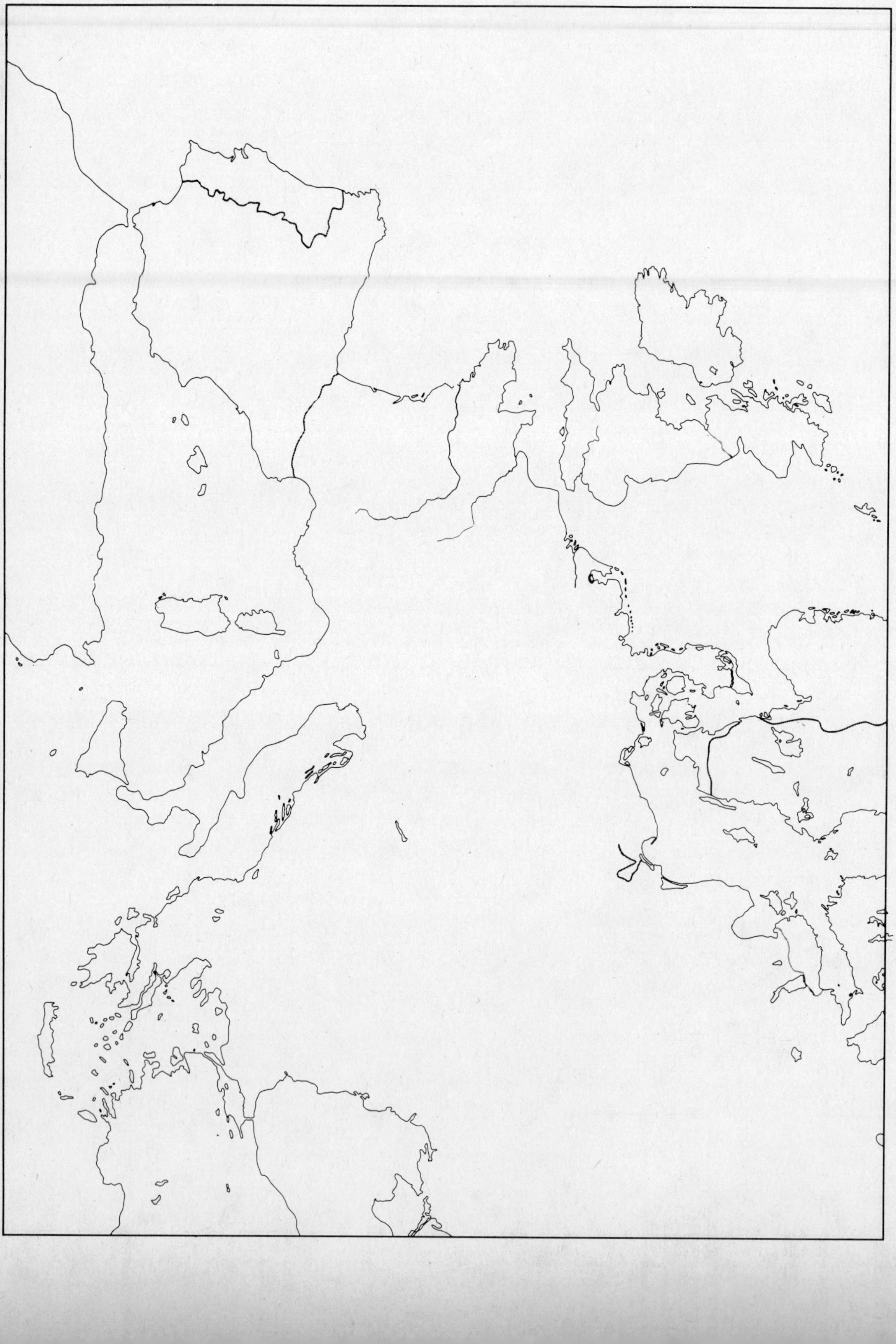

Outline Map 15.3

Understanding History Through the Arts

1. What did the Low Countries contribute to the arts? To investigate this subject, start with W. Gaunt, *Flemish Cities, Their History and Art* (1969), and O. Benesch, *The Art of the Renaissance in Northern Europe* (1945). See also E. Cammaerts, *The Treasure-House of Belgium* (1924).

2. What was the art of the New World like? For the arts of America prior to the European discoveries, see S. K. Lothorp, et al., *Pre-Columbian Art* (1957), and J. E. Thompson, *The Rise and Fall of Maya Civilization* (1954).

Problems for Further Investigation

1. In what ways is Montaigne representative of early modern skepticism? Those interested in skepticism and the life of its finest representative will want to read M. Lowenthal, ed., *Autobiography of Michel de Montaigne* * (1935).

2. Who were the important women of this period? There were a number of extremely important and powerful sixteenth-century women whose biographies make for fascinating reading: R. Roeder, *Catherine de Medici and the Lost Revolution* * (1937); J. E. Neal, *Queen Elizabeth I* * (1934, 1966); and A. Fraser, *Mary Queen of Scots* * (1969). An interesting seventeenth-century woman is Gustavus Adolphus's daughter, whose life is told in G. Masson, *Queen Christina* (1968). N. Harvey, *The Rose and the Thorn* (1977) is an account of the lives and times of Mary and Margaret Tudor.

3. What are the origins of mysogyny and racism? Begin with W. Monter's essay, "Protestant Wives, Catholic Saints, and Devil's Handmaid: Women in the Age of Reformations," in R. Bridenthal, C. Koonz, and S. Stuard, *Becoming Visible: Women in European History* * (1987). To examine the sources of racism see D. B. Davis, *Slavery and Human Progress* (1984), and J. L. Watson, ed., *Asian and African Systems of Slavery* (1980).

4. Why were overseas empires formed in this period? Those interested in doing work in the area of European expansion should begin with D. L. Jensen, ed., *The Expansion of Europe: Motives, Methods, and Meaning* (1967). Students interested in understanding how the vast Spanish Empire worked will want to read C. H. Haring, *The Spanish Empire in America* * (1947, 1963). This book includes an excellent bibliography on the subject.

5. Why were such severe religious wars fought in this era? Some of the problems faced in studying the religious conflict in France are discussed in J. H. M. Sahnon, *The French Wars of Religion* * (1967). Anyone interested in research on the Thirty Years' War should begin with S. H. Steinberg, *The Thirty Years' War and the Conflict for European Hegemony, 1600–1660* * (1966), and T. K. Rabb, *The Thirty Years' War* * (1964).

---

*Available in paperback.

Chapter 16
Absolutism and Constitutionalism in Western Europe (ca 1589–1715)

Chapter Questions

After reading and studying this chapter you should be able to answer the following questions:

How did absolute monarchy and constitutionalism differ from the feudal and dynastic monarchies of earlier centuries? What social and economic factors limited absolute monarchs? Which countries best represent absolutism and constitutionalism?

Chapter Summary

The seventeenth century marks the development of two patterns of government in Europe: absolute monarchy and the constitutional state. This chapter examines how the political system of absolutism succeeded gloriously in France and faded dismally in England in the seventeenth century. Few kings have been as successful in establishing complete monarchial sovereignty as the great Sun King of France, Louis XIV. Louis gave Europe a masterful lesson on how to collaborate with the nobility to strengthen the monarchy and to reinforce the ancient aristocracy. He was a superb actor and propagandist, who built on the earlier achievements of Henry IV and Richelieu and used his magnificent palace of Versailles to imprison the French nobility in a beautiful golden cage. He succeeded in expanding France at the expense of the Habsburgs, and his patronage of the arts helped form the great age of French classicism. However, the economic progress he first made was later checked by his policy of revoking religious toleration.

While the France of Louis was the classic model of absolutism as the last phase of an historic feudal society, Spain was the classic case of imperial decline. By 1600 Spain was in trouble, and by 1700 it was no longer a major European power. Not only did the silver and labor of America run out, but this great American wealth ruined the Spanish economic and social structure. War with the Dutch, the English, and the French also helped turn Spain into a backwater of Europe.

England and the United Provinces of the Netherlands provide a picture of constitutionalism triumphing over absolutism. For England, the seventeenth century was a long period of political conflict, complete with a bitter civil war and a radical experiment with republicanism. The causes of this era of conflict were varied, but it is clear that by 1689 the English army and

Parliament had destroyed the Stuart quest for divine-right absolutism. The period that followed witnessed some important changes in the way the state is managed. The Netherlands was important not only because it became the financial and commercial center of Europe, but also because it provided the period's third model of political development—a loosely federated, middle-class constitutional state.

Study Outline

Use this outline to preview the chapter before you read a particular section in the textbook and then as a self-check to test your reading comprehension after you have read the chapter section.

I. Absolutism
   A. Absolutism defined
      1. In the absolutist state, sovereignty resided in kings—not the nobility or the parliament—who considered themselves responsible to God alone.
      2. Absolute kings created new state bureaucracies and standing armies, regulated all the institutions of government, and secured the cooperation of the nobility.
      3. The absolutist state foreshadowed the modern totalitarian state but lacked its total control over all aspects of its citizens lives.
   B. The foundations of French absolutism: Sully and Richelieu
      1. Henry IV achieved peace and curtailed the power of the nobility.
      2. His minister, Sully, brought about financial stability and economic growth.
      3. Cardinal Richelieu, the ruler of France under King Louis XIII, broke the power of the French nobility.
         a. His policy was total subordination of all groups and institutions to the French monarchy.
         b. He leveled castles and crushed aristocratic conspiracies.
         c. He established an efficient administrative system using intendants, who further weakened the local nobility.
         d. The Huguenot revolt of 1625 led to the destruction of fortified cities in France, eliminating another source of aristocratic power.
      4. Under Richelieu, France sought to break Habsburg power.
         a. He supported the struggle of the Swedish king, Gustavus Adolphus, against the Habsburgs.
         b. He acquired land and influence in Germany.
      5. Richelieu supported the new French Academy, which created a dictionary to standardize the French language.
      6. The French government's ability to tax was severely limited by local rights and the tax-exempt status of much of the nobility and the middle class.
      7. Mazarin continued Richelieu's centralizing policies, but these policies gave rise to a period of civil wars known as the Fronde.
         a. Many people of the aristocracy and the middle classes opposed the government policies of centralization and the huge debt.
         b. The conflicts hurt the economy and convinced the new king, Louis XIV, that civil war was destructive of social order and that absolute monarchy was the only alternative to anarchy.

II. The absolutism of Louis XIV
   A. Louis XIV, the "Sun King," was a devout Catholic who believed that God had established kings as his rulers on earth.
   B. He feared the nobility and was successful in collaboration with them to enhance both aristocratic prestige and royal power.
   C. He made the court at Versailles a fixed institution and used it as a means of preserving royal power and as the center of French absolutism.
      1. The architecture and art of Versailles were a means of carrying out state policy—a way to overawe his subjects and foreign powers.
      2. The French language and culture became the international style.
      3. The court at Versailles was a device to undermine the power of the aristocracy by separating power from status.
      4. A centralized state, administered by a professional class taken from the bourgeoisie, was formed.
   D. Economic management under Louis XIV: Colbert and mercantilism
      1. Mercantilism is a collection of governmental policies for the regulation of economic activities by and for the state.
      2. Louis XIV's finance minister, Colbert, tried to achieve a favorable balance of trade and make France self-sufficient so the flow of gold to other countries would be halted.
         a. Colbert encouraged French industry, enacted high foreign tariffs, and created a strong merchant marine.
         b. He hoped to make Canada part of a French empire.
         c. Though France's industries grew and the commercial classes prospered, its agricultural economy suffered under the burdens of heavy taxation, population decline, and poor harvests.
   E. The revocation of the Edict of Nantes
      1. In 1685, Louis revoked the Edict of Nantes, which had given religious freedom to French Protestants.
      2. This revocation caused many Protestants to flee the country, but it had little effect on the economy.
III. French classicism in art and literature
   A. French classicism imitated and resembled the arts of the ancients and the Renaissance.
   B. Poussin best illustrates classical idealism in painting.
   C. Louis XIV was a patron of the composers Lully, Couperin, and Charpentier.
   D. The comedies of Molière and the tragedies of Racine best illustrate the classicism in French theater.
IV. Louis XIV's wars
   A. The French army under Louis XIV was modern because the state, rather than the nobles, employed the soldiers.
      1. He appointed Louvois to create a professional army.
      2. Louis himself took personal command of the army.
   B. Louis continued Richelieu's expansionist policy.
      1. In 1667, he invaded Flanders and gained twelve towns.
      2. By the treaty of Nijmegen (1678) he gained some Flemish towns and all of Franche-Comté.

3. Strasbourg was taken in 1681 and Lorraine in 1684, but the limits of his expansion had been met.
4. Louis fought the new Dutch king of England, William III, and the League of Augsburg in a war.
    a. The Banks of Amsterdam and England financed his enemies.
    b. Louis's heavy taxes fell on the peasants, who revolted.
5. This led to the War of the Spanish Succession (1701–1713), which was over the issue of the succession to the Spanish throne: Louis claimed Spain but was opposed by the Dutch, English, Austrians, and Prussians.
    a. The war was also an attempt to preserve the balance of power in Europe and to check France's commercial power overseas.
    b. A Grand Alliance of the English, Dutch, Austrians, and Prussians was formed in 1701 to fight the French.
    c. Eugene of Savoy and Churchill of England led the alliance to victory over Louis.
    d. The war was concluded by the Peace of Utrecht in 1713, which forbade the union of France and Spain.
    e. The war ended French expansionism and left France on the brink of bankruptcy, with widespread misery and revolts.

V. The decline of absolutist Spain in the seventeenth century
    A. Factors contributing to Spain's decline
        1. Fiscal disorder, political incompetence, the lack of a strong middle class, population decline, intellectual isolation, and psychological malaise contributed to its decline.
        2. The defeat of the "Invincible Armada" in 1588 was a crushing blow to Spain's morale.
        3. Spain's economy began to decline by 1600.
            a. Royal expenditures increased, but income from the Americas decreased.
            b. Business and agriculture suffered.
        4. Spanish kings lacked force of character and could not deal with all these problems.
    B. The Treaty of the Pyrenees of 1659, which ended the French-Spanish wars, marked the end of Spain as a great power.

VI. Constitutionalism in England and the Netherlands
    A. Constitutionalism defined
        1. Under constitutionalism, the state must be governed according to law, not royal decree.
            a. It implies a balance between the power of the government and the rights of the subjects.
            b. A nation's constitution may be written or unwritten, but the government must respect it.
            c. Constitutional governments may be either republics or monarchies.
        2. Constitutional government is not the same as full democracy because not all of the people have the right to participate.
    B. The decline of royal absolutism in England (1603–1649)
        1. The Stuart kings of England lacked the political wisdom of Elizabeth I.
        2. James I was devoted to the ideal of rule by divine right.
        3. His absolutism ran counter to English belief.

4. The House of Commons wanted a greater say in the government of the state.
   a. Increased wealth had produced a better educated House of Commons.
   b. Between 1603 and 1640, bitter squabbles erupted between the Crown and the Commons.

C. The Protestant, or capitalist, ethic and the problem of religion in England
   1. Many English people, called Puritans, were attracted by the values of hard work, thrift, and self-denial implied by Calvinism.
   2. The Puritans, who were dissatisfied with the Church of England, saw James I as an enemy.
   3. Charles I and his archbishop, Laud, appeared to be pro-Catholic.

D. The English Civil War (1642–1649)
   1. Charles I had ruled without Parliament for eleven years.
   2. A revolt in Scotland over the religious issue forced him to call a new Parliament into session to finance an army.
      a. The Commons passed an act compelling the king to summon Parliament every three years.
      b. It also impeached Archbishop Laud and abolished the House of Lords.
      c. Religious differences in Ireland led to a revolt there, but Parliament would not trust Charles with an army.
   3. Charles initiated military action against Parliament.
      a. The civil war (1642–1649) revolved around the issue of whether sovereignty should reside in the king or in Parliament.
      b. The problem was not resolved, but Charles was beheaded in 1649.

E. Puritanical absolutism in England: Cromwell and the Protectorate
   1. Kingship was abolished in 1649 and a commonwealth proclaimed.
      a. A commonwealth is a government without a king whose power rests in Parliament and a council of state.
      b. In fact, the army controlled the government.
   2. Oliver Cromwell, leader of the "New Model Army" that defeated the royalists, came from the gentry class that dominated the House of Commons.
   3. Cromwell's Protectorate became a military dictatorship, absolutist and puritanical.
      a. Cromwell allowed religious toleration for all Christians, except Roman Catholics, and savagely crushed the revolt in Ireland.
      b. He censored the press and closed the theaters.
      c. He regulated the economy according to mercantilist principles.
      d. The mercantilist navigation act that required English goods to be transported on English ships was a boon to the economy and led to a commercial war with the Dutch.

F. The restoration of the English monarchy
   1. The restoration of the Stuart kings in 1660 failed to solve the problems of religion and the relationship between King and Parliament.
      a. According to the Test Act of 1673, those who refused to join the Church of England could not vote, hold office, preach, teach, attend the universities, or assemble, but these restrictions could not be upheld.
      b. Charles II appointed a council of five men (the "Cabal") to serve as both his major advisers and as members of Parliament.

       c. The Cabal was the forerunner of the cabinet system, and it helped create good relations with the Parliament.

    2. Charles's pro-French policies led to a Catholic scare.

    3. James II, an avowed Catholic, violated the Test Act by appointing Catholics to government and university positions.

    4. Fear of a Catholic monarchy led to the expulsion of James II and the Glorious Revolution.

G. The triumph of England's Parliament: constitutional monarchy and cabinet government

    1. The "Glorious Revolution" that expelled James II and installed William and Mary on the throne ended the idea of divine-right monarchy.

    2. The Bill of Rights of 1689 established the principal of Parliament's sovereignty.

       a. Locke maintained that people set up government to protect life, liberty, and property.

       b. Locke's ideas that there are natural, or universal, rights played a strong role in eighteenth-century Enlightenment thought.

    3. In the cabinet system, which developed in the eighteenth century, both legislative and executive power are held by the leading ministers, who form the government.

H. The Dutch republic in the seventeenth century

    1. The Dutch republic emerged from the sixteenth-century struggle against Spain and flowered in the seventeenth century.

    2. Power in the republic resided in the local Estates.

       a. The republic was a confederation: a weak union of strong provinces.

       b. The republic was based on middle-class ideas and values.

    3. Thrift, frugality, and religious toleration fostered economic growth.

    4. The province of Holland became the commercial and financial center of Europe—much of it based on transport of goods from all over the world.

       a. The Dutch East India Company was formed in 1602; it cut heavily into Portuguese trading in East Asia.

       b. The Dutch West India Company, founded in 1621, traded extensively in Latin America and Africa.

    5. War with France and England in the 1670s hurt the United Provinces.

Review Questions

Check your understanding of this chapter by answering the following questions.

1. In what way does the French minister Richelieu symbolize absolutism? What were his achievements?

2. Why can it be said that the palace of Versailles was used as a device to ruin the nobility of France? Was Versailles a palace or a prison?

3. Define mercantilism. What were the mercantilist policies of the French minister Colbert?

4. Why was the revocation of the Edict of Nantes a great error on the part of Louis XIV?

5. What were the reasons for the fall of the Spanish Empire?

6. Discuss the foreign policy goals of Louis XIV. Was he successful?

7. Define absolutism. How does it differ from totalitarianism?

8. What was the impact of Louis XIV's wars on the French economy and French society?
9. What were the causes of the War of the Spanish Succession? What impact did William III of England have on European events after about 1689?
10. What is constitutionalism? How does it differ from democratic form of government? From absolutism?
11. What were the attitudes and policies of James I that made him so unpopular with his subjects?
12. Who were the Puritans? Why did they come into conflict with James I?
13. What were the immediate and the long-range causes of the English Civil War of 1642–1649? What were the results?
14. Why did James II flee from England in 1688? What happened to the kingship at this point?
15. Were the events of 1688–89 a victory for English democracy? Explain.
16. Why is it said that Locke was the spokesman for the liberal English Revolution of 1689 and for representative government?
17. What accounts for the phenomenal economic success and political stability of the Dutch republic?
18. Describe the Dutch system of government. How was it different from that of other western European states? What was unusual about the Dutch attitudes toward religious beliefs?

Study-Review Exercises

Define the following key concepts and terms.

sovereign

totalitarianism

absolutism

mercantilism

republicanism

constitutionalism

cabinet government

French classicism

quixotic

commonwealth

Identify and explain the significance of each of the following people and terms.
Sully

paulette

Fronde

Cardinal Richelieu

Richelieu's *généralités*

The French Academy

Louis XIV of France

Versailles

Molière

Racine

Poussin

Dutch Estates General

intendants

Peace of Utrecht

Cabal of Charles II

Instrument of Government

Puritans

Oliver Cromwell

James II of England

English Bill of Rights

John Churchill

Philip II of Spain

Explain what each of these men believed about the placement of authority within society.
Cardinal Richelieu

James I of England

Thomas Hobbes

Louis XIV of France

John Locke

Sully

Explain what the following events were and why they were important.
revocation of the Edict of Nantes

Scottish revolt of 1640

War of the Spanish Succession

Glorious Revolution

English Civil War of 1642–1649

Test your understanding of the chapter by providing the correct answers.

1. The highest executive office of the Dutch republic. _____

2. Louis XIV's able minister of finance. _____

3. During the age of economic growth in Spain, a vast number of Spaniards *entered/left* religious orders.

4. For Louis XIV of France the War of the Spanish Succession was a *success/disaster*.

5. The Englishman who inflicted defeat on Louis XIV at Blenheim. _____

6. The archbishop whose goal was to enforce Anglican unity in England and Scotland.

   _____

7. He made the statement "From where do the merchant's profits come except from his own

   diligence and industry." _____

Multiple-Choice Questions

1. Mercantilism
   a. was a military system.
   b. insisted on a favorable balance of trade.
   c. was adopted in England but not in France.
   d. claimed that state power was based on land armies.

2. French Protestants tended to be
   a. poor peasants.
   b. the power behind the throne of Louis XIV.
   c. a financial burden for France.
   d. clever business people.

3. The War of the Spanish Succession began when Charles II of Spain left his territories to
   a. the French heir.
   b. the Spanish heir.
   c. Eugene of Savoy.
   d. the archduke of Austria.

4. Which of the following cities was the commercial and financial capital of Europe in the seventeenth century?
   a. London
   b. Hamburg
   c. Paris
   d. Amsterdam

5. Of the following, the country most centered on middle-class interests was
   a. England.
   b. Spain.
   c. France.
   d. the Netherlands.

6. Which of the following Englishmen was a Catholic?
   a. James II
   b. Oliver Cromwell
   c. Archbishop Laud
   d. William III

7. Which of the following is a characteristic of an absolute state?
   a. Sovereignty embodied in the representative assembly
   b. Bureaucracies solely accountable to the middle classes
   c. A strong voice expressed by the nobility
   d. Permanent standing armies

8. Cardinal Richelieu's most notable accomplishment was
   a. the creation of a strong financial system for France.
   b. the creation of a highly effective administrative system.
   c. winning the total support of the Huguenots.
   d. allying the Catholic church with the government.

9. The statement "There are no privileges and immunities which can stand against a divinely appointed king" forms the basis of the
   a. Stuart notion of absolutism.
   b. Stuart notion of constitutionalism.
   c. English Parliament's notion of democracy.
   d. English Parliament's notion of constitutionalism.

10. The English Long Parliament
    a. enacted legislation supporting absolutism.
    b. supported the Catholic tendencies of Charles I.
    c. supported Charles I as a military leader.
    d. enacted legislation against absolutism.

11. Cromwell's government is best described as a
    a. constitutional state.
    b. democratic state.
    c. military dictatorship.
    d. monarchy.

12. Absolute monarchs secured mastery over the nobility by all of the following *except*
    a. the creation of a standing army.
    b. the creation of a state bureaucracy.
    c. coercive actions.
    d. regulating religious groups.

13. Cardinal Richelieu consolidated the power of the French monarchy by doing all of the following *except*
    a. destroying the castles of the nobility.
    b. ruthlessly treating conspirators who threatened the monarchy.
    c. keeping nobles from gaining high government offices.
    d. eliminating the intendant system of local government.

14. One way in which Louis XIV controlled the French nobility was by
    a. maintaining standing armies in the countryside to crush noble uprisings.
    b. requiring the presence of the major noble families at Versailles for at least part of the year.
    c. periodically visiting the nobility in order to check on their activities.
    d. forcing them to participate in a parliamentary assembly.

15. The French army under Louis XIV
    a. had no standardized uniforms and weapons.
    b. lived off the countryside.
    c. had an ambulance corps to care for the troops.
    d. had no system for recruitment, training, or promotion.

16. The Peace of Utrecht in 1713
    a. shrunk the size of the British Empire significantly.
    b. represented the balance-of-power principle in action.
    c. enhanced Spain's position as a major power in Europe.
    d. marked the beginning of French expansionist policy.

17. The downfall of Spain in the seventeenth century can be blamed on
    a. weak and ineffective monarchs.
    b. an overexpansion of industry and trade.
    c. the growth of slave labor in America.
    d. the rise of a large middle class.

18. When Archbishop Laud tried to make the Presbyterian Scots accept the Anglican *Book of Common Prayer*, the Scots
    a. revolted.
    b. reluctantly accepted the archbishop's directive.
    c. ignored the directive.
    d. heartily adopted the new prayerbook.

19. Who among the following was a proponent of the idea that the purpose of government is to protect life, liberty, and property?
    a. Thomas Hobbes
    b. William of Orange
    c. John Locke
    d. Edmund Burke

20. After the United Provinces of the Netherlands won independence from Spain, their government could best be described as
    a. a strong monarchy.
    b. a centralized parliamentary system.
    c. a weak union of strong provinces.
    d. a democracy.

21. The Dutch economy was based on
    a. fishing, world trade, and banking.
    b. silver mining in Peru.
    c. export of textiles.
    d. a moral and religious disdain of wealth.

22. Dutch economic decline began with
    a. the end of the War of the Spanish Succession.
    b. the formation of the Dutch East India Company.
    c. its practice of religious toleration.
    d. the adoption of the ideas of John Calvin.

23. During the administration of Robert Walpole in Britain, the idea developed that
    a. the monarch was absolute.
    b. the cabinet should be replaced by a legislative parliament.
    c. the king's chief minister be known as the *stadholder*.
    d. the cabinet be responsible to the House of Commons.

24. The Amstel River was the major link between which of the following cities and its world trading system?
    a. London
    b. Amsterdam
    c. Paris
    d. Amiens

25. Which of the following is a book by Cervantes that has as its hero an idealistic but impractical soldier?
    a. *Don Quixote*
    b. *Tarfuffe*
    c. *Te Deum*
    d. *Phèdre*

Major Political Ideas

1. What are the major characteristics of absolutism and how does it, as a political system, differ from totalitarianism?

2. What is constitutionalism? What is the source of power within a constitutional state? How does constitutionalism differ from absolutism?

3. In 1649 England declared itself a commonwealth, or republican form of government. What is a republican state? Where does power reside in such a state?

Issues for Essays and Discussion

1. The seventeenth century saw great political instability and change, during which some modern forms of political organization emerged. Why did political turmoil exist, what new concepts of politics and power emerged, who were the most important participants in this process, and how was stability achieved?

2. Compare and contrast the political development of France, the Netherlands, and England in the seventeenth century. Of these three states, which is the most "modern"?

Interpretation of Visual Sources

Study the reproduction of the woodcut entitled *The Spider and the Fly* on page 508 of your textbook. What is the message the author of this illustration seeks to convey? Does it make a political statement? In your opinion, is there any historical evidence set forth in this chapter to suggest that this print represents historical truth?

Geography

1. On Outline Map 16.1 provided, and using Map 16.1 in the textbook as a reference, mark the territory added to France as a result of the wars and foreign policy of King Louis XIV.

2. Explain how each of the territories was acquired and from whom.

3. What changes in the balance of power occurred as a result of the Treaty of Utrecht in 1713?

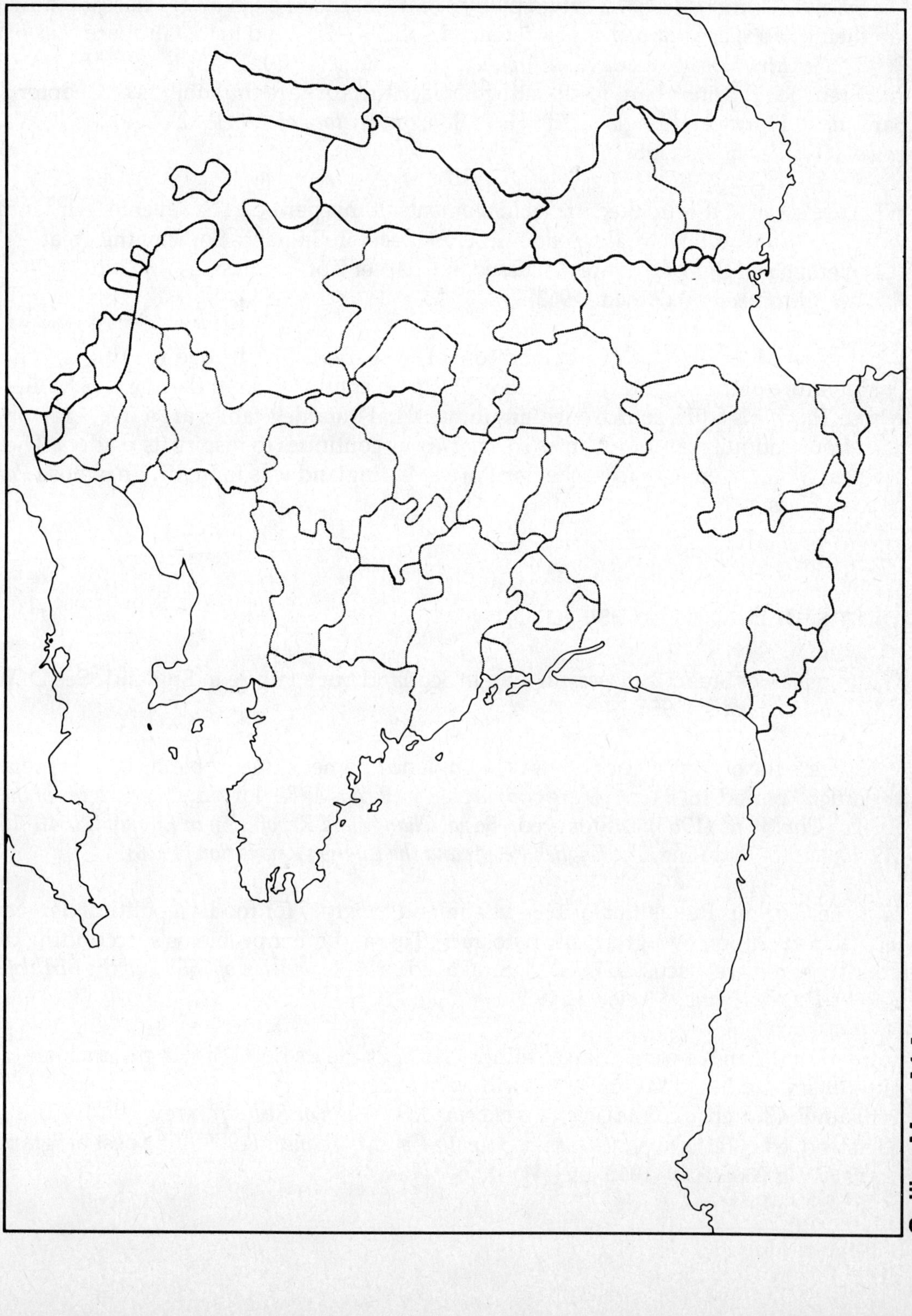

Outline Map 16.1

Understanding History Through the Arts

1. What was life at Versailles like? At the great English estates? Louis XIV and the magnificence of his court at Versailles are re-created with color and spirit in W. H. Lewis, *The Splendid Century** (1953). A vivid picture of life of the English upper classes—how they ran their estates, entertained, and influenced politics—is found in M. Girouard, *Life in the English Country House: A Social and Architectural History* (1979). The splendor of Versailles and French and British baroque painting and architecture are the subjects of Chapter 7, "The Baroque in France and England," in H. W. Janson, *History of Art* (1962). See also G. Walton, *Louis XIV's Versailles** (1986).

2. What are some of the architectural achievements of this period? The seventeenth century was a period of architectural splendor in France and in England. Some of the great achievements of this period are discussed in Chapter 7 of N. Pevsner, *An Outline Of European Architecture** (7th ed., 1963).

3. What can we learn from the great literature of the period? Much good reading is found in the literature of the seventeenth century. The great comic writer of the age was Molière, whose *Tartuffe* is still a source of entertainment. LaFontaine's fables are a lively reworking of tales from antiquity, and Cervantes's *Don Quixote* continues to inspire its readers. The greatest writer to emerge from the Puritan age in England was John Milton, whose *Paradise Lost* is a classic.

Problems for Further Investigation

1. Why was James Stuart a successful king in Scotland but a failure in England? See D. Willson, *King James VI and I** (1956).

2. What were the origins of the civil war in England? Some of the problems in interpretation of the crucial period 1642 to 1649 are considered in P. A. M. Taylor, ed., *The Origins of the English Civil War** (1960); L. Stone, ed., *Social Change and Revolution in England, 1540–1640** (1965); and B. Manning, *The English People and the English Revolution* (1976).

3. Was the Glorious Revolution of 1688 in England a victory for modern political democracy or a palace revolution by a group of aristocrats? This and other problems surrounding this political event are discussed in G. M. Straka, ed., *The Revolution of 1688 and the Birth of the English Political Nation** (rev. ed., 1973).

4. How did the Sun King create an absolutist state? Students interested in research on absolutism and Louis XIV in France will want to consider H. G. Judge, ed., *Louis XIV* (1965); William F. Church, ed., *The Greatness of Louis XIV: Myth or Reality?** (rev. ed., 1972); and R. F. Kierstead, ed., *State and Society in Seventeenth-Century France** (1975). The best biography of Louis XIV is *Louis XIV* (1968) by J. Wolf.

---

*Available in paperback.

5. What were the traditional patterns of military organization and strategy in this age of absolutism? In what ways did warfare change to reflect the political ambitions of Europe's monarchs and economic and social developments? Begin your investigation with M. van Creveld, *Technology and War, from 2000 B.C. to the Present* (1988). A helpful reference for the scholar of military history is R. Dupuy and T. Dupuy, *The Encyclopedia of Military History, from 3500 B.C. to the Present* (1982, 1990).

Chapter 17
Absolutism in Eastern Europe to 1740

Chapter Questions

After reading and studying this chapter you should be able to answer the following questions:

Why did the basic structure of society in eastern Europe move away from that in western Europe? How and why did the rulers of Austria, Prussia, and Russia manage to build more durable absolute monarchies than that of Louis XIV of France? How did the absolute monarchs' interactions with artists and architects contribute to the achievements of baroque culture?

Chapter Summary

This chapter discusses why monarchial absolutism developed with greater lasting strength in eastern Europe than in western Europe. In Russia, Prussia, and Austria monarchs became more powerful as the peasants were pushed back into serfdom. That is, peasants gradually lost the personal and economic freedoms they had built up over several hundred years during the Middle Ages. At the same time that eastern nobles gained greater social and economic control over the enserfed peasants, they lost political power to the rising absolute monarchs. Although there were some economic reasons for the re-emergence of serfdom in the east, it was essentially for political reasons that this strong authoritarian tradition emerged. As opposed to western Europe, it was the common people—the peasants—who were the great losers in the power struggle between nobility and monarchy. Absolutism in Russia, Austria, and Prussia emerged because of war, foreign invasion, and internal struggle. For example, the Austrian monarchs solved the problems arising from external conflicts and a multicultural state by building a strong, centralized military state. Prussian absolutism—intended to check the power of the nobility—was achieved by the Hohenzollern monarchs, while Russian absolutism was largely the outgrowth of the Mongol conquest and internal power struggles.

Some of the absolute monarchs were enlightened reformers, but their good intentions were often thwarted by internal problems. However, if reform from above was not very effective, the absolute monarchs' use of architecture and urban planning—much of it in the baroque style—to enhance their images was a noteworthy success. They created buildings and cities that reflected their growing power, and they hired baroque painters and musicians to glorify them and to fill their palaces with paintings and music.

Study Outline

Use this outline to preview the chapter before you read a particular section in your textbook and then as a self-check to test your reading comprehension after you have read the chapter section.

I. Lords and peasants in eastern Europe
   A. The medieval background (1400–1650)
      1. Personal and economic freedom for peasants increased between 1050 and 1300.
         a. Serfdom nearly disappeared.
         b. Peasants bargained freely with their landlords and moved about as they pleased.
      2. After 1300, powerful lords in eastern Europe revived serfdom to combat their economic problems.
         a. Laws that restricted the peasants' right of free movement were passed.
         b. Lords took more and more of the peasants' land and imposed heavier labor obligations.
   B. The consolidation of serfdom
      1. The re-establishment of hereditary serfdom took place in Poland, Prussia, and Russia between 1500 and 1650.
      2. The consolidation of serfdom was accompanied by the growth of estate agriculture.
         a. Lords seized peasant land for their own estates.
         b. They then demanded unpaid serf labor on those estates.
   C. Political reasons for changes in serfdom in eastern Europe
      1. Serfdom increased because of political, not economic, reasons.
      2. Weak monarchs could not resist the demands of the powerful noble landlords.
      3. The absence of the western concept of sovereignty meant that the king did not think in terms of protecting the people of the nation.
      4. Overall, the peasants had less political power in eastern Europe and less solidarity.
      5. The landlords systematically undermined the medieval privileges of the towns.
         a. The lords sold directly to foreign capitalists instead of to local merchants.
         b. Eastern towns lost their medieval right of refuge.
II. The rise of Austria and Prussia (1650–1750)
   A. Austria and the Ottoman Turks
      1. After the Thirty Years' War, the Austrian Habsburgs turned inward and eastward to unify their holdings.
         a. The Habsburgs replaced the Bohemian Czech (Protestant) nobility with their own warriors.
         b. Serfdom increased, Protestantism was wiped out, and absolutism was achieved.
         c. Ferdinand III created a standing army, centralized the government in Austria, and turned toward Hungary for land.
      2. This eastward turn led Austria to became absorbed in a war against the Turks over Hungary and Transylvania.
      3. Under Suleiman the Magnificent the Turks built the most powerful empire in the world, which included part of central Europe.
         a. The Turkish sultan was the absolute head of the state.

        b.   There was little private property, and a bureaucracy staffed by slaves.

    4.   The Turkish attack on Austria in 1683 was turned back, and the Habsburgs conquered all of Hungary and Transylvania by 1699.

    5.   The Habsburg possessions consisted of Austria, Bohemia, and Hungary, which were joined in a fragile union.

        a.   The Pragmatic Sanction (1713) stated that the possessions should never be divided.

        b.   The Hungarian nobility thwarted the full development of Habsburg absolutism, and Charles VI had to restore many of their traditional privileges after the rebellion led by Rákóczy in 1703.

  B. Prussia in the seventeenth century

    1.   The Hohenzollern family ruled the electorate of Brandenburg but had little real power.

    2.   The Thirty Years' War weakened the representative assemblies of the realm and allowed the Hohenzollerns to consolidate their absolutist rule.

    3.   Frederick William (the Great Elector) used military force and taxation to unify his Rhine holdings, Prussia, and Brandenburg into a strong state.

        a.   The traditional parliaments, or Estates, which were controlled by the Junkers (the nobles and the landowners), were weakened.

        b.   War strengthened the elector, as did the Junkers' unwillingness to join with the towns to block absolutism.

  C. The consolidation of Prussian absolutism

    1.   Frederick William I encouraged Prussian militarism and created the best army in Europe plus an efficient bureaucracy.

    2.   The Junker class became the military elite and Prussia a militarist state.

III. The development of Russia

  A. The Vikings and the Kievan principality

    1.   Eastern Slavs moved into Russia between the fifth and ninth centuries.

    2.   Slavic-Viking settlements grew up in the ninth century.

    3.   The Vikings unified the eastern Slavs politically and religiously, creating a ruling dynasty and accepting Eastern Orthodox Christianity for themselves and the Slavs.

    4.   A strong aristocracy (the boyars) and a free peasantry made it difficult to strengthen the state.

  B. The Mongol yoke and the rise of Moscow

    1.   The Mongols conquered the Kievan state in the thirteenth century and unified it under their harsh rule.

    2.   The Mongols used Russian aristocrats as their servants and tax collectors.

        a.   The princes of Moscow served the Mongols well and became the hereditary great princes.

        b.   Ivan I served the Mongols while using his wealth and power to strengthen the principality of Moscow.

        c.   Ivan III stopped acknowledging the Mongol khan as the supreme ruler and assumed the headship of Orthodox Christianity.

  C. Tsar and people to 1689

    1.   By 1505, the prince of Moscow—the tsar—had emerged as the single hereditary ruler of the eastern Slavs.

2. The tsars and the boyars struggled over who would rule the state; the tsars won and created a new "service nobility," who held the tsar's land on the condition that they serve in his army.
3. Ivan the Terrible was an autocratic tsar who expanded Muscovy and further reduced the power of the boyars.
   a. He murdered leading boyars and confiscated their estates.
   b. Many peasants fled his rule to the newly conquered territories, forming groups called Cossacks.
   c. Businessmen and artisans were bound to their towns and jobs; the middle class did not develop.
4. The Time of Troubles (1598–1613) was a period characterized by internal struggles and invasions.
   a. There was no heir, and relatives of the tsar fought against each other.
   b. Swedish and Polish armies invaded.
   c. Cossack bands slaughtered many nobles and officials.
5. Michael Romanov was elected tsar by the nobles in 1613, and he re-established tsarist autocracy.
6. The Romanovs brought about the total enserfment of the people, while the military obligations on the nobility were relaxed considerably.
7. A split in the church over religious reforms led to mass protests by the peasants, and the church became dependent on the state for its authority.

D. The reforms of Peter the Great
   1. Peter wished to create a strong army for protection and expansion.
      a. He forced the nobility to serve in the army or in the civil service.
      b. He created schools to train technicians for his army.
   2. Army and government became more efficient and powerful as an interlocking military-civilian bureaucracy was created and staffed by talented people.
   3. Russian peasant life under Peter became more harsh.
      a. People replaced land as the primary unit of taxation.
      b. Serfs were arbitrarily assigned to work in the factories and mines.
   4. Modest territorial expansion took place under Peter, and Russia became a European Great Power.
      a. Russia defeated Sweden in 1709 at Poltava to gain control of the Baltic Sea.
      b. Peter borrowed many Western ideas.

IV. Absolutism and the baroque
   A. Palaces and power
      1. Architecture played an important role in politics because it was used by kings to enhance their image and awe their subjects.
      2. The royal palace was the favorite architectural expression of absolutist power.
      3. The dominant artistic style of the age of absolutism was baroque—a dramatic and emotional style.
   B. Royal cities and urban planning
      1. The new St. Petersburg is an excellent example of the tie among architecture, politics, and urban development.
         a. Peter the Great wanted to create a modern, baroque city from which to rule Russia.

      b. The city became a showplace for the tsar paid for by the Russian nobility and built by the peasants.

C. The growth of St. Petersburg

  1. During the eighteenth century, St. Petersburg became one of the world's largest and most influential cities.

  2. The new city was Western and baroque in its layout and design.

    a. It had broad, straight avenues.

    b. Houses were built in a uniform line.

    c. There were parks, canals, and streetlights.

    d. Each social group was to live in a specific section.

  3. All social groups, especially the peasants, bore heavy burdens to construct the city.

  4. Tsarina Elizabeth and the architect Rastrelli crowned the city with great palaces.

Review Questions

Check your understanding of this chapter by answering the following questions.

1. What were the reasons for the re-emergence of serfdom in eastern Europe in the early modern period?

2. In western Europe the conflict between the king and his vassals resulted in gains for the common man. Why did this not happen in eastern Europe?

3. Why would the reign of the Great Elector be regarded as "the most crucial constitutional struggle in Prussian history for hundreds of years"? What did he do to increase royal authority? Who were the losers?

4. Prussia has traditionally been considered one of the most militaristic states in Europe. How do you explain this development? Who or what was responsible?

5. How did the Thirty Years' War and invasion by the Ottoman Turks help the Habsburgs consolidate power?

6. What was the Pragmatic Sanction and why were the Hungarian and Bohemian princes opposed to it?

7. What role, if any, did war play in the evolution of absolutism in eastern Europe?

8. What was the relationship between baroque architecture and European absolutism? Give examples.

9. It has been said that the common man benefited from the magnificent medieval cathedrals as much as the princes. Can the same be said about the common man and the building projects of the absolute kings and princes? Explain.

10. How did the Vikings influence Russian history?

11. How did the Mongols unify the eastern Slavs?

12. What role did Ivan the Terrible play in the rise of absolutism? Peter the Great?

13. Why was territorial expansion "the soul of tsardom"?

Study-Review Exercises

Define the following key concepts and terms.

absolutism

baroque

Prussian Junkers

Hohenzollern

kholops

Romanov

boyar

autocracy

Vikings

Habsburgs

Mongols

Pragmatic Sanction

Identify and explain the significance of the following people.

Suleiman the Magnificent

Frederick the Great

Charles VI of Austria

Prince Francis Rákóczy

Jenghiz Khan

Ivan the Terrible

Frederick William the Great Elector

Frederick William I

Great Prince Iaroslav the Wise

Ivan III

Peter the Great

Prince Eugene of Savoy

Bartolomeo Rastrelli

Explain what the following events were, who participated in them, and why they were important.
building of the Winter Palace of St. Petersburg

siege of Vienna, 1683

War of the Austrian Succession

Time of Troubles

Battle of Poltava

Test your understanding of the chapter by providing the correct answers.

1. The founder of the new Russian city on the coast of the Baltic Sea. _____

2. After 1500, serfdom in eastern Europe *increased/decreased*.

3. The Ottoman Turkish leader who captured Vienna in 1529. _____

4. In the struggle between the Hungarian aristocrats and the Austrian Habsburgs, the Hungarian aristocrats *maintained/lost* their traditional privileges.

5. This Prussian monarch doubled the size of Prussia in 1740 by taking Silesia from Austria.

    _____

6. The monarchs of eastern Europe were generally *stronger/weaker* than the kings of western Europe in the sixteenth and seventeenth centuries.

Place the following events in correct chronological order.

Election of the first Romanov tsar
Establishment of the Kievan state
Time of Troubles
Invasion by the Mongols
Building of St. Petersburg
Battle of Poltava

1.

2.

3.

4.

5.

6.

Multiple-Choice Questions

1. The unifiers and first rulers of the Russians were the
   a. Mongols.
   b. Turks.
   c. Romanovs.
   d. Vikings.

2. By the seventeenth century, commercial activity, manufacturing, and mining in Russia were owned or controlled by the
   a. rising urban capitalists.
   b. Cossacks.
   c. tsar.
   d. Russian church.

3. In eastern Europe the courts were largely controlled by
   a. the peasants.
   b. the monarchs.
   c. the church.
   d. the landlords.

4. The principality called the "sandbox of the Holy Roman Empire" was
   a. Brandenburg-Prussia.
   b. Hungary.
   c. Sweden.
   d. Austria.

5. Ivan the Terrible
   a. failed to conquer the khan.
   b. was afraid to call himself tsar.
   c. monopolized most mining and business activity.
   d. abolished the system of compulsory service for noble landlords.

6. Peter the Great's reforms included
   a. compulsory education away from home for the higher classes.
   b. a lessening of the burdens of serfdom for Russian peasants.
   c. an elimination of the merit-system bureaucracy.
   d. the creation of an independent parliament.

7. The dominant artistic style of the seventeenth and early eighteenth centuries was
   a. Gothic.
   b. romantic.
   c. impressionistic.
   d. baroque.

8. The noble landowners of Prussia were known as
   a. boyars.
   b. Junkers.
   c. Vikings.
   d. Electors.

9. Apparently the most important reason for the return to serfdom in eastern Europe from about 1500 to 1650 was
   a. political.
   b. economic.
   c. military.
   d. religious.

10. The Russian Cossacks were
    a. nobles created by Peter the Great.
    b. free groups and outlaw armies.
    c. private armies of the landlords.
    d. Turkish troops who settled in the Black Sea area.

11. After the disastrous defeat of the Czech nobility by the Habsburgs at the battle of White Mountain in 1618, the
    a. old Czech nobility accepted Catholicism in great numbers.
    b. majority of the Czech nobles' land was given to soldiers who had fought for the Habsburgs.
    c. conditions of the enserfed peasantry improved.
    d. Czech nobles continued their struggle effectively for many years.

12. After the Thirty Years' War and the creation of a large standing army, Austria turned its attention to control of
    a. northern Italy.
    b. Prussia.
    c. Hungary.
    d. Poland.

13. The result of the struggle of the Hungarian nobles against Habsburg oppression was that
    a. they suffered a fate similar to the Czech nobility.
    b. they gained a great deal of autonomy compared with the Austrian and Bohemian nobility.
    c. they won their independence.
    d. their efforts were inconclusive.

14. The monarch who established Prussian absolutism and who was named "the Soldiers' King" was
    a. Peter the Great.
    b. Frederick William I.
    c. Ivan IV.
    d. Elector Frederick III.

15. The Viking invaders of Russia were principally interested in
    a. controlling vast new lands politically.
    b. spreading their religion.
    c. establishing and controlling commercial interests.
    d. the conquest of Vienna.

16. The Muscovite princes gained their initial power through
    a. services rendered to the Vikings.
    b. strategic marriages.
    c. services rendered to the Mongols.
    d. defeat of the rival branches of the house of Ruiruk.

17. The rise of the Russian monarchy was largely a response to the external threat of the
    a. French monarchy.
    b. Asiatic Mongols.
    c. Prussian monarchy.
    d. English monarchy.

18. The Time of Troubles was caused by
    a. a dispute in the line of succession.
    b. Turkish invasions.
    c. Mongol invasions.
    d. severe crop failures resulting in starvation and disease.

19. In order to strengthen the Russian military, Peter the Great
    a. made the nobility serve in the civil administration or army for life.
    b. established a navy in the Atlantic.
    c. excluded foreigners from his service.
    d. turned over political power to the military.

20. The real losers in the growth of eastern Europe absolutism were the
    a. peasants.
    b. peasants and middle classes.
    c. nobility.
    d. nobility and the clergy.

21. The Siege of Vienna of 1683 was undertaken by
    a. the Hungarians under Prince Rákóczy.
    b. the Russians.
    c. the Turks.
    d. Frederick William of Prussia.

22. The Battle of Poltava marks a Russian victory over
    a. Sweden.
    b. Turkey.
    c. Prussia.
    d. Austria.

23. All of the following reflected the power and magnificence of royal absolutism *except*
    a. soaring Gothic cathedrals.
    b. baroque palaces.
    c. royal cities.
    d. broad, urban avenues.

24. The result of the Czech noble revolt of 1618 was
    a. their replacement by Habsburg loyalists.
    b. Czech independence.
    c. Czech autonomy within the Habsburg state.
    d. the rise of Protestantism in Bohemia.

25. The Habsburg state was made up of
    a. Austria, Bohemia, and Hungary.
    b. Austria, Prussia, and Hungary.
    c. Hungary, Brandenburg, and Silesia.
    d. Silesia, Bohemia, and Austria.

Major Political Ideas

1. Why do you think the history of Russia is more a history of servitude than of freedom? Was the major reason for the reinstatement of serfdom political or economic? Explain.

2. Compare and contrast the power of the nobility and the middle class in Russia with that of the nobility and the middle class in of western Europe.

Issues for Essays and Discussion

1. Trace the fortunes and political power of the noble classes in Russia, Austria, and Prussia from about 1300 to about the middle of the 1700s. How did the monarchs gain the upper hand?

2. Peter the Great of Russia and Frederick William the Great Elector of Prussia are often viewed as heroes and reformers in the histories of their own countries. How valid is this assessment?

Interpretation of Visual Sources

Study the print entitled *Molding the Prussian Spirit* on page 543 of the textbook. Describe the scene. Why would this print have been included in a book for children? What were the reasons for Prussia's "obsessive bent for military organization and military scales of value"?

Geography

1. On Outline Map 17.3 provided, and using Map 17.3 in the textbook for reference, mark the following: the area covered by the principality of Moscow in 1300, the territories acquired by the principality of Moscow from 1300 to 1689, the acquisitions of Peter the Great.

2. Looking at Map 17.2 in the textbook, identify the three territorial parts of the Habsburg (Austrian) state and explain how they came to be united.

Outline Map 17.3

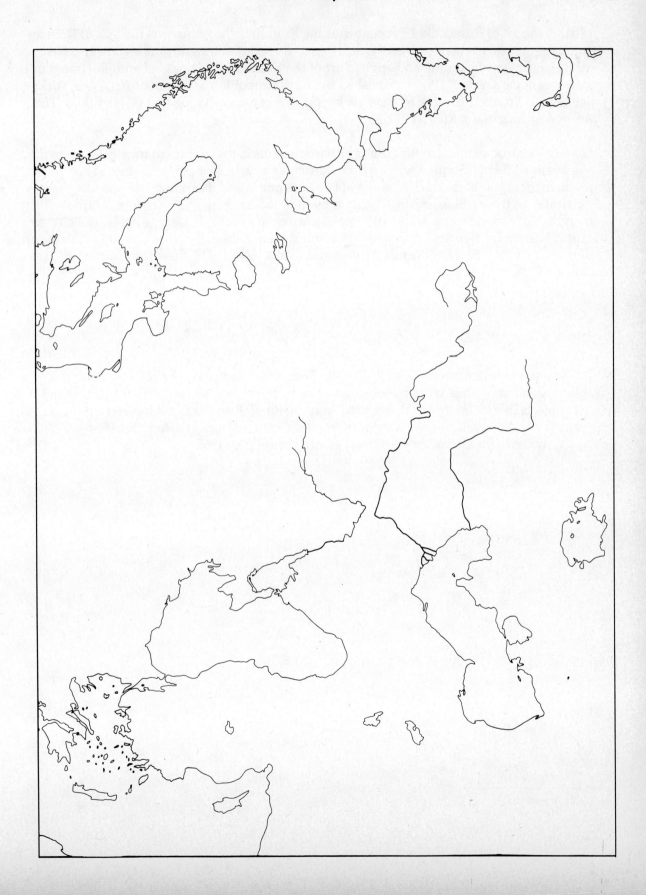

Understanding History Through the Arts

1. What is the art of Russia like? For centuries the Kremlin in Moscow was the axis of Russian culture—the place where works of great historical and artistic significance were amassed. Many examples of painting and applied art of the Kremlin are discussed and illustrated in *Treasures of the Kremlin** (1979), published by the Metropolitan Museum of Art, New York. See also, T. Froncek, ed., *The Horizon Book of the Arts of Russia* (1970), and G. Hamilton, *The Art and Architecture of Russia* (1975).

2. How does baroque music reflect the age? Baroque music, the dominant musical style in the age of absolutism, was often written for a particular monarch or princely court. The mathematical and harmonic emphasis of baroque music and its aristocratic patronage are illustrated in the six *Brandenburg Concertos* by Johann Sebastian Bach, written for the margrave of Brandenburg in the early eighteenth century, and in George F. Handel's *Water Music*, written for George I of England at about the same time. Both of these are available on numerous recordings. For the history of baroque music, see M. F. Bukofzer, *Music in the Baroque Era* (1947).

Problems for Further Investigation

What Western ideas influenced Peter the Great? The personality and reign of Tsar Peter the Great have generated considerable controversy for many years. Ideas for research in this and related subjects in Russian history can be found in M. Raeff, *Peter the Great* (rev. ed., 1972); V. Klyuchevsky and N. Riasanovsky, *Images of Peter the Great in Russian History and Thought* (1985); and L. J. Oliva, ed., *Russia and the West from Peter to Khrushchev* (1965).

---

*Available in paperback.

Chapter 18
Toward a New World-View

Chapter Questions

After reading and studying this chapter you should be able to answer the following questions:

Why did the world-view of the educated classes change from a primarily religious one to one that was primarily secular and scientific? How did this new outlook on life affect society and politics?

Chapter Summary

In the course of the seventeenth and eighteenth centuries the educated classes of Europe moved from a world-view that was basically religious to one that was primarily secular. The development of scientific knowledge was the key cause of this intellectual change. Until about 1500, scientific thought reflected the Aristotelian-medieval world-view, which taught that a motionless earth was at the center of a universe made up of planets and stars in ten crystal spheres. These and many other beliefs showed that science was primarily a branch of religion. Beginning with Copernicus, who taught that the earth revolved around the sun, Europeans slowly began to reject Aristotelian-medieval scientific thought. They developed a new conception of a universe based on natural laws, not on a personal God. Isaac Newton formulated the great scientific synthesis: the law of universal gravitation. This was the culminating point of the scientific revolution.

The new science was more important for intellectual development than for economic activity or everyday life, for above all it promoted critical thinking. Nothing was to be accepted on faith; everything was to be submitted to the rational, scientific way of thinking. This critical examination of everything, from religion and education to war and politics, was the program of the Enlightenment and the accomplishment of the philosophes, a group of thinkers who propagandized the new world-view across Europe and the North American colonies. These writers and thinkers, among them Voltaire, Montesquieu, and Diderot, produced books and articles that influenced all classes and whose primary intent was teaching people how to think critically and objectively about all matters.

The philosophes were reformers, not revolutionaries. Their "enlightened" ideas were adopted by a number of monarchs who sought to promote the advancement of knowledge and improve the lives of their subjects. Most important in this group were Frederick II of Prussia and Catherine II of Russia and the Habsburgs, Maria Theresa and Joseph II. Despite some reforms, particularly in the area of law, Frederick and Catherine's role in the Enlightenment was in the abstract rather than the practical. The Habsburgs were more successful in legal and tax reform, control of the church, and improvement of the lot of the serfs, although much of Joseph's spectacular peasant reform was later undone. Yet reform of society from the top down, that is, by the absolute monarchs through "enlightened absolutism," proved to be impossible because the enlightened monarchs could not ignore the demands of their conservative nobilities. In the end, it was revolution, not enlightened absolutism, that changed and reformed society.

The chapter closes with a discussion of how the middle class of France used the Parlement of Paris and its judgeships as a counterweight to absolutism and the revival of aristocratic power. This opposition was crushed by Louis XV's chancellor Maupeou, only to reappear with the new King Louis XVI.

Study Outline

Use this outline to preview the chapter before you read a particular section and than as a self-check to test your reading comprehension after you have read the chapter section.

  I. The scientific revolution: the origin of the modern world
- A. The scientific revolution of the seventeenth century was the major cause of the change in world-view and one of the key developments in the evolution of Western society.
- B. Scientific thought in the early 1500s
  1. European ideas about the universe were based on Aristotelian-medieval ideas.
     - a. Central to this view was the belief in a motionless earth fixed at the center of the universe.
     - b. Around the earth moved ten crystal spheres, and beyond the spheres was heaven.
  2. Aristotle's scheme suited Christianity because it positioned human beings at the center of the universe and established a home for God.
  3. Science in this period was primarily a branch of theology.
- C. The Copernican hypothesis
  1. Copernicus, a Polish clergyman and astronomer, claimed that the earth revolved around the sun and that the sun was the center of the universe.
  2. This heliocentric theory was a departure from medieval thought and created doubts about traditional Christianity.
- D. From Tycho Brahe to Galileo
  1. Brahe set the stage for the modern study of astronomy by building an observatory and collecting data.
  2. His assistant, Kepler, formulated three laws of planetary motion that proved the precise relationships among planets in a sun-centered universe.
  3. Galileo discovered the laws of motion using the experimental method—the cornerstone of modern science.
     - a. He also applied the experimental method to astronomy, using the newly invented telescope.

   b. Galileo was tried by the Inquisition for heresy in 1633 and forced to recant his views.

 E. Newton's synthesis

  1. Newton integrated the astronomy of Copernicus and Kepler with the physics of Galileo.

   a. He formulated a set of mathematical laws to explain motion and mechanics.

   b. The key feature in his synthesis was the law of universal gravitation.

  2. Henceforth, the universe could be explained through mathematics.

 F. Causes of the scientific revolution

  1. Medieval universities provided the framework for the new science.

  2. The Renaissance stimulated science by rediscovering ancient mathematics and supporting scientific investigations.

  3. The navigational problems of sea voyages generated scientific research and new instruments.

  4. Better ways of obtaining knowledge about the world improved scientific methods.

   a. Bacon advocated empirical, experimental research.

   b. Descartes stressed mathematics and deductive reasoning.

  5. After about 1630 the Catholic church discouraged science while Protestantism tended to favor it.

 G. Some consequences of the scientific revolution

  1. A scientific community emerged whose primary goal was the expansion of knowledge.

  2. A modern scientific method arose that was both theoretical and experimental and refused to base its conclusions on tradition and established sources.

  3. Because the link between pure science and applied technology was weak, the scientific revolution had little effect on daily life before the nineteenth century.

II. The Enlightenment

 A. Enlightenment ideas made up a new world-view.

  1. Natural science and reason can explain all aspects of life.

  2. The scientific method can explain the laws of human society.

  3. Progress—the creation of better societies and better people—is possible.

 B. The emergence of the Enlightenment

  1. Many writers made scientific thought understandable to a large nonscientific audience.

   a. Fontenelle stressed the idea of progress.

   b. He was also cynical about organized religion and absolute religious truth.

  2. Skeptics such as Bayle concluded that nothing can be known beyond all doubt and stressed open-mindedness.

  3. The growth of world travel led Europeans to look at truth and morality in relative, not absolute, terms.

  4. In his *Essay Concerning Human Understanding,* Locke insisted that all ideas are derived from experience—the human mind at birth is like a blank table (*tabula rasa*).

 C. The philosophes and their ideas

  1. The philosophes asked fundamental philosophical questions and were committed to the reformation of society and humanity, although they often had to cloak attacks on church and state in satire.

a. Montesquieu's theory of the separation of powers was extremely influential.
b. Voltaire challenged traditional Catholic theology and exhibited a characteristic philosophe belief in a distant God who let human affairs take their own course.
c. Diderot and d'Alembert edited the *Encyclopedia*, which examined all of human knowledge and attempted to teach people how to think critically and rationally.

2. The later Enlightenment writers built rigid and dogmatic systems.
a. D'Holbach argued that humans were completely controlled by outside forces.
b. Hume argued that the mind is nothing but a bundle of impressions that originate in sense experiences.
c. Rousseau attacked rationalism and civilization; he claimed that children must develop naturally and spontaneously, and in *The Social Contract* argued that the general will of the people is sacred and absolute.

D. The social setting of the Enlightenment
1. Enlightenment ideas—including new ideas about women's rights—were spread by salons of the upper classes.
2. The salons were often presided over by women.
3. These salons seemed to have functioned as informal "schools" for women.

III. The development of absolutism
A. Many philosophes believed that "enlightened" reform would come by way of "enlightened" monarchs.
1. The philosophes believed that a benevolent absolutism offered the best chance for improving society.
2. The rulers seemed to seek the philosophes' advice.
3. The philosophes distrusted the masses and felt that change had to come from above.

B. The "Greats": Frederick II of Prussia and Catherine II of Russia
1. Frederick II used the War of the Austrian Succession (1740–1748) to expand Prussia into a great power by seizing Silesia.
2. The Seven Years' War (1756–1763) saw an attempt by Maria Theresa, with the help of France and Russia, to regain Silesia, but it failed.
3. Frederick allowed religious freedom and promoted education, legal reform, and economic growth but never tried to change Prussia's social structure.
4. Catherine II imported Western culture to Russia, supported the philosophes, and began a program of domestic reform.
5. The Pugachev uprising in 1773 led her to reverse the trend toward reform of serfdom and give nobles absolute control of their serfs.
6. She engaged in a policy of territorial expansion and, with Prussia and Austria, carved up Poland.

C. Absolutism in France and Austria
1. Favored by the duke of Orléans, who governed as a regent until 1723, the French nobility regained much of the power it had lost under Louis XIV.
a. The Parlement of Paris won two decisive victories against taxation.
b. It then asserted that the king could not levy taxes without its consent.
2. Under Louis XV the French minister Maupeou began the restoration of royal absolutism by abolishing the Parlement of Paris.

3. Louis XVI reinstated the Parlement of Paris, and the country drifted toward renewed financial and political crises.
4. Maria Theresa of Austria introduced reforms that limited church power, revised the tax system and the bureaucracy, and reduced the power of the lords over the serfs.
5. Her successor, Joseph II, was a dedicated reformer who abolished serfdom, taxed all equally, and granted religious freedom.
6. Because of opposition from both the nobles and the peasants, Joseph's reforms were short-lived.
D. An overall evaluation of absolutism and the influence of the Enlightenment
1. In France, the rise of judicial and aristocratic opposition combined with liberalism put absolutism on the defensive.
2. In eastern Europe the results of enlightened absolutism were modest and absolutism remained strong.
3. By combining state building with the culture and critical thinking of the Enlightenment, absolute monarchs succeeded in expanding the role of the state in the life of society.

Review Questions

Check your understanding of this chapter by answering the following questions.

1. Contrast the old Aristotelian-medieval world-view with that of the sixteenth and seventeenth centuries. What were the contributions of Copernicus, Brahe, Kepler, Galileo, and Newton? What is meant by Newton's "synthesis"?
2. How did the new scientific theory and discoveries alter the concept of God and religion? Did science, in fact, come to dictate humanity's concept of God?
3. What were the scientific and religious implications of Copernicus's theory?
4. Discuss the origins and the momentum of the scientific revolution in terms of (a) its own "internal logic" and (b) external and nonscientific causes.
5. How did Bacon and Descartes contribute to the development of the modern scientific method?
6. Did the Catholic and Protestant churches retard or foster scientific investigation? Explain.
7. What were the consequences of the rise of modern science?
8. What were the central concepts of the Enlightenment?
9. Who were the philosophes and what did they believe?
10. In what ways were Frederick of Prussia and Catherine of Russia enlightened monarchs?
11. What was the effect of Catherine's reign on (a) the Russian nobility, (b) the Russian serfs, and (c) the position of Russia in the European balance of power?
12. What was the nature of the power struggle between the aristocrats and Louis XV of France?

Study-Review Exercises

Define the following key concepts and terms.

Aristotelian world-view

empirical method

Copernican hypothesis

deductive reasoning

rationalism

progress

secular

skepticism

tabula rasa

Parlement of Paris

Enlightenment

enlightened absolutism

philosophes

Gresham College

Identify and explain the significance of each of the following people.

Diderot

Bayle

Kepler

Galileo

Bacon

Descartes

D'Holbach

Newton

Montesquieu

Voltaire

Copernicus

Brahe

Catherine the Great

Frederick the Great

Maria Theresa

Louis XV

Joseph II

Explain the new ideas of each the following books. What were some of the consequences of these ideas?
On the Revolutions of the Heavenly Spheres

New Astronomy or Celestial Physics

Two New Sciences

Principia

Conversations on the Plurality Of Worlds of 1686

Historical and Critical Dictionary

The Spirit of the Laws

Essay Concerning Human Understanding

Philosophical Dictionary

Encyclopedia: The Rational Dictionary of the Sciences, the Arts, and the Crafts

The Social Contract

Test your understanding of the chapter by providing the correct answers.
1. According to Aristotle, the sublunar world was made up of four elements: air, fire,

   _____ , and _____ .

2. Copernicus *did/did not* attempt to disprove the existence of God.

3. Galileo claimed that *motion/rest* is the natural state of all objects.

4. The key feature in Newton's synthesis was the law of _____ .

5. In the medieval universities, science emerged as a branch of _____ .

6. The method of finding latitude came out of study and experimentation in the country of

   _____ .

7. The idea of "progress" *was/was not* widespread in the Middle Ages.

8. In the seventeenth and eighteenth centuries a close link between pure (theoretical) science and applied technology *did/did not* exist.

9. A _____ is one who believes that nothing can ever be known beyond all doubt.

10. Voltaire believed that _____ was history's greatest man because he used his genius to benefit humanity.

11. Overall, Joseph II of Austria *succeeded/failed* as an enlightened monarch.

Place the following ideas in correct chronological order.

Copernicus's idea that the sun is the center of the universe
Montesquieu's theory of the separation of powers
D'Holbach's theory that human beings were machines
Aristotle's view of a motionless earth at the center of the universe
Newton's law of universal gravitation

1.

2.

3.

4.

5.

Multiple-Choice Questions

1. Catherine the Great accomplished which of the following?
   a. Annexed part of Poland
   b. Freed the Russian serfs
   c. Denied any sort of religious toleration
   d. Persecuted the philosophes of France

2. "Enlightened" monarchs believed in all of the following *except*
   a. reform.
   b. democracy.
   c. cultural values of the Enlightenment.
   d. secularism.

3. Geoffrin and Deffand were
   a. scientific writers.
   b. religious leaders in France.
   c. leaders of the Enlightenment salons.
   d. leaders of the serf uprising in France.

4. The philosophes were
   a. mainly university professors.
   b. generally hostile to monarchial government.
   c. enthusiastic supporters of the Catholic church.
   d. satirists who wished to reform society and humanity.

5. The social setting of the Enlightenment
   a. excluded women.
   b. was characterized by poverty and boredom.
   c. was dominated by government officials.
   d. was characterized by witty and intelligent conversation.

6. Catherine the Great
   a. believed the philosophes were dangerous revolutionaries.
   b. freed the serfs to satisfy Diderot.
   c. increased the size of the Russian Empire.
   d. established a strong constitutional monarchy.

7. According to medieval thought, the center of the universe was the
   a. sun.
   b. earth.
   c. moon.
   d. heaven.

8. The Aristotelian world-view placed emphasis on the idea of
   a. the sun as the center of the universe.
   b. the rejection of Christian theology.
   c. an earth that moves in space.
   d. crystal spheres moving around the earth.

9. Copernicus's theory of a sun-centered universe
   a. suggested the universe was small and closed.
   b. questioned the idea that crystal spheres moved the stars around the earth.
   c. suggested that the worlds of heaven and earth were radically different from each other.
   d. suggested an enormous and possibly infinite universe.

10. The first astronomer to prove his theories through the use of mathematical equations was
    a. Galileo.
    b. Kepler.
    c. Brahe.
    d. Newton.

11. D'Holbach, Hume, and Rousseau are examples of the later Enlightenment trend toward
    a. rigid systems.
    b. social satire.
    c. religion.
    d. the idea of absolutism.

12. The French philosopher who rejected his contemporaries and whose writings influenced the romantic movement was
    a. Rousseau.
    b. Voltaire.
    c. Diderot.
    d. Condorcet.

13. The gathering ground for many who wished to discuss the ideas of the French Enlightenment was the
    a. salon.
    b. lecture hall.
    c. palace at Versailles.
    d. University of Paris.

14. Frederick II is considered an enlightened monarch because he
    a. regained Silesia from Prussia.
    b. wrote poetry and improved the legal and bureaucratic systems.
    c. kept the aristocrats in a dominant position socially and politically.
    d. avoided war.

15. Catherine the Great of Russia hardened her position on serfdom after the
    a. Pugachev rebellion.
    b. Moscow rebellion.
    b. Polish rebellion.
    c. "Five Year" rebellion.

16. After Louis XIV's death
    a. the nobility lost considerable power.
    b. the lower classes secured judicial positions in the Parlement.
    c. the French government struggled with severe economic difficulties.
    d. absolutism remained firmly entrenched during the succeeding reign.

17. Which of the following used the War of the Austrian Succession to expand Prussia into a great power?
    a. Joseph II
    b. Frederick II
    c. Frederick William I
    d. Louis XIV

18. The aggressiveness of Prussia, Austria, and Russia led to the disappearance of which eastern European kingdom from the map after 1795?
    a. Hungary
    b. Sweden
    c. Brandenburg
    d. Poland

19. Francis Bacon's great contribution to scientific methodology was
    a. the geocentric theory.
    b. the notion of logical speculation.
    c. the philosophy of empiricism.
    d. analytic geometry.

20. Which of the following men set the stage for the modern study of astronomy by building an observatory and collecting data?
    a. Darwin
    b. Hume
    c. Newton
    d. Brahe

21. The Parlement of Paris was
    a. a high court dominated by nobles who were formerly middle class.
    b. a center of royal absolutism.
    c. used by Maupeou to strengthen the king's position.
    d. not interested in tax reform or finance.

22. Maria Theresa was a devout Catholic who
    a. sought to limit the church's influence in Austria.
    b. was not interested in the Enlightenment.
    c. did nothing to improve the lot of the agricultural population.
    d. was a weak monarch unable to hold the Austrian Empire together.

23. After 1715 in France, the direction of political change was
    a. toward greater absolutism.
    b. away from Enlightenment political thought.
    c. in favor of opposition forces—largely the nobility and the Parlement of Paris.
    d. toward "enlightened absolutism."

24. In his famous book *Emile*, Rousseau argued that
    a. children are born with corrupting ideas and must be tamed.
    b. women should be taught the same subjects as men.
    c. boys and girls should be taught to operate in separate spheres.
    d. children should be exposed to corruption at an early age so that they know how to reject it.

25. Descartes' idea was that the world consists of two fundamental entities or substances, which we can call
    a. the physical and the spiritual.
    b. water and air.
    c. reason and passion.
    d. deduction and induction.

Major Political Ideas

1. Describe the concept of enlightened absolutism in terms of its political and legal goals. Did it work? What was the response of the aristocracy to this political concept?

2. This chapter emphasizes the difference between a secular and religious view of the world. What is meant by *secular* and what effect did a secular world-view have on political loyalties?

Issues for Essays and Discussion

In the course of the eighteenth century the basic outlook on life and society held by many men and women changed dramatically. In what ways did this transformation affect scientific, political, religious, social, and economic thought? In working out your argument explain how specific new scientific ideas and methods of reasoning led directly to new political and social ideas.

Interpretation of Visual Sources

Study the print of Louis XIV's visit to the Royal Academy in 1671 on page 571 of the textbook. Write a paragraph on how this print illustrates the relationship between science and politics. Did the scientific revolution have a great effect on how kings ran their states? Why were some monarchs interested in science? Does this print give any clues?

Geography

Compare Map 18.1 to Map 17.2. Describe what the "partition of Poland" was, when it took place, why, and who benefited.

Understanding History Through the Arts

How did the Enlightenment affect the arts? This period is often referred to as the age of the baroque style, and the achievements of its great artists are discussed in M. Kitson, *The Age of the Baroque* (1966). See also Chapter 6 in N. Pevsner, *An Outline of European Architecture* (7th ed., 1963), and E. Kaufmann, *Architecture in the Age of Reason—Baroque and Post-Baroque in England, Italy, and France* (1955, *1968). On the subject of the Scottish Enlightenment see T. A. Markus, ed., *Order and Space: Architectural Form and Its Context in the Scottish Enlightenment* (1982). Few artists captured English life as well as the painter Hogarth, whose *Rake's Progress* and *Harlot's Progress* point to the consequences of moral decay. Hogarth's paintings can be seen and studied in W. Gaunt, *The World of William Hogarth* (1978), and D. Bindman, *Hogarth** (1981). For a description of French life by painters of the time, see T. E. Crow, *Painters and Public Life in Eighteenth-Century Paris* (1985).

Problems for Further Investigation

1. Write an essay in which you describe and analyze an important work of the Enlightenment. What were the ideas set forth by the author and how do these ideas reflect or illustrate Enlightenment thought and change? The two greatest philosophes of the age of Enlightenment were Rousseau and Voltaire. Rousseau's ideas on education and natural law are set forth in *Emile,* and Voltaire's most-praised work is *Candide,* a funny and sometimes bawdy parody of eighteenth-century life and thought. Selections from the great *Encyclopedia* are found in S. Gendzier, ed., *Denis Diderot: The Encyclopedia: Selections* (1967). Much of the fiction of the eighteenth century reflects, often in satire, the spirit of the new world-view—Jonathan Swift, *Gulliver's Travels;* Daniel Defoe, *Moll Flanders;* and Henry Fielding, *Tom Jones,* are just a few of the many novels of this period. In Germany, the *Sturm und Drang* (storm and stress) movement embraced the ideas of the Enlightenment and

---

*Available in paperback.

romanticism and produced works such as Lessing's *Nathan the Wise,* which stressed a universal religion.

2. How have historians interpreted the meaning and impact of the Enlightenment? Students interested in this topic will want to begin with two books that set forth some of the major issues and schools of interpretation on the subject: B. Tierney et al., eds., *Enlightenment—The Age of Reason** (1967), and R. Wines, ed., *Enlightened Despotism** (1967).

3. Why was it not until the seventeenth century that rational science emerged? What has been the relationship between science and religion in Western society? What ideas did Darwin and modern biologists draw from the scientific revolution of 1500–1800? These are just a few of the questions asked by scholars of the subject. Begin your investigation with H. Butterfield, *The Origins of Modern Science* (1951); A. R. Hall, *From Galileo to Newton, 1630–1720* (1963); G. Sarton, *Introduction to the History of Science* (1927–1948, 5 vols.); or L. Thorndike, *History of Magic and Experimental Science* (1923–1958). On particular figures in science see F. S. Taylor, *Galileo and the Freedom of Thought* (1938); A. Armitage, *Copernicus, the Founder of Modern Astronomy* (1938); M. Casoar, *Johannes Kepler,* C. Heffman, trans. (1959); L. T. More, *Isaac Newton* (1934); and I. Cohen, *Franklin and Newton* (1956).

---

*Available in paperback.

Studying Effectively—Exercise 4

Learning to Classify Information According to Sequence

As you know, a great deal of historical information is classified by sequence, in which things follow each other in time. This kind of *sequential order* is also known as *time order* or *chronological order*.

Attention to time sequence is important in the study of history for at least two reasons.

1. It helps you organize historical information effectively.

2. It promotes historical understanding. If you know the order in which events happen, you can think intelligently about questions of cause and effect. You can begin to evaluate conflicting interpretations.

Since time sequences are essential in historical study, the authors have placed a number of timelines in the text to help you organize the historical information.

Two Fallacies Regarding Time Sequences

One common fallacy is often known by the famous Latin phrase *post hoc, ergo propter hoc:* "after this, therefore because of this." This fallacy assumes that one happening that follows another *must* be caused by the first happening. Obviously, some great development (such as the Protestant Reformation) could come after another (the Italian Renaissance) without being caused by it. *Causal relationships must be demonstrated, not simply assumed on the basis of the "after this, therefore because of this" fallacy.*

A second common, if old-fashioned, fallacy assumes that time sequences are composed only of political facts with precise data. But in considering social, intellectual, and economic developments, historians must often speak with less chronological exactitude—in terms of decades or even centuries, for example. Yet they still use time sequences, and students of history must recognize them. For example, did you realize that the sections on "The Scientific Revolution" and "The Enlightenment" in Chapter 18 are very conscientious about time sequence, even though they do not deal with political facts?

Exercise

Reread the large section in Chapter 18 on "The Scientific Revolution" with an eye for dates and sequential order. Then take a sheet of notebook paper and with the book open make a "Timeline for the Scientific Revolution." Pick out at least a dozen important events and put them in the time sequence, with a word or two to explain the significance when possible.

Suggestion: Do not confine yourself solely to specific events with specific dates. Also, integrate some items from the subsection on the causes of the scientific revolution into the sequence. You may find that constructing timelines helps you organize your study.

After you have completed your timeline, compare it with the one on the following page, which shows how one of the authors of the text did this assignment.

Timeline on the Scientific Revolution

(1300–1500)	Renaissance stimulates development of mathematics
early 1500s	Aristotle's ideas on movement and universe still dominant
1543	Copernicus publishes *On the Revolution of the Heavenly Spheres*
1572, 1577	New star and comet create more doubts about traditional astronomy
1546–1601	Tycho Brache—famous astronomer, creates mass of observations
1571–1630	Johannes Kepler—his three laws prove Copernican theory and demolish Aristotle's beliefs
1589	Galileo Galilei (1564–1642) named professor of mathematics
1610	Galileo studies moon with telescope and writes of experience
1561–1626	Francis Bacon—English scientific enthusiast, advocates experimental (inductive) method
1596–1650	René Descartes—French philosopher, discovers analytical geometry in 1619 and advocates theoretical (deductive) method
to about 1630	All religious authorities oppose Copernican theory
about 1632	Galileo tried by papal inquisition
1622	Royal Society of London founded—brings scientists and practical men together
1687	Isaac Newton publishes his *Principia,* synthesizing existing knowledge around idea of universal gravitation
to late 1700s	Consequences of scientific revolution primarily intellectual, not economic

Chapter 19
The Expansion of Europe in the Eighteenth Century

Chapter Questions

After reading and studying this chapter you should be able to answer the following questions:

How did the European economy expand and change in the eighteenth century? What were the causes of this expansion? How did these changes affect people and their work?

Chapter Summary

How did our "modern" world begin? This chapter discusses the important economic and demographic changes of the eighteenth century, which led up to the Industrial Revolution. It also prepares us for understanding the life of ordinary people in the eighteenth century, which is the subject of the following chapter.

The chapter covers four important and interrelated subjects. First, the centuries-old open-field system of agricultural production, a system that was both inefficient and unjust, is described. This system was gradually transformed into a more productive system of capitalistic farming, first in the Low Countries and then in England. Some English peasants suffered in the process, but on the whole the changes added up to a highly beneficial agricultural revolution. The second topic is the explosive growth of European population in the eighteenth century. This growth, still imperfectly understood, was probably due largely to the disappearance of the plague and to new and better foods, such as the potato. Doctors and organized medicine played a very minor role in the improvements in health. Third, the chapter discusses the movement of manufacturing from urban shops to cottages in the countryside. Rural families worked there as units in the new domestic system, which provided employment for many in the growing population. The domestic system was particularly effective in the textile industry, which this chapter examines in detail.

Finally, the chapter shows how the mercantilist economic philosophy of the time resulted in world wars for trade and colonies. Mercantilism also led to the acquisition of huge markets for British manufactured goods, especially cloth. The demand from these new markets fostered the continued growth of the domestic system and put pressure on it. This eventually led to important inventions and the development of the more efficient factory system. Thus the modern world was born. It is important to look for the interrelatedness of these changes and to keep in mind that it was in only one country, Great Britain, that all of these forces were fully at work.

Study Outline

Use this outline to preview the chapter before you read a particular section in your textbook and then as a self-check to test your reading comprehension after you have read the chapter section.

I. Agriculture and the land
   A. The hazards of an agrarian economy
      1. The agricultural yields in seventeenth century Europe were not much higher than in ancient Greece.
      2. Frequent poor harvests and bad weather led to famine and disease.
   B. The open-field system
      1. The open-field system, developed during the Middle Ages, divided the land into a few large fields, which were then cut up into long, narrow strips.
      2. The fields were farmed jointly by the community, but a large portion of the arable land was always left fallow.
      3. Common lands were set aside for community use.
      4. The labor and tax system throughout Europe was unjust, but eastern European peasants suffered the most.
         a. There were few limitations on the amount of forced labor the lord could require.
         b. Serfs could be sold.
      5. By the eighteenth century most peasants in western Europe were free from serfdom, and many owned some land.
   C. The agricultural revolution of the late seventeenth and eighteenth centuries
      1. The use of idle fallow land by crop rotation increased cultivation, which meant more food.
         a. The secret was in alternating grain crops with nitrogen-storing crops, such as peas and beans, root crops, and grasses.
         b. This meant more fodder for animals, which meant more meat for the people and more manure for fertilizer.
         c. These improvements necessitated ending the open-field system by "enclosing" the fields.
      2. Enclosure of the open fields to permit crop rotation also meant the disappearance of common land.
         a. Many peasants and noble landowners opposed these changes.
         b. The enclosure process was slow, and enclosed and open fields existed side by side for a long time.
   D. The leadership of the Low Countries and England
      1. By the middle of the seventeenth century, the Low Countries led in intensive farming.
         a. This Dutch lead was due largely to the need to feed a growing population.

b. The growth of the urban population provided good markets for the produce.

2. Dutch engineers such as Vermuyden helped England drain its marshes to create more arable land.

a. Townsend was one of the pioneers of English agricultural improvement.

b. Tull advocated the use of horses for plowing and drilling equipment for sowing seeds.

E. The cost of enclosure

1. Some historians argue that the English landowners were more efficient than continental owners, and that enclosures were fair.

2. Others argue that the enclosure acts forced small peasants and landless cottagers off the land.

3. In reality, the enclosure and the exclusion of cottagers and laborers had begun as early as the sixteenth century.

a. It was the independent peasant farmers who could not compete, and thus began to disappear.

b. The tenant farmers, who rented land from the big landlords, benefited from enclosure.

c. By 1815 a tiny minority of English and Scottish landlords held most of the land—which they rented to tenants, who hired laborers.

4. The eighteenth-century enclosure movement marked the completion of the rise of market-oriented estate agriculture and the emergence of a landless rural proletariat.

II. The beginning of the population explosion

A. The limitations on population growth up to 1700

1. The traditional checks on growth were famine, disease, and war.

2. These checks kept Europe's population growth rate fairly low.

B. The new pattern of population growth in the eighteenth century

1. The basic cause of population growth was fewer deaths, partly owing to the disappearance of the plague.

a. Stricter quarantine measures helped eliminate the plague.

b. The elimination of the black rat by the brown rat was a key reason for the disappearance of the disease.

2. Advances in medicine, such as inoculation against smallpox, did little to reduce the death rate in Europe.

3. Improvements in sanitation promoted better public health.

4. An increase in the food supply meant fewer famines and epidemics, especially as transportation improved.

5. The growing population often led to overpopulation and increased rural poverty.

III. The growth of cottage industry

A. Rural industry

1. The rural poor took in manufacturing work to supplement their income.

2. By the eighteenth century this cottage industry challenged the monopoly of the urban craft industry.

B. The putting-out system

1. The putting-out system was based on rural workers producing cloth in their homes for merchant-capitalists, who supplied the raw materials and paid for the finished goods.

2. This capitalist system reduced the problem of rural unemployment and provided cheap goods.
3. England led the way in the conversion from urban to rural textile production.
C. The textile industry in England as an example of the putting-out system
   1. The English textile industry was a family industry: the women would spin and the men would weave.
   2. A major problem was that there were not enough spinners to make yarn for the weaver.
   3. Strained relations often existed between workers and capitalist employers.
   4. The capitalist found it difficult to control the worker and the quality of the product.
IV. Building the Atlantic economy in the eighteenth century
   A. Mercantilism and colonial wars
      1. Mercantilism is a system of economic regulations aimed at increasing the power of the state, particularly by creating a favorable balance of trade.
      2. English mercantilism was further characterized by the use of government regulations to serve the interests of private individuals.
      3. The Navigation Acts were a form of economic warfare.
         a. They required that most goods exported to England be carried on British ships.
         b. These acts gave England a virtual trade monopoly with its colonies.
      4. The French quest for power in Europe and North America led to international wars.
         a. The loss of the War of the Spanish Succession forced France to cede parts of Canada to Britain.
         b. The Seven Years' War (1756–1763) was the decisive struggle in the French-British competition for colonial empire, and France ended up losing all its North American possessions.
   B. Land and wealth in North America
      1. Colonies helped relieve European poverty and surplus population as settlers eagerly took up farming on the virtually free land.
         a. The availability of land made labor expensive in the colonies.
         b. Cheap land and scarce labor were critical factors in the growth of slavery.
      2. The English mercantilist system benefited American colonists.
         a. They exported food to the West Indies to feed the slaves and sugar and tobacco to Britain.
         b. The American shipping industry grew.
      3. The population of the North American colonies grew very quickly during the eighteenth century, and the standards of living were fairly high.
   C. The growth of foreign trade
      1. Trade with the English colonists compensated for a decline in English trade on the Continent.
      2. The colonies also encouraged industrial growth in England.
   D. Revival in colonial Latin America
      1. Spain's political revitalization was matched by economic improvement in its colonies.
         a. Silver mining recovered in Mexico and Peru.
         b. Trade grew, though industry remained weak.

2. In much of Latin America, Creole landowners dominated the economy and the Indian population by means of debt peonage.
3. Compared to North America, racial mixing was more frequent in Spanish America.

Review Questions

Check your understanding of the chapter by answering the following questions.

1. How did the open-field system work? Why was much of the land left uncultivated while the people sometimes starved?
2. What changes brought the open-field system to an end?
3. Where did the modern agricultural revolution originate? Why?
4. What is meant by *enclosure*? Was this movement a great swindle of the poor by the rich, as some have claimed?
5. Was the dramatic growth of population in the eighteenth century due to a decreasing death rate or an increasing birthrate? Explain.
6. How was the grip of the deadly bubonic plague finally broken?
7. What improvements in the eighteenth century contributed to the decline of disease and famine?
8. How did the putting-out system work and why did it grow?
9. What were the advantages and disadvantages of the putting-out system for the merchant-capitalist? For the worker?
10. What was mercantilism? How could it have been a cause of war? Of economic growth?
11. The eighteenth century witnessed a large number of expensive and drawn-out wars. Who was attempting to alter the balance of power? Were the causes of these wars economic or political?
12. Did the American colonists and the American colonial economy benefit or suffer from the British mercantilistic colonial system?
13. What role did the Creoles play in colonial Latin America? The *mestizos*? The Indians?

Study-Review Exercises

Define the following key concepts and terms.

agrarian economy

famine foods

common land

open-field system

enclosure

mercantilism

cottage industry

putting-out system

fallow fields

agricultural revolution

crop rotation

asiento

mestizos

primogeniture

Creole elite

Identify and explain the significance of each of the following people and terms.
Jethro Tull

Charles Townsend

Cornelius Vermuyden

bubonic plague

Asiatic brown rat

British Navigation Acts

Treaty of Paris

Peace of Utrecht

spinning jenny

turnips

potatoes

Explain the following wars in the age of mercantilism by filling in the appropriate information in the table.

Name of War	Dates	Participants	Causes	Outcome
Anglo-Dutch wars				
War of the Spanish Succession				
War of the Austrian Succession				
Seven Years' War				

Fill in the blank with the letter of the correct answer.

_____ 1. Its disappearance encouraged population growth.

_____ 2. Agricultural land set aside for general village use.

_____ 3. The area with the highest average standard of living in the world.

_____ 4. After 1763 the major power in India.

_____ 5. West African slave trade.

_____ 6. Led Europe in agriucltural improvement.

_____ 7. Offspring of racial intermarriage.

_____ 8. The most important new eighteenth-century food.

a. Low Countries
b. *mestizos*
c. commons
d. Thirty Years' War
e. American colonies
f. potato
g. *asiento*
h. France
i. bubonic plague
j. Britain

Multiple-Choice Questions

1. Dutch agricultural innovation in the eighteenth century was due to
   a. the movement of people from cities to rural areas.
   b. British examples.
   c. population growth and extensive urbanization.
   d. the discovery of the open-field system.

2. Which of the following was a weakness of the cottage textile industry?
   a. An imbalance between spinning and weaving
   b. Shortage of labor
   c. Rigid control of the quality of the product
   d. Not enough demand for the product

3. Which of the following is a characteristic of eighteenth-century economic change?
   a. Decreased world trade
   b. The decline of the cottage system of textile production
   c. The creation of more common lands and open fields for production
   d. The increase in both population and food supply

4. The English enclosure movement ultimately resulted in
   a. more land for a greater number of farmers.
   b. fewer opportunities for the well-off tenant farmers.
   c. the concentration of landowning in the hands of a tiny minority.
   d. opportunity for the landless laborer to purchase small farms.

5. The agricultural improvements of the mid-eighteenth century were based on the elimination of
   a. livestock farming.
   b. the open-field system.
   c. rotation of fields.
   d. nitrogen-producing plants, such as peas and beans.

6. Which of the following prevented eighteenth-century peasants from earning a profit on their land?
   a. The combination of oppressive landlords and poor harvests
   b. The plague
   c. The relatively light taxes imposed on them by landlords
   d. Their reliance on crop rotation

7. The mercantilist attitude toward the state was that
   a. the government should regulate the economy.
   b. governmental power should be increased at the expense of private profit.
   c. using governmental economic power to help private interests is unethical.
   d. the economy should be left to operate according to its natural laws.

8. The new farming system consisting of crop rotation and the use of nitrogen-fixing crops caught on quickly in
   a. the Low Countries and England.
   b. Russia.
   c. eastern Europe as a whole.
   d. Scandinavia.

9. The rapid development of Dutch farming was the result of all of the following *except*
   a. the increasing number of cities and towns.
   b. Dutch reluctance to accept agricultural innovations.
   c. an unencumbered political and economic system.
   d. a dense population.

10. A fair description of the European population before 1700 would be that it
    a. was remarkably uniform in its growth.
    b. increased steadily on account of very young marriages and large families.
    c. decreased slightly on account of war, famine, and disease.
    d. grew slowly and erratically.

11. After 1720, the plague did not reappear because of all of the following *except*
    a. the development of an effective vaccination against the disease in 1718.
    b. the practice of isolating carriers of the dread disease.
    c. the invasion of the Asiatic brown rat.
    d. quarantine in Mediterranean ports.

12. In the mid-seventeenth century, England's major maritime competitor was
    a. France.
    b. the Netherlands.
    c. Spain.
    d. Denmark.

13. The Seven Years' War between France and Britain resulted in
    a. British dominance in North America and India.
    b. French dominance in North America and India.
    c. a stalemate.
    d. British dominance only in North America.

14. The slow growth of industry in North America during the colonial period was caused by
    a. the availability of land and the high cost of labor.
    b. a lack of capital for investment.
    c. a scorn for industry.
    d. British settlers in America had no use for manufactured goods.

15. The black-to-white ratio in America by 1774 was
    a. one to four.
    b. one to eight.
    c. one to ten.
    d. one to two.

16. The abundance of land in the American colonies encouraged all of the following *except*
    a. increased population through natural increase and immigration.
    b. a higher standard of living.
    c. the growth of slavery in the southern colonies.
    d. economic inequality.

17. Which of the following resulted from British mercantilist policies?
    a. A reduction of exports to the Continent
    b. A serious decline of Dutch shipping and commerce
    c. British colonists no longer purchasing all of their goods from Britain
    d. A decline of trade with colonial plantation owners

18. The group that used the new farming methods to the fullest in England was
    a. independent farmers.
    b. well-financed, profit-minded tenant farmers.
    c. large landowners.
    d. small landowning wage laborers.

19. The group who formed the aristocratic elite in Spanish America was the
    a. Creoles.
    b. Indians.
    c. *mestizos.*
    d. Habsburgs

20. The landowners who dominated the economy and the Indian population of Spain's Latin American empire are known as
    a. *mestizos.*
    b. Creoles.
    c. mercantilists.
    d. warlords.

21. Vermuyden's famous "Dutch river" canal was located in
    a. Cambridgeshire, England.
    b. the swampland south of Amsterdam.
    c. the province of Groningen in the Netherlands.
    d. eastern Germany.

22. The initial target of the English Navigation Acts was
    a. France.
    b. Spain.
    c. the American colonists.
    d. the Dutch.

23. As a result of British victory in the War of the Spanish Succession, Spain was forced to give up the *asiento*, meaning
    a. the Isthmus of Panama.
    b. Nova Scotia fishing rights.
    c. Mexico.
    d. the West African slave trade.

24. The Seven Years' War, which ended in 1763, was a victory for
    a. France, who received Louisiana.
    b. Spain, who won the *asiento* back.
    c. Britain, who won territory in North America and India.
    d. the colonists in America, who won free trade rights.

25. British men and women, by the workings of the mercantilist system, were able to purchase goods such as sugar, tobacco, and dried fish
    a. only from plantations within the empire, such as America.
    b. from any country in the world.
    c. from the Continent, largely the Dutch, because of cheapness.
    d. from the Spanish merchants of Central and South America.

Major Political Ideas

1. What was agricultural enclosure? One of the most popular political ramifications of the agricultural revolution was the notion that the rich landowners used their power, including political influence, to swindle the poor cottagers and push farm laborers off the land. Do you agree? What are the arguments on both sides, and which is most convincing?

2. Mercantilism was a form of economic capitalism. Define it in full. What is the impact of mercantilism on political thought and political policy? Did mercantilism lead to war?

Issues for Essays and Discussion

From the late seventeenth century into the eighteenth century, western Europe (particularly the Netherlands and Britain) experienced an agricultural change, population explosion, and a growth of rural industry. Explain these changes. Make reference to specific events. In what way, if any, are these three interrelated?

Interpretation of Visual Sources

Study the photograph entitled *Enclosing the Fields* on page 600 of your textbook. What country do you suspect this is? Distinguish the traditional "open field" from the new "enclosed" organization. Identify the old ridges and furrows. Compare this to the print on page 597 and the illustration on page 599. Why were fields such as these enclosed?

Geography

On Outline Map 19.3 provided, and using Map 19.2 in the textbook as reference, mark the colonial holdings of the European countries in North America in 1755. What territorial changes took place in North America after 1763? Which European country gained most territory after 1763? Which country lost the most territory after 1763? Did the largest colonial holdings go to the largest European countries—or was a position on the Atlantic the key factor?

Outline Map 19.3

Understanding History Through the Arts

What influence did the culture of East have on the imperialist westerners? Begin your inquiry with R. Schwab, *The Oriental Renaissance: Europe's Rediscovery of India and the East, 1680–1880* (1987). Conversely, a study of how the West influenced the architecture of India is found in G. H. R. Tillotson, *The Tradition of Indian Architecture: Continuity, Controversy, and Change Since 1850* (1990), and N. Evenson, *Indian Metropolis: A View Toward the West* (1990).

Problems for Further Investigation

1. What were the motives of those who carved out great new empires in South and North America? Why did the northern Europeans settle in North American and the southern Europeans concentrate on South America? Begin your study with D. K. Fieldhouse, *The Colonial Empires* (1971), and R. Davies, *The Rise of Atlantic Economies* (1973). Students interested in Scottish history will find the subject of how Scotland came to dominate the North American tobacco trade covered in T. Devine, *The Tobacco Lords: A Study of the Tobacco Merchants of Glasgow and Their Trading Activities, 1740–1850* (1975).

2. What were the new patterns of urbanization in this age of population growth and agricultural change? An important work on this subject that shows where urbanization took place over a 350-year period is J. De Vries, *European Urbanisation, 1500–1800* (1987).

3. Why did the agricultural revolution take place? How did agricultural change and rural life differ from place to place within Europe? For more on agricultural life in Britain, start with J. D. Chambers and G. E. Mingay, *The Agricultural Revolution (1750–1880)* (1966), and for the Netherlands, with J. de Vries, *The Dutch Rural Economy in the Golden Age, 1500–1700* (1974). On the subject of soil, climate, land tenure, and the routine of peasant life in Russia before 1917 turn to R. Pipes, *Russia Under the Old Regime** (1974, 1982). For Europe in general, F. Huggett, *The Land Question and European Society Since 1650** (1975), presents a picture of how agricultural changes affected the development of European society.

4. Was enclosure a blessing or a great swindle for the British farmer? This question has been debated by historians and social commentators since the movement toward business agriculture began in sixteenth-century England. The general argument against enclosure was first set out in the sixteenth century by Sir Thomas More, who claimed (in his book *Utopia*) that it resulted in rural unemployment and rural crime. It is the enclosures between 1750 and 1850, however, that are the most controversial. The best contemporary coverage of the debate is G. E. Mingay, *Enclosure and the Small Farmer in the Age of the Industrial Revolution** (1968), which also contains a useful bibliography.

---

*Available in paperback.

Chapter 20
The Life of the People

Chapter Questions

After reading and studying this chapter you should be able to answer the following questions:

How did the peasant masses and the urban poor live in western Europe prior to the late-eighteenth-century age of revolution? Why did traditional marriage and sex practices begin to change in the late eighteenth century? What was it like to be a child in preindustrial society? How adequate was the diet and health care of the people of the eighteenth century? Were there any signs of improvement? What influence did religion hold in everyday life and what was pietism?

Chapter Summary

Until recently scholars have not been very interested in how men and women lived in preindustrial society. The aspects of everyday life, such as family relations, sex, marriage, health, and religion, took a secondary place in history. As a result, much of our understanding of these subjects is often based on myth rather than on solid historical research and interpretations. This chapter corrects some of the long-standing myths and provides a close look at the life of the people.

Contrary to early belief, for example, it appears that in western Europe the nuclear rather than the extended family was very common among preindustrial people. Furthermore, preindustrial people did not marry in their early teens, and illegitimacy was not as common as usually thought, and certainly less so than today. The concept of childhood as we know it hardly existed. The author also shows that when the poor got enough to eat their diet was probably almost as nutritionally sound as that of rich people. As for medical science, it probably did more harm than good in the eighteenth century. Also explained in this chapter are the reasons for a kind of "sexual revolution," particularly for women, beginning in the mid-eighteenth century, when young people began engaging in sex at an earlier age and illegitimacy began to rise. These changes accompanied new patterns of marriage and work—much of which were connected to the growth of new economic opportunities for men and women.

Education and literacy improved significantly, particularly in countries such as Prussia and Scotland. In the area of religion the eighteenth century witnessed a tug of war between the Enlightenment's attempt to demystify Christianity and place it on a more rational basis and a popular movement to retain traditional ritual, superstition, and religious mysteries. In Protestant and Catholic countries alike, rulers and religious leaders sought to purify religion by eliminating many ritualistic practices. The response to this reform by the common people in Catholic countries was a resurgence of religious ritual and mysticism, while in Protestant Germany and England there occurred a popular religious revival based on piety and emotional conversion. Meanwhile, most of Europe—Catholic and Protestant—saw the state increase its control over the church.

Study Outline

Use this outline to preview the chapter before you read a particular section in your textbook and then as a self-check to test your reading comprehension after you have read the chapter section.

I. Marriage and the family
   A. Extended and nuclear families
      1. The nuclear family, not the extended family, was most common in preindustrial western and central Europe.
      2. Early marriage was not common prior to 1750, and many women (perhaps as much as half) never married at all.
      3. Marriage was commonly delayed because of poverty and/or local law and tradition.
   B. Work away from home
      1. Many boys left home to work as craftsmen or laborers.
      2. Girls left to work as servants—where they often were physically and sexually mistreated.
   C. Premarital sex and birth-control practices
      1. Illegitimate children were not common in preindustrial society.
      2. Premarital sex was common, but marriage usually followed.
      3. Coitus interruptus was the most common form of birth control.
   D. New patterns of marriage and illegitimacy
      1. The growth of cottage industry (and later, the factory) resulted in people marrying earlier and for love.
      2. The explosion of births and the growth of prostitution from about 1750 to 1850 had several causes.
         a. Increasing illegitimacy signified rebellion against laws that limited the right of the poor to marry.
         b. Pregnant servant girls often turned to prostitution, which also increased illegitimacy.
   E. The question of sexual emancipation for women
      1. Women in cities and factories had limited economic independence.
      2. Poverty caused many people to remain single—leading to premarital sex and illegitimate births.

II. Infants and children in preindustrial society
  A. Child care and nursing
    1. Infant mortality was very high.
    2. Breast-feeding of children was common among poor women.
    3. Middle- and upper-class women hired wet nurses.
    4. The occupation of wet-nursing was often exploitative of lower-class women.
  B. Foundlings and infanticide
    1. "Killing nurses" and infanticide were forms of population control.
    2. Foundling hospitals were established but could not care for all the abandoned babies.
      a. Some had as many as 25,000 children.
      b. In reality, many were simply a form of legalized infanticide.
  C. Attitudes toward children
    1. Attitudes toward children were different from those of today, partly because of the frequency of death.
      a. Parents and doctors were generally indifferent to children.
      b. Children were often neglected or treated brutally.
    2. The Enlightenment brought about more humane treatment of children.
      a. Critics like Rousseau called for more love and understanding of children.
      b. The practice of swaddling was discouraged.
  D. Schools and education
    1. The beginnings of education for common people were in the seventeenth and eighteenth centuries.
    2. Protestantism encouraged popular education.
    3. Literacy increased, especially in France and Scotland, between 1700 and 1800.
III. The European's food
  A. The life span of Europeans increased from twenty-five years to thirty-five years between 1700 and 1800, partly because diet improved and plagues disappeared.
  B. Diet and nutrition
    1. The diet of ordinary people improved.
      a. Poor people ate mainly grains and vegetables.
      b. Milk and meat were rarely eaten.
    2. Rich people ate quite differently from the poor.
      a. Their diet was rich in meat and wine.
      b. They spurned fruits and vegetables.
  C. The impact of diet on health
    1. There were nutritional advantages and disadvantages to the diet of the poor.
      a. Their breads were very nutritious.
      b. Their main problem was getting enough green vegetables and milk.
    2. The rich often ate too much rich food.
  D. New foods and new knowledge about diet
    1. The potato substantially improved the diet of the poor.
      a. For some poor people, particularly in Ireland, the potato replaced grain as the primary food in the eighteenth century.
      b. Elsewhere in Europe, the potato took hold more slowly, but became a staple by the end of the century.

2. There was a growth in market gardening and an improvement in food variety in the eighteenth century.
3. There was some improvement in knowledge about diet, and Galen's influence declined.
4. Greater affluence caused many to turn to less nutritious food such as white bread and sugar.

IV. Medical science and the sick
   A. The medical professionals
      1. The demonic view of disease was common, and faith healers were used to exorcise the demons.
      2. Pharmacists sold drugs that were often harmful to their patients.
      3. Surgeons often operated without anesthetics and in the midst of dirt.
      4. Physicians frequently bled or purged people to death.
   B. The terrible conditions at hospitals
      1. Patients were crowded together, often several to a bed.
      2. There was no fresh air or hygiene.
      3. Hospital reform began in the late eighteenth century.
   C. Mental illness
      1. Mental illness was misunderstood and treated inhumanely.
      2. Some attempts at reform occurred in the late eighteenth century.
   D. Medical experiments and research
      1. Much medical experimentation was creative quackery.
      2. The conquest of smallpox was the greatest medical triumph of the eighteenth century.
         a. Montague and Jenner's work on inoculation was the beginning of a significant decline in smallpox.
         b. Jenner's work laid the foundation for the science of immunology in the nineteenth century.

V. Religion and Christian churches
   A. The institutional church
      1. Despite the critical spirit of the Enlightenment, the local parish church remained important in daily life, and the priest or pastor was the link between the people and the church hierarchy.
      2. The Protestant belief in individualism in religion was tempered by increased state control over the church and religious life.
      3. Catholic monarchs also increased state control over the church, making it less subject to papal influence.
         a. Spain took control of ecclesiastical appointments and the Inquisition and, with France, pressured Rome to dissolve the Jesuits.
         b. In Austria, Maria Theresa and Joseph II greatly reduced the size and influence of the monasteries and convents.
   B. Catholic piety
      1. In Catholic countries the old religious culture of ritual and superstition remained popular.
      2. Catholic clergy reluctantly allowed traditional religion to survive.

C. Protestant revival
1. Pietism stressed religious enthusiasm, popular education, and individual religious development.
2. In England, Wesley was troubled by religious corruption, decline, and uncertainty.
   a. His Methodist movement rejected the Calvinist idea of predestination and stressed salvation through faith.
   b. Wesley's ministry brought on a religious awakening, particularly among the lower classes.

Review Questions

Check your understanding of this chapter by answering the following questions.

1. Did the typical preindustrial family consist of an extended or a nuclear family? What evidence can you cite to support your answer?
2. In *Romeo and Juliet*, Juliet was just fourteen and Romeo was not too many years older. Is this early marriage typical of preindustrial society? Why did so many people not marry at all?
3. When did the custom of late marriage begin to change? Why?
4. Did preindustrial men and women practice birth control? What methods existed?
5. How do you explain that prior to 1750 there were few illegitimate children but there was a growth of illegitimacy thereafter?
6. It is often claimed that factory women, as opposed to their rural counterparts, were sexually liberated. Is this claim correct? Explain.
7. How and why did life expectancy improve in the eighteenth century?
8. What were the differences in the diets of the rich and the poor in the eighteenth century? What nutritional deficiencies existed?
9. How important was the potato in the eighteenth century? Is it important enough to merit more attention from historians?
10. How important were the eighteenth-century advances in medical science in extending the life span?
11. What was the demonic view of disease?
12. It is said that when it came to medical care, the poor were better off than the rich because they could not afford doctors or hospitals. Why might this have been true?
13. Why was there so much controversy over the smallpox inoculation? Was it safe? What contribution did Edward Jenner make to the elimination of this disease?
14. How was mental illness regarded and treated in the eighteenth century?
15. What effect did changes in church-state relations have on the institutions of the church?
16. Describe the forms in which popular religious culture remained in Catholic Europe.
17. Define pietism and describe how it is reflected in the work and life of John Wesley.

Study-Review Exercises

Define the following key concepts and terms.
extended family

demonic view of disease

nuclear family

preindustrial childhood

illegitimacy explosion

Methodists

coitus interruptus

purging

"killing nurses"

Jesuits

Identify and explain the significance of each of the following people.
Lady Mary Montague

Edward Jenner

James Graham

Joseph II

John Wesley

Test your understanding of the chapter by providing the correct answers.

1. It is apparent that the practice of breast-feeding *increased/limited* the fertility of lower-class women.

2. The teenage bride *was/was not* the general rule in preindustrial Europe.

3. Prior to about 1750, premarital sex usually *did/did not* lead to marriage.

4. In the eighteenth century, the _____ was the primary new food in Europe.

5. People lived *longer/shorter* lives as the eighteenth century progressed.

6. The key to Jenner's discovery was the connection between immunity from smallpox and

   _____ , a mild and noncontagious disease.

7. In Catholic countries it was largely *the clergy/the common people* who wished to hold on to traditional religious rituals and superstitions.

8. The Englishman who brought religious "enthusiasm" to the common folk of England.

   _____

Multiple-Choice Questions

1. One of the chief deficiencies of the diet of both rich and poor Europeans was the absence of sufficient
   a. meat.
   b. fruit and vegetables.
   c. white bread.
   d. wine.

2. A family in which three or four generations live under the same roof under the direction of a patriarch is known as a(n)
   a. nuclear family.
   b. conjugal family.
   c. industrial household.
   d. extended family.

3. Prior to about 1750, marriage between two persons was more often than not
   a. undertaken freely by the couple.
   b. controlled by law and parents.
   c. based on romantic love.
   d. undertaken without economic considerations.

4. The establishment of foundling hospitals in the eighteenth century was an attempt to
   a. prevent the spread of the bubonic plague.
   b. isolate children from smallpox.
   c. prevent willful destruction and abandonment of newborn children.
   d. provide adequate childbirth facilities for rich women.

5. All but which of the following sentences about preindustrial society's attitudes toward children is true?
   a. Parents often treated their children with indifference and brutality.
   b. Poor children were often forced to work in the early factories.
   c. Doctors were the only people interested in the children's welfare.
   d. Killing of children by parents or nurses was common.

6. It appears that the role of doctors and hospital care in bringing about improvement in health in the eighteenth century was
   a. very significant.
   b. minor.
   c. helpful only in the area of surgery.
   d. helpful only in the area of preventive medicine.

7. In the seventeenth and early eighteenth centuries people usually married
   a. surprisingly late.
   b. surprisingly early.
   c. almost never.
   d. and divorced frequently.

8. Which of the following was *not* a general characteristic of the European family of the eighteenth century?
   a. The nuclear family
   b. Late marriages
   c. Many unmarried relatives
   d. The extended family

9. The overwhelming reason for postponement of marriage was
   a. that people didn't like the institution of marriage.
   b. lack of economic independence.
   c. the stipulation of a legal age.
   d. that young men and women valued the independence of a working life.

10. In the second half of the eighteenth century, the earlier pattern of marriage and family life began to break down. Which of the following was *not* a result of this change?
    a. A greater number of illegitimate births
    b. Earlier marriages
    c. Marriages exclusively for economic reasons
    d. Marriages for love

11. The "illegitimacy explosion" of the late eighteenth century was encouraged by all but which one of the following?
    a. The laws, especially in Germany, concerning the right of the poor to marry
    b. The mobility of young people needing to work off the farm
    c. The influence of the French Revolution, which repressed freedom in sexual and marital behavior
    d. The decreasing influence of parental pressure and village tradition.

12. Which of the following statements best describes the attitude toward children in the first part of the eighteenth century?
    a. They were protected and cherished.
    b. They were never disciplined.
    c. They were treated as they were—children living in a child's world.
    d. They were ignored, often brutalized, and often unloved.

13. Most of the popular education in Europe of the eighteenth century was sponsored by
    a. the church.
    b. the state.
    c. private individuals.
    d. parents, in the home.

14. Which of the following would most likely be found in an eighteenth-century hospital?
    a. Isolation of patients
    b. Sanitary conditions
    c. Uncrowded conditions
    d. Uneducated nurses and poor nursing practices

15. The greatest medical triumph of the eighteenth century was the conquest of
    a. starvation.
    b. smallpox.
    c. scurvy.
    d. cholera.

16. The practice of sending one's newborn baby to be suckled by a poor woman in the countryside was known as
    a. the cottage system.
    b. infanticide.
    c. wet-nursing.
    d. overlaying.

17. Which of the following was *not* a common food for the European poor?
    a. Vegetables
    b. Beer
    c. Dark bread
    d. Milk

18. It appears that the chief dietary problem of European society was the lack of an adequate supply of
    a. vitamins A and C.
    b. vitamin B complex.
    c. meat.
    d. sugar.

19. Most probably the best thing an eighteenth-century sick person could do with regard to hospitals would be to
    a. enter only if an operation was suggested by a doctor.
    b. enter only if in need of drugs.
    c. enter only a hospital operating under Galenic theory.
    d. stay away.

20. The country that led the way in the development of universal education was
    a. Britain.
    b. Prussia.
    c. France.
    d. Austria.

21. In which of the following countries did a religious conviction that the path to salvation lay in careful study of the Scriptures led to an effective network of schools and a very high literacy rate by 1800?
    a. Austria
    b. England
    c. France
    d. Scotland

22. The desire for "bread as white as snow" led to
    a. a decline in bacterial diseases.
    b. a significant nutritional advance.
    c. an increase in the supply of bread.
    d. a nutritional decline.

23. The general eighteenth-century attitude toward masturbation was that it
    a. was harmless and perhaps healthy.
    b. unacceptable for women but okay for men.
    c. caused insanity and thereby must be prevented.
    d. did not exist.

24. The general trend in Catholic countries was for monarchs to follow the Protestant lead in
    a. limiting the power and influence of the church.
    b. adopting the idea of predestination.
    c. casting off all allegiance to the papacy.
    d. protecting the poor.

25. During the eighteenth century the Society of Jesus
    a. found its power and position in Europe rise.
    b. gained considerable land in Portugal and France.
    c. was ordered out of France and Spain.
    d. avoided politics and property accumulation altogether.

Major Political Ideas

1. Do you believe that the material circumstances of preindustrial life had any affect on the way people thought and acted politically?

2. Does this chapter suggest that there was a cultural or economic division of society?

3. Was society more or less divided in terms of gender roles? In terms of class?

Issues for Essays and Discussion

1. Did the common people of preindustrial Europe enjoy a life of simple comfort and natural experiences? Or was theirs a life of brutal and cruel exploitation? Discuss this in terms of the nature of family life, childhood, diet and health, and education and religion.

2. In general, was life, by the late eighteenth century, getting better or worse?

Interpretation of Visual Sources

Study the reproduction of the print entitled *The Five Senses* on page 638 of your textbook. What is the theme of this print? What does it tell us about the treatment of children? Is this typical of how society treated children? How does the illustration mirror some of the ideas of the Enlightenment? (Refer to Chapter 18.)

Understanding History Through the Arts

1. What can art tell us about childhood in the preindustrial era? Painting is one of the major sources of information for the history of childhood. Preindustrial childhood is the subject of

Children's Games by Pieter Brueghel the Elder, a lively, action-packed painting of over two hundred children engaged in more than seventy different games. The painting is the subject of an interesting article by A. Eliot, "Games Children Play," *Sports Illustrated* (January 11, 1971): 48–56.

2. How is preindustrial life portrayed in literature and film? Samuel Richardson wrote a novel about the life of a household servant who became the prey of the lecherous son of her master, *Pamela, or Virtue Rewarded** (1740). Tom Jones, eighteenth-century England's most famous foundling, was the fictional hero of Henry Fielding's *Tom Jones* and the subject and title of director Tony Richardson's highly acclaimed, award-winning film version of Fielding's novel. Starring Albert Finney, Susannah York, and Dame Edith Evans, the film re-creates, in amusing and satirical fashion, eighteenth-century English life. A more recent film adaptation is Richardson's *Joseph Andrews*, based on another Fielding novel.

3. Was urban life more comfortable than rural life? What was the great attraction of the city? London was the fastest-growing city in the eighteenth century. How people lived in London is the subject of two highly readable and interesting books: M. D. George, *London Life in the Eighteenth Century** (3rd ed., 1951), and R. J. Mitchell and M. D. R. Leys, *A History of London Life** (1963).

Problems for Further Investigation

1. What was daily life like for poor women in this period? Few men in preindustrial society earned enough to support a family. This, in part, explains why and when women married, and why most women worked. The preindustrial woman, therefore, was not in any modern sense a homemaker. The subject of women and the family economy in eighteenth-century France is discussed by O. Hufton in *The Poor of Eighteenth-Century France* (1974).

2. What was the cause of the so-called population explosion? Did medical science contribute to an improvement in eighteenth-century life? Until about twenty years ago, it was fashionable to believe that the population explosion was due to improvements made by medical science. Although this theory is generally disclaimed today, it appears to be enjoying a slight revival. For both sides of the argument, begin your study with M. Anderson, *Population Change in North-Western Europe, 1750–1850** (1988), and then read the following journal articles (which also have bibliographies): T. McKeown and R. G. Brown, "Medical Evidence Related to English Population Change," *Population Studies 9* (1955); T. McKeown and R. G. Record, "Reasons for the Decline in Mortality in England and Wales During the Nineteenth Century," *Population Studies 16* (1962); and P. Razzell, "Population Change in Eighteenth-Century England: A Reinterpretation," *Economic History Review*, 2nd series, 18-2 (1965). For the history of disease, see D. Hopkins, *Princes and Peasants: Smallpox in History* (1977).

---

*Available in paperback.

Chapter 21
The Revolution in Politics, 1775–1815

Chapter Questions

After reading and studying this chapter you should be able to answer the following questions:

What were the causes of the political revolutions between 1775 and 1815 in America and France? What were the ideas and objectives of the revolutionaries in America and France? Who won and who lost in these revolutions?

Chapter Summary

The French and American revolutions were the most important political events of the eighteenth century. They were also a dramatic conclusion to the Enlightenment, and both revolutions, taken together, form a major turning point in human history. This chapter explains what these great revolutions were all about.

The chapter begins by describing classical liberalism, the fundamental ideology of the revolution in politics. Liberalism, which had deep roots, called for freedom and equality at a time when monarchs and aristocrats took their great privileges for granted. The immediate cause of the American Revolution, the British effort to solve the problem of war debts, was turned into a political struggle by the American colonists, who already had achieved considerable economic and personal freedom. The American Revolution stimulated reform efforts throughout Europe.

It was in France that the ideas of the Enlightenment and liberalism were put to their fullest test. The bankruptcy of the state gave the French aristocracy the chance to grab power from a weak king. This move backfired, however, because the middle class grabbed even harder. It is significant that the revolutionary desires of the middle class depended on the firm support and violent action of aroused peasants and poor urban workers. It was this action of the common people that gave the revolution its driving force.

In the first two years of the French Revolution, the middle class, with its allies from the peasantry and urban poor, achieved unprecedented reforms. The outbreak of an all-European war against France in 1792 then resulted in a reign of terror and a dictatorship by radical moralists, of whom Robespierre was the greatest. By 1795, this radical patriotism wore itself out. The revolutionary momentum slowed, and the Revolution deteriorated into a military dictatorship under the opportunist Napoleon. Yet, until 1815 the history of France was that of war, and that war spread liberalism to the rest of Europe. French conquests also stimulated nationalism. The world of politics was turned upside down.

Study Outline

Use this outline to preview the chapter before you read a particular section in your textbook and then as a self-check to test your reading comprehension after you have read the chapter section.

I. Liberty and equality
   A. In the eighteenth century, liberty meant human rights and freedoms and the sovereignty of the people.
   B. Equality meant equal rights and equality of opportunity.
   C. The roots of liberalism
      1. The Judeo-Christian tradition of individualism, reinforced by the Reformation, supported liberalism.
      2. Liberalism's modern roots are found in the Enlightenment's concern for freedom and legal equality, as best expressed by Locke and Montesquieu.
      3. Liberalism was attractive to both the aristocracy and the middle class, but it lacked the support of the masses.

II. The American Revolution (1775–1789)
   A. Some argue that the American Revolution was not a revolution at all but merely a war for independence.
   B. The origins of the Revolution
      1. The British wanted the Americans to pay their share of imperial expenses.
         a. Americans paid very low taxes.
         b. Parliament passed the Stamp Act (1765) to raise revenue.
         c. Vigorous protest from the colonies forced its repeal (1766).
      2. Although no less represented than Englishmen themselves, many Americans believed they had the right to make their own laws.
         a. Americans have long exercised a great deal of independence.
         b. Their greater political equality was matched by greater social and economic equality—there was no hereditary noble or serf class.
      3. The issue of taxation and representation ultimately led to the outbreak of fighting.
   C. The independence movement was encouraged by several factors.
      1. The British refused to compromise, thus losing the support of many colonists.
      2. The radical ideas of Thomas Paine, expressed in the best-selling *Common Sense*, greatly influenced public opinion in favor of independence.
      3. The Declaration of Independence, written by Thomas Jefferson and passed by the Second Continental Congress (1776), further increased the desire of the colonists for independence.
      4. Although many Americans remained loyal to Britain, the independence movement had wide-based support from all sections of society.
      5. European aid, especially from the French government and from French volunteers, contributed greatly to the American victory in 1783.

D. Framing the Constitution and the Bill of Rights
   1. The federal, or central, government was given important powers—the right to tax, the means to enforce its laws, and the regulation of trade—but the states had important powers too.
   2. The executive, legislative, and judicial branches of the government were designed to balance one another.
   3. The Anti-Federalists feared that the central government had too much power; to placate them, the Federalists wrote the Bill of Rights, which spells out the rights of the individual.
      a. Liberty did not, however, necessarily mean democracy.
      b. Equality meant equality before the law, not equality of political participation or economic well-being.
E. The American Revolution reinforced the Enlightenment idea that a better world was possible, and Europeans watched the new country with fascination.

III. The French Revolution (1789–1791)
A. The influence of the American Revolution
   1. Many French soldiers, such as Lafayette, served in America and were impressed by the ideals of the Revolution.
   2. The American Revolution influenced the French Revolution, but the latter was more violent and more influential; it opened the era of modern politics.
B. The breakdown of the old order
   1. By the 1780s, the government was nearly bankrupt.
   2. The French banking system could not cope with the fiscal problems, leaving the monarchy with no choice but to increase taxes.
C. Legal orders and social realities: the three estates
   1. The first estate, the clergy, had many privileges and much wealth, and it levied an oppressive tax (the tithe) on landowners.
   2. The second estate, the nobility, also had great privileges, wealth, and power, and it taxed the peasantry for its own profit.
   3. The third estate, the commoners, was a mixture of a few rich members of the middle class, urban workers, and the mass of peasants.
D. Revisionist historians challenge the traditional interpretation of the origins of the French Revolution.
   1. They argue that the bourgeoisie were not locked in conflict with the nobility, that both groups were highly fragmented.
      a. The nobility remained fluid and relatively open.
      b. Key sections of the nobility were liberal.
      c. The nobility and the bourgeoisie were not economic rivals.
   2. Nevertheless, the old interpretation, that a new social order was challenging the old, is still convincing and valid.
E. The formation of the National Assembly of 1789
   1. Louis XVI's plan to tax landed property was opposed by the Assembly of Notables and the Parlement of Paris.
   2. Louis then gave in and called for a meeting of the Estates General, the representative body of the three estates.
      a. Two-thirds of the delegates from the clergy were parish priests.

      b. A majority of the noble representatives were conservative, but fully a third were liberals committed to major change.

      c. The third estate representatives were largely lawyers and government officials.

      d. The third estate wanted the three estates to meet together to ensure the passage of fundamental reforms.

      e. According to Sieyès in *What Is the Third Estate?*, the third estate constituted the true strength of the French nation.

   3. The dispute over voting in the Estates General led the third estate to break away and form the National Assembly, which pledged, in the Oath of the Tennis Court, not to disband until they had written a new constitution.

   4. Louis tried to reassert his monarchical authority and assembled an army.

  F. The revolt of the poor and the oppressed

   1. Rising bread prices in 1788–89 stirred the people to action.

   2. Fearing attack by the king's army, angry Parisians stormed the Bastille on July 14, 1789.

      a. The people took the Bastille, and the king was forced to recall his troops.

      b. This uprising of the masses saved the National Assembly.

      c. All across France peasants began to rise up against their lords.

      d. The Great Fear seized the countryside.

   3. The peasant revolt forced the National Assembly to abolish feudal obligations.

  G. A limited monarchy established by the bourgeoisie

   1. The National Assembly's Declaration of the Rights of Man (1789) proclaimed the rights of all citizens and guaranteed equality before the law and a representative government.

   2. Meanwhile, the poor women of Paris marched on Versailles and forced the royal family and the government to move to Paris.

   3. The National Assembly established a constitutional monarchy and passed major reforms.

      a. The nobility was abolished as a separate legal order.

      b. All lawmaking power was placed in the hands of the National Assembly.

      c. The jumble of provinces was replaced by 83 departments.

      d. The metric system was introduced.

      e. Economic freedom was promoted.

   4. The National Assembly nationalized the property of the church and abolished the monasteries.

   5. This attack on the church turned many people against the Revolution.

IV. World war and republican France (1791–1799)

  A. Foreign reactions and the beginning of war

   1. Outside France, liberals and radicals hoped that the revolution would lead to a reordering of society everywhere, but conservatives such as Burke (in *Reflections on the Revolution in France*) predicted it would lead to chaos and tyranny.

   2. Wollstonecraft challenged Burke (in *A Vindication of the Rights of Woman*), arguing that it was time for women to demand equal rights.

   3. Fear among European kings and nobility that the revolution would spread resulted in the Declaration of Pillnitz (1791), which threatened the invasion of France by Austria and Prussia.

4. In retaliation, the patriotic French deputies, most of them Jacobins, declared war on Austria in 1792.
   a. France was soon retreating before the armies of the First Coalition.
   b. A war of patriotic fervor swept France.
5. In 1792 a new National Convention proclaimed France a republic and imprisoned the king.

B. The "second revolution" and rapid radicalization in France
1. The National Convention proclaimed France a republic in 1792.
2. However, the convention was split between the Girondists and the Mountain, led by Robespierre and Danton.
3. Louis XVI was tried and convicted of treason by the National Convention and guillotined in early 1793.
4. French armies continued the "war against tyranny" by declaring war on nearly all of Europe.
5. In Paris, the struggle between the Girondists and the Mountain for political power led to the political rise of the laboring poor.
6. The sans-culottes—the laboring poor—allied with the Mountain and helped Robespierre and the Committee of Public Safety gain power.

C. Total war and the Terror (1793–1794)
1. Robespierre established a planned economy to wage total war and aid the poor.
   a. The government fixed prices on key products and instituted rationing.
   b. Workshops were nationalized to produce goods for the war effort, and raw materials were requisitioned.
2. The Reign of Terror was instituted to eliminate opposition to the Revolution, and many people were jailed or executed.
3. The war became a national mission against evil within and outside of France, and not a class war.
   a. The danger of foreign and internal foes encouraged nationalism.
   b. A huge army of patriots was led by young generals who relied on mass attack.

D. The Thermidorian reaction and the Directory (1794–1799)
1. Fear of the Reign of Terror led to the execution of its leader, Robespierre.
2. The period of the Thermidorian reaction following Robespierre's death was marked by a return to bourgeois liberalism.
   a. Economic controls were abolished.
   b. Riots by the poor were put down.
   c. The Directory, a five-man executive body, was established.
3. The poor lost their fervor for revolution.
4. A military dictatorship was established in order to prevent a return to peace and monarchy.

V. The Napoleonic era (1799–1815)
A. Napoleon's rule
1. Napoleon appealed to many, like Abbé Sieyès, who looked for a strong military leader to end the country's upheaval.
2. Napoleon was named first consul of the republic in 1799.
3. He maintained order and worked out important compromises.
   a. His Civil Code of 1804 granted the middle class equality under the law and safeguarded their right to own property.

      b. He confirmed the gains of the peasants.

      c. He centralized the government, strengthened the bureaucracy, and granted amnesty to nobles.

      d. He signed the Concordat of 1801, which guaranteed freedom of worship for Catholics.

    4. Napoleon brought order and stability to France but betrayed the ideals of the Revolution by violating the rights of free speech and press and free elections.

      a. Women had no political rights.

      b. There were harsh penalties for political offenses.

  B. Napoleon's wars and foreign policy

    1. He defeated Austria (1801) and made peace with Britain (1802), the two remaining members of the Second Coalition.

    2. Another war (against the Third Coalition—Austria, Russia, Sweden, and Britain) resulted in British naval dominance at the Battle of Trafalgar (1805).

    3. Napoleon used the fear of a conspiracy to return the Bourbons to power to get himself proclaimed emperor in 1804.

    4. The Third Coalition collapsed at Austerlitz (1805), and Napoleon reorganized the German states into the Confederation of the Rhine.

    5. In 1806, Napoleon defeated the Prussians at Jena and Auerstädt.

      a. In the Treaty of Tilsit (1807), Prussia lost half its population, while Russia accepted Napoleon's reorganization of western and central Europe.

      b. Russia also joined with France in a blockade against British goods.

    6. Napoleon's Grand Empire in Europe meant French control of continental Europe.

      a. Napoleon introduced many French laws, abolishing feudal dues and serfdom in the process.

      b. However, he also levied heavy taxes.

    7. The beginning of the end for Napoleon came with the Spanish revolt (1808) and the British blockade.

    8. The French invasion of Russia in 1812 was a disaster for Napoleon.

    9. Napoleon was defeated by the Fourth Coalition (Austria, Prussia, Russia, and Great Britain) and abdicated his throne in 1814, only to be defeated again at Waterloo in 1815.

   10. The Bourbon dynasty was restored in France under Louis XVIII.

Review Questions

Check your understanding of the chapter by answering the following questions.

1. The ideas of liberty and equality were the central ideas of classical liberalism. Define these ideas. Are they the same as democracy?
2. According to Locke, what is the function of government?
3. Did the Americans or the British have the better argument with regard to the taxation problem?
4. Why is the Declaration of Independence sometimes called the world's greatest political editorial?
5. What role did the European powers play in the American victory? Did they gain anything?

6. What was the major issue in the debate between the Federalists and the Anti-Federalists?
7. Did the American Revolution have any effect on France?
8. Describe the three estates of France. Who paid the taxes? Who held the wealth and power in France?
9. With the calling of the Estates General, "the nobility of France expected that history would repeat itself." Did it? What actually did happen?
10. What were the reforms of the National Assembly. Do they display the application of liberalism to society?
11. What were the cause and the outcome of the peasants' uprising of 1789?
12. What role did the poor women of Paris play in the Revolution?
13. Why were France and Europe overcome with feelings of fear and mistrust?
14. Why did the Revolution turn into war in 1792?
15. Who were the sans-culottes? Why were they important to radical leaders such as Robespierre? What role did the common people play in the Revolution?
16. Why did the Committee of Public Safety need to institute a Reign of Terror?
17. Describe the Grand Empire of Napoleon in terms of its three parts. Was Napoleon a liberator or a tyrant?
18. What caused Napoleon's downfall? Was it inevitable?

Study-Review Exercises

Define the following key concepts and terms.

liberalism

checks and balances

natural or universal rights

republican

popular sovereignty

tithe

Identify and explain the significance of each of the following people and terms.

Stamp Act

Battle of Trafalgar

American Bill of Rights

Loyalists

Constitutional Convention of 1787

Jacobins

Girondists

Mountain

Reign of Terror

National Assembly

Declaration of the Rights of Woman

Bastille

sans-culottes

Girondists

Mountain

"the baker, the baker's wife, and the baker's boy"

Lord Nelson

352 / Chapter 21

Mary Wollstonecraft

Edmund Burke

Marie Antoinette

Marquis de Lafayette

Thomas Jefferson

Robespierre

John Locke

Abbé Sieyès

Test your understanding of the chapter by providing the correct answers.

1. Napoleon's plan to invade England was made impossible by the defeat of the French and

   Spanish navies in the Battle of _____ in 1805.

2. Overall, the common people of Paris played *a minor/an important* role in the French Revolution.

3. The author of the best-selling radical book *Common Sense*. _____

4. Prior to the crisis of the 1760s, American colonists had exercised *little/a great deal of* political and economic independence from Britain.

5. The peasant uprising of 1789 in France ended in *victory/defeat* for the peasant class.

6. By the 1790s, people like Sieyès were increasingly looking to *the people/a military ruler* to bring order to France.

Multiple-Choice Questions

1. Eighteenth-century liberals stressed
   a. economic equality.
   b. equality in property holding.
   c. equality of opportunity
   d. racial and sexual equality.

2. Which came first?
   a. Formation of the French National Assembly
   b. Execution of King Louis XVI
   c. American Bill of Rights
   d. Seven Years' War

3. The French Jacobins were
   a. aristocrats who fled France.
   b. monarchists.
   c. priests who supported the Revolution.
   d. revolutionary radicals.

4. The French National Assembly was established by
   a. the middle class of the Third Estate.
   b. King Louis XVI.
   c. the aristocracy.
   d. the sans-culottes.

5. The National Assembly did all but which of the following?
   a. Nationalized church land
   b. Issued the Declaration of the Rights of Man
   c. Established the metric system of weights and measures
   d. Brought about the Reign of Terror

6. In 1789 the influential Abbé Sieyès wrote a pamphlet in which he argued that France should be ruled by the
   a. nobility.
   b. clergy.
   c. people.
   d. king.

7. In 1799 Sieyès argued that authority in society should come from
   a. the people.
   b. the leaders of the Third Estate.
   c. a strong military leader.
   d. the Directory.

8. In the first stage of the Revolution the French established
   a. a constitutional monarchy.
   b. an absolutist monarchy.
   c. a republic.
   d. a military dictatorship.

9. Edmund Burke's *Reflections on the Revolution in France* is a defense of
   a. the Catholic church.
   b. Robespierre and the Terror.
   c. the working classes of France.
   d. the English monarchy and aristocracy.

10. Generally, the people who did not support eighteenth-century liberalism were the
    a. elite.
    b. members of the middle class.
    c. masses.
    d. intellectuals.

11. Most eighteenth-century demands for liberty centered on
    a. the equalization of wealth.
    b. a classless society.
    c. better welfare systems.
    d. equality of opportunity.

12. Americans objected to the Stamp Act because the tax it proposed
    a. was exorbitant.
    b. was not required of people in Britain.
    c. would have required great expense to collect.
    d. was imposed without their consent.

13. The American Revolution
    a. had very little impact on Europe.
    b. was supported by the French monarchy.
    c. was not influenced by Locke or Montesquieu.
    d. was supported by almost everyone living in the United States.

14. Which of the following was a cause of the outbreak of revolution in France in 1789?
    a. Peasant revolt in the countryside
    b. The death of Louis XVI
    c. The demand of the nobility for greater power and influence
    d. The invasion of France by foreign armies

15. The first successful revolt against Napoleon began in 1808 in
    a. Spain.
    b. Russia.
    c. Germany.
    d. Italy.

16. Prior to about 1765, the American people were
    a. fairly independent of the British government.
    b. subject to heavy and punitive British controls.
    c. paying a majority share of British military costs.
    d. under the direct control of the East India Company.

17. The major share of the tax burden in France was carried by the
    a. peasants.
    b. bourgeoisie.
    c. clergy.
    d. nobility.

18. The participation of the common people of Paris in the revolution was initially attributable to
    a. their desire to be represented in the Estates General.
    b. the soaring price of food.
    c. the murder of Marat.
    d. the large number of people imprisoned by the king.

19. For the French peasants, the Revolution of 1789 meant
    a. a general movement from the countryside to urban areas.
    b. greater landownership.
    c. significant political power.
    d. few, if any, gains.

20. The group that announced that it was going to cut off Marie Antoinette's head, "tear out her heart, and fry her liver" was the
    a. National Guard.
    b. Robespierre radicals.
    c. revolutionary committee.
    d. women of Paris.

21. The group that had the task of ridding France of any internal opposition to the revolutionary cause was the
    a. Revolutionary Army.
    b. secret police.
    c. republican mob of Paris.
    d. Committee of Public Safety.

22. In her writings, Mary Wollstonecraft argues that
    a. the liberating promise of the French Revolution must be extended to women.
    b. British life is threatened by the revolutionary chaos in France.
    c. Burke is correct in his defense of inherited privilege.
    d. women should devote themselves to education, not politics.

23. Some historians have questioned the traditional interpretation of the French Revolution by arguing that
    a. the Revolution was solely the result of a clash of economic classes.
    b. the key to the Revolution was the social and economic isolation of the nobility.
    c. fundamental to the Revolution was the clash between the bourgeois and noble classes.
    d. the nobility and the bourgeois had common political and economic interests.

24. The abolition of many tiny German states and the old Holy Roman Empire and the reorganization of fifteen German states into a Confederation of the Rhine was the work of
    a. the Congress of Vienna.
    b. Frederick William III of Prussia.
    c. the Continental system.
    d. Napoleon.

25. Napoleon's plan to invade Britain was scrapped as a result of
    a. the Treaty of Amiens.
    b. the Battle of Trafalgar.
    c. the fall of the Third Coalition.
    d. economic restraints in France.

Major Political Ideas

1. Define liberalism. What did it mean to be a liberal in the eighteenth and nineteenth century sense? How does this liberalism compare to twentieth-century liberalism? To democracy? What is the relationship between liberalism and the Enlightenment idea of natural law?

2. How did Americans interpret the term *equality* in 1789? Has it changed since then? Are the definitions of *liberalism* and *equality* unchangeable, or do they undergo periodic redefinition?

Issues for Essays and Discussion

1. What were the causes, both immediate and long term, of the French Revolution? Was it basically an economic event? A social or political struggle? Support your argument by making reference to specific events and ideas.

2. Why did the French Revolution become violent? Is it inevitable that all revolutions turn into violence and dictatorship?

3. Was the American Revolution a true revolution or a war of independence? Support your argument with reference to specific events and ideas.

Interpretation of Visual Sources

Study the reproduction of the print *To Versailles* on page 673 of your textbook. Who are the participants and what are their motives? Is a recognizable social class represented here? Did demonstrations such as this have any impact on the course of the Revolution?

Geography

1. On Outline Map 21.1 provided, and using Map 21.1 in the textbook as a reference, mark the following: the boundaries of France before the outbreak of war in 1792, and the areas acquired by France by 1810.

2. Look closely at Map 21.1 in the text. Can you find the four small British outposts scattered throughout Europe? How were these outposts necessary to and a reflection of Britain's military power? What did these outposts mean for smugglers and Napoleon's efforts to stop British trade with continental countries?

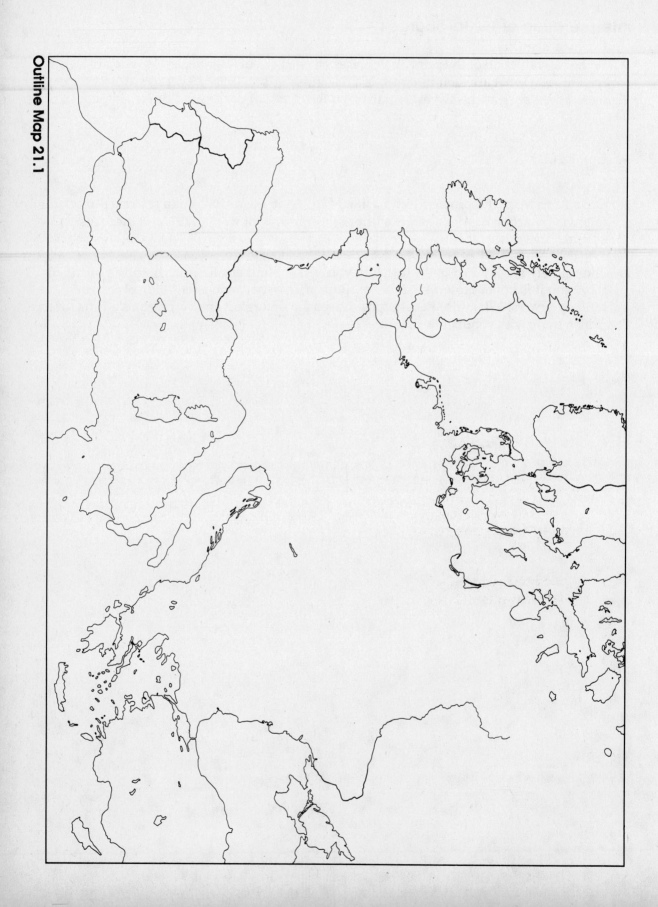

Outline Map 21.1

Understanding History Through the Arts

1. How did the era of revolution affect architecture? Out of the Enlightenment and the upheaval of the Revolution, and in response to the desire to create a new social order based on principles of natural law, French architects took traditional classical and baroque features and merged them with an interest in natural geometrical shapes. The result was an original architecture of bold and gigantic buildings. The leading architects in this movement were Etienne-Louis Boullée and Claude-Nicolas Ledoux. Their work can be found in most general histories of architecture, but the student may wish to begin with E. Kaufmann, *Architecture in the Age of Reason** (1954), and A. Vidler, *Claude-Nicolas Ledoux, Architecture and Social Reform at the End of the Ancien Régime* (1990).

2. What was the impact of the French Revolution on art? The Revolution in France forced art to become a statement of politics and political ideals. The style was a "new classicism" based on simplicity and rationality, with references to Roman civic virtue. This new style, whose goal was to inspire patriotism, was made popular by Jacques Louis David. David, a member of the National Convention, painted a number of emotional masterpieces that glorified first the Revolution—such as *Oath in the Tennis Court* and *The Death of Marat*—and later the patriotic aims of Napoleon. For a view of David and other revolutionary artists of the late eighteenth century, see E. Kennedy, *A Cultural History of the French Revolution* (1989), and R. Paulson, *Representations of Revolution, 1789–1820** (1987).

Problems for Further Investigation

1. Do individuals determine history, or is history the product of the environment? The various arguments of scholars over the motives and contributions of Napoleon are brought together in D. H. Pinkney, ed., *Napoleon: Historical Enigma** (1969). The story of Admiral Lord Nelson, Britain's hero and victor of great sea battles, is interestingly told in R. Hough, *Nelson, A Biography* (1980).

2. King George III of Britain has often been viewed, in American history, as the archenemy of liberty and constitutionalism. Is this a fair assessment? The debate over his role has gone on for a number of years and is the subject of a book of collected opinions, *George III: Tyrant or Constitutional Monarch?** (1964), edited by E. A. Reitan.

3. How important were women in the French Revolution? Did the people of Paris play a role in determining the Revolution's political ideas? Group action in a revolution makes for an interesting study. The role of women in the Revolution in France (and in other times) is well handled in E. Boulding, *The Underside of History: A View of Women Through Time* (1976). The people (which includes the Paris mob) who participated in the Revolution in France are the subject of the interesting study by George Rude, *The Crowd in the French Revolution** (1959).

---

*Available in paperback.

4. How did the French Revolution start? Students interested in the origins of the French Revolution will want to check R. W. Greenlaw, ed., *The Economic Origins of the French Revolution** (1958), and those interested in political theory may want to consider a study of liberalism, beginning with H. Schultz, ed., *English Liberalism and the State: Individualism or Collectivism** (1972).

---

*Available in paperback.

Primary Sources
The Rights of Man and of Woman

Drawing upon the ideas of the Enlightenment, particularly those of John Locke and Jean-Jacques Rousseau, the bourgeois-dominated French National Assembly issued on August 26, 1789, *The Declaration of the Right of Man and of the Citizen*. Thousands of copies of this document circulated in France, and it became the ideological manifesto of the Revolution. Its influence on the rest of Europe and the world was equally noteworthy. In 1792 an English-woman, Mary Wollstonecraft, wrote *A Vindication of the Rights of Woman*, which was a reply to Edmund Burke's attack on the French Revolution and the starting point for the debate over whether the natural rights of man should apply, in full, to women.

What, according to these documents, are the principle rights of man and woman? In what principles are these rights grounded? What Enlightenment views do these documents illustrate?

Declaration of the Rights of Man and of the Citizen, 1789

The representatives of the French people, organized as a National Assembly, believing that the ignorance, neglect, or contempt of the rights of man are the sole cause of public calamities and of the corruption of governments, have determined to set forth in a solemn declaration the natural, unalienable, and sacred rights of man, in order that this declaration, being constantly before all the members of the Social body, shall remind them continually of their rights and duties; in order that the acts of the legislative power, as well as those of the executive power, may be compared at any moment with the objects and purposes of all political institutions and may thus be more respected, and, lastly, in order that the grievances of the citizens, based here-after upon simple and incontestable principles, shall tend to the maintenance of the constitution and redound to the happiness of all. Therefore the National Assembly recognizes and proclaims, in the presence and under the auspices of the Supreme Being, the following rights of man and of the citizen:

Article

1. Men are born and remain free and equal in rights. Social distinctions may be founded only upon the general good.

2. The aim of all political association is the preservation of the natural and imprescriptible rights of man. These rights are liberty, property, security, and resistance to oppression.

3. The principle of all sovereignty resides essentially in the nation. No body nor individual may exercise any authority which does not proceed directly from the nation.

4. Liberty consists in the freedom to do everything which injures no one else; hence the exercise of the natural rights of each man has no limits except those which assure to the other members of the society the enjoyment of the same rights. These limits can only be determined by law.

5. Law can only prohibit such actions as are hurtful to society. Nothing may be prevented which is not forbidden by law, and no one may be forced to do anything not provided for by law.

6. Law is the expression of the general will. Every citizen has a right to participate personally, or through his representative, in its foundation. It must be the same for all, whether it protects or punishes. All citizens, being equal in the eyes of the law, are equally eligible to all dignities and to all public positions and occupations, according to their abilities, and without distinction except that of their virtues and talents.

7. No person shall be accused, arrested, or imprisoned except in the cases and according to the forms prescribed by law. Any one soliciting, transmitting, executing, or causing to be executed, any arbitrary order, shall be punished. But any citizen summoned or arrested in virtue of the law shall submit without delay, as resistance constitutes an offense.

8. The law shall provide for such punishments only as are strictly and obviously necessary, and no one shall suffer punishment except it be legally inflicted in virtue of a law passed and promulgated before the commission of the offense.

9. As all persons are held innocent until they shall have been declared guilty, if arrest shall be deemed indispensable, all harshness not essential to the securing of the prisoner's person shall be severely repressed by law.

10. No one shall be disquieted on account of his opinions, including his religious views, provided their manifestation does not disturb the public order established by law.

11. The free communication of ideas and opinions is one of the most precious of the rights of man. Every citizen may, accordingly, speak, write, and print with freedom, but shall be responsible for such abuses of this freedom as shall be defined by law.

12. The security of the rights of man and of the citizen requires public military forces. These forces are, therefore, established for the good of all and not the personal advantage of those to whom they shall be intrusted.

13. A common contribution is essential for the maintenance of the public forces and for the cost of administration. This should be equitably distributed among all the citizens in proportion to their means.

14. All the citizens have a right to decide, either personally or by their representatives, as to the necessity of the public contribution; to grant this freely; to know to what uses it is put; and to fix the proportion, the mode of assessment and of collection and the duration of the taxes.

15. Society has the right to require of every public agent an account of his administration.

16. A society in which the observance of the law is not assured, nor the separation of powers defined, has no constitution at all.

17. Since property is an inviolable and sacred right, no one shall be deprived thereof except where public necessity, legally determined, shall clearly demand it, and then only on condition that the owner shall have been previously and equitably indemnified.

Mary Wollstonecraft, *The Vindication of the Rights of Woman*, 1792*

Contending for the rights of woman, my main argument is built on this simple principle, that if she be not prepared by education to become the companion of man, she will stop the progress of knowledge and virtue; for truth must be common to all, or it will be inefficacious with respect to its influence on general practice. And how can woman be expected to co-operate unless she know why she ought to be virtuous? Unless freedom strengthen her reason till she comprehend her duty, and see in what manner it is connected with her real good? If children are to be educated to understand the true principle of patriotism, their mother must be a patriot; and the love of mankind, from which an orderly train of virtues spring, can only be produced by considering the moral and civil interest of mankind; but the education and situation of woman, at present, shuts her out from such investigations.

In this work I have produced many arguments, which to me were conclusive, to prove that the prevailing notion respecting a sexual character was subversive of morality, and I have contended, that to render the human body and mind more perfect, chastity must more universally prevail, and that chastity will never be respected in the male world till the person of woman is not, as it were, idolized, when little virtue sense embellish it with the grand traces of mental beauty, or the interesting simplicity of affection.

Consider, sir, dispassionately, these observations—for a glimpse of this truth seemed to open before you when you observed, "that to see one half of the human race excluded by the other from all participation of government, was a political phenomenon that, according to abstract principles, it was impossible to explain." If so, on what does your constitution rest? If the abstract rights of man will bear discussion and explanation, those of woman, by a parity of

Source: Mary Wollstonecraft, from the Dedication of the first edition, *The Vindication of the Rights of Woman* (1792).

reasoning, will not shrink from the same test: though a different opinion prevails in this country, built on the very arguments which you use to justify the oppression of woman—prescription.

Consider—I address you as a legislator—whether, when men contend for their freedom, and to be allowed to judge for themselves respecting their own happiness, it be not inconsistent and unjust to subjugate women, even though you firmly believe that you are acting in the manner best calculated to promote their happiness? Who made man the exclusive judge, if woman partake with him the gift of reason?

But, if women are to be excluded, without having a voice, from a participation of the natural rights of mankind, prove first, to ward off the charge of injustice and inconsistency, that they want reason—else this flaw in your NEW CONSTITUTION will ever show that man must, in some shape, act like a tyrant; and tyranny, in whatever part of society it rears its brazen front, will ever undermine morality.

I have repeatedly asserted, and produced what appeared to me irrefragable arguments drawn from matters of fact, to prove my assertion, that women cannot, by force, be confined to domestic concerns; for they will, however ignorant, intermeddle with more weighty affairs, neglecting private duties only to disturb, by cunning tricks, the orderly plans of reason which rise above their comprehension.

Besides, whilst they are only made to acquire personal accomplishments, men will seek for pleasure in variety, and faithless husbands will make faithless wives: such ignorant beings, indeed, will be very excusable when, not taught to respect public good, nor allowed any civil rights, they attempt to do themselves justice by retaliation.

The box of mischief thus opened in society, what is to preserve private virtue, the only security of public freedom and universal happiness?

Let there be then no coercion established in society, and the common law of gravity prevailing, the sexes will fall into their proper places. And, now that more equitable laws are forming your citizens, marriage may become more sacred: your young men may choose wives from motives of affection, and your maidens allow love to root out vanity.

The father of a family will not then weaken his constitution and debase his sentiments by visiting the harlot, nor forget, in obeying the call of appetite, the purpose for which it was implanted. And, the mother will not neglect her children to practise the arts of coquetry, when sense and modesty secure her the friendship of her husband.

But, till men become attentive to the duty of a father, it is vain to expect women to spend that time in their nursery which they, "wise in their generation," choose to spend at their glass; for this exertion of cunning is only an instinct of nature to enable them to obtain indirectly a little of that power of which they are unjustly denied a share: for, if women are not permitted to enjoy legitimate rights, they will render both men and themselves vicious, to obtain illicit privileges.

I wish, sir, to set some investigations of this kind afloat in France; and should they lead to a confirmation of my principles, when your constitution is revised the Rights of Woman may be respected, if it be fully proved that reason calls for this respect, and loudly demands JUSTICE for one half of the human race.—I am, sir, your respectfully,

M. W.

Chapter 22
The Revolution in Energy and Industry

Chapter Questions

After reading and studying this chapter you should be able to answer the following questions:

What was the Industrial Revolution, what caused it, and how did it evolve? How did the Industrial Revolution affect people and society in an era of continued population growth? Was it a blessing or a disaster?

Chapter Summary

The world we live in today is largely a product of a revolution in industry and energy that began in England in the 1780s and lasted until about 1850. A number of important problems of interpretation relating to this Industrial Revolution are discussed in this chapter.

The chapter first considers why the Industrial Revolution occurred when it did and why it began in England. Important causes of English industrialization, some of which were discussed in detail in Chapter 19, were foreign and home demand for manufactured goods, agricultural improvements, a large free-trade area, good transportation, and a fairly advanced banking system. The pressure of a growing demand for textiles led to better spinning and weaving machinery, which, in turn, led to the creation of the world's first modern factories. In addition, a severe energy crisis resulted in new production methods: abundant coal replaced scarce wood in the all-important iron industry and fueled Watt's magnificent new steam engine. For the first time, the English people had almost unlimited energy for useful work.

The chapter next considers the gradual spread of the new industrial methods from England to continental Europe. It was not easy for continental countries to copy the English achievement, but with the coming of the railroad rapid progress was made by the 1840s. The difficult problem of assessing the impact of the Industrial Revolution on the lives of the men and women of the working class is then examined. Was industrialization mainly a blessing or a disaster for the workers? After evaluating consumption patterns, the text concludes, with qualifications, that the lot of ordinary men and women improved only after about 1820, and more particularly between 1840 and 1850. Equally important, the Industrial Revolution affected women differently than it did men, as a sexual division of labor created "separate spheres," wherein women were assigned to low-paying and dead-end jobs or became homemakers. Several theories about why this happened are examined.

Study Outline

Use this outline to preview the chapter before you read a particular section in your textbook and then as a self-check to test your reading comprehension after you have read the chapter section.

I. The Industrial Revolution in England
   A. The eighteenth-century origins of the Industrial Revolution
      1. A colonial empire, the expanding Atlantic trade, and a strong and tariff-free home market created new demands for English manufactured goods.
      2. Cheap food also increased this demand.
      3. Available capital, stable government, economic freedom, and mobile labor in England encouraged growth.
      4. The Industrial Revolution began in England in the 1780s and on the Continent after 1815.
   B. The first factories in the cotton textile industry
      1. Growing demand for textiles led to the creation of the world's first large factories.
        a. The putting-out system could not keep up with demand.
        b. Hargreaves's spinning jenny and Arkwright's water frame speeded up the spinning process.
        c. Cotton spinning was gradually concentrated in factories.
      2. Cotton goods became cheaper and more widely available.
      3. The wages of weavers rose rapidly, and many agricultural workers became handloom weavers.
      4. Abandoned children became a prime source of labor in the early factories.
   C. The problem of energy
      1. The search for a solution to the energy problem was a major cause of industrialization.
      2. From prehistoric to medieval times the major energy sources were plants and animals, and human beings and animals did most of the work.
      3. Energy from the land was limited.
        a. By the eighteenth century, England's major source of fuel, wood, was nearly gone.
        b. A new source of power and energy was needed, so people turned to coal.
   D. The steam engine breakthrough
      1. Before about 1700, coal was used for heat but not to produce mechanical energy or to run machinery.
      2. Early steam engines, such as those of Savery (1698) and Newcomen (1705), were inefficient but revolutionary converters of coal into energy.
      3. In the 1760s, in Scotland, James Watt increased the efficiency of the steam engine and began to produce them.

4. Steam power was used in many industries, and it encouraged other breakthroughs.
   a. It enabled the textile industry to expand.
   b. The iron industry was transformed as steam power made coke available.
   c. Cort's puddling furnace led to increased production of pig iron.
E. The coming of the railroads
   1. Stephenson's steam-powered *Rocket* (1825) was Europe's first locomotive, and the Liverpool and Manchester Railway was the first important railroad.
   2. The railroad boom (1830–1850) meant lower transportation costs, larger markets, and cheaper goods.
   3. Railroad building took workers from their rural life and made them more inclined to become urban dwellers.
   4. The railroad changed the outlook and values of the entire society.
F. Industry and population
   1. The 1851 Great Exposition, held in the Crystal Palace, reflected the growth of industry and population in Britain and confirmed that Britain was the "workshop of the world."
   2. GNP grew by 400 percent and population boomed, but average consumption grew only by 75 percent.
      a. Malthus argued that the population would always exceed the food supply.
      b. Ricardo said that wages would always be low.
II. Industrialization in continental Europe
   A. National variations
      1. Statistics show that between 1750 and 1830, Britain industrialized more rapidly than other countries.
      2. Belgium followed Britain's lead, with France showing gradual growth.
      3. By 1913 Germany and the United States were closing in on Britain; the rest of Europe (along with Japan) grew, while some Asian states (India, China) lost ground.
   B. The challenge of industrialization
      1. Revolutions and wars on the Continent retarded economic growth after 1789.
      2. Continental countries found it difficult to compete with Britain after 1815 because it was so economically and technologically advanced.
      3. However, continental countries had three advantages.
         a. Most continental countries had a rich tradition of putting-out enterprise, merchant-capitalists, and urban artisans.
         b. Britain had done the developmental pathbreaking, so other countries could simply copy the British way of doing things.
         c. The power of strong central governments could be used to promote industry.
   C. Agents of industrialization in continental Europe
      1. Cockerill, in Belgium, was one of many Englishmen who brought British industrial secrets to other parts of Europe.
      2. In Germany, Harkort's failed attempt to industrialize Germany illustrates the difficulty of duplicating the British achievements.
      3. Governments aided industrialists by erecting tariffs, building roads and canals, and financing railroads.

4. Many thinkers and writers, such as List in Germany, believed that industrialization would advance the welfare of the nation.
    a. List supported the idea of a tariff-free zone in Germany, the Zollverein (1834).
    b. Henceforth, goods could move among the German member states without tariffs, but goods from other nations were subject to a tariff.
5. Banks played a more important role in industrialization on the Continent than in Britain.
    a. Industrial banks, such as the Crédit Mobilier, became important in France and Germany in the 1850s.
    b. These industrial banks mobilized the savings of thousands of small investors and invested them in transportation and industry.

III. Capital and labor in the age of the Industrial Revolution
  A. The new class of factory owners
    1. Capitalist owners were locked into a highly competitive system.
    2. The early industrialists came from a variety of backgrounds.
    3. As factories grew larger, opportunities declined.
  B. The new factory workers and their working conditions
    1. Many observers claimed that the Industrial Revolution brought misery to the workers.
        a. The romantic poets Blake and Wordsworth protested the life of the workers and the pollution of the land and water.
        b. The Luddites smashed the new machines they believed were putting them out of work.
        c. Engels wrote a blistering attack on the middle classes, *The Condition of the Working Class in England* (1844).
    2. Others, such as Ure and Chadwick, claimed that life was improving for the working class.
    3. The statistics with regard to purchasing power of the worker (real wages) shows that there was little or no improvement between 1780 and 1820.
        a. Between 1792 and 1815, living conditions actually declined as food prices rose faster than wages.
        b. Only after 1840 did a substantial improvement in real wages occur.
        c. Even in this era of improving purchasing power, hours of labor increased and unemployment was present.
    4. Diet probably improved, as did the supply of clothing, but housing did not.
  C. Conditions of work
    1. Working in the factory meant more discipline and less personal freedom.
    2. The refusal of cottage workers to work in factories led to child labor.
        a. The use of pauper children was forbidden in 1802.
        b. Urban factories attracted whole families, as did coal mining, and tended to preserve kinship ties.
        c. Children and parents worked long hours.
    3. Parliament acted to limit child labor.
        a. Robert Owen, a successful manufacturer in Scotland, proposed limiting the hours of labor and child labor.
        b. The Factory Act of 1833 limited child labor and the number of hours children could work in textile factories.

      c. Factory owners were required to establish elementary schools for the children of their employees.

    4. Subcontracting led to a close relationship between the subcontractor and his work crew, many of whom were friends and relations.

      a. Subcontracting helped maintain kinship ties.

      b. Many workers (such as in Liverpool and Glasgow) were Irish and were thus held together by ethnic and religious ties.

    5. Some firms were large, but the survival of small workshops and artisan crafts gave many workers an alternative to factory employment.

    6. Many traditional jobs, such as farming and domestic service, lived on.

    7. Workers created a labor movement to improve working conditions.

      a. The Combination Acts, which outlawed unions and strikes, were repealed in 1824.

      b. Robert Owen experimented with cooperative and socialist communities and then formed a national union in 1834 in Britain.

      c. The British labor movement moved once again, after 1851, in the direction of craft unions.

    8. Chartism was a workers' political movement that sought universal male suffrage, shorter work hours, and cheap bread.

  D. The sexual division of labor

    1. A new pattern of "separate spheres" emerged.

      a. The man emerged as the family's primary wage earner, while the woman found only limited job opportunities.

      b. Married women were much less likely to work outside the house after the first child arrived.

      c. Women were confined to low-paying, dead-end jobs.

    2. The reasons for this reorganization of paid work along gender lines are debated.

      a. One argument centers on the idea of a deeply ingrained patriarchal tradition, which predates the economic transformation.

      b. Others claim that the factory conflicted with strong incentives on the part of mothers to concentrate on child care.

      c. This theory centers on the claim that women saw division of labor as the best strategy for family survival in the industrializing society.

      d. Others argue that sexual division of labor was part of an effort to control the sexuality of working-class youth.

Review Questions

Check your understanding of the chapter by answering the following questions.

1. Why did the Industrial Revolution begin in England?
2. Describe the energy crisis in England. How was it solved?
3. What was the relationship between the steam engine and the coal mine? The railroad and the coal mine?
4. What impact did the railroad have on (a) the factory system, (b) the rural workers, and (c) the outlook and values of society?

5. What did James Watt do to increase the efficiency of the steam engine?
6. How did the change in textile production affect employment in spinning and weaving for adults and children?
7. What effect did the French Revolution and the wars of 1792–1815 have on the economies of the continental states? What were the variations in the timing and extent of industrialization in the United States, Belgium, Germany, and France?
8. What disadvantages and advantages were felt by countries that industrialized after Great Britain?
9. What do the careers of Cockerill, Harkort, and List tell us about the problems and methods of industrialization on the Continent?
10. What was the purpose of the Zollverein? Of the Crédit Mobilier?
11. Did Britain's new industrial middle class ruthlessly exploit the workers?
12. Did the standard of living improve or decline between 1790 and 1850? What about other factors, such as diet and working conditions?
13. What was the effect of the factory system in Britain on the family?
14. What was the subcontract system and how did it work? Did it have a negative or a positive impact on working-class life?
15. What were the goals and accomplishments of the Chartists?
16. What is meant by the term *sexual division of labor*? What are the various theories about its emergence?

Study-Review Exercises

Define the following key concepts and terms.

cottage workers

domestic system

Industrial Revolution

protective tariff

Chartist movement

energy crisis of the eighteenth century

real wages

sexual division of labor

Identify and explain the significance of the following people and terms.
Thomas Malthus

David Ricardo

Andrew Ure

Crystal Palace

Cartwright's power loom

spinning jenny

Zollverein

Factory Act of 1833

Crédit Mobilier

Combination Acts

parish "apprentices" in cotton mills

Henry Cort

James Hargreaves

Robert Owen

James Watt

Friedrich List

George Stephenson

Grand National Consolidated Trades Union

Emile and Isaac Pereire

Friedrich Engels

craft union

Test your understanding of the chapter by providing the correct answers.

1. The Industrial Revolution began in England in about _____ in the

   _____ industry.

2. A decrease in food prices led to an *increased/decreased* demand for manufactured goods.

3. The Scotsman who improved the steam engine. _____

4. Henry Cort developed a new process of using coke to improve the output of

   _____ .

5. The first railroad line was the _____ line, and the first effective locomotive

   was Stephenson's _____ .

6. The railroads tended to *increase/decrease* the number of cottage workers.

7. The architectural wonder of the 1851 industrial fair in London. _____

8. Between 1780 and 1820, purchasing power in Britain *increased/decreased*.

9. The role of the government in bringing about industrialization was *greater/less* in continental countries than in Britain.

10. The economic and trade agreement formed in 1834 that allowed goods to move among

    German member states without tariffs. _____

11. The possibility of a worker becoming a successful industrialist *increased/decreased* as the nineteenth century wore on.

12. With the _____ Act of 1833, the employment of children in British factories tended to *increase/decrease*.

Multiple-Choice Questions

1. In the 1830s, the most technologically advanced country in the world was
   a. Belgium.
   b. the United States.
   c. France.
   d. Britain.

2. Which of the following was a period of falling real wages for English workers?
   a. 1792–1815
   b. 1815–1850
   c. 1840–1850
   d. 1850–1890

3. Which of the following was used by continental countries to meet British competition?
   a. The adoption of free trade
   b. Closing the doors to skilled British workers
   c. Exchanging the secrets of technology with one another
   d. Government grants and loans

4. Which of the following was most likely to characterize a cottage worker?
   a. Worked at his or her own pace
   b. Never worked alongside other members of his or her family
   c. Worked at a steady and constant rate
   d. Would probably prefer factory work to domestic industry work

5. Which of the following contributed to England's early industrialization?
   a. Colonial trade
   b. Very weak central banking system
   c. High food prices due to inadequate crops
   d. A domestic market with many local protective barriers

6. The energy crisis of the eighteenth and nineteenth centuries was solved by reliance on
   a. wood.
   b. coal and steam.
   c. electricity.
   d. water power.

7. According to Friedrich List, the promotion of industry
   a. was dangerous for the well-being of the peasants.
   b. was vital for the defense of the nation.
   c. increased the poverty of the population.
   d. required free trade between nations.

8. The most significant technological advance made during the Industrial Revolution was the
   a. first large factory.
   b. cotton-spinning jenny.
   c. steam engine.
   d. water frame.

9. Which of the following was passed by the British Parliament to outlaw unions and strikes?
   a. The Factory Act of 1833
   b. The Combination Acts
   c. The Mines Act of 1842
   d. The Grand National Consolidated Trades Union Act

10. The Industrial Revolution in France
    a. developed at a faster pace than it did in Germany.
    b. developed more rapidly than in Britain.
    c. occurred largely prior to 1780.
    d. lagged behind that of Britain.

11. The growth of the railroad caused all of the following *except*
    a. a reduction in the cost of overland freight.
    b. an increase in the demand for cottage industry goods.
    c. the growth of a class of urban workers.
    d. the widening of markets.

12. The first continental country to industrialize was
    a. Belgium.
    b. France.
    c. Italy.
    d. Germany.

13. The industrial development of continental Europe was delayed by
    a. a lack of resources.
    b. the French Revolution and Napoleonic wars.
    c. the plague.
    d. a labor shortage.

14. To understand more fully the impact of the Industrial Revolution, historians concentrate their studies on
    a. England.
    b. France.
    c. Ireland.
    d. Belgium.

15. Before the 1830s, the
    a. family continued to work as a unit in the factories.
    b. factory employed only females.
    c. mother and father worked together while their children went to factory schools.
    d. factory employed only the males.

16. The British workers' campaign to gain the franchise between 1838 and 1848 was called the
    a. Ten-Hours' movement.
    b. Luddite movement.
    c. Chartist movement.
    d. democratic movement.

17. Which of the following was *not* characteristic of Robert Owen?
    a. He was a scholar who wanted to implement his socialist ideas.
    b. He experimented with cooperative and socialist communities.
    c. He organized one of Britain's first national unions.
    d. He tried to improve the working conditions of his workers.

18. The first factories were
    a. steel mills.
    b. chemical firms.
    c. clothing companies.
    d. textile mills.

19. The early industrialists in Britain very often were
    a. aristocrats taking advantage of new economic opportunities.
    b. members of the established church.
    c. Irish immigrants.
    d. Quakers and Scots.

20. Workers who smashed the machines that put them out of work were known as
    a. Luddites.
    b. anti-Modernists.
    c. Chartists.
    d. apprentices.

21. William Cockerill, a Lancashire carpenter, built an industrial empire in
    a. the English Midlands.
    b. London.
    c. Belgium.
    d. North America.

22. By the end of the nineteenth century large decreases in per capita industrial levels had occurred in
    a. India and China.
    b. France.
    c. Britain.
    d. Germany.

23. For women, the Industrial Revolution
    a. provided a greater chance of economic equality with men.
    b. discouraged marriage and children.
    c. provided new career opportunities in high-level jobs.
    d. caused them to be confined to low-paying, dead-end jobs.

24. It appears that during the Industrial Revolution in Britain the gross national product
    a. rose at about the same rate as the per capita consumption of goods.
    b. rose more rapidly than the per capita consumption of goods.
    c. rose less rapidly than the per capita consumption of goods.
    d. fell below the per capita consumption of goods.

25. The daily requirement of calories that adult men and women need to fuel their bodies, work, and survive is
    a. 1,000.
    b. 5,000 to 6,000.
    c. 200 to 400.
    d. 2,000 to 4,000.

Major Political Ideas

1. What role did the government play in the process of industrialization? Did this role vary from country to country?

2. Why, with the Factory Act 1833, did the British government turn toward some state intervention?

Issues for Essays and Discussion

1. What were the causes of the Industrial Revolution in Britain? Which of the causes, in your opinion, were the most important?

2. Historians have long argued whether the Industrial Revolution was a blessing or a disaster for the workers who lived through it. What is your opinion? What information exists that allows us to measure the impact of industrialization? Did the Industrial Revolution affect women and men alike?

Interpretation of Visual Sources

Study the reproduction of the engraving titled *Girl Dragging Coal Tubs* on page 712 of your textbook. What seems to be the motive of those who produced and published this print? Could this illustration have supported the argument for "separate spheres" for men and women?

Geography

1. Compare maps 22.1 and 22.2 in the textbook in terms of the major industrial areas and transportation networks shown on each. How do these maps explain why an ever-greater portion of the English population lived in the north as time passed? What different stages in the development of English transportation are illustrated by these maps? Write your answers in the space provided below.

2. Study maps 22.2 and 22.3 in the textbook. Using the space below, compare British and continental industrialization by 1850 in terms of (a) railroads, (b) coal deposits, and (c) industrial centers. What role did geography play in Britain's early industrial lead?

3. Four of Europe's most important centers of modern industry are (a) the Manchester-Sheffield area, (b) the Ruhr valley, (c) the Liège region, and (d) the Roubaix region. Locate these regions on maps 22.2 and 22.3. What countries are they in? What do they have in common?

Understanding History Through the Arts

1. What was the impact of photography on society? Few nineteenth-century inventions had as great an impact on society as did the invention of the camera in 1839. Photography allowed society to examine itself with a closeness never before experienced. In the late 1860s, for example, Thomas Annan took a series of photographs of the slums of Glasgow, and thus encouraged interest in sanitary reform and urban improvement. Annan's photographs have been reproduced by Dover Press as T. Annan, *Photographs Of the Old Closes and Streets of Glasgow, 1868–1877** (1977). M. Hiley, *Victorian Working Women* (1980), is a view of the habits and life of Victorian women through photography.

2. How did the artist face the changes brought forth by the Industrial Revolution? Begin your study with the path-breaking study by F. D. Klingender, *Art and the Industrial Revolution*,* edited and revised by A. Elton (1970). An unrivaled source of visual material associated with Britain's early industrial history is A. Briggs, *Iron Bridge to Crystal Palace, Impact and Images of the Industrial Revolution* (1979), and more recently his book *Victorian Things* (1988).

Problems for Further Investigation

1. When did the Industrial Revolution begin? Some historians do not agree with the traditional interpretation that the Industrial Revolution began in the late eighteenth century. One such historian is John Nef, who argues that it actually began in the sixteenth century. He places considerable emphasis on the importance of the coal industry and the early energy crisis. Some of his ideas are found in J. Nef, "The Early Energy Crisis and Its Consequences," *Scientific American* (November 1977), and "The Progress of Technology and the Growth of Large-Scale Industry in Great Britain, 1540–1640," *Economic History Review 5* (October 1934). Students interested in the causes of the Industrial Revolution will also want to read the series of debates by six historians in R. M. Hartwell, ed., *The Causes of the Industrial Revolution in England** (1967).

2. What was the impact of the Industrial Revolution on the working class? No facet of the Industrial Revolution has been as controversial and long-lasting as the debate over whether it was a blessing or a curse for the working class. Many of the arguments of the optimists and the pessimists are collected in two small books: P. A. M. Taylor, ed., *The Industrial Revolution in Britain** (rev. ed., 1970), and C. S. Doty, ed., *The Industrial Revolution** (1969). The impact of industrialization on women is one of the themes of Louise Tilly and Joan Scott in *Women, Work and Family** (1978). The most important (and controversial) book on the impact of industrialization on the working class is E. P. Thompson, *The Making of the English Working Class** (1966). Emile Zola's *Germinal** is a powerful novel about life and conditions in Belgian and French coal mines. Popular novels by Charles Dickens and Elizabeth Gaskill are among the suggested readings in the text. The machine breakers in England (1811–1817) are the subject of M. I. Thomis's *The Luddites** (1970–1972). Those interested in reading about the

---

*Available in paperback.

new industrial working class may want to begin with J. Kuczynski, *The Rise of the Working Class* (1967), or two collections of essays on the subject—M. L. McDougal, ed., *The Working Class in Modern Europe* (1975), and E. J. Hobsbawm, ed., *Labouring Men: Studies in the History of Labour** (1964).

---

*Available in paperback.

Studying Effectively—Exercise 5

Learning to Identify Main Points That Are Causes or Reasons

In Exercise 3 we considered cause and effect and underlined a passage dealing with effects or results. This exercise continues in this direction by focusing on causes or reasons.

Exercise

Read the following passage in its entirety. Then reread it and underline or highlight each cause (or factor) contributing to the Industrial Revolution in England.

Note that there are several causes and that they are rather compressed. (This is because the author is summarizing material presented in previous chapters before going on to discuss other causes or factors—notably technology and the energy problem—in greater detail.) Since several causal points are presented in a short space, this is a very good place to number the points (and key subpoints) in the margin. After you have finished, compare your underlining or highlighting with that in the suggested model that follows.

Eighteenth-Century Origins

Although many aspects of the English Industrial Revolution are still matters for scholarly debate, it is generally agreed that the industrial changes that did occur grew out of a long process of development. First of all, the expanding Atlantic economy of the eighteenth century served mercantilist England remarkably well. The colonial empire that England aggressively built, augmented by a strong position in Latin America and in the African slave trade, provided a growing market for English manufactured goods. So did England itself. In an age when it was much cheaper to ship goods by water than by land, no part of England was more than 20 miles from navigable water. Beginning in the 1770s, a canal-building boom greatly enhanced this natural advantage (see Map 22.1). Nor were there any tariffs within the country to hinder trade, as there were in France before 1789 and in politically fragmented Germany.

Agriculture played a central role in bringing about the Industrial Revolution in England. English farmers were second only to the Dutch in productivity in 1700, and they were continuously adopting new methods of farming as the century went on. The result, especially before 1760, was a period of bountiful crops and low food prices. The ordinary English family did not have to spend almost everything it earned just to buy bread. It could spend more on other items, on manufactured goods—leather shoes or a razor for the man, a bonnet or a shawl for the woman, toy soldiers for the son, and a doll for the daughter. Thus demand for goods within the country complemented the demand from the colonies.

England had other assets that helped give rise to industrial leadership. Unlike eighteenth-century France, England had an effective central bank and well-developed credit markets. The monarchy and the aristocratic oligarchy, which had jointly ruled the country since 1688, provided stable and predictable government. At the same time the government let the domestic economy operate fairly freely and with few controls, encouraging personal initiative, technical change, and a free market. Finally, England had long had a large class of hired agricultural laborers, rural proletarians whose numbers were further increased by the enclosure movement of the late eighteenth century. These rural wage earners were relatively mobile—compared to village-bound peasants in France and western Germany, for example—and along with cottage workers they formed a potential industrial labor force for capitalist entrepreneurs.

All these factors combined to initiate the Industrial Revolution, a term first coined by awed contemporaries in the 1830s to describe the burst of major inventions and technical changes they had witnessed in certain industries. This technical revolution went hand in hand with an impressive quickening in the annual rate of industrial growth in England. Thus industry grew at only 0.7 percent between 1700 and 1760—before the Industrial Revolution—but it grew at the much higher rate of 3 percent between 1801 and 1831, when industrial transformation was in full swing. The decisive quickening of growth probably came in the 1780s, after the American war for independence and before the French Revolution.

Eighteenth-Century Origins

causes

1

a

b

c

2

a

b

c

3

4

5

6

The Industrial Revolution grew out of the expanding Atlantic economy of the eighteenth century, which served mercantilist England remarkably well. The colonial empire, augmented by a strong position in Latin America and in the African slave trade, provided a growing market for English manufactured goods. So did England itself. In an age when it was much cheaper to ship goods by water than by land, no part of England was more than 20 miles from navigable water. Beginning in the 1770s, a canal building boom greatly enhanced this natural advantage (see Map 22.1). Nor were there any tariffs within the country to hinder trade, as there were in France before 1789 and in politically fragmented Germany.

Agriculture played a central role in bringing about the Industrial Revolution in England. English farmers were second only to the Dutch in productivity in 1700, and they were continuously adopting new methods of farming as the century went on. The result, especially before 1760, was a period of bountiful crops and low food prices. The ordinary English family did not have to spend almost everything it earned just to buy bread. It could spend more on other items, on manufactured goods—leather shoes or a razor for the man, a bonnet or a shawl for the woman, toy soldiers for the son, and a doll for the daughter. Thus, demand for goods within the country complemented the demand from the colonies. England had other assets that helped give rise to industrial leadership. Unlike eighteenth-century France, England had an effective central bank and well-developed credit markets. The monarchy and the aristocratic oligarchy, which had jointly ruled the country since 1688, provided stable and predictable government. At the same time the government let the domestic economy operate fairly freely and with few controls, encouraging personal initiative, technical change, and a free market. Finally, England had long had a large class of hired agricultural laborers, rural proletarians, whose numbers were further increased by the enclosure movement of the late eighteenth century. These rural wage earners were relatively mobile—compared to village-bound peasants in France and western Germany, for example—and along with cottage workers they formed a potential industrial labor force for capitalist entrepreneurs. All these factors combined to initiate the Industrial Revolution, a term first coined by awed contemporaries in the 1830s to describe the burst of major inventions and technical changes they had witnessed in certain industries. This technical revolution went hand in hand with an impressive quickening in the annual rate of industrial growth in England. Thus industry grew at only 0.7 percent between 1700 and 1760—before the Industrial Revolution—but it grew at the much higher rate of 3 percent between 1801 and 1831, when industrial transformation was in full swing. The decisive quickening of growth probably came in the 1780s, after the American war for independence and just before the French Revolution.

Primary Sources
Industrialization and Urban Life for the Working Classes

Most historians agree that, given the poverty and uncertainty of preindustrial life, the process of urbanization and industrialization brought more benefits than hardships. Nevertheless, a large number of people continued to live in filthy environments and work under exploitative conditions. The following readings do two things. First, they show how the state, in this case the British state, became increasingly absorbed in defining and solving the problems faced by the less advantaged classes. Second, they show what life and labor was like for many people at the bottom—particularly women, children, and elderly people, who gained the least from the economic advances of the time. All of these excerpts are from parliamentary hearings, and all led to specific legislative reform.

Child Labor in the Textile Factories, 1832*

Eldin Hargrave was a boy from the great city of Leeds, which was the center of Britain's wool cloth manufacture. He was brought to London on April 13, 1832, to testify before the parliamentary committee of Mr. Sadler, M.P., a committee that was set up to uncover the evils of child labor in order to gain public support for a factory protection act. It appears they provided him with a new suit—and it also appears that he may have lost his job for testifying. The act, passed in 1833, was the first effective factory legislation in Britain.

If Hargrave is typical of children who worked in the early textile factories, what are the ages at which children began their work? Their hours of labor? Wages? What effect did factory work have on their health and morals?

Eldin Hargrave, called in; and Examined (13 April, 1832):

755.   What age are you?—I shall be 15 next month.
756.   Have you a father?—No.

*Source: "Report from the Select Committee on the Bill to Regulate the Labour of Children in Mills and Factories of the United Kingdom, with Minutes of Evidence, August, 1832," *Parliamentary Papers, 1831–32, Vol. XV.*

757. Your father is dead?—Yes.
758. Have you a mother?—Yes, I have a mother.
759. What age were you when you were sent to the mill?—I was about eight years old.
760. You come from Leeds?—Yes.
761. To whose mill did you go?—I went to Messrs. Shaun & Driver's.
762. Did you work there as a premer?—Yes.
763. What were your hours of labour there?—I worked from 6 to 7.
764. You worked 13 hours, with two hours for meals?—Yes.
765. How long did you stop at that work?—A year.
766. What wages did you have for that?—Three shillings a week.
767. Where did you go then?—I went to Lord & Robinson's.
768. What did you do there?—I was a carper there.
769. What is a carper?—There are some prickles on the top of the tassels, and they had a pair of scissors to clear them off.
770. Did you find that work easier?—Yes.
771. Had you less wages for that?—I had half-a-crown.
772. How many hours did you work at Lord & Robinson's?—From 5 to 9.
773. Why did you leave Shaun & Driver's?—Because they went to a fresh mill, and one of the master's cousins went in my place.
774. How long did you stop at Lord & Robinson's?—About half a year.
775. Why did you leave that?—Because I could not clip tassels fast enough.
776. Did they discharge you?—Yes.
777. Where did you seek for employment then?—At Mr. Brown's mill.
778. What age were you then?—About 10 years old.
779. In what situation were you there?—I was a sweeper and errand-boy.
780. What were your wages there?—Three shillings.
781. What hours did you work there?—I went from 6 to 7.
782. How long were you a sweeper?—About a year.
783. What situation did you get after that?—I was a brusher.
784. What wages did you get as a brusher?—I had 3s. 6d.* a week; and I had sometimes 1s. for over-hours, and sometimes 1s. 3d.; I had three-farthings an hour.
785. How long did you work when you worked over-hours?—I went from 5 to 10.
786. Supposing you had refused to work over-hours, what would have happened?—I was forced to work over-hours, otherwise I must seek a fresh shop.
787. For what length of time did you so work?—I worked for that time for a year round.
788. What did you do after that?—I went to mind Lewises.
789. At the same mill?—Yes.
790. Did you work at the broad or the narrow Lewis?—I worked at the broad.
791. What had you for working at the Lewis?—I had 5s. a week and over-hours.
792. How much had you for over-hours?—I had a penny an hour.

---

*There were 12 pence ("d") in a shilling and 20 shillings ("s") in a pound (£).

793. Will you describe the labour you had to do in attending to the Lewis.—I had a stool to stand on, and then I had to reach over as far as I could reach to put the list on.

794. Did you find that harder work than brushing?—Yes, that was harder work than any that I had.

795. In attending to this machine, are you not always upon the stretch, and upon the move?—Yes, always.

796. Do not you use your hand a good deal in stretching it out?—Yes.

797. What effect had this long labour upon you?—I had a pain across my knee, and I got crooked.

798. Was it the back of your knee, or the side of your knee?—All round.

799. Will you show your limbs?—[Here the Witness exposed his legs and knees.]

800. Were your knees ever straight at any time?—They were straight before I went to Mr. Brown's mill.

801. Are there any other boys at work at that mill that have crooked knees beside yourself?—Yes, there is one.

802. Did you ever hear any boys in the mill complain that by working there they got crooked knees or bad legs?—Yes, one.

803. Have you had bad health generally, besides the pain in your knee?—Yes; I have been very weak and poorly sometimes.

804. What sort of clothes had you before you put these on?—They were middling good trousers.

805. Have you only one suit?—No, I have only one suit.

806. You have no better suit for Sunday?—Not before I got this.

807. You say that you worked for 17 hours a day all the year round; did you do that without interruption?—Yes.

808. Could you attend any day or night-school?—No.

809. Can you write?—No.

810. Can you read?—I can read a little in a spelling book.

811. Where did you learn that; did you go to a Sunday-school?—No, I had not clothes to go in.

812. Did you ever go to church?—Yes, sometimes.

813. When you were a sweeper and errand-boy, had you any thing to do with the manufacturing?—Yes; I took one of the boys' places at the Lewises when they went out.*

814. What situation did you like best?—I liked sweeping best.

815. What is the most you have earned in a week, since you have worked at the broad Lewises?—I have earned 6s. 3d. and 6s. 6d. sometimes; very seldom 6s. 6d.

816. Have you any brothers?—I have four.

817. Are they working in manufactories?—No; I have only a sister working.

818. Where are your brothers working?—I have not a brother working at present.

819. You say that your regular hours of working at the broad Lewises were from 6 in the morning to 6 at night, and that you had four extra hours, and that you

---

*On strike.

get a penny an hour; how much did you ever get extra?—Sometimes 1s. 3d. and sometimes 1s. 6d.; but very seldom 1s. 6d.

820. Were you paid for every extra hour you worked?—Yes.

821. What time did you leave off on Saturday?—Sometimes at half-past 4, sometimes 5.

822. Did you get paid for all the over-hours that you worked?—Yes.

823. They never cheated you out of any time?—No.

824. When did you begin on Saturday?—Sometimes at 5, and sometimes at 6; but I went a great deal oftener at 5 than at 6.

825. Are you still working at Mr. Brown's?—I have got turned off for going to London.

826. Till you came, did you work at Mr. Brown's, at the Lewis?—Yes.

827. How came you to be turned off; what did they tell you?—They told me I was to go no more.

828. Did you ask to leave to go away?—Yes, I told the overlooker a day or two before.

829. When they turned you away, did they tell you that you could not come back because they must put another boy in your place, or did they seem angry with you for going?—They looked very cross with me for going.

830. Did they say any thing?—They say that I was not to come any more again, if I went.

831. Have you been working at this last place from 5 to 10?—No; we have been going from 8 to half-past 5.

832. Did they ever beat you at Mr. Brown's mill?—Yes; the overlooker used to beat us for not going to school.

833. Did they ever beat you for not working?—No.

834. Did Mr. Brown desire you to go to school?—I do not know; but the overlooker used to beat us for not going.

835. Did Mr. Brown keep a school upon the premises?—No.

836. Had you any other school to go to but the Sunday-school?—No.

837. Was it then for not going to the Sunday-school that you were beat?—Yes, it was.

838. What were you flogged with?—With a strap.

839. Did it hurt you very much?—Yes.

840. When was it he beat you for not going to the Sunday-school, was it upon a Sunday?—No, Monday morning.

841. Did the schoolmaster tell that you had not been there?—He used to ask us all every Monday morning, and I used to always tell him the truth.

842. What Sunday-school did you go to?—I did not go to any, because I had no clothes.

843. What Sunday-school should you have gone to if you had gone to any?—I might have gone to any that I liked.

844. When did you work last from 5 till 10?—About a year and a half since.

845. Were you working at the broad Lewis when you came away?—Yes.

846. Are you pretty well in health?—No, I am very weak.

847. Have you no appetite?—No, I do not eat much.

848. When you were an errand-boy and sweeper, was that hard work?—It was middling hard work.

849. When you came to be a brusher, did that tire you very much?—Yes, I was rather tired, but brushing is a good deal easier than minding Lewises.

850. Did you feel fatigued with 12 hours of daily labour?—Yes.

851. Has it affected your health?—Yes.

852. And you believe that it has deformed your limbs?—Yes, it has.

853. Were you obliged either to work those long hours, or to leave your employment?—Yes.

854. Would you have liked it better to have worked a smaller length of time, even though your wages would have been less?—Yes, I would have liked to have worked less, but then the wages would have lower.

855. When you were a brusher, how came you to go the Lewises; did you wish to go there?—Yes, it was not work that I looked at, but wages.

856. How far did you live from the mill?—About half a mile.

857. Did you go home when you left work?—Yes.

858. What time was that?—Sometimes 10, and sometimes 9.

859. When you went home, what did you do?—I got my supper, and went to bed.

860. What time did you get up?—About half-past 4, and sometimes a quarter to 5, and then I went to work at 5.

861. Who waked you in the morning?—My mother.

862. At this place you have been working short hours?—Yes.

863. What wages have your got?—I have got 4s. from 8 till half-past 5.

864. If you had left these manufactories could you have got any other work?—No, I do not think I could.

865. Do you know what boys got that worked with farmers?—I do not know.

866. Had you rather work now as you are doing, from 8 to half-past 5, and get 4s., or work the 11 hours and get 5s.?—I had gather go 11 hours and get 5s., because it is more wages; we have very little coming in at our house; there is only another sister besides me working, and she has 7s. 6d. a week.

867. What is the most wages you ever got when you were working the 17 hours?—I sometimes got 6s. 3d. and sometimes 6s. 6d.

868. Would you rather work the long hours and get the 6s. 3d. or work the short hours and get the 4s?—I would as lief work the short hours.

869. Would your health enable you to endure the 17 hours of labour?—No, it would not.

870. Has your mother any parochial relief*?—Yes, she has 5s. a fortnight.

871. Does your mother work at the mill?—No, she goes out washing.

872. How old is your sister?—Going on 24.

873. Does she work the same length of time that you do?—She goes at 7 in the morning and works till half-past 6 at night.

874. You said that the working 17 hours fatigued you, does working from 8 till half-past 5 fatigue you?—No.

875. When you go back, shall you go to Mr. Brown's mill and ask for the work again?—Yes, I shall go and ask.

---

*Welfare subsidy provided by the local poor law guardians.

876. Do you hope they will take you in again?—Yes, I do.
877. Are you capable of doing any other work but working in a manufactory?—No, nothing but working in a manufactory of cloths.

Working-Class Life in Glasgow, 1842*

In the early 1840s a British civil servant by the name of Edwin Chadwick undertook, for the government, an investigation into the "sanitary condition of the labouring population" in various cities of Britain. Following is an excerpt from a report on the city of Glasgow, in Scotland, by one of Chadwick's fellow researchers, Charles Baird, in March 1841. Glasgow was the second largest city in Britain—a city of great wealth but also of great poverty. What impression does Baird convey with regard to the standard of living of the average working-class family in Glasgow? What were the "many causes" by which the workers could be reduced to poverty? What proportion of Glasgow's population was working class? How did people survive in times of distress?

That many of the operatives in Glasgow live in comfort and are able to clothe themselves and families, and to educate their children, is well known to all who know anything of them, and must be evident even to the passing stranger who sees the thousands pouring along the streets on the sabbath-day, apparently well fed and well clad, to their respective places of worship. I rejoice to be able to add, that numbers of them can do more—they give their quota of charity (far more in proportion than the higher classes do)—they assist in supporting their clergymen, as witness the payments for church-seats, and the donations, especially at the dissenting churches, and not a few of them save money. In proof of this last fact I call attention to our savings banks, and to the class of depositors therein. By the last Report (dated 2nd January, 1841) of the National Security Savings Bank of Glasgow, I find that, out of 20,076 individual depositors, there were—

Mechanics, artificers, and their wives	6,736
Factory operatives	1,574
Labourers, carters, and their wives	867
In all, of these descriptions	9,177

And it is proper to mention, that there are nearly 2,000 other depositors, whose "descriptions are not stated."

While, however, many of the working classes in Glasgow are able to live in comfort, and a number of them, by proper economy and prudence, to save money, it must be kept in view that they are subject to many causes by which even the most prudent and economical may be reduced to penury, such, for instance, as the want of employment: it may be from the inclemency of the weather, which almost every winter (and peculiarly during the last winter) interrupts the masons, slaters, and out-door labourers; the sudden convulsions and fluctuations of trade, by which the means of subsistence are frequently withdrawn from large masses; the high price of provisions; and, above all, their liability to diseases, especially those of an

---

*Source: Charles Baird, "On the General and Sanitary Condition of the Working Classes and the Poor in the City of Glasgow," included in *Reports of the Sanitary Conditions of the Labouring Populations of Scotland, 1842*, 165–168.

epidemic nature.

Like the population of every other manufacturing city or town, the working classes of Glasgow have frequently suffered very severely from sudden depressions and fluctuations of trade, and the consequent want of employment. In 1816–17 the distress was such that it was found necessary to raise a large sum of voluntary subscription. At that time 9,6531. 6s. 2d. was distributed among 23,130 persons. In 1819–20 large distributions of clothing, meal, and fuel were made to persons who could find no employment. Upwards of 600 men were employed in breaking stones for the roads, and 340 weavers at spade-work in the public green. From April, 1826, till October, 1827, was another period of great mercantile distress, and about 9,0001. was laid out for the amelioration of the working classes. In 1829, 2,9501. for the like purpose. In 1832, the memorable cholera year, the condition of these classes was most lamentable. About 10,0001. was then raised by voluntary subscription, and 8,0001. Under the Cholera Assessment Act, and (with the exception of 1,8541.) was expended in feeding and clothing the destitute, washing the houses, attending to the sick, and providing coffins, &c. &c. Down till 1837 there was no other period of great distress; but in the spring of that year, owing to the depressed state of trade, the want of employment, and the high price of provisions, a large number of the working classes in Glasgow were reduced to very necessitous circumstances: 5,2001. was raised by voluntary subscription, with which, and 3,0001. handed over by a former relief committee, 3,072 adults were employed at out door work, as preparing road-metal, or at weaving, and 3,800 adults, besides children, in all about 18,500 persons, were daily supplied with food at the soup-kitchens then established; besides which considerable sums were expended in providing fuel, and in redeeming bedding and clothes from pawn. Even during last winter, although it was generally admitted that there was no great scarcity of employment, and that the operatives were in a much better condition than they had been at previous times, owing to the great severity of the weather the relief committee thought it was necessary to give extraordinary aid; and accordingly, in the city and suburbs, upwards of 3,000 persons were assisted in various ways, particularly with food, during the months of January and February last.

Much, however, as the working classes in Glasgow have suffered from the depressions or fluctuations of trade, the want of employment, and the high prices of provisions, I conceive that their sufferings from these causes have been trifling indeed when compared to what they have annually suffered from disease, especially of an epidemic nature.

From deductions made on an extensive scale by our most eminent statists, it may be said to be established that "when 1 person in 100 dies annually, 2 are constantly sick." Let this axiom be applied to Glasgow, in which, last year, the deaths were as 1 to 31 969, or 3128 per cent (and the mean annual mortality for the last 5 years 1 in 31738). Let it be taken into account that the deaths from fever alone, in 1840, were 1229, being 1 to 7177, or 13921 per cent of the whole deaths. Let it be also considered the fever here, as elsewhere, chooses its victims in the prime of life, and consequently most frequently the parents of large young families; and let it be recollected that, as above stated, at least four-fifths of the population of Glasgow and suburbs consist of the working classes, or their families: so that if, as is too often the case, the father is laid on a bed of sickness or cut off by death, there is no provision for the other members of the family, I say let these considerations be duly weighed, and even a passing thought given to the sufferings, the watching, want and wretchedness which accompanies sickness and death, especially in the poor man's house, and any right-constituted mind will contemplate with horror the amount of misery which must have been the lot of countless thousands of our working classes.

Instead of dwelling longer here upon the vast amount of suffering incident to these classes from the fearful extent of disease and mortality which has afflicted our city for many years past,

I shall now proceed to the next head of my report, viz., on the sanitary state of Glasgow, and there give tables, or data, from which any person interested in the condition of the working and poorer classes may draw deductions; and I may here mention that I make a separate chapter, and place it in position I do, as the tables and statements in it illustrate the condition of both the working classes and the poor, and also show the great extent of destitution which must exist in the city of Glasgow. With these characteristics, the chapter on the sanitary condition of our city will form an intermediate and proper connecting link in my report.

Women in "Sweated Labor" in London, 1888*

Mary Hayes was a widow who lived in London and worked as a tailoress (a "trouser finisher") in what was called a "sweated industry." "Sweated" work was very common in most large cities of Europe and America, and for the most part undertaken in their homes by women, children, and immigrant Jews. What were the circumstances under which Mrs. Hayes worked? Can you tell from this testimony what her work consisted of? What her hours of labor were? Wages? Diet? How did she get her work from the business for whom she worked? What were the advantages of this sort of work to the manufacturer who hired her?

Mrs. MARY HAYES, is called in; and, having been sworn, is Examined, as follows
(24th, April 1888):

1563. [Chairman.] Where do you live?
14, Maplin-street.

1564. What is your trade?
Trouser finishing.

1565. Your husband was a soldier, was he not?
Yes.

1566. How long have you been in this trade?
I was in the trade before I was married, but when I got married to my husband of course I had to do the army work, such as washing; and since the death of my husband of course I have done the work, because I knew it from a girl; I was always in the line.

1567. How long is it since your husband died?
Nineteen years on the 5th of next June.

---

*Source: "First Report from the Select Committee of the House of Lords on the Sweating System, together with Proceedings of the Committee, Minutes of Evidence, and Appendix," *Parliamentary Papers, 188, Vol. XX.*

1568. You have been 19 years at trouser finishing?
Yes.

1569. Have you any children?
Yes.

1570. What ages, and how many?
I have got three children; I say "children." I have two daughters at home. I have got one that has been in the infirmary since she has left a situation. Off and on she has been laid up with rheumatism, and likewise with rheumatic fever.

1571. And the other?
The other has been a delicate girl from the birth; she has never been fit for any situation, but she assists me with the work as far as she can.

1572. Perhaps you will tell the Committee the prices you get for these trousers?
I get from 2 3/4d. to 3d.* I have had more years ago; I have had 4 1/2d. for twist holes, and I have had 4d. for all cotton holes; but then that is some years ago.

1573. You have had 4d. and 4 1/2d. for what you now get 2 3/4d. and 3d. for?
Yes, for what I now get 2 3/4d. for I used five years ago to get 4d.; they are all cotton holes.

1574. How many can you make a week?
With me and my assistant, my daughter, I do about eight pair a day. I call it a day, but it is not a day; I do not feel able to sit the hours I used to do. Sometimes I sit from eight in the morning until 10, or sometimes 11 at night.

1575. Did you hear what the witness before you said as to the price of materials, and so on; I suppose you would have to pay the same price?
The same price; because I suppose, to take the trimmings of the work, that there is hardly a farthing difference in all the work so far as that goes.

1576. How much can you make a day?
With me and my daughter, the hours that we sit, we do about eight pairs a day; that is when I can get them.

1577. What will that come to?
If they are 2 3/4d.; if I have a day's work, that is 1s. 10d. for the day.

1578. And out of that you find materials?
Yes, I have to find threads and cottons.

---

*There were 12 pence ("d") in a shilling and 20 shillings ("s") in a pound (£).

1579. And what do you consider you can clear?
Of course, when I take my trimmings and all that out, it leaves me but a very little clear; to take the average I do not suppose it leaves above 5s. 6d. a week when trimmings are taken; I do not think I am much out of the way in saying that.

1580. During the winter have you good work?
No, I lose a deal by slack time in the winter.

1581. How long is the slack time?
About two months before Christmas; this year it has been very bad indeed.

1582. Do you find any other kind of work to do then?
I do not feel able to do much other sort of work; I have not very good health myself since I have been left a widow. I have got now, at this present time, an abscess at the back of the left eye that I have been suffering from for years.

1583. You work now from about eight in the morning till 10 or 11 at night?
Yes.

1584. Used you ever to work longer hours than that?
I used to work longer when I was younger.

1585. You used to work harder?
Yes; of course I cannot do that now.

1586. What could you earn when prices were better, five or six years ago?
When the children were little I could earn, I dare say, from 10s. to 11s. a week at that time; but then that is some years ago.

1587. When did prices begin to get so bad?
That is a good many years ago now; but then I daresay for this last five years they have come down a great deal more than that.

1588. Do you think there are more people engaged in the same business now than there were then?
I think so.

1589. What is your ordinary food?
I am almost ashamed to tell the gentlemen. Of course you must know that it cannot be very good food; I know that very little meat comes to the house out of it.

1590. What do you pay for meat?
When I do get any it is 8d. a pound, and if I get a pound of it, it has to be for Sunday; that is as much as I can get when I can afford to be out of that little money.

1591. Do you have meat once a week?
Sometimes I do, and sometimes I do not. I generally try to struggle to have a bit on a Sunday, if I can possibly at all.

1592. And what is your ordinary diet, bread?
Bread and a cup of tea, and such as a bit of fish, or anything of that sort.

1593. What rent do you pay?
Two shillings a week.

1594. How do you manage to pay that during the slack times in the winter?
I have to pay it as well as I possibly can; I owe nothing of it.

1595. Do you have to fetch your work?
My daughter, she goes after the work.

1596. How far has she to go?
It is not a great distance from where I am living.

1597. [Earl of Aberdeen.] About the rent, if you get into arrears, how much time are you allowed?
She is a very good landlady that I am now living with; she will not compel me to any particular time; I could pay it the best way I could get it.

1598. [Lord Monkswell.] What were your former hours when you were strong; how many used you to work?
Perhaps it might be 12 o'clock at night and much earlier, beginning in the morning.

1599. How early beginning?
I might begin, perhaps, at six, sometimes at seven.

1600. And work generally till 12, or only sometimes?
Only sometimes.

1601. When did you leave off, usually, if you began at six or seven, when you were strong?
Sometimes about 10 o'clock.

1602. Then your hours would be usually from 6 or 7 to 10 at night?
Yes.

1603. How many days a week did you work like that?
I might have a little time just to do a bit of cleaning, either me or my daughter.

1604. Otherwise you would work the whole seven days; could you afford not to work on Sunday?
I never do any work on a Sunday, not such as that work.

1605. You say you earn 5s. 6d. a week; does that include your daughter's earnings?
That is with me; she does not do much, because she has to run about.

1606. When you get 1s. 10d. a day, that must make more than 5s. 6d. a week?
Sometimes I have trousers that I get 3d. for.

1607. Then how much would you deduct for materials?
There is firing, and the thread and the twist, and the oil; I know it comes to 1s. 6d.;
that is with the firing and the trimming.

1608. One shilling and sixpence a week?
Yes, because I have all colours of thread and cotton to find.

1609. [Chairman] Do you work by gas light?
With a lamp.

1610. I forgot to ask you whether you use a sewing machine in your work?
No.

1611. Why not?
I do not use any sewing machine; I am a finisher.

1612. Do you mean that a sewing machine could not be used in finishing?
Of course it can be, but I am too old to do it now; I could not use the machine.

1613. Why not?
My nerves would never let me; I have hard work sometimes to see to thread the
needle, much more a machine.

1614. Other finishers do use a machine?
Oh, yes; there are some that can finish and machine together.

1615. Could you earn better wages if you were able to use a machine?
I dare say I could, if I was able to do such a thing; but I cannot properly sit in a room
when I hear the noise of a machine.

The Witness is directed to withdraw.

Chapter 23
Ideologies and Upheavals, 1815–1850

Chapter Questions

After reading and studying this chapter you should be able to answer the following questions:

What ideas did thinkers develop to describe and shape the great political and economic transformation that was taking place? How and why did conservatives and radicals view liberalism and nationalism differently? How did the artists and writers of the Romantic movement reflect and influence the era? How and why did political revolution break out once again? Why did the revolutionary surge triumph in 1848, then fail almost completely?

Chapter Summary

This chapter examines a number of extremely important ideas: liberalism, nationalism, socialism, and romanticism. Studying these ideas helps us understand the historical process in the nineteenth and twentieth centuries. A key aspect of that process was the bitter and intense struggle between the conservative aristocrats, who wanted to maintain the status quo, and the middle- and working-class liberals and nationalists, who wanted to carry on the destruction of the old regime of Europe that had begun in France in 1789. The symbol of conservatism was Prince Metternich of Austria, Europe's leading diplomat. Metternich was convinced that liberalism and nationalism had to be repressed, or else Europe would break up into warring states. In opposition to Metternich, liberals and nationalists saw their creeds as the way to free humanity from the burden of supporting the aristocracy and from foreign oppression. Metternich's convictions were shared by the other peacemakers at Vienna in 1814, while those of the liberals fanned the fires of revolution, first in 1830 and, more spectacularly, in 1848. Political liberalism, combined with the principles of economic liberalism, with its stress on unrestricted economic self-interest as the avenue to human happiness, was extremely attractive to the middle class. Of the major powers, only Britain was transformed by reform and untouched by revolution.

The chapter shows that although many believed nationalism led toward human happiness, it contained in reality the dangerous ideas of national and racial superiority. To make the turbulent intellectual world even more complex, socialism emerged as another, equally powerful set of ideas regarding the creation of a just and happy society. Early socialists were idealistic and utopian, but the socialism of Karl Marx, which later became dominant, claimed to be realistic and scientific. Socialism contributed to the split between the middle and lower classes. This split explains the failure of these classes in the face of the common enemies in the revolutions of 1848. The chapter also discusses romanticism, which was a reaction to the rationalism of the previous century. Romanticism was the central mood of the nineteenth century and the emotional background of its painting, music, and literature.

Study Outline

Use this outline to preview the chapter before you read a particular section in your textbook and then as a self-check to test your reading comprehension after you have read the chapter section.

I. The peace settlement
    A. The Congress of Vienna
        1. By 1814 the conservative monarchs of Europe had defeated French armies and checked the spread of the French Revolution.
        2. The victors restored the French boundaries of 1792 and the Bourbon dynasty.
        3. They made other changes in the boundaries of Europe, establishing Prussia as a "sentinel" against France, and created a new kingdom out of Belgium and Holland.
        4. It was believed that the concept of the balance of power—an international equilibrium of political and military forces—would preserve peace in Europe.
        5. But the demands of the victors, especially the Prussians and the Russians, for compensation threatened the balance.
            a. The Russian demands for Poland and the Prussian wish for Saxony led to conflict among the powers.
            b. Castlereigh, Metternich, and Tallyrand forced Russian and Prussia into a compromise whereby Russia got part of Poland and Prussia received two-fifths of Saxony.
    B. Intervention and repression
        1. Under Metternich, Austria, Prussia, and Russia led a crusade against liberalism.
            a. They formed a Holy Alliance to check future liberal and revolutionary activity.
            b. When liberals succeeded in Spain and in the Two Sicilies, these powers intervened to restore conservatism.
            c. However, Britain blocked intervention in Latin America and encouraged the Monroe Doctrine (1823).
        2. Metternich's policies also dominated the German Confederation.
            a. Metternich had the Carlsbad Decrees issued in 1819.
            b. These decrees repressed subversive ideas and organizations.
    C. Metternich and conservatism
        1. Metternich represented the view that the best state blended monarchy, bureaucracy, and aristocracy.
        2. He hated liberalism, which he claimed stirred up the lower classes and caused war and bloodshed.
            a. Liberalism also stirred up national aspirations in central Europe, which could lead to war and the breakup of the Austrian Empire.

    b. The empire, which was dominated by the minority Germans, contained many ethnic groups, including Hungarians and Czechs, which was a potential source of weakness and dissatisfaction.

II. Radical ideas and early socialism
  A. Liberalism
    1. Liberalism demanded representative government, equality before the law, and individual freedoms such as freedom of speech and assembly.
    2. Early nineteenth-century liberalism opposed government intervention in social and economic affairs.
    3. Economic liberalism was known as laissez-faire—the principle that the economy should be left unregulated.
      a. Adam Smith was critical of mercantilism and argued that a free economy would bring wealth for all, including workers.
      b. British businessmen often used the principle of laissez-faire in self-serving ways, backed up by the theories of Malthus, who believed that marrying late in life was the best means of population control, and Ricardo, who claimed that because of the pressure of population, wages would always be low.
    4. After 1815, political liberalism became increasingly a middle-class doctrine, used to exclude the lower classes from government and business.
      a. Some foes of conservatism called for universal voting rights for men.
      b. Many people who believed in democracy also believed in the republican form of government and were more radical than the liberals.
  B. Nationalism
    1. Nationalism was a second radical idea in the years after 1815.
      a. It evolved from cultural unity.
      b. Nationalists sought to turn cultural unity into political reality, so the territory of each people coincides with its state boundaries.
      c. Modern nationalism had its roots in the French Revolution and the Napoleonic wars.
    2. Nationalists believed that common language and traditions would bring about unity and common loyalties and, therefore, self-government.
    3. On the negative side, nationalism generated ideas of racial and cultural superiority.
      a. The German pastor Herder claimed that nationalities are different.
      b. Palacký, Mazzini, and Michelet all spoke of national mission and the superiority of one nation over others.
  C. French utopian socialism.
    1. Early French socialists proposed a system of greater economic equality planned by the government.
      a. They believed the rich and poor should be more nearly equal economically.
      b. They believed that private property should be abolished.
    2. Saint-Simon and Fourier proposed a planned economy and socialist communities.
      a. Saint-Simon was a moralist who believed that a planned society would bring about improved conditions for the poor.
      b. Fourier proposed new planned towns; he also criticized middle-class family life and sexual and marriage customs.

3. Blanc believed that the state should set up government-backed workshops and factories to guarantee employment.

4. Proudhon, often considered an anarchist, claimed that the worker was the source of all wealth.

D. The birth of Marxian socialism

1. The *Communist Manifesto* (1848), by Marx and Engels, is the key work of socialism.

   a. Marx saw all of previous history in terms of an economic class struggle.

   b. The industrial society was characterized, according to Marx, by the exploitation of the proletariat (workers) by the bourgeoisie (middle class).

2. He predicted that the future would bring a violent revolution by workers to overthrow the capitalists.

3. Marx argued that profits were really wages stolen from the workers.

4. His theory of historical evolution came from Hegel.

   a. Hegel believed that each age is characterized by a dominant set of ideas, which produces opposing ideas and eventually a synthesis.

   b. Marx retained Hegel's view of history as a dialectic process of change but made economic relationships between classes the driving force.

III. The romantic movement

A. Romanticism was partly a revolt against classicism and the Enlightenment.

1. Romantics rejected the classical emphasis on order and rationality.

   a. Romanticism was characterized by a belief in emotional exuberance, imagination, and spontaneity.

   b. Romantics stressed individualism and the rejection of materialism.

2. Romantics used nature as a source of inspiration, and they emphasized the study of history.

   a. History was seen as the key to an organic, dynamic universe.

   b. Reading and writing history was viewed as the way to understand national destiny.

B. Romanticism in literature

1. Romantic literature first developed fully in Britain, as exemplified by the poets Wordsworth, Coleridge, Scott, Byron, Shelley, and Keats.

   a. Wordsworth and Coleridge rejected classical rules of poetry; Wordsworth's work points to the power of nature to elevate and instruct.

   b. The Scottish novelist and poet Walter Scott romanticized history.

2. In France, Victor Hugo emphasized strange settings and human emotions.

3. Romantics such as the Frenchwoman George Sand rebelled against social conventions.

4. In central Europe romanticism reinforced nationalism.

C. Romanticism in art and music

1. Delacroix, Turner, and Constable were three of the greatest romantic painters.

2. Romantic composers rejected well-defined structure in their efforts to find maximum range and emotional intensity.

   a. Liszt was the greatest pianist of his age.

   b. Beethoven was the first master of romantic music.

IV. Reforms and revolutions

A. National liberation in Greece

1. Greek nationalists led by Ypsilanti in 1821 fought for freedom from Turkey.

2. The Great Powers supported the Ottoman Empire, but Britain, France, and Russia supported Greek nationalism, and Greece became independent in 1830.

B. Liberal reform in Great Britain

1. The British aristocracy, which controlled the Tory party, feared liberalism and worked to repress it.

2. The Corn Law (1815), which protected the English landowners by prohibiting the importation of foreign grain unless the domestic price rose above a certain level, is an example of aristocratic class power and selfishness.

   a. The change in the Corn Laws led to protests by urban laborers, supported by radical intellectuals.

   b. Parliament responded by passing the Six Acts (1819), which eliminated all mass meetings.

3. The growth of the middle class and its desire for reform led to the Reform Bill of 1832, which increased the number of voters significantly.

   a. The House of Commons emerged as the major legislative body.

   b. The new industrial areas of the country gained representation in Commons.

   c. Many "rotten boroughs" were eliminated.

4. The Chartist demand for universal male suffrage failed, but the Anti-Corn Law League succeeded in getting the Corn Laws repealed in 1846 and free trade established.

5. By 1846, both the Tory and Whig parties were interested in reform.

   a. The Ten Hours Act (1847) limited the workday for women and young people in factories to ten hours.

   b. The reform efforts did not extend to Ireland, where potato crops failed in 1846, 1848, and 1851, causing the Great Famine.

C. The revolution of 1830 in France

1. Louis XVIII's Constitutional Charter of 1814, although undemocratic, protected the people against a return to royal absolutism and aristocratic privilege.

2. Charles X, Louis's successor, tried to re-establish the old order and repudiated the Constitutional Charter in 1830.

3. The reaction was an immediate insurrection that brought the expulsion of Charles X.

4. The new king, Louis Philippe, accepted the Constitutional Charter but did little more than protect the rich upper middle class.

V. The revolutions of 1848

A. A democratic republic in France

1. The refusal of King Louis Philippe and his chief minister, Guizot, to bring about electoral reform sparked a revolt in Paris in 1848.

2. The revolt led to the establishment of a provisional republic that granted universal male suffrage and other reforms.

3. The revolutionary coalition couldn't agree on a common program, as the moderate, liberal republicans split with the socialist republicans.

4. National workshops were a compromise between the socialists' demands for work for all and the moderates' determination to provide only temporary relief for the massive unemployment.

5. The fear of socialism led to a clash of classes.
   a. The workers invaded the Constituent Assembly and tried to proclaim a new revolutionary government.
   b. The Assembly dissolved the workshops in Paris.
6. The closing down of the workshops led to a violent uprising (the June Days).
7. Class war led to the election of a strongman, Louis Napoleon, as president in 1848.

B. The Austrian Empire
1. The revolution in France resulted in popular upheaval throughout central Europe, but in the end conservative reaction won.
2. Hungarian nationalism resulted in revolution against the Austrian overlords.
   a. Under Kossuth, the Hungarians demanded national autonomy, civil liberties, and universal suffrage.
   b. Emperor Ferdinand I promised reforms and a liberal constitution.
   c. Serfdom was abolished.
3. Conflict among the different nationalities (Hungarians against Croats, Serbs and Rumanians; Czechs against Germans), encouraged by the monarchy, weakened the revolution.
4. The alliance of the working and middle classes soon collapsed.
5. The conservative aristocrats crushed the revolution.
6. Frances Joseph was crowned emperor in 1848.
7. The Russian army helped defeat the Hungarians.

C. Prussia and the Frankfurt Assembly
1. Middle-class Prussians wanted to create a unified, liberal Germany.
2. Inspired by events in France, the working-class people of Prussia demanded and received a liberal constitution.
3. Further worker demands for suffrage and socialist reforms caused fear among the aristocracy.
4. The Frankfurt National Assembly of 1848 was a middle-class liberal body that began writing a constitution for a unified Germany.
5. War with Denmark over the provinces of Schleswig and Holstein ended with a rejection of the Frankfurt Assembly by the newly elected Frederick William and the failure of German liberalism.

Review Questions

Check your understanding of this chapter by answering the following questions.

1. What is the "dual revolution"?
2. Describe the treatment of defeated France by the victors in 1814. Why wasn't the treatment harsher?
3. What is meant by the term *balance of power*? What methods were used by the Great Powers to preserve the balance of power?
4. What were the Hundred Days?
5. Who were the participants and what was the purpose of the Holy Alliance and the congress system?

6. Describe the make-up of the Austrian Empire. How and why were nationalism and liberalism regarded as dangerous to those in power?
7. Describe laissez-faire economic philosophy. Why did the laissez-faire liberals see mercantilism as undesirable?
8. Define nationalism. What were its links to liberalism?
9. What are the goals of socialism? How do the ideas of Saint-Simon, Fourier, Blanc, and Proudhon illustrate socialist thought?
10. What was Marx's view of history? What was the role of the proletariat?
11. What is romanticism? What were the romantics rebelling against?
12. In what ways was romantic music a radical departure from the past? What was the purpose of romantic music?
13. Compare and contrast the political developments in Britain and France between 1814–15 and 1832. Who were the winners and the losers?
14. What were the causes and the outcome of the Greek revolution of 1821–1832?
15. What were the goals of the Chartists? The Anti-Corn Law League?
16. What was the Reform Bill of 1832?
17. Why did Charles X lose his throne?
18. Describe what happened in France in 1848. Why did the French voters turn their backs on the Revolution and elect a strongman as president?
19. Was the national workshop plan a wise compromise for the French socialists?
20. Why did the revolutionary coalition in Hungary in 1848 break down?
21. Why couldn't the middle-class liberals and the urban poor in Austria cooperate in destroying their common enemies?
22. What was the role of the Archduchess Sophia in the preservation of the Austrian Empire?
23. What were the goals of the Frankfurt Assembly? Why did it fail?

Study-Review Exercises

Define the following key concepts and terms.

romanticism

conservatism

dual revolution

liberalism

nationalism

radicalism

laissez faire

iron law of wages

socialism

Marx's theory of historical evolution

classicism

republicanism

Identify and explain the significance of the following people and terms.
Quadruple Alliance

Constitutional Charter of 1814 (France)

Napoleon's Hundred Days

Congress of Troppau

congress system

Corn Law

Ten Hours Act of 1847 (Britain)

national workshops

Wealth of Nations

Frankfurt Assembly

Schleswig-Holstein question

Louis Kossuth

Jules Michelet

Johann Herder

Frederick William IV

Alexander Ypsilanti

Chartists

Thomas Malthus

Karl Marx

Louis Philippe

Communist Manifesto

Robert Peel

Explain what ideas the following romantic figures attempted to convey to their audiences.
William Wordsworth

Walter Scott

George Sand

Victor Hugo

Eugène Delacroix

Ludwig van Beethoven

Explain the objectives of the participants at the peace conferences of 1814–15 by completing the following table.

Name of Diplomat	Country	Objective
Metternich		
Castlereagh		
Alexander I		
Talleyrand		
Hardenburg	Prussia	

Explain the objectives of the revolutionaries in the following countries and how successful they were. In each case explain why the revolution failed or succeeded.

Country	Year	Revolutionary Goals and Outcome
Spain	1820–1823	
Two Sicilies	1820–1821	
Greece	1821–1832	
France	1830	
France	1848	
Hungary	1848	
Prussia	1848	

Test your understanding of the chapter by providing the correct answers.

1. In the long run, the revolutions in Germany in 1848 resulted in the *victory/defeat* of German liberalism.

2. The new president of France in 1848. _____

3. The romantic painter whose masterpiece was *Liberty Leading the People.*

   _____

4. Laissez-faire economists believed that the state *should/should not* regulate the economy.

5. Hungary was a part of the _____ Empire.

6. This German pastor and philosopher argued that every national group has its own

   particular spirit and genius. _____

7. This mid-nineteenth-century Frenchman, author of *Organization of Work*, believed that the

   right to work was sacred and should be guaranteed by the state. _____

8. The revolutions of 1848 in Austria saw *cooperation/competition* between national groups and
   the eventual *victory/defeat* of the old aristocracy and conservatism.

Multiple-Choice Questions

1. Which of the following people was part of the romantic movement of the nineteenth
   century?
   a. George Sand
   b. Count Metternich
   c. Louis Blanc
   d. Alexis de Tocqueville

2. The British Corn Laws were passed to give economic advantage to the
   a. landed aristocracy.
   b. middle class.
   c. urban working class.
   d. agricultural workers.

3. The term *dual revolution* refers to
   a. political revolution in France and Russia.
   b. an economic and political revolution.
   c. a joint revolution in improved health care and population increase.
   d. a revolution in both literature and music.

4. Which of the following statements about the peace settlement worked out at the Congress
   of Vienna is true?
   a. It was harsh toward the defeated French and rejected the restoration of the Bourbon
      monarchy.
   b. France gained a few colonies in addition to territories it had conquered in Italy,
      Germany, and the Low Countries.
   c. Belgium and Holland were united, and Prussia received territory on France's eastern
      border.
   d. Russia lost some western territory to Poland.

5. The problem that almost led to war among the major powers in 1815 was
   a. the refusal of France to participate in the Vienna conference.
   b. the British takeover of the South American trade routes.
   c. Russian and Prussian territorial demands.
   d. the traditional idea about balance of power.

6. The major demand of the English Chartists was for
   a. universal male suffrage.
   b. improved prison conditions.
   c. tariff protection for poor farmers.
   d. government-sponsored cooperative workshops.

7. The Holy Alliance consisted of
   a. Russia, Britain, and Austria.
   b. Britain, France, and Prussia.
   c. Prussia, Austria, and Russia.
   d. France, Austria, and Prussia.

8. Metternich's conservative policies prevailed in
   a. South America.
   b. western Europe.
   c. central Europe.
   d. Great Britain and its colonies.

9. Adam Smith would have been likely to agree that
   a. monopolies are good for a state.
   b. increased competition benefits all classes of society.
   c. increasing workers' wages is harmful in the long run.
   d. population will always grow too fast.

10. The Vienna peace settlement was largely the product of
    a. liberals.
    b. nationalists.
    c. socialists.
    d. conservatives.

11. One of the most influential French utopian socialists was
    a. the count de Saint-Simon.
    b. Talleyrand.
    c. Louis Philippe.
    d. Eugène Delacroix.

12. In 1848, great revolutions occurred in all of the following countries *except*
    a. Prussia.
    b. Hungary.
    c. Italy.
    d. Great Britain.

13. After the peace settlement of Vienna there were
    a. still over three hundred independent German political entities.
    b. thirty-eight independent German states, including Austria and Prussia.
    c. only two German states: Austria and Prussia.
    d. approximately one hundred independent German states dominated by Austria.

14. Those conservatives who opposed liberal thought would have supported
    a. representative government.
    b. equality before the law.
    c. individual freedoms, e.g., freedom of the press, freedom of speech.
    d. legally separated classes.

15. In his writings, Karl Marx drew heavily on the ideas of
    a. French writers on absolutism.
    b. English mercantilist economists.
    c. Hegel, especially the dialectic process of history.
    d. Christianity and middle-class views of the family.

16. The first great nationalist rebellion of the 1820s involved the
    a. Germans against the Austrians.
    b. Greeks against the Turks.
    c. Irish against the English.
    d. Greeks against the Russians.

17. The English Corn Laws prohibited
    a. the exporting of British grain.
    b. raising the price of British grain above that of continental prices.
    c. the importing of foreign grain unless the price of British grain reached harvest-disaster prices.
    d. the domination of the British grain market by the aristocracy.

18. The English Reform Bill of 1832 provided for
    a. representation in Parliament for the new industrial areas.
    b. the working-class vote.
    c. the supremacy of the House of Lords over the House of Commons.
    d. universal womanhood suffrage.

19. Generally, the revolutions of 1848 resulted in
    a. success for the liberal forces in France.
    b. slow gains at first for the liberals, followed by complete realization of their goals.
    c. a consolidation of moderate, nationalistic middle classes.
    d. the end of the age of romantic revolution.

20. The nineteenth-century romantic writer who is famous for his fascination with fantastic characters, (including his "human gargoyle"), strange settings, and human emotion was
    a. William Wordsworth.
    b. Walter Scott.
    c. Victor Hugo.
    d. J. M. W. Turner.

21. The writer and poet influenced by German romanticism who wrote novels and poems based on romantic history, particularly that of Scotland, was
    a. William Wordsworth.
    b. Walter Scott.
    c. Adam Smith.
    d. Samuel Coleridge.

22. The greatest master of romantic music was
    a. Liszt.
    b. Paganini.
    c. Hugo.
    d. Beethoven.

23. Romanticism originated in
    a. Britain and Germany.
    b. France.
    c. Italy.
    d. Russia.

24. Marx believed that the key to understanding history is
    a. religion.
    b. feudalism.
    c. the power of the aristocracy.
    d. class struggle.

25. The Austrian Empire and Austrian society were dominated by which of the following ethnic groups?
    a. German
    b. Hungarian
    c. Czech
    d. Bohemian

Major Political Ideas

1. Compare and contrast conservatism and liberalism. What are the principal beliefs of each, who were their major supporters, and how successful was each?

2. Define nationalism. Why did it become a major political force in the nineteenth century?

Why did many conservatives oppose it? Did nationalism exist in the eighteenth century or earlier?

3. How were the ideas of economic liberals like Smith, Malthus, and Ricardo used by the industrialist middle class to further its own interests?

Issues for Essays and Discussion

The early nineteenth century saw the rise of a number of profoundly influential ideologies—conservatism, liberalism, nationalism, and socialism. What are these ideologies and what are their origins? Are there any connections between them? Which were the most influential?

Interpretation of Visual Sources

Study the reproduction of the painting *Liberty Leading the People* by Delacroix on page 743 of your textbook. What is the "message" of this painting? Could it be described as an ideological painting? What are some of the characteristics of the painting in terms of composition and subject portrayal that have caused it to be described as romantic.

Geography

Study carefully Map 23.1, "Europe in 1815," to better understand the Vienna peace settlement and the balance of power in the nineteenth century. Identify the five Great Powers and fix their boundaries in your mind. Also study the boundaries of the reorganized German Confederation. What are the two main states in the confederation, and what are some of the smaller ones? Now, refer to Map 21.1 and see how France had lost and Prussia had gained in the Rhineland area. Note how Poland virtually disappeared as an independent state. How do you explain this? Finally, were Italy, Germany, and Austria clearly defined national states?

Now close the text and test your understanding with Outline Map 23.1 provided. Shade in the five Great Powers and their boundaries, trace the boundary of the German confederation, and name and locate (approximately) the capital cities of the five Great Powers.

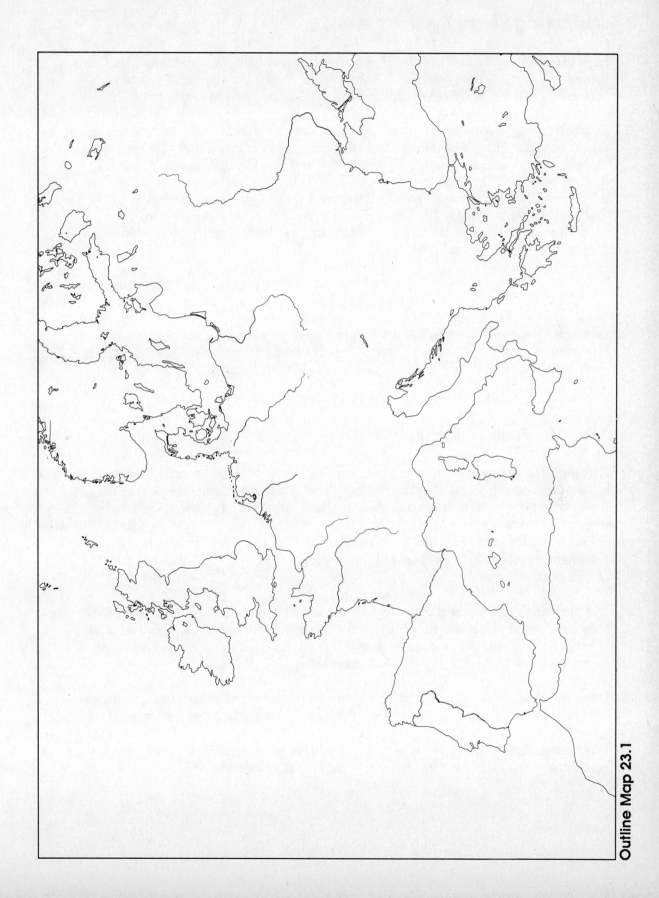

Outline Map 23.1

Understanding History Through the Arts

1. How did politics affect art in France? Begin your investigation with M. Marrian, *Painting Politics for Louis-Philippe* (1988), N. Athanassoglou, *French Images from the Greek War of Independence* (1989), and P. Mainardi, *Art and Politics of the Second Empire** (1987).

2. What do novels reveal about the period? Great novels that accurately portray aspects of the times are Victor Hugo's *Les Miserables,** an exciting story of crime and passion among France's poor; Honoré de Balzac's *Cousin Bette** and *Pere Goriot**; Thomas Mann's *Buddenbrooks** (1902), a wonderful historical novel that traces the rise and fall of a prosperous German family over three generations during the nineteenth century; and Charles Dickens's *A Tale of Two Cities*, a portrait of London and Paris during the dual revolution. A more recent historical novel about nineteenth-century life is J. Fowles's *The French Lieutenant's Woman** (1969).

3. How does Beethoven's music exemplify romantic ideals? Beethoven was the first great master of romantic music, even though in his early period he was influenced by the classical works of Haydn and Mozart. Beethoven's Ninth Symphony, the Choral Symphony, was greatly influenced by the ideas of the French Revolution—liberty, equality, and fraternity—and the symphony's "Ode to Joy" is based on Schiller's "Ode to Freedom. " The score was dedicated to Frederick William III, the king of Prussia.

Problems for Further Investigation

1. Was the 1848 revolution in France a modern class struggle in the Marxist sense? Much of the answer depends on whether or not one can show that the working class was of the new proletarian type—that is, modern factory workers rather than traditional artisan craftsmen. Begin your investigation with G. Rude, *The Crowd in History: A Study of Popular Disturbances in France and England, 1730–1848** (1964), Chapters 9 and 11. For the other side of the argument, see C. Tilly, "The People of June, 1848," in R. Price, ed., *Revolution and Reaction* (1977).

2. Did the British aristocrats give power to the middle class (in the Reform Bill of 1832) because they were afraid that it was the only alternative to violent revolution? This and other questions of interpretation of the famous bill are considered by seventeen different historians in W. H. Maehl, Jr., ed., *The Reform Bill of 1832** (1967).

3. What were the origins of romanticism? Those interested in the subject of romanticism should see J. B. Halsted, ed., *Romanticism: Definition, Explanation, and Evaluation** (1965).

4. Has nationalism been a force for good or for evil? A good starting point for an investigation of nationalism is H. Kohn, *Nationalism: Its Meaning and History** (1955).

---

*Available in paperback.

Chapter 24
Life in Urban Society

Chapter Questions

After reading and studying this chapter you should be able to answer the following questions:

What was life like in the cities? What did the emerging urban-industrial society mean for its rich, poor, and in-between members? Did the quality of life improve? What impact did the city have on family life, sexuality, marriage, and child rearing? What changes in science and thought and culture grew out of the new urban civilization?

Chapter Summary

Life in the new urban society was exciting and complex—as well as full of problems. This chapter shows that although the urban environment had long been crowded and unhealthy, the rapid growth of urban population made such problems worse. However, by the 1840s, urban problems were attacked and partly solved in both Great Britain and the continental countries. For example, throughout Europe a movement for better public health brought about sewer and water systems and gradually cleaned up the worst filth. Likewise, there were revolutionary breakthroughs in preventive medicine in the 1860s and after as Pasteur and his followers discovered how germs spread disease and how disease could be controlled. Urban planning and public transportation helped people move to better, less crowded housing. Thus, by the late nineteenth century the quality of life in cities had improved dramatically for ordinary people and the working classes.

However, enormous social and economic differences between upper and lower classes continued to exist as urban and industrial growth created new classes, class conflict, and a more complex social hierarchy. The chapter illustrates these differences by describing the different classes and some of the fascinating details of their distinctive lifestyles. During this period family life, sexual practices and the role of women changed dramatically. In general, family life became more stable and affectionate in the later nineteenth century, but economic activities became rigidly separated according to sex—with most women relegated to the position of mother and homemaker. Only in poor families did women work. Women were subordinated to their husbands in law as well, although it appears that their power in the home increased. The result of this discrimination was the emergence of a feminist movement among middle- and working-class women. At the same time family size declined and children were treated in a more affectionate (and more calculated) manner—so much so that family life in the nineteenth century became tremendously intense.

Major intellectual developments in the urban society included an expansion of scientific knowledge and the rise of realism as the dominant literary mood. Scientific thought scored theoretical triumphs, which resulted in practical improvements, a growing faith in progress, and great prestige for scientists and their methods. Influential social thinkers such as Comte and Marx sought to determine society's unalterable scientific laws, while Social Darwinists applied Darwin's theory of natural selection to human affairs. The trend toward secular thinking strengthened. Literary realism, fascinated by scientific laws, ordinary people, and urban problems, fully reflected the spirit of the age.

Study Outline

Use this outline to preview the chapter before you read a particular section in your textbook and then as a self-check to test your reading comprehension after you have read the chapter section.

I. Taming the city
   A. Industry and the growth of cities
      1. Deplorable urban conditions of congestion, filth, and disease existed long before the Industrial Revolution.
      2. The Industrial Revolution and population growth made urban reform necessary.
         a. In Britain, the percent of population living in cities of 20,000 or more jumped from 17 percent in 1801 to 54 percent in 1891.
         b. Housing was crowded and poor, and living conditions unhealthy.
         c. Many people lived in sewerage and excrement.
      3. What was responsible for the awful conditions?
         a. A lack of transportation, which necessitated the crowding, and the slowness of government enforcement of sanitary codes contributed to the problem.
         b. The legacy of rural housing also contributed to the problem.
   B. The public health movement
      1. The reformer Chadwick was influenced by Bentham's ideas of the greatest good for the greatest number.
         a. He believed that cleaning the city would curtail disease.
         b. He proposed the installation of running water and sewers.
      2. New sanitation methods and public health laws were adopted all over Europe from the 1840s on.
   C. The bacterial revolution
      1. The prevailing theory of disease (the miasmatic theory) was that it was caused by bad odors.
      2. Pasteur's theory that germs caused disease was a major breakthrough, and its application meant disease could be controlled through vaccines.
      3. Based on the work of Koch and others, the organisms responsible for many diseases were identified and effective vaccines developed.
      4. Lister developed the concept of sterilization of wounds.
      5. Mortality rates began to decline rapidly in European countries.

D. Urban planning and public transportation
   1. Better urban planning contributed to improved living conditions.
   2. After 1850, Paris was transformed by the urban planning of Haussmann and became a model city.
      a. Broad, straight, tree-lined boulevards cut through the center of the city.
      b. Parks were created throughout the city.
      c. Sewers were improved and aqueducts built.
   3. Zoning expropriation laws were a major tool of the new urbanism.
   4. Electric streetcars revolutionized urban life and enabled the cities to expand.

II. Rich and poor and in between
   A. Social structure
      1. Between about 1850 and 1906, the standard of living for the average person improved substantially.
      2. But differences in wealth continued to be enormous; society remained stratified in a number of classes.
   B. The middle classes
      1. The upper middle class was composed of successful business families who were attracted to the aristocratic lifestyle.
      2. The middle middle-class group contained merchants, lawyers, and doctors—people who were well off but not wealthy.
      3. Next came the lower middle class: shopkeepers, small businessmen, white-collar workers.
      4. Experts, such as engineers, chemists, accountants, and managers, were also considered members of the middle class.
      5. The middle-class lifestyle included large meals, dinner parties, servants, an interest in fashionable dressing, and good education.
      6. Their code of expected behavior stressed hard work, self-discipline, religion, and restraint from vices.
   C. The working classes
      1. The vast majority of people belonged to the working class, yet the class had varying lifestyles and little unity.
      2. The most highly skilled workers constituted a fluid "labor aristocracy."
         a. They developed a lifestyle of stern morality.
         b. They considered themselves the leaders of the working class.
         c. They had strong political and philosophical beliefs.
      3. Next came the semiskilled and unskilled urban workers.
         a. Workers in the crafts and factory workers constituted the semiskilled workers.
         b. Domestic servants, mostly female, were one of the largest subgroups of the unskilled workers.
         c. Women employed in the "sweated industries" were another large group.
         d. Drinking was a favorite leisure activity of the working class; other pastimes included sports and music halls.
      4. In Europe, church attendance by the working class declined, while in the United States churches thrived and were a way to assert ethnic identity.

III. The family
   A. Premarital sex and marriage
      1. "Romantic love" had triumphed over economic considerations in the working class by 1850.
      2. Economic considerations remained important to the middle class.
      3. Both premarital sex and illegitimacy increased.
      4. After 1850, illegitimacy decreased, indicating the growing morality and stability of the working class.
   B. Prostitution
      1. Men commonly turned to prostitutes because marriages were so often made later in life, especially in the middle and upper classes.
      2. Brutal sexist behavior was a part of life.
   C. Kinship ties
      1. Marriage and family ties were often strong.
      2. Kinship networks were an important source of mutual support and welfare.
   D. Women and family life
      1. The preindustrial pattern of women working outside the home disappeared except for working-class women.
      2. Women became full-time mothers and homemakers, not wage earners.
      3. Women were excluded from good jobs; the law placed women in an inferior position.
         a. A wife in England had no legal identity and no right to own property.
         b. The Napoleonic Code gave women few legal rights in France.
      4. Women's struggle for rights occurred on two fronts.
         a. Middle-class feminists campaigned for equal legal rights, equal opportunities in education and the professions, and the right to vote.
         b. Socialist women, especially in Germany, called for the liberation of working-class women through revolution.
      5. Meanwhile, women's control and influence in the home increased.
         a. The wife usually determined how the family's money was spent and made all the major domestic decisions.
         b. Running the household was complicated and demanding, and many women sacrificed for the welfare and comfort of their husband.
      6. The home increased in emotional importance in all social classes; it symbolized shelter from the harsh working world.
      7. Strong emotional bonds between mothers and children and between wives and husbands developed.
   E. Child rearing
      1. There was more breast-feeding and less swaddling and abandonment of babies.
      2. The birthrate declined, so each child became more important and could receive more advantages.
         a. The main reason for the reduction in family size was the parents' desire to improve their economic and social position and that of their children.
         b. Children were no longer seen as an economic asset.

  3. Many children were too controlled by parents, however, and suffered the effects of excessive parental concern.
      a. Parents were obsessed with the child's sexual behavior—particularly the possibility of masturbation.
      b. Relations between fathers and children were often tense; fathers tended to be very demanding.
  4. In studying family dynamics, Freud developed his theory of the Oedipal complex: that sons compete with their fathers for their mothers' love.
  5. Working-class youths probably had more avenues of escape from family tensions than middle-class youths.

IV. Science and thought
  A. The triumph of science
      1. Theoretical discoveries resulted increasingly in practical benefits, as in thermodynamics, chemistry, and electricity.
      2. Scientific achievements strengthened faith in progress and gave science unrivaled prestige.
  B. Social science and evolution
      1. Many thinkers, such as Comte, tried to study society scientifically—using data collected by the government—and find general social laws.
          a. Comte argued that the third and final stage of knowledge is that of science, or what he called the "positivist method."
          b. Positivism would allow social scientists to develop a disciplined and harmonic society ruled by science and experts.
      2. Theories of dynamic development and evolution fascinated the nineteenth century.
          a. Building on the ideas of Lyell and Lamarck, Charles Darwin theorized that all life had evolved gradually from a common origin through an unending "struggle for survival" that led to the survival of the fittest by natural selection.
          b. Social Darwinists, such as Herbert Spencer, applied Darwin's ideas to human affairs.
  C. Realism in literature
      1. Realism, which stressed that heredity and environment determined human behavior, replaced romanticism as the dominant literary trend from the 1840s through the 1890s.
      2. Realist writers, led by Zola, gloried in everyday life, taboo subjects, and the urban working class.
      3. The realists were strict determinists and believed that human actions were caused by unalterable natural laws.
      4. Balzac and Flaubert, along with Zola, were the leading French realists.
      5. Mary Ann Evans (George Eliot) and Hardy in Britain, Tolstoy in Russia, and Dreiser in America were also great realists.

Review Questions

Check your understanding of this chapter by answering the following questions.

1. To what extent was industrialization responsible for the deplorable conditions of the cities in the early nineteenth century?
2. Who was Edwin Chadwick? What role did he play in the health movement?
3. What was the miasmatic theory of disease? How did it retard progress?
4. What contributions did Pasteur, Koch, and Lister make to life in urban Europe? Give examples.
5. What were the reasons for the rebuilding of Paris? Who was responsible for this change?
6. Why was the electric streetcar so important in improving urban life?
7. Marx claimed that as a result of industrialization there was an increasing polarization of society into rich and poor. Do the facts warrant such a conclusion?
8. Describe the differences and similarities between groups within the middle class. What separated and what united them?
9. What were the goals of the middle class?
10. Describe the "labor aristocracy." What were the interests of its members? How did they differ from the rest of the working class?
11. What were the interests, motives, and lifestyle of the working class? How were they changing by the late nineteenth century?
12. Why was there a decline in illegitimacy after 1850?
13. Why did middle-class men marry late? What effect did this have on their sexual behavior?
14. How common was prostitution in the nineteenth century? What sort of evidence on the subject exists?
15. Did kinship ties disappear in the new urban environment? Explain.
16. What was the social and economic position of women in the nineteenth century? Were they better off than in preindustrial society?
17. What changes occurred in child care and the attitudes toward children in the nineteenth century?
18. What was the nineteenth-century view of masturbation?
19. Overall, did family life improve in the nineteenth century? Explain.
20. In what practical ways did breakthroughs in scientific inquiry transform life for the general population of the nineteenth century?
21. What impact did science have on the study of society?
22. Explain the new evolutionary views of biological development and how these views influenced religious and social thought.
23. What was the realist movement in literature? Who were the major writers of this movement, and how did they differ from previous writers?

Study-Review Exercises

Define the following key concepts and terms.

antiseptic principle

Darwin's theory of biological evolution

sweated industries

labor aristocracy

realist movement

miasmatic theory

middle-class morality

Comte's positivism

Study figures 24.2 and 24.4 in the text. What important characteristics of nineteenth-century society do they reveal?

_____

_____

_____

Explain how each of the following people contributed to the improvement of nineteenth-century life.
Edwin Chadwick

Louis Pasteur

Robert Koch

Jean Baptiste Lamarck

Charles Darwin

Sigmund Freud

Gustave Flaubert

Emile Zola

Auguste Comte

Joseph Lister

Baron Haussmann

Gustave Droz

Test your understanding of the chapter by providing the correct answers.

1. The birthrate *increased/decreased* in the last half of the nineteenth century.

2. He advocated the principle of "the greatest good for the greatest number."

   _____

3. Lister believed that infection could be controlled by the application of the

   "_____ principle."

4. Electric streetcars first came to the city in about the year _____ .

5. Overall, treatment of children and infants *improved/deteriorated* in the nineteenth century.

6. Generally speaking, the European aristocracy experienced *no change/a decrease* in relative income in the nineteenth century.

7. The highly skilled upper 15 percent of the working class was known as the

   _____ .

8. The status and income of schoolteachers and nurses *rose/fell* during the nineteenth century.

9. "It is to the _____ that the vast body of the working people look for recreation and entertainment."

10. By 1850, working-class young people tended to marry for *love/economic reasons*.

11. Kinship ties tended to grow *stronger/weaker* as a result of urban society.

12. Sex roles for men and women in the nineteenth century tended to become *more/less* rigid.

13. Women's economic power in the nineteenth century *increased/decreased* compared to the eighteenth century.

Multiple-Choice Questions

1. Compared to preindustrial society, the relative distribution of wealth among the three classes in industrial society
   a. probably did not change.
   b. shifted in favor of the working class.
   c. shifted significantly in favor of the middle class.
   d. shifted toward the aristocracy.

2. Which group was most opposed to drinking?
   a. Aristocracy
   b. Middle class
   c. Working class
   d. Slumdwellers

3. Comte's "stages of knowledge" theory held that the third and final stage of all intellectual activity was
   a. scientific.
   b. theological, or fictitious.
   c. metaphysical, or abstract.
   d. ideological.

4. The new movement in writing, found in the works of Zola, Flaubert, and Hardy, which pursued the typical and commonplace and claimed that human action was a result of heredity and environment, was called
   a. romanticism.
   b. secularism.
   c. realism.
   d. the positivist method.

5. Which of the following factors was a reason for the deplorable conditions of English cities up to the 1850s?
   a. People's acceptance of dirt
   b. The abundance of urban land
   c. The presence of too many urban transportation facilities
   d. The slow growth of urban population

6. The development of urban society between 1850 and 1900 brought
   a. a decrease in wages.
   b. a drop in the average standard of living.
   c. less of a gap between the income of rich and poor.
   d. more diversity of occupation in the middle and lower classes.

7. By 1900, people of the working class
   a. were divided into well-defined subclasses.
   b. had generally similar lifestyles.
   c. were united against the rich.
   d. were largely agricultural workers.

8. One change the nineteenth century brought to women was
   a. less distinction between the duties of husband and wife.
   b. a rise in factory employment after marriage.
   c. more equal employment opportunities.
   d. legal insubordination to men.

9. The birthrate declined in the later nineteenth century for all of the following reasons
   except the
   a. desire to give more individual care and attention to children.
   b. desire to give more educational opportunities to children.
   c. acceptance of birth-control practices by the Catholic church.
   d. declining value of children as an economic asset.

10. After 1850, ordinary women
    a. were more likely to marry for money.
    b. were more likely to breast-feed their babies.
    c. hardly ever got pregnant before marriage.
    d. generally cut themselves off from parents and relatives after they got married.

11. White-collar workers generally
    a. grew in importance in the nineteenth century.
    b. were uninterested in moving up in society.
    c. kept many servants.
    d. felt a common tie with manual workers.

12. The country in which the problems of urban congestion and deplorable conditions
    occurred first and most acutely was
    a. France.
    b. Germany.
    c. Great Britain.
    d. Ireland.

13. Freud's most revolutionary idea was that
    a. unconscious psychological energy was sexual energy.
    b. masturbation was a source of psychological disturbance.
    c. spontaneous affection was damaging.
    d. family life had little to do with mental illness.

14. Comte's social philosophy of positivism was based on the idea that the laws of human relations were discoverable through
    a. God.
    b. political action.
    c. social science.
    d. Marxism.

15. The realist writers held to which of the following principles in their writing?
    a. The romantic search for the sublime
    b. An emphasis on rural life
    c. A general approval of middle-class values and life
    d. A focus on everyday life, particularly that of the working classes

16. The transformation of Paris in the 1850s encompassed all of the following *except*
    a. new streets and boulevards.
    b. improved sewer and water systems.
    c. a decrease in the number of parks and the amount of open space.
    d. comprehensive urban planning.

17. After the Industrial Revolution, the general standard of living
    a. decreased for everyone except the very rich.
    b. increased for everyone except for the middle class.
    c. stayed about the same for most people.
    d. improved, but did not close the gap between rich and poor.

18. The typical nineteenth-century middle-class social occasion was
    a. a trip to the music hall.
    b. gambling.
    c. a dinner party.
    d. a relaxing evening at the local pub.

19. By the late nineteenth century, indulging in heavy drinking and practicing cruel sports like cockfighting
    a. were on the increase because of more leisure time.
    b. were both in decline.
    c. fluctuated from year to year.
    d. resulted in the prohibition of such activities.

20. After 1850, the illegitimacy rate in Europe
    a. increased.
    b. decreased.
    c. remained about the same.
    d. fluctuated depending upon economic conditions.

21. During the nineteenth century, the working class viewed which of the following as the most important consideration for marriage?
    a. Mercenary concerns
    b. Pregnancy
    c. Romantic love
    d. Social improvement

22. It is most likely that kinship ties within the typical nineteenth-century working-class family
    a. hardly existed.
    b. were greater than often believed.
    c. did not exist after marriage.
    d. existed only in crisis situations.

23. The division of labor by sex in the last half of the nineteenth century tended to
    a. increase.
    b. decrease.
    c. not change from the earlier period.
    d. decrease only for middle-class women.

24. Late nineteenth-century roles of father and mother tended to become
    a. more alike.
    b. more rigid and defined.
    c. more democratic, with the father showing more affection.
    d. more equal as economic power shifted to women.

25. In nineteenth-century Europe, the working classes consisted of about
    a. four out of every five people.
    b. half the population.
    c. one out of every three people.
    d. one-quarter of the population.

Major Political Ideas

1. Define working class and working classes. Which term best describes nineteenth-century society? Many historians and political thinkers have argued that industrialization produced a single, unified working class. Do you agree? Was there such a thing as a working-class culture with values and beliefs different from other classes in society?

2. Was there a gender division of power within nineteenth-century society? Compared to previous societies, were women better or worse off in terms of their power within society? What changes had taken place?

Issues for Essays and Discussion

What was life like in the new urban society and in what ways had it changed from previous centuries? Discuss this by describing developments in the area of (1) public health and transportation, (2) class structure, (3) family life, and (3) science and thought. Who were the winners and who were the losers in this process—or did all members of society gain?

Interpretation of Visual Sources

Study the drawing entitled *Apartment Living in Paris* on page 762 of your textbook. Name the various classes shown. Besides showing the social hierarchy, how does this illustration show the social and gender division of labor?

Geography

Study Map 24.1 in your textbook. Approximately how many more cities of 100,000 or more population existed in 1900 as compared to 1800? Where did the new concentration of urban growth take place? Why?

Understanding History Through the Arts

1. How does the art of the era reflect the times? Victorian social and moral codes were expressed in narrative, or "modern-life," paintings. These highly popular works of the time (they have since fallen out of fashion) are interestingly described (and shown) in C. Wood, *Victorian Panorama: Paintings of Victorian Life* (1977), and J. Hadfield, *Every Picture Tells a Story: Images of Victorian Life* (1985). Impressionist painting is very popular today but a new light on how it related to social change of the time is sketched out in T. Clark, *The Painting of Modern Life: Paris in the Art of Manet and His Followers* (1985). Socialism and art was a subject taken up by the influential Englishman William Morris, who is himself the subject of A. Briggs, *William Morris, Selected Writings and Designs* (1957).

2. How does nineteenth-century architecture mirror nineteenth-century urban life? The student interested in architecture and the city should begin with M. Girouard, *Cities and People* (1985), D. Olsen, *The City as a Work of Art* (1986); A. Sutcliffe, ed., *Metropolis, 1890–1940* (1984); and F. Loyer, *Paris, Nineteenth-Century Architecture and Urbanism* (1988), C. L. Clark,

trans. For an important development in nineteenth-century German architecture, see D. Watkin and T. Mellinghoff, *German Architecture and the Classical Ideal* (1987); and for a discussion of how architects viewed the society within which they worked, see J. Schmiechen, "The Victorians, the Historians, and the Idea of Modernism," in *The American Historical Review* 93, No. 2, April 1988.

3. How does music reflect the social changes of the nineteenth century? The tragedy of industrial-urban life for the lower classes is woven into Puccini's highly popular and romantic opera *La Bohème*, which takes place in Paris. Many recordings of this opera are available.

4. What can fiction reveal about the nineteenth century? The best way to learn about life for the common people is to read historical novels. The life of a family in early twentieth-century Scotland (Ayrshire) is told in W. McIlvanney's *Docherty* (1975); the London underworld of crime is mixed with upper-class life in M. Crichton's exciting *The Great Train Robbery** (1975); and life in a slum is the subject of Robert Robert's autobiography, *The Classic Slum** (1973). Charles Dickens's *Hard Times** has become a classic statement about life in the new industrial society, as has E. Gaskill's *Mary Barton**. A. Trollope's six novels of the *Chronicles of Barsetshire*, of which *Barchester Towers** (1857) is the most popular, tell of middle-class intrigues of ambition and love. An interesting fictional account of hardship and survival among the nineteenth-century working class is C. Kingsley, *Alton Locke**.

Problems for Further Investigation

1. What was life like for members of the nineteenth-century working class? Historians are just now beginning to understand how they lived. One of the problems, however, is that the working people wrote little about themselves. Some autobiographical and biographical material that exists for the British working classes is H. Mayhew, *London Labour and London Poor** (reprint, 3 vols., 1969); E. Yeo, *The Unknown Mayhew** (1972); J. Burnett, ed., *Annals of Labour* (1974); P. Thompson, *The Edwardians* (1975); and J. Saville and J. Bellamy, eds., *Dictionary of Labour Biography* (6 vols., 1973–1988). For accounts of the lives of two German women, see P. Knight (with R. Knight), *A Very Ordinary Life* (1974), and A. Pott, *The Autobiography of a Working Woman*, trans. by E. C. Harvey (1913).

2. In what ways did male and female roles change in Germany during this age of urbanization? Begin your study with R. Evans and W. R. Lee, *The German Family* (1981).

3. What were some of the problems faced by women in German society in the nineteenth century? Begin your inquiry with J. Fout, ed., *German Women in the Nineteenth Century: A Social History* (1984); R. Evans, *The Feminist Movement in Germany, 1884–1933* (1976); and J. Quataert, *Reluctant Feminists in German Social Democracy, 1885–1917* (1979).

---

*Available in paperback.

Chapter 25
The Age of Nationalism, 1850–1914

Chapter Questions

After reading and studying this chapter you should be able to answer the following questions:

How did nation building transform the major states of nineteenth-century Europe? Why did nationalism become a universal faith in Europe and the United States between 1850 and 1914? How did it evolve so that it gained the support of the broad masses of society?

Chapter Summary

The theme of this chapter is the triumph of nationalism after the unsuccessful nationalist revolutions of 1848. Between 1850 and 1914, strong nation-states developed, which won the enthusiastic support of all the social classes, caused a shift in the balance of international political power, and pulled the masses away from the socialist doctrine of class war. Napoleon III of France played a pioneering role in this triumph of nationalism. His mild dictatorship, which came into being illegally and which lasted from 1852 to 1870, showed how the national state and its programs could appeal to rich and poor, conservative and radical. In this way, the national state became a way of coping with the challenge of rapid political and economic change. In Italy, Count Cavour, the moderate nationalist leader of the kingdom of Sardinia, managed to unify most of Italy in 1860 into a single political state that was far from radical in social and economic matters. Shortly thereafter, in 1862, Otto von Bismarck became chief minister of Prussia. A master of power politics, Bismarck skillfully fought three wars to unify the states of Germany into a single nation under Prussian leadership. In doing so, Bismarck strengthened German nationalism and gave it a conservative and antiliberal thrust. In the United States competing national aspirations led to bitter civil war. In the South a slave-based cotton economy, rapidly expanding as new land was opened and industrialization generated new demands for cotton, came into conflict with the urban culture and family farm agriculture of the North. A Northern victory meant the end of slavery, but it did not mean land reform or the end of discrimination against blacks. Nationalism was also important in Russia. There it led to major reforms after the Crimean War: in 1861 the serfs were freed, and the government encouraged the development of railroads and modern industry. Frustrated nationalism was an important factor in the Russian revolution of 1905, after defeat in a war with Japan.

Nationalism continued to grow in strength in the emerging urban society of the late nineteenth century. This was because national governments and politicians responded effectively to many of the political demands and social needs of the people. Throughout most of Europe socialists and socialist political parties looked increasingly toward unions and parliaments for continued gradual improvement. They paid only lip service to the idea of radical, violent revolution and class war. The growing moderation of European socialists reflected the great appeal of nationalism for the masses. Only in multinational states, most notably the Austro-Hungarian Empire, did the growth of competing nationalisms promote fragmentation as opposed to unity.

Study Outline

Use this outline to preview the chapter before you read a particular section in your textbook and then as a self-check to test your reading comprehension after you have read the chapter section.

I. Napoleon III in France
   A. The Second Republic and Louis Napoleon
      1. The reasons for Napoleon's election include middle-class and peasant fears of socialism and a disgust with class politics.
      2. Many people wanted a strong national leader who would serve all the people and help them economically.
      3. Louis Napoleon believed the state had an obligation to provide jobs and stimulate the economy.
      4. Napoleon cooperated with the conservative National Assembly, but it refused to change the constitution so he could run for another term.
      5. Therefore, he seized power in a *coup d'état* in 1851 and dismissed the Assembly; these actions were approved by the voters.
   B. Napoleon III's Second Empire
      1. Napoleon III's greatest success was improving the economy of France.
         a. His government encouraged new investment banks and massive railroad construction.
         b. The government also sponsored an ambitious program of public works, including the rebuilding of Paris.
         c. He granted workers the right to form unions and to strike.
      2. His political system allowed only limited opposition.
         a. He restricted the Assembly and tied reform to support of his candidates.
         b. In the 1860s he allowed the Assembly greater power and gave the opposition more freedom.
II. Nation building in Italy and Germany
   A. Italy to 1850: a battleground for great powers
      1. Italy prior to 1860 was divided; much of it was under the control of Austria and the pope.
      2. Between 1815 and 1848, the goal of national unity began to appeal to Italians.
      3. Sardinia was the logical leader in the nationalist movement.
      4. Pope Pius IX opposed nationalism and other modern ideas.

B. Cavour and Garibaldi
1. Count Cavour, the liberal minister of Sardinia, built Sardinia into a liberal and economically sound state.
   a. He was a moderate nationalist who sought unity only for the northern and perhaps central areas of Italy.
   b. He worked in the 1850s to consolidate Sardinia as a liberal state capable of leading northern Italy.
2. Cavour used France to engineer a war with Austria to further his plans for unification.
3. Central Italy was united with Sardinia in 1860.
4. Garibaldi "liberated" southern Italy and Sicily, and Italy was further unified.
5. Except for Rome and Venice, Italy was politically united by 1860.
   a. However, there were strong class divisions.
   b. There were also strong cultural divisions between the northern and southern areas.
C. Germany before Bismarck
1. In the aftermath of 1848, the German states were locked in a political stalemate.
2. The Zollverein became a crucial factor in the Austro-Prussian rivalry.
3. William I of Prussia wanted to double the size of the army, but he was opposed by the parliament, which rejected the military budget in 1862.
D. Bismarck takes command
1. Bismarck was an ultraconservative Junker politician whose main goal was to strengthen Prussia's power and status.
2. He concluded that the path to this goal was to weaken Austria.
   a. He supported German nationalism.
   b. His view was that middle-class parliamentary liberalism was not the way to unify Germany—"blood and iron" was.
E. The Austro-Prussian War of 1866—the first step toward unification
1. Denmark's attempted annexation of Schleswig-Holstein led first to an alliance with Austria in a war against Denmark (1864) and then to a war with Austria in 1866.
   a. The German Confederation was dissolved and a new North German Confederation, led by Prussia, formed.
   b. Austria withdrew from German affairs.
2. Bismarck's goal of Prussian expansion was being realized.
F. The taming of Parliament
1. Bismarck believed the middle class could be led to prefer national unity to liberal institutions.
2. Bismarck outmaneuvered the liberals in the parliament, and the middle class ended up supporting monarchial authority.
G. The Franco-Prussian War (1870–71)
1. Bismarck used war with France to bring southern Germany into the union.
2. As a result of military success, semi-authoritarian nationalism in Germany won out over liberalism.

III. Nation-building in the United States
    A. Slavery and territorial expansion
       1. The Northwest Ordinance of 1787 extended the seaboard patterns of free and slave labor further west.
       2. The purchase of the Louisiana Territory from France in 1803 opened another enormous area for settlement.
          a. In the North, white settlers extended the pattern of family farm agriculture and began the process of industrialization.
          b. In the South, industry and cities did not develop, and slave-owning plantation farmers dominated the economy and society.
       3. The growth of a slave-based cotton economy meant great profits and encouraged the defense of slavery in the South.
       4. New territory in 1848 led to a national debate over slavery and a "house divided" by conflicting values.
    B. Civil war and reunification
       1. Lincoln's election led to Southern agitation for independence.
       2. The long Civil War (1861–1865) was the bloodiest conflict in American history.
       3. The Northern victory was due to superior resources, to the disillusionment of ordinary whites in the South, and to the South's inability to use blacks in the military.
       4. In the North, most people prospered during the war years.
          a. Powerful business corporations emerged, supported by the Republican party.
          b. The Homestead Act (1862) and the Emancipation Proclamation (1863) reinforced the concept of free labor.
          c. A new American nationalism, based on the concept of "manifest destiny," emerged from the war.
       5. With Northern victory, Congress guaranteed the freedom of blacks but did not institute land reform, so blacks continued as poor sharecroppers and still faced a great deal of discrimination.
IV. The modernization of Russia
    A. The "Great Reforms"
       1. Serfdom was still the basic social institution of agrarian nineteenth-century Russia.
       2. The Crimean War (1853–1856) speeded up the modernization of Russia.
          a. Russia's defeat showed how badly the country had fallen behind the industrializing West.
          b. The war also created the need for reforms because its hardships led to the threat of peasant uprisings.
       3. Serfdom was abolished in 1861, collective ownership of the land established, and other reforms undertaken.
          a. Local assemblies (*zemstvos*) were established.
          b. The legal system was reformed.
    B. The industrialization of Russia
       1. Railroad construction stimulated the economy and inspired nationalism and imperialism.
       2. The assassination of Alexander III (1881) brought political reform to an end.
       3. Economic reform was carried out by Sergei Witte, the minister of finance from 1892 to 1903.

     a. More railroads were built, notably the trans-Siberian line.

     b. Protective tariffs were raised.

     c. Foreign ideas and money were used to build factories and create modern coal, steel, and petroleum industries.

  C. The revolution of 1905

    1. Imperialist ambitions brought defeat at the hands of Japan in 1905 and political upheaval at home.

     a. The "Bloody Sunday" massacre, when the tsar's troops fired on a crowd of protesting workers, produced a wave of indignation.

     b. By the summer of 1905, strikes, uprisings, revolts, and mutinies were sweeping the country.

    2. A general strike in October forced Nicholas II to issue the October Manifesto, which granted full civil liberties and promised a popularly elected parliament (Duma).

    3. The Social Democrats rejected he manifesto and led a bloody workers' uprising in Moscow in December.

    4. Middle-class moderates helped the government repress the uprising and survive as a constitutional monarchy.

V. The responsive national state, 1871–1914

  A. Characteristics of the new national state

    1. Ordinary people felt increasing loyalty to their governments.

    2. By 1914, universal male suffrage was the rule, and women were beginning to demand the right to vote too.

  B. The German Empire

    1. The German Empire was a union of twenty-five German states in 1871 governed by a chancellor (Bismarck) and a parliament (the Reichstag).

    2. Bismarck and the liberals attacked the Catholic church (the *Kulturkampf*) in an effort to maintain the superiority of state over church, but abandoned the attack in 1878.

    3. Worldwide agricultural depression after 1873 resulted in the policy of economic protectionism in Germany.

    4. Bismarck outlawed socialist parties in 1878.

    5. Bismarck gave Germany an impressive system of social-welfare legislation, partly to weaken socialism's appeal to the workers.

    6. William II dismissed Bismarck in 1890 to try to win the support of the workers, but he couldn't stem the rising tide of socialism.

    7. The Social Democratic Party became the largest party in the parliament, but it was strongly nationalistic, not revolutionary.

  C. Republican France (the Third Republic)

    1. The defeat of France in 1871 led to revolution in Paris (the Commune).

    2. The Paris Commune was brutally crushed by the National Assembly.

    3. A new Third Republic was established and led by skilled men such as Gambetta and Ferry.

    4. The Third Republic passed considerable reforms, including legalizing trade unions and creating state schools, and it built a colonial empire.

    5. The Dreyfus affair (1898–99) weakened France and caused anti-Catholic reaction.

      a. Between 1901 and 1905, the government severed all ties between the state and the Catholic church.

      b. Catholic schools were put on their own financially and lost many students.

D. Great Britain and Ireland

  1. The reform bills of 1867 and 1884 further extended the franchise in Britain, and political views and the party system became more democratic.

      a. Nevertheless, some, like John Stuart Mill, explored the problem of safeguarding individual differences and unpopular opinions.

      b. The conservative leader Disraeli supported extending the vote.

      c. The Third Reform Bill of 1884 gave the vote to almost every adult male.

  2. Led by David Lloyd George, the Liberal party ushered in social-welfare legislation between 1906 and 1914 by taxing the rich.

  3. The issue of home rule (self-government) divided Ireland into the northern Protestant Ulsterites, who opposed it, and the southern Catholic nationalists, who favored it.

      a. Gladstone supported home rule for Ireland in 1886 and 1893, but the bills failed to pass.

      b. The question of home rule was postponed because of war in 1914.

E. The Austro-Hungarian Empire

  1. After 1866, the empire was divided in two, and the nationalistic Magyars ruled Hungary.

  2. Austria suffered from competing nationalisms, which pitted ethnic groups against one another and weakened the state.

      a. A particularly divisive issue was the language used in government and elementary education.

      b. From 1900 to 1914 the parliament was so divided that a majority could not be obtained.

      c. Anti-Semitism grew rapidly, especially in Vienna.

VI. Marxism and the socialist movement

A. The Socialist International

  1. A rapid growth of socialist parties occurred throughout Europe after 1871.

  2. With Marx's help, socialists united in 1864 to form an international socialist organization known as the First International; it was short-lived but had a great psychological impact.

  3. The Second International—a federation of national socialist parties—lasted until 1914.

B. Unions and revisionism

  1. There was a general rise in the standard of living and quality of life for workers in the late nineteenth century, so they became less revolutionary.

  2. Unions were gradually legalized in Europe, and they were another factor in the trend toward moderation.

  3. Revisionist socialists believed in working within capitalism (through labor unions, for example) and no longer saw the future in terms of capitalist-worker warfare.

  4. In the late nineteenth century, the socialist movements within each nation became different from one another and thereby more and more nationalistic.

Review Questions

Check your understanding of this chapter by answering the following questions.

1. How was Germany unified? Describe Bismarck's methods. What were the long-term results?
2. Why did nationalism become a universal faith in Europe between 1850 and 1914?
3. How did nationalism gain the support of the broad masses of society?
4. Why did the voters of France elect Louis Napoleon president in 1848? Why did they elect him emperor a few years later?
5. What were some of the benefits Napoleon bestowed on his subjects?
6. Did Napoleon allow any political opposition to exist? Explain his political system and why it eventually broke down.
7. Why was Italy before 1860 merely a "geographical expression"?
8. What were the three basic approaches to Italian unification? Which one prevailed?
9. What was the nature and significance of Garibaldi's liberation of Sicily and Naples in 1860? Why was Cavour so nervous about Garibaldi?
10. What were the causes and results of the Austro-Prussian War?
11. What was the significance of the Zollverein in German history?
12. Why did the Prussian liberals make an about-face and support their old enemy Bismarck after 1866?
13. How were territorial expansion and the issue of slavery related in the United States?
14. What enabled the North to defeat the South in the Civil War? How did a new American nationalism grow out of the war?
15. What was the status of the Russian serf in the early nineteenth century? How beneficial was the reform of 1861 to the serf?
16. Why was the Crimean War a turning point in Russian history?
17. How did Russia use the West to catch up with the West?
18. Was the new Germany a democracy? Where did power reside in the Germany of 1871?
19. What was Bismarck's relationship (after 1871) with (a) the Catholic church, (b) the liberals, and (c) the socialists?
20. What were the German social-welfare laws? What were their origins?
21. What were the causes and outcome of the Dreyfus affair in France?
22. What were the major political developments and issues in Britain and Ireland in the late nineteenth century? Was the Irish problem solvable?
23. In what ways were ethnic rivalries and growing anti-Semitism related in Austro-Hungary?
24. How does one account for the rapid growth of socialist parties in Europe in the last quarter of the nineteenth century?
25. What was the purpose of the socialist internationals? To what degree did they represent working-class unity?
26. What were the general arguments of the revisionist socialists? Were they true Marxists?

Study-Review Exercises

Identify and explain the significance of the following people.

Benjamin Disraeli

Emmeline Pankhurst

Jules Ferry

Sergei Witte

Alexander II

Camillo Benso di Cavour

Edward Bernstein

Pius IX

William Gladstone

Giuseppe Garibaldi

William II

John Stuart Mill

Explain what the following events were, who participated in them, and why they were important.

The People's Budget (Britain)

Napoleon III's *coup d'état*

May Day

assassination of Tsar Alexander II

establishment of the Zollverein (1834)

establishment of the Austro-Hungarian monarchy

Treaty of Villafranca

Paris Commune of 1871

Ulster revolt of December 1913

Explain the outcome and significance of each of the following wars by completing the following table.

	Year	Outcome and Significance
Danish War		
Austro-Prussian War		
Franco-Prussian War		
Crimean War		
Russo-Japanese War		

Test your understanding of the chapter by providing the correct answers.

1. In 1851, the French voters *approved/disapproved* of Louis Napoleon's seizure of power.

2. Increasingly, the main opposition to Napoleon III came from the *middle class/working class/upper class*.

3. The Russian *victory/defeat* in the Crimean War of 1853–1856 contributed to *freedom/serfdom* for the Russian peasants after 1861.

4. After 1848, the pope *supported/opposed* Italian unification.

5. After 1873, the price of wheat on the world market *rose/fell* dramatically.

6. The minority Irish Ulsterites were *Catholic/Protestant* and *for/against* home rule.

7. Bismarck used war with *Austria/France/Russia* in order to bring the south Germans into a united Germany.

Multiple-Choice Questions

1. The most industrialized, socialized, and unionized continental country by 1914 was
   a. France.
   b. Germany.
   c. Italy.
   d. Belgium.

2. The Russian *zemstvo* was a(n)
   a. industrial workers' council.
   b. local government assembly.
   c. terrorist group.
   d. village priest.

3. The *Kulturkampf* in Germany was an attack on
   a. liberals.
   b. socialists.
   c. the Catholic church.
   d. Prussian culture.

4. The first modern social security laws were passed in the 1880s in
   a. Britain.
   b. France.
   c. Russia.
   d. Germany.

5. The general tendency of unions toward the end of the century was
   a. to move closer to Marxism.
   b. to move toward evolutionary socialism.
   c. to reject socialism altogether.
   d. increasingly to favor revolution.

6. After 1850, the disciples of nationalism in Italy looked for leadership from
   a. Prussia.
   b. the papacy.
   c. Sardinia-Piedmont.
   d. the kingdom of the Two Sicilies.

7. Cavour's program for the unification of northern Italy included
   a. improved transportation.
   b. increased power for the Catholic church.
   c. restriction of civil liberties.
   d. compromise and cooperation with Austria.

8. Russian social and political reforms in the 1860s could best be described as
   a. revolutionary.
   b. totally ineffective.
   c. halfway measures.
   d. extremely effective.

9. Witte's plans for the economic development of Russia included
   a. lowering protective tariffs.
   b. taking Russia off the gold standard.
   c. encouraging foreign investment.
   d. bringing Russian Marxists into the government.

10. Bismarck's fundamental goal for Prussia was
    a. democratic reform.
    b. expansion.
    c. the elimination of nationalism.
    d. the elimination of the monarchy.

11. Which of the following groups fought for the defense of Captain Dreyfus in France?
    a. The Catholics
    b. The army
    c. The radical republicans
    d. The anti-Semites

12. Among those opposing home rule in Ireland were
    a. Catholics.
    b. Ulsterites.
    c. Irish peasants.
    d. William Gladstone.

13. After 1870, Marxian socialists
    a. accepted the revisionist theories of Eduard Bernstein.
    b. failed to grow in number.
    c. formed a second international organization.
    d. refused to participate in national elections.

14. Which of the following statements about German unification is true?
    a. It was completed in 1891 with a war between Prussia and Russia.
    b. The chief architect of the movement was the emperor of Austria.
    c. The unification process was directed by the German state of Austria.
    d. Unification did not include liberal and democratic ideas and methods.

15. A new institution of local government established in Russia in 1864 was the
    a. zemstvo.
    b. Reichstag.
    c. Duma.
    d. Zollverein.

16. Changes that enable a country to compete effectively with leading countries at a given time are called
    a. nationalism.
    b. modernization.
    c. revisionism.
    d. Reconstruction.

17. Which of the following was *not* an action taken by the Third French Republic?
    a. Crushing the Paris Commune of 1871.
    b. Passing considerable reforms.
    c. Legalization of trade unions.
    d. Expansion of the traditional Catholic school system.

18. The Russian defeat in the Crimean War of 1853–1856
    a. signalled the end of the modernization of Russia for nearly fifty years.
    b. resulted in legal and local political reform.
    c. delayed the abolition of serfdom.
    d. was relatively insignificant militarily and politically.

19. The German Zollverein was
    a. a trade union.
    b. a customs union.
    c. an "all-German" parliament.
    d. a political party.

20. Bismarck's policy toward the Social Democrats was one of
    a. limited support.
    b. political alliance to defeat the military party.
    c. total repression.
    d. official tolerance.

21. The sometime popular emperor-dictator of France who granted France a new constitution in 1869 was
    a. Napoleon III.
    b. Baron Haussmann.
    c. Alexander H. Stephens.
    d. Sergei Witte.

22. The new popularly-elected parliament in Russia after 1805 was known as the
    a. House of Commons.
    b. National Assembly.
    c. Reichstag.
    d. Duma.

23. The People's Budget of David Lloyd George in Britain was, in effect, a tax on
    a. the rich.
    b. those who wanted national health insurance.
    c. the urban masses.
    d. the middle classes.

24. After the adoption of the 1867 constitution, Hungary was dominated by
    a. the peasantry.
    b. the middle classes.
    c. the Croatians and Rumanians.
    d. the Magyar nobility.

25. Between 1906 and 1913 in Germany, the working classes
    a. increasingly rejected unions and unionism.
    b. adopted revolutionary Marxist principles.
    c. looked to collective bargaining as a substitute for revolution.
    d. rejected Bernstein's revisionist thought.

Major Political Ideas

1. What is meant by the term *responsive national state*? Why did it come to serve as a new unifying principle? Give examples of how this new concept of state worked. How did this state differ from earlier ones in terms of its objectives and its appeal? Which nation best exemplifies this development?

2. By 1914 a large number of Europeans had adopted social democracy as their political and cultural ideology. What were the goals of the Social Democratic party in Germany and elsewhere? How revolutionary was this socialist movement and what were the ideas behind revisionism, or evolutionary socialism?

Issues for Essays and Discussion

Between about 1850 and 1914 nationalism became almost a new religion in Europe and the United States. Why? What were the characteristics of nationalism that were so appealing? Define the goals of nationalism and then compare and contrast how nationalist goals were implemented in France, Germany, Italy, and Russia. Was nationalism, in your opinion, a positive or negative force in history?

Interpretation of Visual Sources

Study the reproduction of the print entitled *Rebuilding Paris* on page 792 of your textbook. What appears to be the purpose of this demolition? What do you imagine the original site looked like compared to its successor? Note the irregular thoroughfare to the center right. Why do you think this sort of passage was regarded as undesirable? How is this project tied to the idea of the responsive national state? (This topic is also discussed in Chapter 24 under the heading "Urban Planning and Public Transportation.")

Geography

On Outline Map 25.2, and using maps 25.2 and 25.3 in the textbook for reference, mark the following: the boundaries of both the old German Confederation and the new Germany of 1871, Prussia before 1866, the territory added to Prussia as a result of the Austro-Prussian War in 1866, the territory joined to Prussia to form the North German Confederation of 1867, the territory joined to all of the preceding to make up the new German Empire in 1871, Berlin, Bavaria, Wurtenburg, Baden, Hanover, Mecklenburg, Oldenburg, Schleswig, Saxony, and the Oder, Rhine, Danube, and Elbe rivers.

Outline Map 25.2

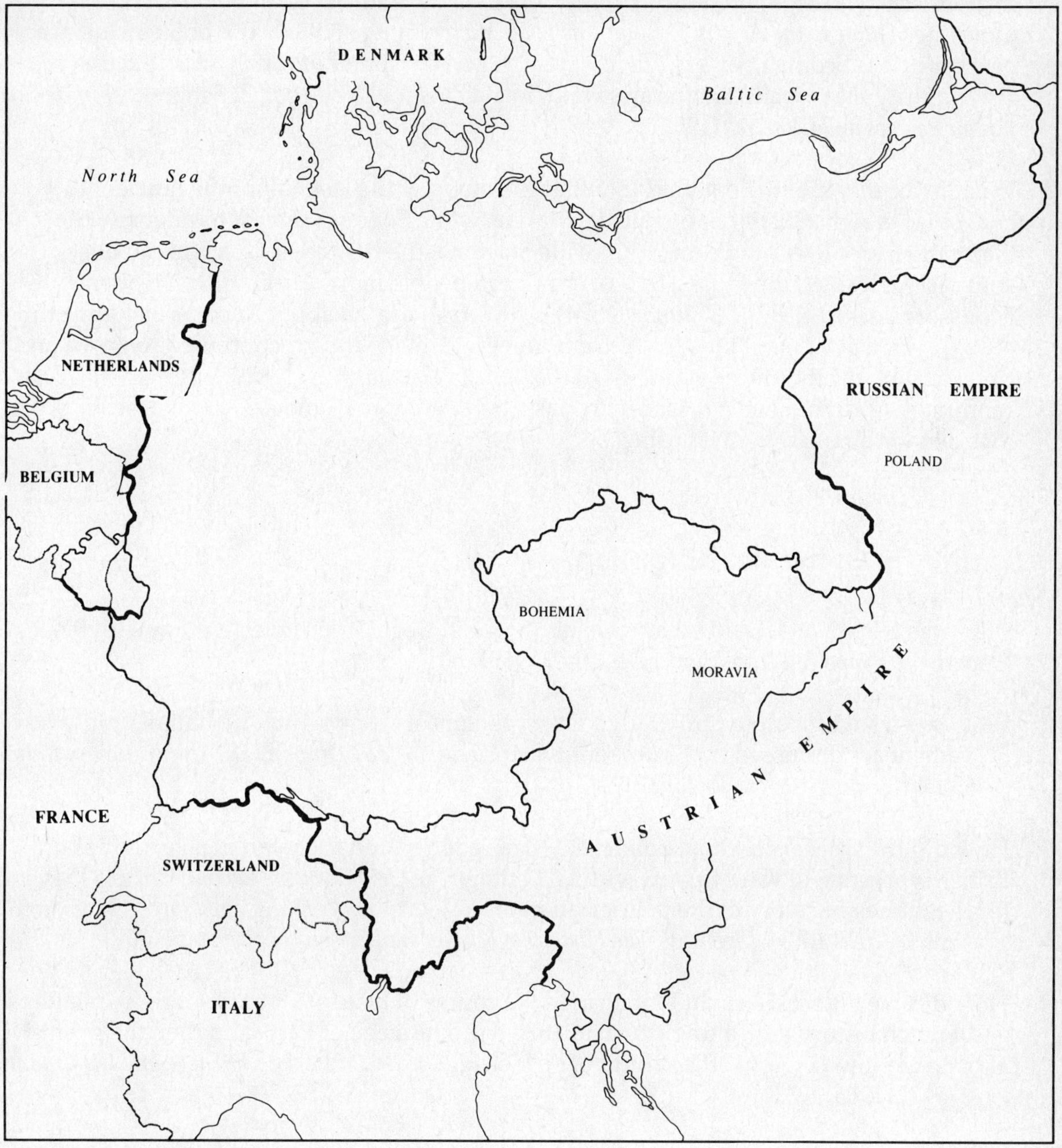
DENMARK
Baltic Sea
North Sea
NETHERLANDS
RUSSIAN EMPIRE
POLAND
BELGIUM
BOHEMIA
MORAVIA
AUSTRIAN EMPIRE
FRANCE
SWITZERLAND
ITALY

Understanding History Through the Arts

1. What were the achievements in the arts in the nineteenth century? The late-nineteenth-century achievements in the visual and applied arts were spectacular. British achievements in architecture, design, literature, drama, and music are surveyed in B. Ford, ed., *The Cambridge Guide to the Arts in Britain: The Later Victorian Age* (1989). The book includes a chapter on the Scottish city of Glasgow, which was the center of much artistic activity. Another city that excelled in the arts was Vienna; it is the subject of C. Schorske, *Fin-de-Siècle Urban Politics and Culture** (1980).

2. What is the music of the era like? In music the mood of the last half of the nineteenth century was romantically nationalistic. Brahms wrote *Song of Triumph* to celebrate the German victory over France in 1870, while Smetana, the first great Czech nationalist composer, glorified the folk history of the Czech people in his *My Country*. In opera Moussorgsky wrote *Boris Godunov* (1874), a historical drama about Russia during the time of Ivan the Terrible. The popularity of German heroic music-drama continued to grow, and it drew added inspiration from Wagner's *The Ring of the Nibelung* (four parts, 1869–1876), a monumental national epic of Germany based on Nordic mythology. All of these works are available on a number of recordings.

Problems for Further Investigation

1. Who was Napoleon III and what were his motives? Begin your investigation with B. D. Gooch, ed., *Napoleon III—Man of Destiny** (1963).

2. Why was it so difficult to unify Italy? The problems of interpreting the Italian unification movement are discussed by a number of historians in C. F. Delzell, *The Unification of Italy** (1963).

3. How did the workers become politicized? Those interested in the political activities of British workers will want to start with H. Pelling, *The Origins of the Labour Party* (1954), and for the interesting story of the politicization of the German working class, from Marx to the present, begin with H. Grebing, *The History of the German Labour Movement* (1969).

4. How did the Franco-German War change the course of history? French-German relations and French history took a tragic turn in 1870 with the siege of Paris and then the grim civil war that followed. This is the subject of A. Horne, *The Fall of Paris: The Siege and the Commune of 1870–1** (1965, 1981).

5. What were the goals and interests of women in the nineteenth century? Begin with T. Lloyd, *Suffragettes International: The World Wide Campaign for Women's Rights** (1971); M. Thomis and J. Grimmett, *Women in Protest, 1800–1850** (1983); and O. Banks, *Faces of Feminism* (1981). Further, in an era in which most women were confined to either the kitchen or drawing

---

*Available in paperback.

room, three Victorian women (Josephine Butler, Octavia Hill, and Florence Nightingale) became important makers of social policy. This is the subject of N. Boyd, *Three Victorian Women Who Changed Their World* (1982). Women and socialism is the subject of C. Sowerwine, "The Socialist Women's Movement from 1850 to 1940," in R. Bridenthal, C. Koonz, and S. Stuard, eds., *Becoming Visible: Women in European History** (1987). One of the most interesting women of the century was Queen Victoria of Britain, whose life is dealt with in the lively biography *Queen Victoria** (1964) by E. Longford.

6. Was socialism a positive or negative force in the struggle for reform? The nineteenth century saw the publication of many books based on the idea that humanity could transform itself and build a new world ruled by justice and equality. One of the most popular of these utopian works in Europe was the American author Edward Bellamy's *Looking Backward,** which was first published in 1888. One of the most influential socialist thinkers and writers in Britain was William Morris, whose book *News From Nowhere** (1890) is a masterpiece of the socialist utopian style of writing that inspired many to work for reform of the present system. Also important were H. H. Hyndman's *England for All** (1883) and the very popular socialist (but not Marxist) little book *Merrie England* (1894) by R. Blatchford. Blatchford's aim was to explain the meaning of socialism to the common man.

---

*Available in paperback.

Primary Sources
Varieties of Socialism

One of the most important political developments of late-nineteenth-century Europe was the popularity of socialism as an alternative to the capitalist organization of society. Although Karl Marx was important in this process, he was neither the most popular nor the most influential of the socialist writers. The documents that follow illustrate the varieties of socialist thought that existed in the late nineteenth century.

Eduard Bernstein, *Evolutionary Socialism**

Eduard Bernstein (1850–1932) was a German Social Democrat who challenged the predictions of Marx that capitalism would end in catastrophe and that the bourgeois parliamentary state is an enemy of the working classes. According to Bernstein, what advances have the workers made that were not anticipated by Marx and Engels? What goals should the working class set for itself? What are the predictions of Marx and Engels that Bernstein believes to be mistaken or contradictory?

I set myself against the notion that we have to expect shortly a collapse of the bourgeois economy, and that social democracy should be induced by the prospect of such an imminent, great, social catastrophe.[†] . . .

The adherents of this theory of a catastrophe base it especially on the conclusions of the *Communist Manifesto*. This is a mistake in every respect.

The theory which the *Communist Manifesto* sets forth of the evolution of modern society was correct as far as it characterised the general tendencies of that evolution. But it was mistaken in several special deductions, above all in the estimate of the time the evolution would take. The last has been unreservedly acknowledged by Friedrich Engels, the joint author with Marx of the *Manifesto,* in his preface to the *Class War in France*. But it is evident that if social evolution takes a

---

*Source: Eduard Bernstein, *Evolutionary Socialism, A Criticism and Affirmation*, intro. Sidney Hook, trans. E. C. Harvey (Schocken Books, first paper edition, 1961).
[†]The Marxists held that a great economic crash or revolution or some other internal disorder within capitalism, such as revolution, would cause capitalism to collapse.

much greater period of time than was assumed, it must also take upon itself forms and lead to forms that were not foreseen and could not be foreseen then.

Social conditions have not developed to such an acute opposition of things and classes as is depicted in the *Manifesto*. It is not only useless, it is the greatest folly to attempt to conceal this from ourselves. The number of members of the possessing classes is to-day not smaller but larger. The enormous increase of social wealth is not accompanied by an decreasing number of capitalists but by an increasing number of capitalists of all degrees. The middle classes change their character but they do not disappear from the social scale.

The concentration in productive industry is not being accomplished even to-day in all its departments with equal thoroughness and at an equal rate. In a great many branches of production it certainly justifies the forecasts of the socialist critic of society; but in other branches it lags even to-day behind them. The process of concentration in agriculture proceeds still more slowly. . . .

In all advanced countries we see the privileges of the capitalist bourgeoisie yielding step by step to democratic organisations. Under the influence of this, and driven by the movement of the working classes which is daily becoming stronger, a social reaction has set in against the exploiting tendencies of capital, a counteraction which, although it still proceeds timidly and feebly, yet does exist, and is always drawing more departments of economic life under its influence. Factory legislation, the democratising of local government, and the extension of its area of work, the freeing of trade unions and systems of co-operative trading from legal restrictions, the consideration of standard conditions of labour in the work undertaken by public authorities—all these characterise this phase of the evolution.

But the more the political organisations of modern nations are democratised the more the needs and opportunities of great political catastrophes are diminished. He who holds firmly to the catastrophic theory of evolution must, with all his power, withstand and hinder the evolution described above, which, indeed, the logical defenders of that theory formerly did. But is the conquest of political power by the proletariat simply to be by a political catastrophe? Is it to be the appropriation and utilisation of the power of the State by the proletariat exclusively against the whole non-proletarian world?

He who replies in the affirmative must be reminded of two things. In 1872 Marx and Engels announced in the preface to the new edition of the *Communist Manifesto* that the Paris Commune had exhibited a proof that "the working classes cannot simply take possession of the ready-made State machine and set it in motion of their own aims." And in 1895 Friedrich Engels stated in detail in the preface to *War of the Classes* that the time of political surprises, of the "revolutions of small conscious minorities at the head of unconscious masses" was to-day at an end, that a collision on a large scale with the military would be the means of checking the steady growth of social democracy and of even throwing it back for a time—in short, that social democracy would flourish far better by lawful than by unlawful means and by violent revolution. And he points out in conformity with this opinion that the next task of the party should be "to work for an uninterrupted increase of its votes" or to carry on a slow propaganda of parliamentary activity. . . .

[To Engels] the task of social democracy is, instead of speculating on a great economic crash, "to organise the working classes politically and develop them as a democracy and to fight for all reforms in the State which are adapted to raise the working classes and transform the State in the direction of democracy."

That is what I have said in my impugned article and what I still maintain in its full import. . . .

The conquest of political power by the working classes, the expropriation of capitalists, are not ends in themselves but only means for the accomplishment of certain aims and endeavours. . . . The conquest of political power necessitates the possession of political rights; and the most important problem of tactics which German social democracy has at the present time to solve, appears to me to be to devise the best ways for the extension of the political and economic rights of the German working class.

Robert Blatchford, "What Is Socialism"*

Robert Blatchford was a British journalist who was influenced by Carlyle, Ruskin, Mill, the Christian socialists, and Karl Marx. In his enormously popular little book, *Merrie England* (1894), he sought to explain the meaning of socialism to the average man and woman (the "John Smith" of the following excerpt). How does he define socialism? What, in effect, would practical socialism be like? How, to his mind, does this differ from the system of the time? What do you believe to be the strengths and weaknesses of this argument?

John Smith, do you know what Socialism is? You have heard it denounced many a time, and it is said that you do not believe in it; but do you know what it is?

But before I tell you what Socialism is, I must tell you what Socialism is not. For half our time as champions of Socialism is wasted in denials of false descriptions of Socialism; and to a large extent the anger, the ridicule, and the argument of the opponents of Socialism are hurled against a Socialism which has no existence except in their own heated minds.

Socialism does not consist in violently seizing upon the property of the rich and sharing it out amongst the poor.

Socialists do not propose by a single Act of Parliament, or by a sudden revolution, to put all men on an equality, and compel them to remain so. Socialism is not a wild dream of a happy land where the apples will drop off the trees into our open mouths, the fish come out of the rivers and fry themselves for dinner, and the looms turn out ready-made suits of velvet with golden buttons without the trouble of coaling the engine. Neither is it a dream of a nation of stained-glass angels, who never say damn, who always love their neighbours better than themselves, and who never need to work unless they wish to.

No, Socialism is none of those things. It is a scientific scheme of national Government, entirely wise, just, and practical. And now let us see. . . .

Practical Socialism is so simple that a child may understand it. It is a kind of national scheme of co-operation, managed by the State. Its programme consists, essentially, of one demand, that the land and other instruments of production shall be the common property of the people, and shall be used and governed by the people for the people.

Make the land and all the instruments of production State property; put all farms, mines, mills, ships, railways, and shops, under State control, as you have already put the postal and telegraphic services under State control, and Practical Socialism is accomplished.

The postal and telegraphic service is the standing proof of the capacity of the State to manage the public business with economy and success.

---

*Source: Robert Blatchford, *Merrie England* (London, 1894), 98–102.

That which has been done with the post-offices may be done with mines, trams, railways, and factories.

The differences between Socialism and the state of things now in existence will now be plain to you.

At present the land—that is, England—does not belong to the people—to the English—but to a few rich men. The mines, mills, ships, shops, canals, railways, houses, docks, harbours, and machinery do not belong to the people, but to a few rich men.

Therefore the land, the factories, the railways, ships and machinery are not used for the general good of the people, but are used to make wealth for the few rich men who own them. Socialists say that this arrangement is unjust and unwise, that it entails waste as well as misery, and that it would be better for all, even for the rich, that the land and other instruments of production should become the property of the State, just as the post-office and the telegraphs have become the property of the State.

Socialists demand that the State shall manage the railways and the mines and the mills just as it now manages the post-offices and the telegraphs.

Socialists declare that if it is wicked and foolish and impossible for the State to manage the factories, mines, and railways, then it is wicked and foolish and impossible for the State to manage the telegraphs.

Socialists declare that as the State carries the people's letters and telegrams more cheaply and more efficiently than they were carried by private enterprise, so it could grow corn and weave cloth and work the railway systems more cheaply and more efficiently than they are now worked by private enterprise.

Socialists declare that as our Government now makes food and clothing and arms and accoutrements for the army and navy and police, so it could make them for the people.

Socialists declare that as many corporations make gas, provide and manage the water-supply, look after the paving and lighting and cleansing of the streets, and often do a good deal of building and farming, so there is no reason why they should not get coal, and spin yarn, and make boots, and bread, and beer for the people.

Socialists point out that if all the industries of the nation were put under State control, all the profit, which now goes into the hands of a few idle men, would go into the coffers of the State—which means that the people would enjoy the benefits of all the wealth they create.

This, then, is the basis of Socialism, that England should be owned by the English, and managed for the benefit of the English, instead of being owned by a few rich idlers, and mismanaged by them for the benefit of themselves.

But Socialism means more than the mere transference of the wealth of the nation to the nation.

Socialism would not endure competition. Where it found two factories engaged in under-cutting each other at the price of long hours and low wages to the workers, it would step in and fuse the two concerns into one, save an immense sum in cost of working, and finally produce more goods and better goods at a lower figure than were produced before.

But Practical Socialism would do more than that. It would educate the people. It would provide cheap and pure food. It would extend and elevate the means of study and amusement. It would foster literature and science and art. It would encourage and reward genius and industry. It would abolish sweating and jerry work. It would demolish the slums and erect good and handsome dwellings. It would compel all men to do some kind of useful work. It would recreate and nourish the craftsman's pride in his craft. It would protect women and children. It would raise the standard of health and morality; and it would take the sting out of pauperism by paying pensions to honest workers no longer able to work.

Why nationalise the land and instruments of production? To save waste; to save panics; to avert trade depressions, famines, strikes, and congestion of industrial centres; and to prevent greedy and unscrupulous sharpers from enriching themselves at the cost of the national health and prosperity. In short, to replace anarchy and war by law and order. To keep the wolves out of the fold, to tend and fertilise the field of labour instead of allowing the wheat to be strangled by the tares, and to regulate wisely the distribution of the seed-corn of industry so that it might no longer be scattered broadcast—some falling on rocks, and some being eaten up by the birds of the air.

Chapter 26
The West and the World

Chapter Questions

After reading and studying this chapter you should be able to answer the following questions:

What was the "new imperialism" and how and why did it occur? What were its consequences for Europe and the new colonial peoples?

Chapter Summary

We live in a world today in which the consequences of nineteenth-century Western imperialism are still being felt. In the nineteenth century, Western civilization reached the high point of its long-standing global expansion. Western expansion in this period took many forms. There was, first of all, economic expansion. Europeans invested large sums of money abroad, building railroads and ports, mines and plantations, factories and public utilities. Trade between nations grew greatly, and a world economy developed. Between 1750 and 1900 the gap in income disparities between industrialized Europe and America and the rest of the world grew at an astounding rate. Part of this was due, first, to a rearrangement of land use that accompanied Western colonialism and to Western success in preventing industrialization in areas Westerners saw as markets for their manufactured goods. European economic penetration was very often peaceful, but Europeans (and Americans) were also quite willing to force isolationist nations such as China and Japan to throw open their doors to Westerners. Second, millions of Europeans migrated abroad. The pressure of poverty and overpopulation in rural areas encouraged this migration, but once in the United States and Australia, European settlers passed laws to prevent similar mass migration from Asia.

A third aspect of Western expansion was that European states established vast political empires, mainly in Africa but also in Asia. This "new imperialism" occurred primarily between 1880 and 1900, when European governments scrambled frantically for territory. White people came, therefore, to rule millions of black and brown people in Africa and Asia. The causes of the new imperialism are still hotly debated. Competition for trade, superior military force, European power politics, and a racist belief in European superiority were among the most important. Some Europeans bitterly criticized imperialism as a betrayal of Western ideals of freedom and equality.

Western imperialism produced various reactions in Africa and Asia. The first response was simply to try to drive the foreigners away. The general failure of this traditionalist response then led large masses to accept European rule, which did bring some improvements. A third response was the modernist response of Western-educated natives, who were repelled by Western racism and attracted by Western ideals of national independence and economic progress. Thus, imperialism and reactions to it spread Western civilization to non-Western lands.

Study Outline

Use this outline to preview the chapter before you read a particular section in your textbook and then as a self-check to test your reading comprehension after you have read the chapter section.

I. Industrialization and the world economy
    A. The rise of global inequality
        1. The Industrial Revolution caused a great and steadily growing gap between Europe and North America and the nonindustrializing regions of Africa, Asia, and Latin America.
            a. In 1750 the average standard of living in Europe was no higher than the rest of the world.
            b. By 1970 the average person in the rich countries had twenty-five times the wealth of the average person in the poor countries.
            c. This gap, seen first between Britain and the rest of Europe, was the product of industrialization.
            d. Only after 1945 did Third World regions begin to make gains.
        2. Some argue that these disparities are the result of the West using science and capitalism; others argue that the West used its economic and political power to steal its riches.
    B. Trade and foreign investment
        1. World trade, which by 1913 was twenty-five times what it had been in 1800, meant an interlocking economy centered in and directed by Europe.
        2. Britain played a key role in using trade to link the world.
            a. It used its empire as a market for its manufactured goods.
            b. It prohibited its colonies from raising protective tariffs.
            c. Britain sought to eliminate all tariffs on traded goods, and this free-trade policy stimulated world trade.
        3. The railroad, the steamship, refrigeration, and other technological innovations revolutionized trade patterns.
        4. The Suez and Panama canals and modern port facilities fostered intercontinental trade.
        5. Beginning about 1840, Europeans invested large amounts of capital abroad and in other European countries.
            a. Most of the exported capital went to the United States, Canada, Australia, New Zealand, and Latin America, where it built ports and railroads.
            b. This investment enabled still more land to be settled by Europeans, pushing out the native peoples already living there.

C. The opening of China and Japan
   1. European trade with China increased, but not without a struggle.
      a. China was self-sufficient and had never been interested in European goods, and the Manchu Dynasty carefully regulated trade.
      b. British merchants and the Chinese clashed over the sale of opium and the opening of Chinese ports to Europeans.
      c. The opium war in 1839–1842 led to the British acquisition of Hong Kong and the opening of four cities to trade (the Treaty of Nanking).
      d. A second war in 1856–1860 resulted in more gains for Europeans.
   2. Japan also was unwilling to trade or have diplomatic relations with the West.
      a. Japan wanted to maintain its long-standing isolation.
      b. An American fleet under Perry "opened" Japan in 1853 with threats of naval bombardment.

D. Western penetration of Egypt
   1. Muhammad Ali built a modern state in Turkish-held Egypt that attracted European traders.
      a. He drafted the peasants, reformed the government, and improved communications.
      b. The peasants lost out because the land was converted from self-sufficient farms to large, private landholdings to grow cash crops for export.
   2. Ismail continued the modernization of Egypt, including the completion of the Suez Canal, but also drew the country deeply into debt.
   3. To prevent Egypt from going bankrupt, Britain and France intervened politically.
   4. Foreign financial control provoked a violent nationalistic reaction in Egypt that led to British occupation of the country until 1956.

II. The great migration from Europe and Asia
A. The pressure of population
   1. The population of Europe more than doubled between 1800 and 1900.
   2. This population growth was the impetus behind emigration.
   3. Migration patterns varied from country to country, reflecting the differing social and economic conditions.
      a. Five times as many people migrated in 1900–1910 as in the 1850s.
      b. Between 1840 and 1920 one-third of all migrants came from Britain; German migration was greatest between 1830 and the 1880s, while Italian migration continued high until 1914.
      c. The United States absorbed about half the migrants from Europe, while in other countries an even larger proportion of their population was new arrivals.

B. European migrants
   1. Most European migrants were peasants lacking adequate landholdings or craftsmen threatened by industrialization.
      a. Most were young and unmarried, and many returned home after some time abroad.
      b. Many were spurred on by the desire for freedom; many Jews left Russia after the pogroms of the 1880s.
      c. Italian migrants were typical in that they were small landowning peasants who left because of agricultural decline; many of them went to Brazil and Argentina, but later returned to Italy.

2. Ties of friendship and family often determined where people would settle.

3. Many migrated because they resented the power of the privileged classes.

C. Asian migrants

   1. Many Asians became exploited laborers.

   2. Asian migration led to racist reactions, such as "whites only" laws in the West.

III. Western imperialism

A. The new imperialism

   1. Between 1880 and 1914, European nations scrambled for political as well as economic control over foreign nations.

   2. This scramble led to new tensions among competing European states and wars with non-European powers.

B. The scramble for Africa

   1. Prior to 1880, European penetration of Africa was limited.

   2. British occupation of Egypt and Belgian penetration into the Congo started the race for colonial possessions.

      a. Leopold II of Belgium sent explorers into the Congo and planted the Belgian flag.

      b. Other countries, such as France and Britain, rushed to follow.

   3. The Berlin conference (1884–85) laid ground rules for this new imperialism.

      a. European claims to African territory had to be based on military occupation.

      b. No single European power could claim the whole continent.

   4. Germany entered the race for colonies and cooperated with France against Britain; the French goal was control of Lake Chad.

   5. The British under Kitchener massacred Muslim tribesmen at Omdurman (1898) in their drive to conquer the Sudan and nearly went to war with the French at Fashoda.

C. Imperialism in Asia

   1. The Dutch extended their control in the East Indies while the French took Indochina.

   2. Russia and the United States also penetrated Asia.

D. Causes of the new imperialism

   1. Economic motives—especially trade opportunities—were important, but in the end general economic benefits were limited because the new colonies were too poor to buy much.

   2. Political and diplomatic factors also encouraged imperialism.

      a. Colonies were believed to be crucial for national security, military power, and international prestige.

      b. Many people believed that colonies were essential to great nations.

   3. Nationalism, racism, and Social Darwinism contributed to imperialism.

      a. The German historian Treitschke claimed that colonies were essential to show racial superiority and national greatness.

      b. Special-interest groups favored expansion, as did military men and adventurers.

   4. Imperialists also felt they had a duty to "civilize" more primitive, nonwhite peoples.

      a. Kipling set forth the notion of the "white man's burden."

      b. Missionaries brought Christianity and education, but also European racism.

E. Critics of imperialism
    1. The British economist J. A. Hobson set forth the argument that imperialism was the result of capitalism and that only special-interest groups benefited from colonial possessions.
    2. Others condemned imperialism on moral grounds.
       a. They rebelled against the crude Social Darwinism of the imperialists.
       b. They accused the imperialists of applying a double standard: liberty and equality at home, military dictatorship and discrimination in the colonies.

IV. Responses to Western imperialism
  A. Imperialism threatened traditional society.
    1. Traditionalists wanted to drive Western culture out and preserve the old culture and society.
    2. Modernizers believed it was necessary to adopt Western practices.
    3. Anti-imperialist leaders found inspiration in Western liberalism and nationalism.
  B. The British Empire in India
    1. The last traditionalist response in India was broken by crushing the Great Rebellion of 1857–58.
    2. After 1858, India was administered by a white elite that considered itself superior to the Indians.
    3. An Indian elite was educated to aid the British in administration.
    4. Imperialism brought many benefits, including economic development, unity, and peace.
    5. But nationalistic sentiments and demands for equality and self-government grew among the Western-educated Indian elite.
  C. The example of Japan
    1. The Meiji Restoration (1867) was a reaction to American intrusion, unequal treaties, and the humiliation of the shogun (military governor).
    2. The Meiji leaders were modernizers who brought liberal and economic reforms.
       a. They abolished the old decentralized government and formed a strong, unified state.
       b. They declared social equality and allowed freedom of movement.
       c. They created a free, competitive, government-stimulated economy.
       d. They built a powerful modern navy and reorganized the army.
    3. In the 1890s, Japan looked increasingly toward the German empire and rejected democracy in favor of authoritarianism.
    4. Japan became an imperial power in the Far East.
       a. Japan defeated China in a war over Korea in 1894–95.
       b. In 1904, Japan attacked Russia and took Manchuria.
  D. Toward revolution in China
    1. The traditionalist Manchu rulers staged a comeback after the opium wars.
       a. The traditional ruling groups produced effective leaders.
       b. Destructive foreign aggression lessened, and some Europeans helped the Manchus.
    2. The Chinese defeat by Japan in 1894–95 led to imperialist penetration and unrest.
    3. Modernizers hoped to take over and strengthen China.
    4. Boxer traditionalists caused violence (1900–1903) and a harsh European reaction.
    5. Revolutionary modernizers overthrew the Manchu Dynasty in 1912.

Review Questions

Check your understanding of the chapter by answering the following questions.

1. How large was the income gap between industrializing and nonindustrializing regions? What was the cause of this gap?
2. What factors facilitated intercontinental trade in the late nineteenth century? Where did most of the foreign investments in this period go?
3. What were the motives of both the British merchants and the Chinese government in the opium wars of 1839–1842 and 1856–1860?
4. What were some of the differences in migration patterns among the various European states?
5. Where did the European migrants go?
6. Why did the migrants leave? Why did so many return?
7. Why was migration from Italy so heavy? Who were the migrants and where did they go?
8. Khedive Ismail once said, "My country is no longer in Africa, we now form part of Europe." What did he mean?
9. Explain the British-Egyptian conflict of 1882. What were the causes and the results?
10. What distinguished the "new imperialism" from earlier forms of European expansion in the nineteenth century?
11. Why was Leopold II of Belgium interested in Africa?
12. What was meant by "effective occupation"? Did it cause or curtail further imperialism?
13. In 1898, a British army faced a French army at Fashoda in north-central Africa. How did each power get to such a location, and how was the confrontation solved?
14. What impact did Christianity have on imperialism?
15. What was the purpose of the Great Rebellion in India in 1857–58?
16. What were the advantages and disadvantages of British rule for the Indians?
17. What was the Meiji Restoration in Japan? Why was it a turning point in Japanese history?
18. How well did the Japanese copy the Europeans? What European ideas were most attractive to them?
19. Does the Manchu Dynasty in the period 1860–1912 represent a traditionalist or modernist response to Europe and imperialism?

Study-Review Exercises

Define the following key concepts and terms.

"new imperialism"

traditionalist response to imperialism

modernist response to imperialism

Social Darwinism

racism

"the white man's burden"

Identify and explain the significance of the following people and terms.
Manchu Dynasty

Pale of [Jewish] Settlement

International Association for the Exploration and Civilization of Central Africa

Egyptian Nationalist Party

Suez Canal

Omdurman

British opium trade

Pierre de Brazza

Muhammad Ali

Leopold II

Matthew Perry

Boers

Dowager Empress Tzu Hsi

John Hobson

Heinrich von Treitschke

Explain what the following events were, who participated in them, and why they were important.
Japanese "opening" of Korea in 1876

Berlin conference of 1884–85

Fashoda crisis of 1989

Great Trek of the Boers

Treaty of Nanking, 1842

Clermont experiment of 1807

Meiji Restoration of 1867

Sino-Japanese War (1894–95)

Test your understanding of this chapter by providing the correct answers.

1. He took the Sudan for the British with his victory at Omdurman. _____

2. His attempt to modernize Egypt resulted in bankruptcy and foreign intervention.

    _____

3. He was a journalist, explorer, and employee of Leopold III. _____

4. He was a British paternalistic reformer in Egypt. _____

5. He argued that the strongest nations tend to be the best. _____

6. He "opened" Japan to the West in 1853. _____

7. He was a Chinese revolutionary and republican. _____

8. Under her leadership China was able to strengthen itself and maintain its traditional culture.

_____

Multiple-Choice Questions

1. The Treaty of Nanking (1842) ended a war between Great Britain and China that had started over
   a. Chinese expulsion of British diplomats from Canton.
   b. disagreement over shipping rights in Chinese ports.
   c. opium smuggled into China from British India.
   d. the British annexation of Manchuria.

2. The great European migration of the nineteenth century was caused by all of the following *except*
   a. population pressure.
   b. desire for political and social rights.
   c. the desire of wealthy Europeans to emigrate and settle in non-European lands.
   d. lack of employment.

3. The most persuasive Western argument against European imperialism was that
   a. it was not economically profitable.
   b. European control of nonwhites was immoral and hypocritical.
   c. not enough investment was made in colonies.
   d. it was unworthy of great nations.

4. Western influence on Japan resulted in
   a. a Westernized country that began to practice its own form of imperialism.
   b. a country subject to Britain in the same way that India was.
   c. a country subject to the United States in the same way that India was subject to Britain.
   d. no effect at all.

5. After the wars over the opium trade, China
   a. began to industrialize rapidly.
   b. recovered for a number of years under the empress dowager.
   c. defeated Japan in the Sino-Japanese war of 1894–95.
   d. established a communist dictatorship to crush the Boxer Rebellion.

6. After 1840, world trade
   a. grew slowly as prices increased.
   b. grew rapidly as prices decreased.
   c. remained about the same as during the early decades of the century.
   d. declined because of the rise of protective barriers.

7. Which of the following promoted the growth of world trade after 1840?
   a. The British policy of high tariffs and trade barriers
   b. The increase in transportation costs
   c. The opening of the Suez and Panama canals
   d. The rise in price of raw materials and food

8. Which of the following characterizes the traditional attitude of Chinese society toward Western society?
   a. Great interest in European products
   b. A desire to open trade ports to European capitalists
   c. A need for Europe as a source of capital and market for Chinese tea
   d. Considerable disinterest in Europe

9. The war between Britain and China, which ended in 1842, was caused by
   a. Chinese penetration into southeast Asia.
   b. British merchants' demand to sell opium to the Chinese.
   c. the Chinese naval blockade of the Japanese coast.
   d. British refusal to sell European goods in China.

10. Japan was "opened" by the United States as a result of
    a. a military display of force.
    b. long and arduous negotiations.
    c. a willingness of the part of Japan.
    d. the opium wars.

11. Throughout the nineteenth century, European population and emigration tended to
    a. increase.
    b. decrease slightly.
    c. remain about the same.
    d. decrease significantly.

12. The country that was most affected by the immigration of Europeans was
    a. the United States.
    b. Argentina.
    c. Russia.
    d. Peru.

13. For the most part, the people who left Europe to settle elsewhere were
    a. the poorest and least skilled of society.
    b. middle-class adventurers in search of new fortunes.
    c. small landowners and village craftsmen.
    d. urban factory workers.

14. The return of the migrant to his or her native land was
    a. rare.
    b. not uncommon.
    c. common only among the Irish.
    d. common only among those migrating to Argentina.

15. In the nineteenth century, two out of three migrants to Argentina and Brazil came from
    a. Italy.
    b. Africa.
    c. Ireland.
    d. northern Europe.

16. The groups of east European migrants *least* likely to return to Europe were
    a. Poles.
    b. Jews.
    c. Germans.
    d. migrants from the Balkan lands.

17. The great European scramble for possession of Africa occurred
    a. prior to 1850.
    b. after 1900.
    c. between 1880 and 1900.
    d. around 1850.

18. The victor of the Fashoda incident in Africa was
    a. Britain.
    b. France.
    c. Germany.
    d. Belgium.

19. Reasons for British colonial expansion in the late 1870s and 1880s include all of the following *except*
    a. the desire to spread Christianity to Africa and Asia.
    b. the rise of France, Germany, and America as industrial powers.
    c. the fear of "protectionism" on the part of other European powers and the United States.
    d. the increased belief that colonies were necessary to support naval supremacy.

20. The radical English economist J. S. Hobson argued in his book *Imperialism* that the motive for colonial imperialism was
    a. economic.
    b. political.
    c. military.
    d. overpopulation.

21. Between 1750 and 1913 the gap in average income between the industrializing and nonindustrializing regions
    a. stayed about the same.
    b. narrowed considerably.
    c. increased slightly.
    d. increased enormously.

22. The application of steam power to transportation affected the general economy in that it resulted in
    a. lower prices for raw materials and manufactured goods.
    b. higher prices for raw materials.
    c. decreased demand for manufactured products.
    d. higher passenger and freight rates.

23. The effect of Muhammad Ali's modernization on the average peasant was that it
    a. improved the peasants' economic independence.
    b. caused a rise in peasant income.
    c. resulted in a loss of land.
    d. allowed the peasant to become a wealthy landlord.

24. The German historian Treitschke believed that imperialism was
    a. morally wrong but historically inevitable.
    b. the result of "pure selfishness."
    c. a way for the superior races to fulfill their greatness.
    d. due to the economic needs of unregulated capitalism.

25. It appears that the nineteenth-century British policy of free trade
    a. successfully replaced mercantilism.
    b. was nothing but a hindrance and caused economic loss.
    c. caused many wars.
    d. resulted in economic growth.

Major Political Ideas

1. Define imperialism. Was it largely a political or an economic phenomenon? What was the political impact of imperialism on those who were subject to imperialist activity? How valid is the claim that imperialism caused a shift in world power in favor of the Europeans and Americans?

2. Non-Westerners responded to imperialism in a variety of ways, but it is possible to think of their responses as a spectrum, with traditionalists at one end and modernizers at the other. What do these two terms mean and how were they implemented. Which approach was the most successful?

Issues for Essays and Discussion

Was Western imperialism "pure selfishness" and the product of unregulated capitalism, as its critics claimed? Provide evidence to back up your argument.

Interpretation of Visual Sources

Study the cartoon entitled *The Chinese Exclusion Act* on page 837 of your textbook. What is the message here? What images are used to convey this message? Is this racism? What migration patterns and economic circumstances brought this issue to this point?

Geography

1. On Outline Map 26.2 provided, locate and label the following and indicate to which European nation it belonged: Union of South Africa, Madagascar, Algeria, French Equatorial Africa, Belgian Congo, Orange Free State, Libya, Nigeria, German East Africa, Transvaal, Egypt, British East Africa, Gold Coast, Morocco.

2. On Outline Map 26.3 provided, locate and label the following places and indicate which Western nation exercised control or domination: French Indochina, Philippine Islands, Port Arthur, Korea, India, Canton, Macao, Manchuria, Dutch East Indies, Hong Kong, Formosa, Vladivostok.

Outline Map 26.2

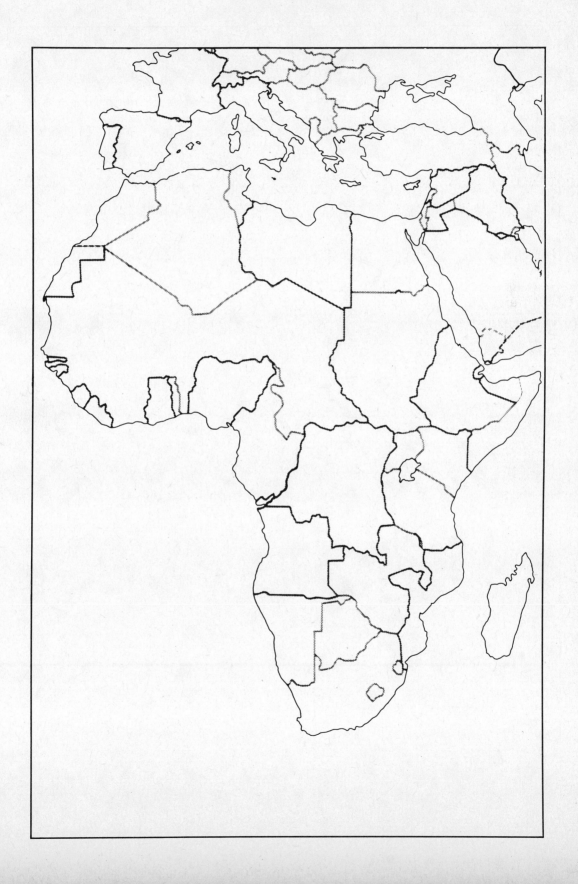

Outline Map 26.3

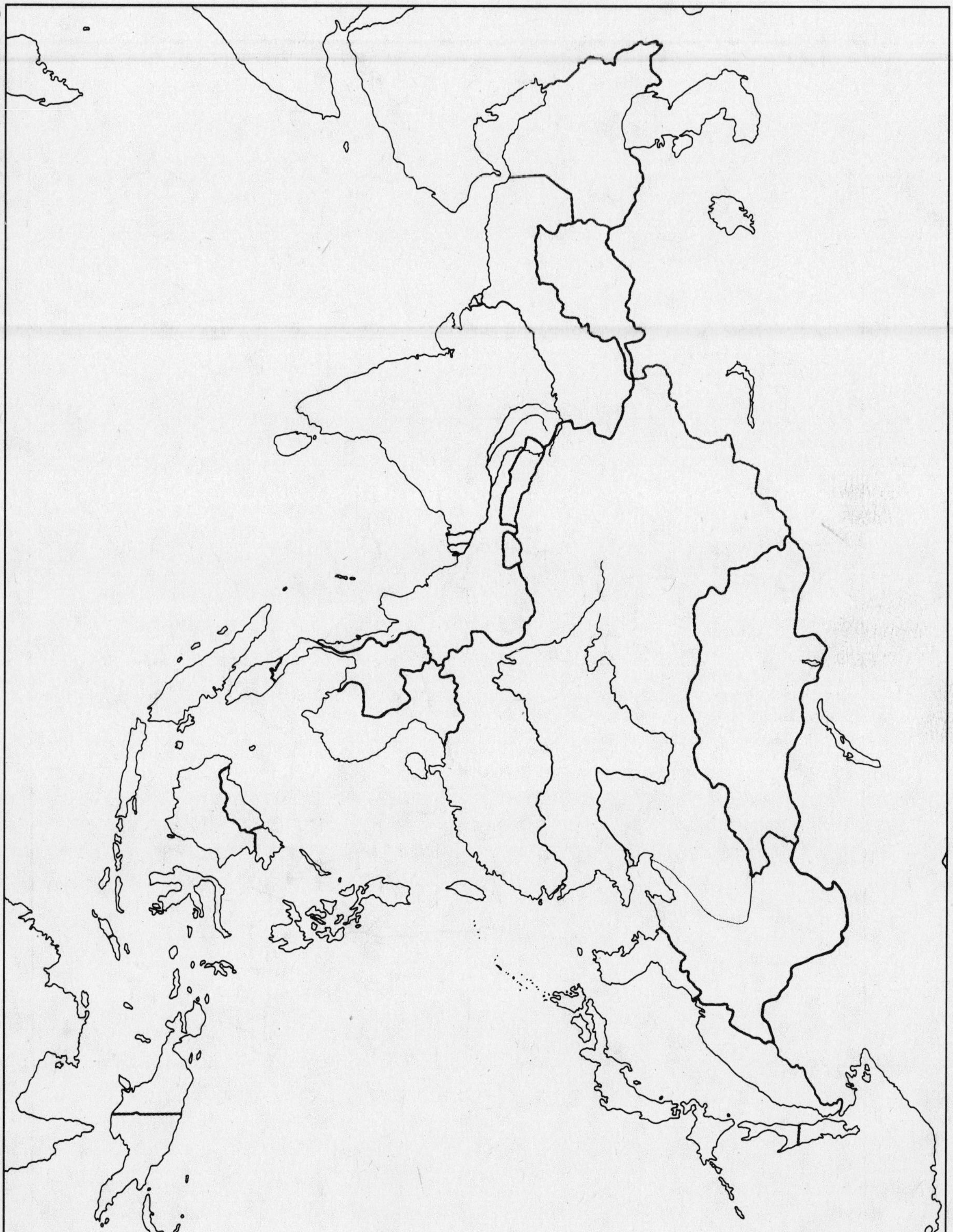

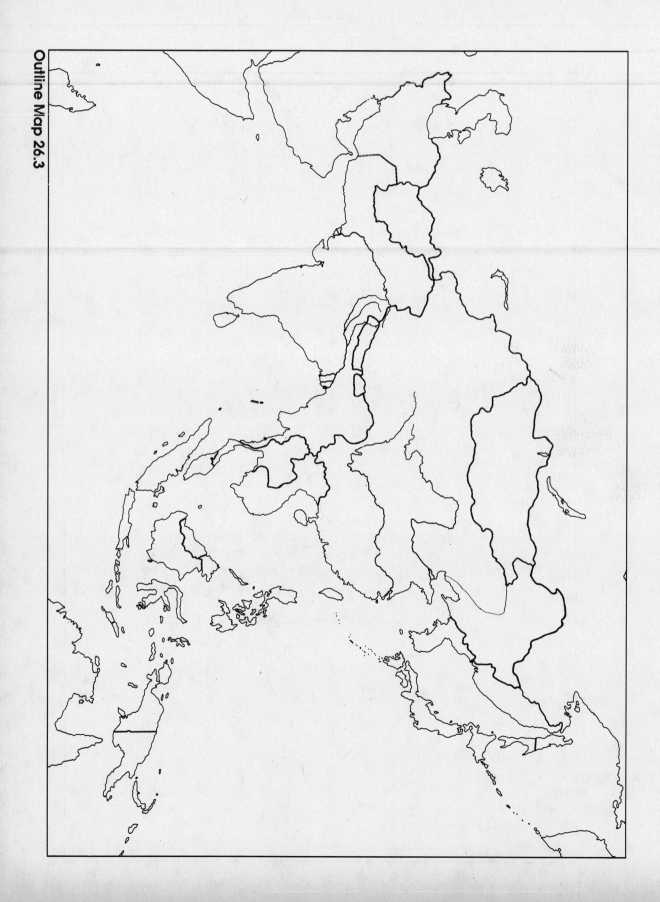

Understanding History Through the Arts

How has imperialism been depicted in opera and the movies? Few operas have enjoyed the popularity of Puccini's *Madame Butterfly* (1904). Set in Japan, the opera centers on the marriage of an American naval lieutenant and a Japanese woman.

Imperialist adventure, and more recently imperialist exploitation, have long been subjects of filmmakers. Several recent films, available on video, are *Gandhi, The Last Emperor*, and *Empire in the Sun*.

Problems for Further Investigation

1. What impact did Western imperialism have on Chinese society? This is among the questions addressed in J. Grey, *Rebellions and Revolutions, China from the 1800s to the 1980s** (1990).

2. What were the causes of imperialism and what made the system of "empire" work? What were the motives of its participants? The various causes for the changed nature of imperialism in the 1880s are discussed in H. M. Wright, ed., The *"New Imperialism"** (1961). Imperialism in Africa is analyzed by a number of historians in R. F. Betts, ed., The *"Scramble" for Africa** (1966), and a good general description of the greatest imperialist nation, Great Britain, can be found in B. Porter, *The Lion's Share, A Short History of British Imperialism, 1850–1970** (1975). A striking and fascinating study of one of the greatest of the imperialist-militarists is P. Magnus, *Kitchener: Portrait of an Imperialist** (1959, 1968). Imperialist adventure, as found in works such as R. Kipling, *Kim* and *In Black and White*, and J. Conrad, *Lord Jim*, has become part of the classical literature of our time. One woman's life in Africa is the subject of the award-winning film *Out of Africa* (1984), based on I. Dinesen, *Letters from Africa, 1914–1931** (1981), trans. by A. Born.

3. How were immigrants treated in their new homelands? The American experience is treated in L. Dinnerstein and D. Reimers, *Ethnic Americans: A History of Immigration** (1988), and Y. Ichioka, *The Issei: The World of First-Generation Japanese Immigrants, 1885–1924** (1988).

---

*Available in paperback.

Chapter 27
The Great Break: War and Revolution

Chapter Questions

After reading and studying this chapter you should be able to answer the following questions:

What were the causes of the First World War? How and why did the war have such enormous and destructive consequences? What impact did the war have on the ways in which people lived and thought? What were the causes of the great revolution in Russia, and what changes did this event bring to Russian society?

Chapter Summary

The First World War had enormous consequences. Western civilization changed decisively, as the war caused not only death and destruction but a variety of revolutions as well. Thus, the First World War opened a new era in European history. This chapter shows how and why this was so. Beginning with the system of alliances that had formed two hostile military blocs by 1914, the text explains how nationalism and fears of nationalism touched off a world war. Contrary to expectations, the First World War became a ghastly military stalemate. The stalemate forced each government to make a total war effort, which demanded great sacrifices and major social changes. Economic life was strictly controlled, women entered defense plants, and nationalistic propaganda strengthened genuine popular support for the war. By 1916, however, there was growing discontent and war weariness in all countries.

Russia broke first under the enormous strains of total war. In March 1917, a moderate patriotic revolution established a Russian republic. In November 1917, Lenin and the Bolsheviks took power in a socialist revolution. Lenin was a dedicated revolutionary who had reinterpreted Marxism in a radical way before 1914, and he took Russia out of the war and established a harsh dictatorship. This dictatorship allowed the Bolshevik government to survive and to defeat many different foes in a bloody civil war. Revolution also occurred in Germany and Austria. Germany established a republic, and Austria-Hungary broke into pieces. In 1919, the world of 1914 lay in ruins, due to the impact of total war and radical revolution. Nor did the peace settlement of Versailles bring stability, since the defeated Germans hated the peace treaty, and the victorious Americans rejected it.

Study Outline

Use this outline to preview the chapter before you read a particular section in your textbook and then as a self-check to test your reading comprehension after you have read the chapter section.

I. The First World War (1914–1918)
   A. The Bismarckian system of alliances
      1. Germany was the most powerful European country after 1871.
      2. Bismarck sought to guarantee European peace through alliances.
      3. The Three Emperors' League (Austria, Russia, and Germany) was created in 1873 to maintain the status quo; this was followed by an Austrian-German Alliance of 1879 and the Alliance of the Three Emperors in 1881.
      4. Because of tensions with France, Italy joined Germany and Austria in the Triple Alliance (1882).
      5. In 1887, the Russian-German Reinsurance Treaty promised neutrality by each state if the other were attacked.
   B. The rival blocs
      1. William II dismissed Bismarck, and his termination of the German-Russian Reinsurance Treaty led to a new Russian-French alliance.
      2. Under William II, the British-German "natural alliance" deteriorated into a bitter rivalry.
         a. The Boer War, German envy of British imperialism, and economic and military rivalry drove the British and the Germans apart.
         b. Then Britain allied with Japan and turned to France and formed the Anglo-French Entente of 1904, which further alienated Germany.
         c. Germany tested this entente in a diplomatic struggle over Morocco.
         d. The Algeciras Conference (1906) left Germany empty-handed and isolated.
      3. As a result, Germany became increasingly distrustful, and other European countries began to see Germany as a threat.
      4. German naval buildup, under Tirpitz, led to an arms race with Britain and a cycle of paranoia.
   C. The outbreak of war (August 1914)
      1. Nationalism in the Balkans threatened the Ottoman Empire and European peace.
      2. Independence was acquired by Serbia, Rumania, and part of Bulgaria in 1878.
      3. Austria's annexation of Bosnia and Herzegovina in 1908 greatly angered Serbia, which was forced to turn southward against the Ottomans in its nationalistic desire to expand—this was the first Balkan War (1912).
      4. Serbia's dispute with Bulgaria over the spoils of victory led to the Second Balkan War in 1913.
      5. The Balkan wars of 1912–13 were a victory for Balkan nationalism.
      6. The assassination of the Austrian archduke Francis Ferdinand (1914) resulted in a war between Serbia and Austria as Austria tried to stem the rising tide of hostile nationalism.
      7. Germany gave Austria unconditional support.
      8. Military considerations dictated policy, and an all-European war resulted.
         a. Russia ordered full mobilization against Austria and Germany.

  b. Germany invaded France via Belgium.

  c. Great Britain joined France and declared war on Germany.

 D. Reflections on the origins of the war

  1. Austria-Hungary deliberately started the war, goaded by Germany.

  2. German aggression in 1914 reflected the failure of all European leaders to incorporate Bismark's empire into the international system.

  3. Nationalism contributed to war fever.

  4. All the European leaders underestimated the consequences of war.

 E. The first Battle of the Marne (September 1914)

  1. The original Schlieffen plan—a German invasion of France through Belgium—had to be altered when British troops landed to help the Belgians.

  2. The Battle of the Marne turned the war into a long stalemate.

 F. Stalemate and slaughter

  1. Trench warfare meant much horrible death but no end to the war.

   a. The battles of Somme and Verdun cost thousands of lives but no significant gains in territory for either side.

   b. The French army was almost destroyed at Champagne (1917), while the British lost many men at Passchendaele.

  2. The war's horrors caused a profound disillusionment with society and mankind.

   a. The war shattered an entire generation of young men.

   b. It created a gulf between veterans and civilians.

 G. The widening war

  1. Despite huge Austrian losses, Austria and Germany defeated Russia and Serbia on the eastern front (1914–15).

  2. Italy and Bulgaria entered the war (1915).

  3. With Arab help, Britain defeated the Ottoman Empire (1918).

  4. The European war extended around the globe as Great Britain, France, and Japan seized Germany's colonies.

  5. The United States entered the war in 1917 because of German submarine warfare.

II. The home front

 A. Mobilizing for total war

  1. Most people saw the war in nationalistic terms and believed their nation was defending itself against aggression.

  2. Total war meant that economic planning was necessary.

   a. Rationing, price and wage controls, and restrictions on workers' freedom of movement were imposed by government.

   b. The economy of total war blurred the distinctions between soldiers and civilians—all were involved in the war effort.

   c. The ability of governments to manage economies strengthened the cause of socialism.

  3. In Germany, food and raw materials were rationed and universal draft was initiated.

   a. Hindenburg and Ludendorff became the real rulers of Germany.

   b. Total war led to the establishment of a totalitarian society.

  4. By 1916, the British economy was largely planned.

 B. The social impact

  1. Labor shortages brought about benefits for organized labor.

   2. The role of women changed dramatically as many women entered the labor force.
      a. Some European women gained the right to vote after the war.
      b. Women displayed a growing spirit of independence.
   3. War brought about greater social equality.
   C. Growing political tensions
      1. Wartime propaganda to maintain popular support of the war was widespread.
      2. By 1916, people were growing weary of war; morale declined.
         a. In France, Clemenceau established a virtual dictatorship to deal with strikes and those who wanted compromise to end the war.
         b. In Germany, the social conflict of the prewar years emerged.
III. The Russian Revolution (1917)
   A. The fall of imperial Russia
      1. War losses and mistakes pointed to the weak leadership of the tsar and the unresponsiveness of the Russian government.
      2. The influence of Rasputin on the royal family further weakened the government and created a national scandal.
      3. Food shortages led to revolution in March 1917.
         a. A provisional government was proclaimed by the Duma.
         b. The tsar abdicated.
   B. The provisional government (March 1917)
      1. After the March revolution, Russia became the freest country in the world.
      2. Yet the new revolutionary government, led by Kerensky, wanted to postpone land reform, fearing it would further weaken the peasant army; the continuation of the war was Kerensky's primary concern.
      3. The provisional government had to share power with the Petrograd Soviet of Workers' and Soldiers' Deputies.
         a. The Petrograd Soviet's Army Order No. 1 placed military authority in the hands of ordinary soldiers.
         b. Army discipline broke down completely, and massive desertions began.
      4. Liberty was rapidly turning into anarchy.
   C. Lenin and the Bolshevik Revolution
      1. Lenin believed that revolution was necessary to destroy capitalism.
      2. He also believed that Marxist revolution could occur in Russia despite its absence of advanced capitalism if led by an intellectual elite.
      3. Russian Marxists became divided over Lenin's theories.
         a. Lenin's Bolsheviks demanded a small, disciplined, elitist party.
         b. The Mensheviks wanted a democratic party with mass membership.
      4. Lenin led an attack against the provisional government in July 1917, but it failed and he went into hiding.
      5. Kerensky's power was weakened by an attack on the provisional government by his commander in chief, Kornilov, and he lost favor with the army.
   D. Trotsky and the seizure of power
      1. A radical Marxist and supporter of Lenin, Trotsky centered his power in the Petrograd Soviet.
         a. The Bolsheviks gained a majority in the Petrograd Soviet.
         b. Bolsheviks controlled the military in the capital.

2. Trotsky engineered a Soviet overthrow of the provisional government (November 1917).
3. The Bolsheviks came to power because they were the answer to anarchy, they had superior leaders, and they appealed to many soldiers and urban workers exhausted by war.

E. Dictatorship and civil war
1. Lenin gave approval to the peasants' seizure of land and the urban workers' takeover of the factories.
2. Lenin arranged for an end of the war with Germany, but at a high price: the sacrifice of all of Russia's western territories (the Treaty of Brest-Litovsk, 1918).
3. Free elections produced a stunning loss for the Bolsheviks, and Lenin dissolved the Constituent Assembly.
4. Opposition to the Bolsheviks led to civil war (1918–1921).
   a. The officers of the old army (the Whites) organized the opposition to the Bolsheviks (the Reds).
   b. The Whites came from many social groups and wanted self-rule, not Bolshevik dictatorship.
5. The Bolshevik victory in the civil war was due to a number of factors: unity, a better army, a well-defined political program, mobilization of the home front, an effective secret police force (the Cheka), and an appeal to nationalism in the face of foreign aid to the Whites.
6. World War I brought the conditions that led to the Russian Revolution and a radically new government based on socialism and one-party dictatorship.

IV. The Versailles peace settlement (1918–1919)
A. The end of the war
1. By early 1917, the German populace was weary of war, and the German army was decisively defeated in the second Battle of the Marne (1918).
2. The Allies were strengthened by American intervention, and by September, the Allies were advancing on all fronts.
3. The German military arranged for a new liberal German government to accept defeat.
4. German soldiers and workers began to demonstrate for peace, and Germany surrendered in November 1918.

B. Revolution in Germany
1. Revolution in Austria-Hungary led to the breakup of the Austro-Hungarian Empire into new national states: Austria, Hungary, Czechoslovakia, and Yugoslavia.
2. Revolution in Germany (November 1918) led to a victory for the moderate socialists, the Social Democrats.
   a. There was little popular support for a radical revolution.
   b. The Social Democrats wanted the gradual elimination of capitalism.
   c. They accepted defeat and used the army to crush a radical uprising led by Leibknecht and Luxemburg.

C. The Treaty of Versailles
1. President Wilson was obsessed with creating a League of Nations to avert future wars.

2. Clemenceau of France and Lloyd George of England were more interested in permanently weakening Germany and making it pay for the war.
3. The conflicting desires of the Allies led to a deadlock and finally a compromise.
   a. France gave up its demand for a protective buffer state in return for a defensive alliance with Britain and the United States.
   b. The League of Nations was created.
4. Germany lost her colonies and territory in Europe—largely Alsace-Lorraine, Danzig, and eastern land to Poland.
5. Germany had to limit its army, admit responsibility for the war, and pay enormous damages.
6. Austria-Hungary and Turkey were the big losers in the separate peace treaties; the principle of self-determination still applied only to Europeans, and thus Western imperialism lived on.

D. American rejection of the Versailles treaty
1. The Versailles settlement rested on the principle of national self-determination, the League of Nations, and fear that the Bolshevik Revolution might spread.
2. Republican senators refused to ratify the treaty largely because of the issue of the League's power.
   a. Henry Cabot Lodge and others believed that requiring member states of the League of Nations to take collective action against aggression violated Congress's right to declare war.
   b. Wilson refused to compromise, and the Senate did not ratify the treaty.
3. The Senate also refused to ratify the defensive alliance with Britain and France.
   a. Britain also refused to ratify the defensive alliance.
   b. France felt betrayed and isolated.

Review Questions

Check your understanding of this chapter by answering the following questions.

1. How did Bismarck's system of alliances help maintain peace?
2. What was the purpose of the German-Russian Reinsurance Treaty? Why did it end in 1890 and with what results?
3. What were the reasons for Britain and Germany's love-hate relationship?
4. Why was the Moroccan crisis of 1905 a turning point in European diplomacy?
5. What impact did the Congress of Berlin (1878) have on the Balkan area? Who was bound to be the loser in the Balkans?
6. What were the origins and causes of the "third Balkan war" in 1914?
7. Which of the major powers do you believe most responsible and least responsible for the war? Explain.
8. What impact did the war have on the economy and the people at home? How cooperative was the population?
9. Did the war have any effect on the power of organized labor? On women in society?
10. How did the war tend to have an equalizing effect on society?
11. What evidence is there that the strain of war was beginning to take its toll on the home front in Russia, Austria, France, and Germany by 1916?

12. What were the reasons for the Russian Revolution in March 1917? Was revolution inevitable?
13. What were the soviets? What role did they play in the Bolshevik Revolution?
14. What was it about Lenin's character that made him a successful revolutionary? Why were his ideas popular with peasants and urban workers?
15. Why did Kerensky and the provisional government fail?
16. What were the reasons for the Bolshevik victory in the civil war?
17. Were there one, two, or many Russian revolutions in 1917? Explain.
18. What happened to the Austro-Hungarian and Turkish empires after 1918?
19. What were the goals of Wilson, Lloyd George, and Clemenceau at the Versailles peace conference?
20. The Treaty of Versailles is often seen as a major reason for World War II. Do you agree? Why?
21. Compare and contrast the Versailles settlement of 1919 with the Vienna settlement of 1815. What similarities do you see? What were the most striking differences?

Study-Review Questions

Define the following key concepts and terms.

Congress of Berlin, 1878

Schlieffen Plan

"total war"

totalitarian

western front

Bolsheviks

principle of national self-determination

war reparations

Identify and explain the significance of the following people and terms.
First Balkan War, 1912

Lawrence of Arabia

Reinsurance Treaty

Algeciras Conference of 1906

Anglo-French Entente of 1904

"Third Balkan War" (1914)

Lusitania

Admiral Tirpitz

(German) Auxiliary Service Law of 1916

David Lloyd George

Rasputin

Georges Clemenceau

Duma

Explain what role each of the following played in the Russian Revolution.
Tsar Nicholas II

Petrograd Soviet

Leon Trotsky

Petrograd bread riots (1917)

Congress of the Soviets

Kiev mutiny (1918)

Alexander Kerensky

Vladimir Lenin

Army Order No. 1

Constituent Assembly

White opposition

Treaty of Brest-Litovsk (1918)

Test your understanding of the chapter by providing the correct answers.

1. Germany violated this country's neutrality in 1914. _____

2. He was exiled to Siberia for socialist agitation. _____

3. Called "the tiger," he wanted to punish Germany. _____

4. He was the Bolshevik war commissar. _____

5. This Russian was called "our Friend Grigori." _____

6. The name of the important German war plan designed for a two-front war.

    _____

7. The date of the assassination of Archduke Francis Ferdinand. _____

8. The president of the revolutionary provisional government in Russia.

   _____

9. Russian workers' councils. _____

10. He aroused the Arab princes to revolt in 1917. _____

11. The name of the treaty between the Germans and the Russian Bolshevik government in

    1918. _____

12. The German chancellor fired by William II. _____

13. A Serbian revolutionary group. _____

14. The first country to mobilize for European war in 1914. _____

15. The Russian parliament that Nicholas adjourned in 1914. _____

Place the following events in correct chronological order.

Marx writes the *Communist Manifesto*
Lenin's return from Switzerland
establishment of the provisional government
outbreak of war between Russia and Germany
Kornilov plot
abolishment of the Constituent Assembly
overthrow of Kerensky and the provisional government

1.

2.

3.

4.

5.

6.

7.

Multiple-Choice Questions

1. The Bismarckian system of alliances was meant to
   a. expand Germany's borders.
   b. help German allies expand their borders.
   c. restrain Russia and Austria-Hungary and isolate France.
   d. encourage relations with France.

2. Which group of events is in correct chronological order?
   a. The Three Emperors' League, the Alliance of the Three Emperors, the Russian-German Reinsurance Treaty
   b. The Russian-German Reinsurance Treaty, the Alliance of the Three Emperors, the Three Emperors' League
   c. The Alliance of the Three Emperors, the Russian-German Reinsurance treaty, the Three Emperors' League
   d. The Russian-German Reinsurance Treaty, the Three Emperors' League, the Alliance of the Three Emperors

3. Which of the following strained German-British relations before the First World War?
   a. The Greek Revolution
   b. A German-French entente
   c. The German naval buildup
   d. British occupation of Belgium

4. The Schlieffen Plan called for Germany to knock out
   a. England by marching through France.
   b. Russia by marching through Poland.
   c. France by marching through Belgium.
   d. Belgium by marching through France.

5. Which of the following is usually considered a cause of the First World War?
   a. British appeasement of the Germans
   b. Nationalism
   c. Germany deliberately starting the "Third Balkan War"
   d. German control over the international alliance system

6. Which of the following was a consequence of the First World War?
   a. The weakening of socialism
   b. The exclusion of labor leaders and socialists from government
   c. The right to vote for women
   d. A widening of the gap between rich and poor

7. Which of the following was a central idea of Lenin?
   a. Revolution cannot occur in a backward country.
   b. Revolution is determined by an elite leadership.
   c. A broad-based democratic workers' party is necessary.
   d. The war against Germany must continue.

8. The end of the war in 1918 brought revolution to which of the following countries?
   a. France and Britain
   b. Germany and Italy
   c. Germany and Austria-Hungary
   d. France and Italy

9. Which of the following was an accomplishment of the peace conference at Versailles after the war?
   a. The division of Germany into an East and West Germany
   b. A defensive alliance in favor of France signed by the United States and Britain
   c. The re-establishment of Russian borders
   d. The establishment of the principle of German reparations payments

10. The phrase that best describes Bismarck's attitude toward German expansion after 1871 is
    a. German control of Europe.
    b. the annexation of Austria-Hungary to Germany.
    c. no territorial ambitions.
    d. a great German navy and German colonies.

11. The young Emperor William II of Germany made the fateful decision to reverse Bismarck's foreign policy by refusing to renew the treaty between Germany and
    a. Austria.
    b. Britain.
    c. France.
    d. Russia.

12. As a result of the Moroccan crisis, European powers viewed which of the following countries as a threat to peace and stability?
    a. France
    b. Germany
    c. Britain
    d. Japan

13. The countries with the most at stake in the Balkans and who were most fearful of nationalism were
    a. Germany and Austria.
    b. France and Turkey.
    c. Turkey and Austria.
    d. Russia and Germany.

14. The first country to mobilize in 1914 for general warfare was
    a. France.
    b. Germany.
    c. Russia.
    d. Britain.

15. The chief feature of the war on the western front was
    a. inconclusive battles fought in ceaseless trench warfare.
    b. the invasion of Germany by French and British troops.
    c. a series of German victories at the German-French border.
    d. a propaganda war with little actual fighting.

16. The major impact of World War I on economic thought was the
    a. promotion of government planning and involvement in the economy.
    b. strengthening of capitalism based on laissez-faire principles.
    c. reaffirmation of imperialism.
    d. proof that civilian populations were unimportant to the war economy.

17. For women in European society, the First World War brought about
    a. overall economic and political improvement.
    b. some economic gains but no political gains.
    c. a setback in the struggle for women's rights.
    d. a deterioration of their economic position.

18. The Petrograd Soviet's Army Order No. 1 resulted in
    a. a renewed and effective war effort.
    b. a complete breakdown of army discipline.
    c. increased authority of the Russian military elite.
    d. large numbers of new recruits.

19. Lenin's appeal to the people of Russia centered on
    a. ending the war and giving land to the peasants and power to the soviets.
    b. giving all power to the Duma.
    c. victory over Germany through renewed war effort.
    d. support of the Kornilov plot against Kerensky.

20. As a result of the Treaty of Brest-Litovsk, Russia
    a. acquired considerable territory.
    b. re-entered the war on the German side.
    c. agreed to spread the revolution to western Europe.
    d. lost one-third of its population.

21. Which of the following was *not* included in the Treaty of Versailles?
    a. A clause that placed blame for the war on Germany and her allies
    b. German colonies taken away
    c. German territory given to Poland
    d. Germany allowed to keep Alsace-Lorraine but forced to give up the city of Danzig

22. The most anti-German of the major powers represented at the Versailles treaty conference in 1919 was
    a. Clemenceau of France.
    b. Lloyd George of Britain.
    c. Wilson of the United States.
    d. Orlando of Italy.

23. The second Battle of the Marne resulted in
    a. a virtual stalemate.
    b. an impressive German victory that boosted morale at home.
    c. a Russian victory at the eastern front, but a French loss in the west.
    d. a decisive loss for the Germans.

24. This leader of the German left scorned moderate socialism and stressed the revolutionary character of Marxism.
    a. Theobald von Bethmann-Hollweg
    b. Tsarina Alexandra
    c. Rosa Luxemburg
    d. Alexander Kerensky

25. Which of the following battles resulted in a stalemate and the end of the German dream to use the Schlieffen Plan to capture France?
    a. The Battle of Verdun
    b. The first Battle of the Marne
    c. The Battle of the Somme
    d. The second Battle of the Marne

Major Political Ideas

1. What is Leninist Bolshevism? Define it by describing Lenin's principal ideas with regard to revolutionary change. How did Lenin differ from other Marxists and why, in your view, did Lenin prevail?

2. What is a soviet and what role did these organizations play in the Russian Revolution of 1917?

Issues for Essays and Discussion

The First World War has been called "the great turning point in government and society." Do you agree? Discuss this by making reference to the political, social, physical, and psychological impact of the war. Which country was most affected by the war, Russia, Austria, France, or Britain? Provide evidence to support your argument.

Interpretation of Visual Sources

Study the wartime posters on page 873 of your textbook. What is the message of the poster on the left? Is this propaganda? Why were posters such as the French one on the right necessary?

Geography

1. Study maps 27.1 and 27.2. Referring to the textbook when necessary, answer the following questions.
   a. Describe the ethnic make-up of the Balkans.
   b. Locate the extent of Ottoman (Turkish) control in the Balkans in 1878 and in 1914. Describe how and why the Turks lost territory.
   c. What were the territorial ambitions of Serbia and Austria-Hungary in the Balkans?

2. Study Map 27.3. Referring to the textbook when necessary, answer the following questions.
   a. What was the western front and where did it exist? Compare it with the eastern front.
   b. Locate the following important battles of the First World War: Gallipoli, Passchendaele, Tannenburg, and Verdun. In each case, who fought, what was the outcome, and what was the significance?
   c. Describe the German offensive of August–September 1914 and the first Battle of the Marne. What were the strengths and the weaknesses of the German military and the Schlieffen Plan?

3. Study Map 27.4 to understand some of the changes brought by the First World War. Use Outline Map 27.4 provided to answer the following questions.
   a. The boundaries of 1926 are indicated on this map. Mark the boundaries of Europe in 1914. Next, mark the location of the Polish corridor, Alsace and Lorraine, the three new Baltic states, and Galicia. What happened to each of these areas because of the First World War and what was the significance?
   b. Mark the location of the demilitarized zone along the Rhine. How did this zone strengthen the French military position?
   c. Mark the territorial losses experienced by Germany, Austria, and Russia. How did the losses reflect the principle of self-determination?
   d. Mark the location of Paris, Berlin, Warsaw, Budapest, Vienna, Belgrade, Brussels, Amsterdam, Leningrad, Danzig, Rome, Bucharest, and Sofia.

Outline Map 27.4

Understanding History Through the Arts

1. What effect did the Russian Revolution have on art? One of the most important cultural developments to emerge from the revolution in Russia was a revolution in art. What forms did this revolution take and who were its participants? Begin your research with C. Lodder, *Russian Constructivism** (1983); J. Milner, *Vladimir Tatlin and the Russian Avant-Garde** (1983); S. O. Dhan-Magomedov, *Rodchenko, The Complete Work* (1986); and S. White, *The Bolshevik Poster** (1988).

2. How was the First World War portrayed in fiction? Few books have captured the tragedy of the First World War as well as Erich Remarque's novel *All Quiet on the Western Front,** while A. Home's *The Price of Glory: Verdun 1916* (1979) recounts the horror of the western-front battle that cost 700,000 lives.

Problems for Further Investigation

1. Was Germany responsible for the Great War? The German people of the postwar era felt that they had been unjustly blamed. Some historians argue that the "war guilt" issue led to the rise of Hitler. Do you agree? This has been one of the most-debated subjects in political-diplomatic history in recent years. One of the chief revisionists is A. J. P. Taylor, *The Struggle for Mastery in Europe, 1848–1919* (1954), while an anti-German argument has come from E. Fischer, *The German War Aims in World War I* (1967). The debate is discussed in D. E. Lee, *The Outbreak of the First World War** (1970), and in R. Henig, *The Origins of the First World War* (1989).

2. What were the motives of the leaders of the Bolshevik Revolution? The problem of interpreting the revolution in Russia, current interpretations, and key themes are examined in a valuable anthology with a bibliography: R. Suny and A. Adams, *The Russian Revolution and Bolshevik Victory** (1990). The war, the hemophiliac child, Rasputin, and the murder of the royal family by the Bolsheviks are all brought together in an interesting book about Russia in the era of the revolution, *Nicholas and Alexandra** (1971) by R. Massie. Lenin's impact on history is best covered in L. Fischer, *The Life Of Lenin** (1964, 1965), and in C. Hill, *Lenin and the Russian Revolution** (1947, 1971), while the standard work on Leon Trotsky is a three-volume work (1954–1963) by I. Deutscher. Other books on the Bolshevik leaders are R. Conquest, *V. I. Lenin* (1972), and B. Wolfe, *Three Who Made a Revolution* (1955).

---

*Available in paperback.

Studying Effectively—Exercise 6

Learning to Make Historical Comparisons

An important part of studying history is learning how to *compare* two (or more) related historical developments. Such comparisons not only demonstrate a basic understanding of the two objects being compared, but also permit the student historian to draw distinctions that indicate real insight.

For these reasons, "compare-and-contrast" questions have long been favorites of history professors, and they often appear on essay exams. Even when they do not, they are an excellent study device for synthesizing historical information and testing your understanding. Therefore, as the introductory essay suggests, try to *anticipate* what compare-and-contrast questions your instructor might ask. Then work up your own study outlines that summarize the points your essay answer would discuss and develop. The preparation of study outlines, of course, is also a useful preparation for essay questions that do not require you to compare and contrast.

Exercise

Read the following brief passage. Reread it and underline or highlight it for main points. Now study the passage in terms of comparison and contrast. Prepare a brief outline (solely on the basis of this material) that will allow you to compare and contrast the Russian and German revolutions of 1917–1918. After you have finished, compare your outline with the model on the following page. Remember: the model provides a *good* answer, not the *only* answer.

The German Revolution of November 1918 resembled the Russian Revolution of March 1917. In both cases, a genuine popular uprising toppled an authoritarian monarchy and established a liberal provisional republic. In both countries, liberals and moderate socialists took control of the central government, while workers' and soldiers' councils formed a counter-government. In Germany, however, the moderate socialists won and the Lenin-like radical revolutionaries in the councils lost. In communist terms, the liberal, republican revolution in Germany in 1918 was only half a revolution: a bourgeois political revolution without a communist second installment. It was Russia without Lenin's Bolshevik triumph.

There were several reasons for the German outcome. The great majority of Marxian socialist leaders in the Social Democratic party were, as before the war, really pink and not red. They wanted to establish real political democracy and civil liberties, and they favored the gradual elimination of capitalism. They were also German nationalists, appalled by the prospect of civil war and revolutionary terror. Moreover, there was much less popular support among workers and soldiers for the extreme radicals than in Russia. Nor did the German peasantry, which already had most of the land, at least in western Germany, provide the elemental force that has driven all great modern revolutions, from the French to the Chinese.

Of crucial importance also was the fact that the moderate German Social Democrats, unlike Kerensky and company, accepted defeat and ended the war the day they took power. This act ended the decline in morale among soldiers and prevented the regular army with its conservative officer corps from disintegrating. When radicals headed by Karl Liebknecht and Rosa Luxemburg and their supporters in the councils tried to seize control of the government in Berlin in January, the moderate socialists called on the army to crush the uprising. Liebknecht and Luxemburg were arrested and then brutally murdered by army leaders, an act that caused the radicals in the Social Democratic party to break away in anger and form a pro-Lenin German Communist party shortly thereafter. Finally, even if the moderate socialists had followed Liebknecht and Luxemburg on the Leninist path, it is very unlikely they would have succeeded. Civil war in Germany would certainly have followed, and the Allies, who were already occupying western Germany according to the terms of the armistice, would have marched on to Berlin and ruled Germany directly. Historians have often been unduly hard on Germany's moderate socialists.

Comparison of Russian and German Revolutions (1917–1918)

Similarities	Differences
1. Both countries had genuine liberal revolutions. a. Russia—March 1917 b. Germany—November 1918	1. Russia had a second, radical (Bolshevik) revolution; Germany did not.
2. In both countries moderate socialists took control.	2. In Germany workers and peasants gave radicals less support than in Russia.
	3. In Germany the moderate socialists stopped the war immediately and therefore the German army, unlike the Russian army, remained intact to put down radical uprisings.

Chapter 28
The Age of Anxiety

Chapter Questions

After reading and studying this chapter you should be able to answer the following questions:

Why did so many people in the postwar era feel adrift in an uncertain world? How were the postwar feelings of crisis and anxiety reflected in Western thought, art, and culture? How did political leaders try to maintain peace and prosperity between 1919 and 1939? Why did they fail?

Chapter Summary

Because war and revolution had shattered so many traditional ideas, beliefs, and institutions, many people of the postwar era found themselves living in an age of anxiety and continuous crisis. Many developments in thought, science, and the arts after the war encouraged this crisis even further.

The first half of this chapter deals with major changes in ideas and in culture that were connected to this age of anxiety. Some of these changes began before 1900, but they became widespread only after the great upheaval of the First World War affected millions of ordinary people and opened an era of uncertainty and searching. People generally became less optimistic and had less faith in rational thinking. Radically new theories in physics associated with Albert Einstein and Werner Heisenberg took form, while Sigmund Freud's psychology gave a new and disturbing interpretation of human behavior. Philosophy and literature developed in new ways, and Christianity took on renewed meaning for thinking people. There was also great searching and experimentation in architecture, painting, and music, all of which went in new directions. Much painting became abstract, as did some music. Movies and radio programs, which offered entertainment and escape, gained enormous popularity among the general public. In short, there were revolutionary changes in thought, art, and popular culture.

The second half of this chapter discusses efforts to re-establish real peace and political stability in the troubled era after 1918. In 1923, hostility between France and Germany led to an undeclared war when French armies occupied Germany's industrial heartland, the Ruhr. This crisis was resolved, though, and followed by a period of cautious hope in international politics between 1924 and 1929. The stock market crash in the United States in 1929, however, brought renewed economic and political crisis to the Western world. Attempts to meet this crisis in the

United States, Sweden, Britain, and France were only partly successful. Thus, economic and political difficulties accompanied and reinforced the revolution in thought and culture. It was a hard time in Western society.

Study Outline

Use this outline to preview the chapter before you read a particular section in your textbook and then as a self-check to test your reading comprehension after you have read the chapter section.

I. Uncertainty in modern thought
   A. The effects of World War I
      1. Western society began to question values and beliefs that had guided it since the Enlightenment.
      2. Many people rejected the long-accepted beliefs in progress and the power of the rational mind to understand a logical universe and an orderly society.
         a. Valéry wrote about the crisis of the cruelly injured mind; to him the war ("storm") had left a "terrible uncertainty."
         b. New ideas and discoveries in philosophy, physics, psychology, and literature encouraged this general intellectual crisis.
   B. Modern philosophy
      1. The traditional belief in progress and the rational human was attacked by Nietzsche, Bergson, and Sorel before 1914.
         a. Nietzsche believed that Western civilization was in decline because of Christian humility and the overstress on rational thinking at the expense of emotion and passion; he believed that a few superior individuals—supermen—had to become the leaders of the herd of inferior men and women.
         b. Bergson added to this the idea that immediate experience and intuition are as important as rational and scientific thinking.
         c. Sorel argued that socialism, led by an elite, would succeed through a great violent strike of all working people.
      2. The two main developments in philosophy were logical empiricism (logical positivism) in English-speaking countries, and existentialism on the Continent.
         a. Logical empiricism, as defined by Wittgenstein, claimed that philosophy was nothing more than the logical clarification of thoughts–the study of language; it could not answer the great issues of the ages such as the meaning of life.
         b. Existentialism, first developed in Germany by Heidegger and Jaspers, and then by Sartre and Camus in France, stressed that humans can overcome the meaninglessness of life by individual action.
         c. Existentialism was popular in France after the Second World War because it advocated positive human action at a time of hopelessness.
   C. The revival of Christianity
      1. Before 1914, Protestant theologians, such as Schweitzer, stressed the human nature of Jesus and turned away from the supernatural aspects of his divinity; they sought to harmonize religious belief with scientific findings.

2. A revitalization of fundamental Christianity took place after the First World War.
   a. Kierkegaard was rediscovered; he had criticized the worldliness of the church and stressed commitment to a remote and majestic God.
   b. Barth stressed the imperfect and sinful nature of man and the need to accept God's truth through trust, not reason.
   c. Catholic existential theologians, such as Marcel, found new hope in religion by emphasizing the need for its hope and piety in a broken world.

D. The new physics
   1. Prior to the 1920s, science was one of the main supports of Western society's optimistic and rational world-view.
   2. The challenge to Newtonian physics by scientists such as Planck and Einstein undermined belief in constant natural laws.
      a. Plank's work with subatomic energy showed that atoms were not the basic building blocks of nature.
      b. Einstein postulated that time and space are relative, the universe is infinite, and matter and energy are interchangeable.
   3. The 1920s was the "heroic age of physics."
      a. Rutherford split the atom.
      b. Subatomic particles were identified, notably the neutron.
      c. The new physics described a universe that lacked absolute objective reality; Heisenberg claimed that instead of Newton's rational laws, there are only tendencies and probabilities.
      d. In short, science seemed to have little to do with human experience and human problems.

E. Freudian psychology
   1. Prior to Freud, it was assumed that the conscious mind processed experiences in a rational and logical way.
   2. According to Freud, human behavior is basically irrational.
      a. The key to understanding the mind is the irrational unconscious (the id), which is driven by sexual, aggressive, and pleasure-seeking desires.
      b. Behavior is a compromise between the needs of the id and the rationalizing conscious (the ego), which mediates what a person *can* do, and ingrained moral values (the superego), which tell what a person *should* do.
   3. Instinctual drives can easily overwhelm the control mechanisms; yet rational thinking and traditional moral values can cripple people with guilt and neuroses.
   4. Many interpreted Freudian thought as an encouragement of an uninhibited sex life.

F. Twentieth-century literature
   1. The postwar moods of pessimism, relativism, and alienation influenced novelists.
   2. Literature focused on the complexity and irrationality of the human mind.
   3. Writers such as Proust embraced psychological relativity—the attempt to understand oneself by looking at one's past.
   4. Novelists like Woolf, Faulkner, and Joyce adopted the stream-of-consciousness technique, in which ideas and emotions from different time periods bubble up randomly.
   5. Some literature, such as that of Spengler, Kafka, and Orwell, was anti-utopian—it predicted a future of doom.

II. Modern art and music
   A. Architecture and design
      1. The new idea of functionalism, exemplified by Loos and Le Corbusier, revolutionized architecture by emphasizing efficiency and clean lines instead of ornamentation.
      2. The Chicago school of architects, led by Sullivan, pioneered in the building of skyscrapers.
      3. Frank Lloyd Wright designed truly modern houses featuring low lines, open interiors, and mass-produced building materials.
      4. In Germany, the Bauhaus school under Gropius became the major proponent of functional and industrial forms.
         a. It combined the study of fine art with the study of applied art.
         b. The Bauhaus stressed good design for everyday life.
      5. Le Corbusier was inspired by industrial forms, while van der Rohe brought European functionalism to Chicago.
   B. Modern painting
      1. French impressionism yielded to nonrepresentational expressionism, which sought to portray the worlds of emotion and imagination, as in the works of van Gogh, Gauguin, Cézanne, and Matisse.
      2. Cubism, founded by Picasso, concentrated on zigzagging lines and overlapping planes.
      3. Nonrepresentational art turned away from nature completely; it focused on mood, not objects.
      4. Dadaism and surrealism became prominent in the 1920s and 1930s.
         a. Dadaism delighted in outrageous conduct.
         b. Surrealists, inspired by Freud, painted wild dreams and complex symbols.
         c. Picasso's great mural *Guernica* unites cubism, surrealism, and expressionism.
   C. Modern music
      1. The concept of expressionism also affected music, as in the work of Stravinsky and Berg.
      2. Some composers, led by Schönberg, abandoned traditional harmony and tonality.
   D. Movies and radio
      1. The general public embraced movies and radio enthusiastically.
      2. The movie factories and stars like Mary Pickford, Lillian Gish, Douglas Fairbanks, Rudolph Valentino, and Charlie Chaplin created a new medium and a new culture.
      3. Moviegoing became a form of escapism and the main entertainment of the masses.
      4. Radio, which became possible with Marconi's "wireless" communication and the development of the vacuum tube, permitted transmission of speech and music, but major broadcasting did not begin until 1920.
         a. Then every country established national broadcasting networks; by the late 1930s three of four households in Britain and Germany had a radio.
         b. Dictators and presidents used the radio for political propaganda.
      5. Movies also became tools of indoctrination.
         a. Eisenstein used film to dramatize the communist view of Russian history.
         b. In Germany, Riefenstahl created a propaganda film for Hitler.

III. The search for peace and political stability
  A. Germany and the Western powers
    1. Germany was the key to lasting peace, and the Germans hated the Treaty of Versailles.
    2. France believed that an economically weak Germany was necessary for its security and wanted massive reparations to repair devastated northern France.
    3. Britain needed a prosperous Germany in order to maintain the British economy.
       a. J. M. Keynes, an economist, argued that the Versailles treaty crippled the European economy and needed revision.
       b. His attack on the treaty contributed to guilt feelings about Germany in Britain.
       c. As a result, France and Britain drifted apart.
    4. When Germany refused to continue its heavy reparation payments, French and Belgian armies occupied the Ruhr (1923).
  B. The occupation of the Ruhr
    1. Since Germany would not pay gold, France wanted to collect reparations in coal, steel, and machinery.
    2. The Germans stopped work in the factories and France could not collect reparations, but the French occupation affected the German economy drastically.
       a. Inflation skyrocketed.
       b. Resentment and political unrest among the Germans grew.
    3. Under Stresemann, Germany agreed to revised reparations payments and France withdrew its troops, but many Germans were left financially ruined and humiliated.
  C. Hope in foreign affairs (1924–1929)
    1. The Dawes Plan (1924) provided a solution to the reparations problem: the United States loaned money to Germany so it could pay France and Britain so they could pay the United States.
    2. In 1929 the Young Plan further reduced German reparations.
    3. The treaties of Locarno (1925) eased European disputes.
       a. Germany and France accepted their common border.
       b. Britain and Italy agreed to fight if either country invaded the other.
    4. The Kellogg-Briand Pact (1928) condemned war, and the signing states agreed to settle international disputes peacefully.
  D. Hope in democratic government
    1. After 1923, democracy seemed to take root in Germany as the economy boomed.
    2. However, there were sharp political divisions in the country.
       a. The right consisted of nationalists and monarchists.
       b. The communists remained active on the left.
       c. Most working-class people supported the socialist Social Democrats.
    3. In France, the democratically elected government rested in the hands of the middle-class-oriented moderates, while Communists and Socialists battled for the support of the workers.
    4. Northern France was rebuilt, and Paris became the world's cultural center.
    5. Britain's major problem was unemployment, and the government's efforts to ease it led the country gradually toward state-sponsored welfare plans.
       a. Britain's Labour party, committed to revisionist socialism, replaced the Liberals as the main opposition party to the Conservatives.

        b. Labour, under MacDonald, won in 1924 and 1929, yet moved toward socialism gradually.

IV. The Great Depression (1929–1939)

    A. The economic crisis

        1. The depression began with the American stock market crash (October 1929).

            a. Many investors and speculators had bought stocks on margin (paying only a small part of the purchase price and borrowing the rest from their stockbrokers).

            b. When prices started to fall, thousands of people had to sell their shares at once to pay their brokers, and a financial panic started.

        2. Financial crisis led to a decline in production in first the United States and then Europe and an unwise turn to protective tariffs.

        3. The absence of international leadership and poor national economic policies added to the depression.

    B. Mass unemployment

        1. As production decreased, workers lost their jobs and had no money to buy goods, which cut production even more.

        2. Mass unemployment also caused great social and psychological problems.

    C. The New Deal in the United States

        1. Roosevelt's goal was to preserve capitalism through reform.

        2. Government intervention in and regulation of the economy first took place through the National Recovery Administration (NRA), whose goal was to reduce competition and fix prices and wages for everyone's benefit.

        3. The NRA was declared unconstitutional (1935), and Roosevelt decided to attack the problem of mass unemployment directly by using the federal government to employ as many people as possible.

            a. The Work Projects Administration (1935) employed millions of people.

            b. It was very popular and helped check the threat of social revolution.

        4. Other social measures, such as social security and government support for labor unions, also eased the hardships of the depression.

        5. Although the New Deal helped, it failed to pull the United States out of the depression.

            a. Some believe Roosevelt should have nationalized industry so national economic planning could have worked.

            b. Many economists argued that the New Deal did not put enough money into the economy through deficit financing.

    D. The Scandinavian response to depression

        1. Backed by a strong tradition of community cooperation, socialist parties were firmly established in Sweden and Norway by the 1920s.

        2. Deficit spending to finance public works and create jobs was used to check unemployment and revive the economy after 1929.

        3. Scandinavia's welfare socialism, though it depended on a large bureaucracy and high taxes, offered an appealing middle way between capitalism and communism or fascism in the 1930s.

    E. Recovery and reform in Britain and France

        1. Britain's concentration on its national market aided its economic recovery.

        2. Government instability in France prevented recovery and needed reform.

a. The Socialists, led by Blum, became the strongest party in France, and his Popular Front government attempted New Deal–type reforms.
b. France was drawn to the brink of civil war, and Blum was forced to resign (1937), leaving the country to drift aimlessly.

Review Questions

Check your understanding of this chapter by answering the following questions.

1. Describe how Nietzsche, Bergson, and Sorel began the revolt against the idea of progress and the general faith in the rational human mind. How did Wittgenstein add to this belief?
2. What does Sartre's statement that "man is condemned to be free" mean? How is this thought connected to the existential belief that man must seek to define himself?
3. What impact did the loss of faith in reason and progress have on twentieth-century Christian thought?
4. Define *quanta* and explain its implications for the definition of matter and energy.
5. Define and discuss the relationship among the id, ego, and superego.
6. Freud's view that human beings are basically irrational coincides with the picture of the universe drawn by modern physics. Discuss this relationship between psychology and science.
7. What was the stream-of-consciousness technique and how was it used in twentieth-century literature?
8. Compare and contrast Gauguin's and Le Corbusier's concepts of art.
9. How do impressionism and expressionism reflect the rationality and irrationality of the nineteenth and twentieth centuries, respectively?
10. What influence did Freud have on twentieth-century painting?
11. What was the political impact of radio and film?
12. What were the attitudes of Britain, France, and Germany toward the Treaty of Versailles?
13. The most serious international crisis of the 1920s occurred in the Ruhr in January 1923. What was the crisis and what were its consequences?
14. What part was played by the United States in the economic and political settlements of the mid-1920s in Europe?
15. What problems faced the British governments of the 1920s and with what ideas did the Labour party approach these problems?
16. Discuss the origins, interests, and goals of the Labor and Liberal parties in Britain.
17. What were the causes of the Great Depression?
18. What was the effect of the recall of public and private loans to European countries?
19. What was the NRA and why did it not work well?
20. The New Deal ultimately failed to halt mass unemployment. Why? Why is it said that the WPA helped prevent social revolution in the United States?
21. Why was the Scandinavian response to the economic crisis the most successful one in the Western democracies?

Study-Review Exercises

Identify and explain the significance of the following people and terms.

Gustav Stresemann

Ramsay MacDonald

"Little Entente" of 1921

Ruhr crisis of 1923

Locarno meetings of 1925

Munich beer hall "revolution" of 1923

principle of uncertainty

French Popular Front

National Recovery Administration

BBC

Raymond Poincaré

John Maynard Keynes

Guglielmo Marconi

Leni Riefenstahl

Sergei Eisenstein

Kellogg-Briand Pact, 1928

Adolf Hitler

Explain who the following people were and note how their work contributed to and reflected the uncertainty and anxiety in modern thought.

Paul Valéry

Friedrich Nietzsche

Georges Sorel

Henri Bergson

Ludwig Wittgenstein

Jean-Paul Sartre

Max Planck

Albert Einstein

Ernest Rutherford

Werner Heisenberg

Sigmund Freud

James Joyce

Marcel Proust

George Orwell

Oswald Spengler

Define the following philosophic and artistic schools and movements by describing their basic aims and characteristics and naming some participants and works.

logical empiricism

modern existentialism

functionalism in architecture

Chicago school of architecture

expressionism in painting

cubism

dadaism

surrealism

expressionism in music

atonality in music

Test your understanding of the chapter by providing the correct answers.

1. Most modern (postimpressionist) artistic movements *were/were not* concerned with the visible world of fact.

2. The Dawes Plan provided that _____ would get loans from the United States to pay reparations to _____ and _____ so that they could repay their loans to _____ .

3. The French poet and critic who wrote that "almost all the affairs of men remain in terrible uncertainty. We think of what has disappeared, and we are almost destroyed by what has been destroyed." _____

4. After 1914, people tended to *strengthen/discard* their belief in progress.

5. The works of modern physics tended to *confirm/challenge* the dependable laws of Newton.

6. The British economist who criticized the Versailles treaty and advocated a "counter-cyclical policy" to deal with depressed economies. _____

Multiple-Choice Questions

1. The country most interested in strict implementation of the Treaty of Versailles was
    a. France.
    b. Britain.
    c. the United States.
    d. Italy.

2. Which one of the following occurred during the early years of the Great Depression?
    a. Most countries went on the gold standard.
    b. Most countries raised tariffs.
    c. Americans issued massive loans to European states.
    d. Most governments increased their budgets and spending.

3. Which of the following countries was the most effective in dealing with the depression?
    a. France
    b. Britain
    c. Sweden
    d. The United States

4. Existentialists believed that
    a. the world was perfectible.
    b. only God was certain in this lost world.
    c. human beings can conquer life's absurdity.
    d. no human action can bring meaning to life.

5. The trend in literature in the postwar period was
   a. toward a new faith in God and mankind.
   b. the glorification of the state.
   c. the new belief in a world of growing desolation.
   d. utopian dreams of the future.

6. The German philosopher Friedrich Nietzsche believed that Western civilization
   a. had lost its creativity by neglecting emotion.
   b. should be rebuilt around Christian morality.
   c. needed to increase political democracy.
   d. should place more stress on social equality.

7. The modern, or international, style in architecture emphasized
   a. practical and functional construction.
   b. freedom from town planning.
   c. massive exterior ornamentation.
   d. separation of fine from applied arts.

8. The British economist J. M. Keynes argued that to ensure lasting peace and prosperity in Europe after World War I emphasis should be placed on
   a. a powerful France and Russia.
   b. the growth of the British Empire.
   c. the enforcement of the Treaty of Versailles.
   d. a prosperous and strong Germany.

9. Which of the following was *not* a cause of the Great Depression?
   a. Financial panic in the United States
   b. The absence of world financial leadership
   c. Unemployment
   d. The reduction of national spending

10. The British Labour party leader and prime minister in 1924 and 1929 was
    a. MacDonald.
    b. Blum.
    c. Sartre.
    d. Keynes.

11. The "spirit of Locarno" after 1924 was a general feeling in Europe that
    a. the communist overthrow of European governments was inevitable.
    b. Germany must be forced to pay her original reparation debts.
    c. European peace and security were possible.
    d. Hitler would bring about the recovery of Germany.

12. The decade following World War I was generally a period of
    a. uncertainty and dissatisfaction with established ideas.
    b. increasing belief in the goodness and perfectibility of humanity.
    c. emphasis on the idea that a new science and technology would build a more democratic and liberal world.
    d. religious revival based on the human nature of Christ and the basic goodness of human beings.

13. The philosophy of logical empiricism held that
    a. great philosophical issues can never be decided.
    b. humanity must accept all truths as being absolute.
    c. humanity is basically sinful.
    d. there is no God.

14. The writings of Virginia Woolf, Marcel Proust, James Joyce, and William Faulkner all reflect the postwar concern with
    a. the reconstruction of society.
    b. an attempt to discover the reasons for the loss of faith in God.
    c. the conflict between materialism and spiritualism.
    d. the complexity and irrationality of the human mind.

15. Modern painting grew out of a revolt against
    a. classicism.
    b. capitalism.
    c. French impressionism.
    d. German romanticism.

16. The movement in painting that attacked all accepted standards of art and behavior and delighted in outrageous conduct was
    a. the Bauhaus movement.
    b. brutalism.
    c. dadaism.
    d. cubism.

17. The great maker of Nazi propaganda films in Germany was
    a. Sergei Eisenstein.
    b. Mack Sennett.
    c. Alban Berg.
    d. Leni Riefenstahl.

18. For the people of Britain, the greatest problem of the 1920s was
    a. increased class tension.
    b. the Irish problem.
    c. the rise of socialist dictatorship.
    d. unemployment.

19. The antifascist movement in France in 1936–37, led by Leon Blum, was known as the
    a. Radical Alliance.
    b. Communist Coalition.
    c. Popular Front.
    d. New Deal Republic.

20. In January 1923 the German Ruhr was occupied by
    a. Russia.
    b. France.
    c. Britain.
    d. Austria.

21. The main entertainment of the masses until the Second World War was
    a. football.
    b. motion pictures.
    c. the music hall.
    d. the pub.

22. After 1914, religion became
    a. less popular and was largely abandoned.
    b. more interested in a reconciliation with science.
    c. more relevant and meaningful to thinking people than before the war.
    d. less occupied with spiritual matters and more worldly.

23. Surrealism in painting was inspired to a great extent by
    a. ordinary visual reality.
    b. traditional landscape painting and attention to historical accuracy.
    c. the movement to deny the concepts of anxiety and alienation.
    d. Freudian psychology.

24. The British Labour party was strongly tied to the idea of
    a. competitive capitalism.
    b. limited government control.
    c. democracy and a gradual move toward socialism.
    d. revolution and the rejection of revisionist socialism.

25. With Russia no longer a possible ally, France turned to which of the following for diplomatic support in the 1920s?
    a. Italy
    b. The new eastern European states
    c. Germany
    d. Turkey

Major Political Ideas

1. One of the most controversial political ideas in the 1920s was John Maynard Keynes's argument that the Treaty of Versailles was harsh and foolish in its treatment of Germany. Do you agree? What positions did the French, Germans, and British take on this issue?

2. The 1920s saw democracy in both Germany and France undergo considerable strain, but relative harmony in Britain. Describe the various political parties in each of these nations. Who supported them, and what were their objectives?

Issues for Essays and Discussion

1. The period from 1919 to 1939 was one of both hope and anxiety. Discuss this period by describing the events and ideas that pointed to a better world. What forces and events pointed in the other direction? What, in your view, were the factors that pushed Europe in the direction of another war?

2. After about 1919, European (and American) society witnessed an unprecedented upheaval in thought and the arts. What were some of these developments and how did they reflect postwar society? Make sure you mention developments in philosophy, religion, psychology, music, architecture, and painting.

Interpretation of Visual Sources

1. Study the illustration entitled *Guernica"* on page 903 of your textbook. Describe the event and then describe how Picasso used expressionism, cubism, and surrealism in this painting.

2. Study the poster entitled "Hands Off the Ruhr" that is reproduced on page 907 of your textbook. Describe the event it portrays (you may need to refer to your textbook discussion of the Ruhr crisis). What does the female figure symbolize? What is she doing and to whom? Is this poster (1) a true indication of German public opinion? and (2) a true indication of what really happened? (You may wish to refer to Map 27.4, which shows the general area of the Ruhr.)

Understanding History Through the Arts

1. What can we learn about the age of anxiety from the novels of the period? The message of existentialist philosophy is movingly told in Albert Camus's *The Myth of Sisyphus*,* and the Paris Gertrude Stein claimed was "where the twentieth century was" is the subject of Ernest Hemingway's *A Moveable Feast** and Janet Flanner's *Paris Was Yesterday** (1972). The text

---

*Available in paperback.

bibliography lists a number of excellent books, including several on life during the depression. George Orwell's *Animal Farm** and *1984** are classics for good reason, and his *Road to Wigan Pier** is a view of British working-class life in the era of the Great Depression.

2. What are the distinguishing characteristics of modern architecture? Functionalism in architecture (including the Chicago school) is treated in N. Pevsner, *Pioneers of Modern Design** (1960). The international style and the Bauhaus leader who made Chicago the most important architectural center in America are the subjects of P. Blacke, *Mies van de Rohe: Architecture and Structure** (1964), and more recently, F. Schulze, *Mies van der Rohe, A Critical Biography* (1985). An important Dutch movement in design is covered in C. Blotkamp et al., *De Stijl: The Formative Years** (1986, 1990). An excellent review of Le Corbusier's buildings and his writings is found in S. von Moos, *Le Corbusier** (1985), and the aims and achievements of the German Bauhaus movement are examined in H. Wingler, *Bauhaus: Weimar, Dessau, Berlin, Chicago** (1978), and in two books by G. Naylor: *The Bauhaus** (1968) and *The Bauhaus Re-assessed** (1985). A revolution in photography is covered in E. Marzona and R. Fricke, eds., *Bauhaus Photography* (1987). For a more critical view, perhaps the most famous and the most outspoken critic of modern functionalist architecture and urban planning is the Prince of Wales, whose book on the subject is *A Vision of Britain, A Personal View of Architecture* (1989).

3. How was film used for propaganda in this period? One of the most chilling examples of the use of film for the ideological transformation of a country is Leni Riefenstahl's documentary *The Triumph of the Will*, showing the 1934 Nazi party rally at Nuremburg. It reveals a great deal about what Nazis wanted to believe about themselves and their leader, Adolf Hitler. It is available on video film.

Problems for Further Investigation

1. How did events following the First World War lead to the Second World War? Those interested in the complexities of interwar economic history will find B. W. E. Alford, *Depression and Recovery: British Economic Growth, 1918–1939** (1972), a short and readable discussion of a number of interpretations of the British economy. The Versailles treaty is dealt with in the Problems in European History book *The Versailles Settlement** (1960), edited by I. J. Lederer.

2. What was daily life like in this period? The dramatic changes in domestic life, sport, amusement, politics, sex, and other aspects of life in the twenty-one-year period between the two great wars make a stimulating subject for student research. Begin your investigation with R. Graves and A. Hodge, *The Long Week End, A Social History of Great Britain, 1918–1939** (1940, 1963). For two aspects of the so-called sex revolution of the interwar era, see R. Bridenthal, "Something Old, Something New: Women Between the Two World Wars," in R. Bridenthal et al., *Becoming Visible: Women in European History* (1987), and J. Steakley, *The Homosexual Emancipation Movement in Germany* (1975).

---

*Available in paperback.

Chapter 29
Dictatorships and the Second World War

Chapter Questions

After reading and studying this chapter you should be able to answer the following questions:

What are the characteristics of the twentieth-century totalitarian state? How did the totalitarian state affect ordinary people and how did it lead to another war? How did the great coalition, called the Grand Alliance, defeat Germany and its allies? What were the strengths and weaknesses of this alliance?

Chapter Summary

The anxiety and crisis that followed the First World War contributed to the rise of powerful dictatorships in parts of Europe, and, unfortunately, an even more horrible Second World War. Some of these dictatorships were old-fashioned and conservative, but there were new totalitarian dictatorships as well, notably in Soviet Russia and Nazi Germany. This chapter examines the different kinds of dictatorship in a general way and then looks at Stalin's Russia and Hitler's Germany in detail. It goes on to describe the Second World War and why and how the great coalition of the Soviet Union, Britain, and the United States defeated Germany and its allies.

In Soviet Russia, Lenin relaxed rigid state controls in 1921 after the civil war in order to revive the economy. After defeating Trotsky in a struggle for power, Stalin established a harsh totalitarian dictatorship, which demanded great sacrifices from the people. Soviet Russia built up its industry while peasants lost their land and a radically new socialist society came into being. Mussolini's government in Italy was much less radical and totalitarian.

This chapter then examines Adolf Hitler and the totalitarian government of the Nazis in Germany. The roots of Nazism are found in racism, extreme nationalism, and violent irrationality, all of which drove Hitler relentlessly. Hitler was also a master politician, and this helped him gain power legally. His government was popular, especially because it appeared to solve the economic problems of the Great Depression. Hitler also had the support of many of the German people because of his success in foreign affairs. He used bullying and fears of communism in Britain and France to rearm and expand, until finally war broke out over Poland in 1939. By 1942, Hitler and the Nazis had temporarily forged a great empire and were putting their anti-Jewish racism into operation.

The Grand Alliance, consisting of the Soviet Union, Britain, and the United States, was able to wage a successful war against Hitler partly because it postponed political questions and adopted the principle of unconditional surrender of Germany and Japan, and partly because of the great and heroic contributions of the British and Soviet peoples and American resources. The beginning of the end for Germany came in 1942, when its offensive into the Soviet Union was turned into a retreat, and the end, became certain in 1944, when the American and British forces began to push into Hitler's empire from the west.

Study Outline

Use this outline to preview the chapter before you read a particular section in your textbook and then as a self-check to test your reading comprehension after you have read the chapter section.

I. Authoritarianism and totalitarianism in Europe after the First World War
   A. Conservative authoritarianism
      1. Conservative authoritarianism had deep roots in European history and led to an antidemocratic form of government that believed in avoiding change but was limited in its power and objectives.
      2. Conservative authoritarianism revived after the First World War in eastern Europe, Spain, and Portugal.
         a. These countries lacked a strong tradition of self-government.
         b. Many were torn by ethnic conflicts.
         c. Large landowners and the church looked to dictators to save them from land reform.
      3. The new authoritarian governments were more concerned with maintaining the status quo than with forcing society into rapid change.
   B. Modern totalitarianism
      1. Modern totalitarianism emerged from the First World War and the Russian civil war, when individual liberties were subordinated to a total war effort.
      2. Nothing was outside of the control of the totalitarian state: it was a dictatorship that used modern technology and communications to try to control the political, economic, social, intellectual, and cultural components of its subjects' lives.
      3. Unlike old-fashioned authoritarianism, which was based on elites, modern totalitarianism was based on the masses.
      4. Totalitarian regimes believed in mobilizing society toward some great goal.
   C. Totalitarianism of the left and right
      1. In Stalinist Russia, the leftists prevailed; private property was taken over by the state, and the middle class lost its status and power.
      2. In Nazi Germany, private property was maintained.
II. Stalin's Russia
   A. From Lenin to Stalin
      1. By 1921, the economy of Russia had been destroyed.
      2. In 1921, Lenin's New Economic Policy (NEP) re-established limited economic freedom in an attempt to rebuild agriculture and industry.

       a. Peasants bought and sold goods on the free market.

       b. Agricultural production grew, and industrial production surpassed the prewar level.

  3. Economic recovery and Lenin's death in 1924 brought a struggle for power between Stalin and Trotsky, which Stalin won.

       a. Stalin met the ethnic demands for independence within the multinational Soviet state by granting minority groups limited freedoms.

       b. Stalin's theory of "socialism in one country," or Russia building its own socialist society, was more attractive to many Communists than Trotsky's theory of "permanent revolution," or the overthrow of other European states.

  4. By 1927, Stalin had crushed all opposition and was ready to launch an economic-social revolution.

B. The five-year plans

  1. The first five-year plan (1928) to increase industrial and agricultural production was extremely ambitious, but Stalin wanted to erase the NEP, spur the economy, and catch up with the West.

  2. Stalin waged a preventive war against the better-off peasants, the kulaks, to bring them and their land under state control.

       a. Collectivization of the peasants' land—forcible consolidation of individual peasant farms into large, state-controlled enterprises—resulted in disaster for agriculture and unparalled human tragedy.

       b. But it was a political victory for Stalin and the Communist party, as the peasants were eliminated as a potential threat.

  3. The five-year plans brought about a spectacular growth of heavy industry, especially with the aid of government control of the workers and foreign technological experts.

  4. Massive investment in heavy industry, however, meant low standards of living for workers.

C. Life in Stalinist society

  1. The Communists wanted to create a new kind of society and human personality.

  2. Stalin's reign of terror and mass purges created fear and eliminated any opposition.

  3. Propaganda and indoctrination were common features of life, and even art and literature became highly political.

  4. Life was hard, but people were often inspired by socialist ideals and did gain some social benefits and the possibility of personal advancement through education.

D. Women in Soviet Russia

  1. Women were given much greater opportunities in industry and education.

       a. The 1917 revolution proclaimed complete equality of rights for women.

       b. In the 1920s, divorce and abortion were made easy, and women were urged to work outside the home and liberate themselves sexually.

  2. Medicine and other professions were opened to them.

  3. Most women had to work to help support their families in addition to caring for the home and the children.

III. Mussolini's Italy
  A. The fascist seizure of power
    1. The First World War and postwar problems ended the move toward democracy in Italy.
    2. By 1922, most Italians were opposed to liberal, parliamentary government.
    3. Mussolini's Fascists opposed the "Socialist threat" with physical force (the Black Shirts).
    4. Mussolini marched on Rome in 1922 and forced the king to name him head of the government.
  B. The regime in action
    1. Mussolini's Fascists manipulated elections and killed the Socialist leader Matteotti.
    2. Between 1924 and 1926, Mussolini built a one-party Fascist dictatorship but did not establish a fully totalitarian state.
      a. Much of the old power structure remained, particularly the conservatives, who controlled the army, economy, and state.
      b. The Catholic church supported Mussolini because he recognized the Vatican as an independent state and gave the church heavy financial support.
      c. Women were repressed, but Jews were not persecuted until late in the Second World War.
IV. Hitler's Germany
  A. The roots of Nazism
    1. Hitler became a fanatical nationalist while in Vienna, where he absorbed anti-Semitic and racist ideas.
    2. He believed that Jews and Marxists lost the First World War for Germany.
    3. By 1921, he had reshaped the tiny extremist German Workers' group into the Nazi party using the mass rally as a particularly effective tool of propaganda.
      a. The party grew rapidly.
      b. Hitler and the party attempted to overthrow the Weimar government, but he was defeated and sent to jail (1923).
  B. Hitler's road to power
    1. The trial after Hitler's attempted coup brought him much publicity, but the Nazi party remained small until 1929.
    2. Written in jail, his autobiography, *Mein Kampf*, was an outline of his desire to achieve German racial supremacy and domination of Europe, under the leadership of a dictator (Führer).
    3. The depression made the Nazi party attractive to the lower middle class and to young people, who were seized by panic as unemployment soared and Communists made election gains.
    4. By 1932, the Nazi party was the largest in the Reichstag.
    5. The Weimar government's orthodox economic policies intensified the economic collapse and convinced the middle class that its leaders were incompetent; hence, they welcomed Hitler's attacks on the republican system.
    6. The Communists refused to ally with the Social Democrats to block Hitler.
    7. Hitler was a skilled politician, a master of propaganda and mass psychology who generated enormous emotional support with his speeches.
    8. Hitler was legally appointed chancellor in 1933.

C. The Nazi state and society
   1. The Enabling Act of March 1933 gave Hitler absolute dictatorial power.
   2. Nazis took over every aspect of German life—political, social, economic, cultural, and intellectual.
      a. Germany became a one-party state—only the Nazi party was legal.
      b. Strikes were forbidden and labor unions abolished.
      c. Publishing houses and universities were brought under Nazi control, and life became violently anti-intellectual.
   3. Hitler took over total control of the military by purging the storm troopers.
   4. The Gestapo, or secret police, used terror and purges to strengthen Hitler's hold on power.
   5. Hitler set out to eliminate the Jews.
      a. The Nuremberg Laws (1935) deprived Jews of their citizenship.
      b. Jews were constant victims of violence and outrages.
D. Hitler's popularity
   1. Hitler promised and delivered economic recovery through public works projects and military spending.
   2. Hitler reduced Germany's traditional class distinctions.
   3. He appealed to Germans for nationalistic reasons.
   4. Communists, trade unionists, and some Christians opposed Hitler; many who opposed him were executed.
V. Nazi expansion and the Second World War
   A. Aggression and appeasement (1933–1939)
      1. Hitler's main goal was territorial expansion for the superior German race.
         a. He withdrew from the League of Nations in 1933.
         b. An Anglo-German naval agreement in 1935 broke Germany's isolation.
         c. In violation of the Treaty of Versailles, Hitler occupied the demilitarized Rhineland in 1936.
      2. The British policy of appeasement, motivated by both guilt and pacifism, lasted far into 1939.
      3. Mussolini attacked Ethiopia in 1935 and joined Germany in supporting the fascists in Spain.
      4. Germany, Italy, and Japan formed an alliance.
      5. Hitler annexed Austria and demanded part of Czechoslovakia in 1938.
      6. Chamberlain flew to Munich to appease Hitler and agree to his territorial demands.
      7. Hitler accelerated his aggression and occupied all of Czechoslovakia in 1939.
      8. In 1939, Hitler and Stalin signed a public nonaggression pack and a secret pact that divided eastern Europe into German and Russian zones.
      9. Germany attacked Poland, and Britain and France declared war on Germany (1939).
   B. Hitler's empire (1939–1942)
      1. The key to Hitler's military success was speed and force (the blitzkrieg).
      2. He crushed Poland quickly and then France; by July 1940 the Nazis ruled nearly all of Europe except Britain.
      3. He bombed British cities in an attempt to break British morale but did not succeed.

4. In 1941 Hitler's forces invaded Russia and conquered the Ukraine and got as far as Leningrad and Moscow until stopped by the severe winter weather.
5. After Japan attacked Pearl Harbor (1941) Hitler also declared war on the United States.
6. Hitler began building a New Order based on racial imperialism.
   a. Nordic peoples were treated with preference; the French were heavily taxed; the Slavs were treated as "subhumans."
   b. The S.S. evacuated Polish peasants to create a German "settlement space."
   c. Polish workers and Russian prisoners of war did most of the heavy labor.
   d. Jews, gypsies, Jehovah's witnesses, and communists were condemned to death—six million Jews were murdered in concentration camps.
C. The Grand Alliance
   1. The allies had three policies that led them to victory.
      a. The United States concentrated on European victory first, then Japan.
      b. The Americans and British put military needs before political questions, thus avoiding conflict over postwar settlements.
      c. The Allies adopted the principle of "unconditional surrender" of Germany and Japan, denying Hitler the possibility of dividing his foes.
   2. American aid to Britain and the Soviets, along with the heroic support of the British and Soviet peoples and the assistance of resistance groups throughout Europe, contributed to the eventual victory.
D. The tide of battle
   1. The Germans were defeated at Stalingrad at the end of 1942, and from there on the Soviets took the offensive.
   2. At the same time American, British, and Australian victories in the Pacific put Japan on the defensive.
      a. The Battle of the Coral Sea (1942) stopped the Japanese advance.
      b. The Battle of Midway Island (1942) established American naval superiority in the Pacific.
   3. The British defeat of Rommel at the Battle of El Alamein (1942) helped drive the Axis powers from North Africa in 1943.
   4. Italy surrendered in 1943, but fighting continued as the Germans seized Rome and northern Italy.
   5. Bombing of Germany and Hitler's brutal elimination of opposition caused the Germans to fight on.
   6. The British and Americans invaded German-held France in June 1944, but did not cross into Germany until March 1945.
      a. The Soviets pushed from the east, crossing the Elbe and meeting the Americans on the other side on April 26, 1945; Hitler committed suicide, and Germany surrendered on May 7, 1945.
      b. The United States dropped two atomic bombs on Japan in August 1945, and it too surrendered.

Review Questions

Check your understanding of this chapter by answering the following questions.

1. Why did conservative authoritarian governments develop in Poland, Hungary, Yugoslavia, and Portugal?
2. What are the characteristics of modern totalitarianism? How does it differ from conservative authoritarianism?
3. What was the purpose of Lenin's New Economic Policy?
4. How successful was Stalin's program of five-year plans for the industrialization of Soviet Russia? What were its strengths and weaknesses?
5. How does one explain that despite a falling standard of living, many Russians in the 1920s and 1930s willingly worked harder and were happy?
6. Generally, did women gain or lose status and power in the new Stalinist Russian state?
7. What were the circumstances under which Mussolini rose to power in Italy? What were his goals and tactics?
8. Many Germans in the 1920s and 1930s viewed Hitler as a reformer. What were his ideas about the problems and the future of Germany?
9. How did the Great Depression affect German political life?
10. What was the role of mass propaganda and psychology in Hitler's rise to power?
11. Why did Hitler acquire such a mass appeal? Did he improve German life?
12. Describe the Munich Conference of 1938 and Chamberlain's policy of appeasement. Why were so many British willing to appease Hitler? What was the result of the Munich Conference?
13. What was Hitler's foreign and military policy up to 1938? Was there enough evidence of aggression to convince the world that Hitler was dangerous?
14. What was the "final solution of the Jewish question"?
15. Describe German-Soviet relations between 1939 and 1941. Was war between the two inevitable?
16. What were the strengths of the Grand Alliance?
17. How did the Allies finally defeat Hitler?

Study-Review Exercises

Define the following key concepts and terms.

Hitler's final solution

modern totalitarianism

"socialism in one country"

appeasement

fascism

anti-Semitism

Identify and explain the significance of the following people and terms.
Weimar Republic

National Socialist German Workers' party

Benito Mussolini

Leon Trotsky

General Paul Hindenburg

Neville Chamberlain

kulaks

Nazi Storm Troopers (the SA)

Joseph Goebbels

German Social Democrats

Explain what the following events were, who participated in them, and why they were important.
Stalin's collectivization program

Lenin's New Economic Policy (1921)

Mussolini's march on Rome (1922)

Hitler's Munich plot (1923)

Great Depression in Germany (1929–1933)

Munich Conference (1938)

Russio-German ("Nazi-Soviet") nonaggression pact (1939)

Stalin's five-year plans

Grand Alliance

Battle of Stalingrad, 1942

Battle of El Alamein, 1942

Battle of the Coral Sea, 1942

Normandy invasion, June 6, 1944

Hiroshima and Nagasaki

Test your understanding of the chapter by providing the correct answers.

1. Unlike his rival Trotsky, Stalin *favored/opposed* the policy of "socialism in one country."

2. In Germany, the Communists *agreed/refused* to cooperate with the Social Democrats in opposition to Hitler.

3. Stalin's forced collectivization of peasant farms was a political *victory/failure* and an economic *success/disaster*.

4. Hitler's Nazi party ruled a modern totalitarian state of the *right/left*.

5. Totalitarian states of the right usually *do/do not* advocate state takeover of private property.

6. He was an antisocialist and the leader of the Italian Black Shirts. _____

7. Lenin's New Economic Policy *was/was* not a return to capitalism.

8. He was legally appointed chancellor of Germany in 1933. _____

9. The standard of living of the average Russian worker in the 1930s *improved/declined* as a result of Stalin's five-year plans.

10. The foreign policy of Prime Minister Chamberlain tended to be *pro-German/anti-German.*

11. Mussolini's Italy *did/did not* have all the characteristics of a modern totalitarian state.

Multiple-Choice Questions

1. The Nuremberg laws related to
   a. antidepression programs.
   b. the Versailles treaty.
   c. the elimination of the fascists.
   d. Jewish citizenship.

2. The Vichy government of 1940 was established in
   a. Poland.
   b. Germany.
   c. Czechoslovakia.
   d. France.

3. Which of the following was *not* a modern totalitarian state in the 1930s?
   a. Germany
   b. Italy
   c. Russia
   d. France

4. The two countries in which modern totalitarianism reached its most complete form in the 1930s were
   a. Russia and Germany.
   b. Italy and France.
   c. Germany and Italy.
   d. Russia and Italy.

5. Before the modern totalitarian state, the traditional form of antidemocratic government in Europe was
   a. conservative authoritarianism.
   b. absolutism.
   c. republicanism.
   d. military government.

6. The modern totalitarian state is
   a. lethargic in its approach.
   b. built on elite groups.
   c. concerned only with survival.
   d. characterized by rapid and profound changes.

7. Lenin's New Economic Policy of 1921
   a. nationalized industries.
   b. called for the collectivization of agriculture.
   c. restored limited economic freedom.
   d. set five-year goals.

8. Before Lenin died, he named which of the following as his successor?
   a. Stalin
   b. Trotsky
   c. No one
   d. Dzhugashvili

9. Stalin became Lenin's successor because he
   a. was chosen by Lenin.
   b. was able to work outside the party.
   c. successfully related Russian realities to Marxist teachings.
   d. devised a system whereby minorities enjoyed total freedom.

10. Stalin's plans for rapid industrialization were based on
    a. importing coal from Japan.
    b. factories staffed exclusively by party members.
    c. depriving peasants in order to feed workers.
    d. a huge domestic market for consumer goods.

11. Under Stalin, women's greatest real benefits were
    a. sexual liberation and abortion.
    b. easy divorce and day-care centers.
    c. work freedom and accessible education.
    d. easier work than in the past and freedom from family worries.

12. Most Germans reacted to Hitler's purge of Jews with
    a. hostility and anger.
    b. protests and demonstrations.
    c. apathy and indifference.
    d. joy and celebration.

13. Which of the following characterized Stalinist society?
    a. Very slow economic and industrial growth
    b. The encouragement of religion
    c. The politicization of art and literature
    d. Large-scale discrimination against women in the job market

14. For Italian women, the fascist regime of Mussolini meant
    a. no improvement and a probable decline in status.
    b. considerable gains, especially in finding new careers in industry.
    c. more birth control and better-paying jobs.
    d. greater political participation and legal rights.

15. The social class within German society to whom Hitler appealed most was the
    a. industrial working class.
    b. poor.
    c. Jewish banking class.
    d. middle class.

16. Which of the following would have most likely supported Hitler?
    a. Communists
    b. Social Democrats
    c. Conservatives
    d. Nationalists

17. Conservative authoritarianism differs from modern totalitarianism in that it
    a. did not result in dictatorships.
    b. allowed popular participation in government.
    c. was more concerned with maintaining the status quo than with rapid change or war.
    d. did not persecute liberals or socialists.

18. Which of the following countries experienced a revival of conservative authoritarianism in the 1920s?
    a. Hungary
    b. Russia
    c. France
    d. Germany

19. In essence, the totalitarian state was
    a. a form of liberalism.
    b. an extension of the dictatorial state.
    c. a rigid, conservative society rooted in tradition.
    d. a form of government built on the power of the elite.

20. One major reason for British appeasement of Hitler was that
    a. he was seen as a way to block German capitalist expansion.
    b. he was seen as the bulwark against communism.
    c. the British government was prosocialist.
    d. Britain wanted time to prepare for war.

21. The Russians defeated the Germans at
    a. Leningrad.
    b. Brest-Litovsk.
    c. Stalingrad.
    d. El Alamein.

22. Prior to June 1944, most of the fighting against Germany on the Continent was carried out by
    a. France.
    b. Britain.
    c. the Soviet Union.
    d. the United States.

23. American policy during World War Two can be best described as
    a. a conditional war against Germany.
    b. massive use of American troops on the eastern front.
    c. "Europe first" and the war in the Pacific second.
    d. pursue political goals first, military goals second.

24. The turning point in the North African war was the British defeat of the Germans in the Battle of
    a. the Coral Sea.
    b. Kursk.
    c. El Alamein.
    d. Leningrad.

25. It appears that rapid industrialization in the Soviet Union under Stalin was accompanied by
    a. a significant rise in the standard of living.
    b. a strengthening of trade unionism.
    c. an overall rise in real wages.
    d. a fall in the standard of living.

Major Political Ideas

Define totalitarianism. What are its fundamental characteristics and its origins? What is the difference between totalitarianism of the left and totalitarianism of the right? Compare totalitarianism to liberalism.

Issues for Essays and Discussion

1. The 1920s and the 1930s witnessed the rise of totalitarian states in Europe. How did it differ from authoritarian regimes of the past, and what were the goals and motives of the totalitarian state? In your answers, refer to the Soviet Union, Germany, and Italy.

2. Was the Second World War and the accompanying Holocaust the fault of the German people or the product of the evil mind of Adolf Hitler? Discuss this by describing the roots of Nazism and the reason for German expansionism.

Interpretation of Visual Sources

Study the photographs in your textbook labeled "Nazi Mass Rally, 1936" and "Hitler, Our Last Hope," on pages 923 and 938, respectively. What do the Hitler propagandists mean by the phrase "our last hope"? Do the people in the photo seem to fit the poster? How does this photograph help explain the photograph entitled "Nazi Mass Rally"? Contrast the portrayal of the individual in the two photos.

Geography

On Outline Map 29.1 provided, and using maps 29.1 and 29.2 in the textbook for reference, mark the following: Germany in 1933, the step-by-step growth of Nazi Germany through September 1939 (shade in each area taken and give the date of acquisition), the extent of German penetration into the Soviet Union, Leningrad, Moscow, the Elbe River, the Ruhr, Poland, Austria, the Rhine, East Prussia, Czechoslovakia, Sudetenland, Munich, the Rhineland, Danzig, the Normandy beachhead.

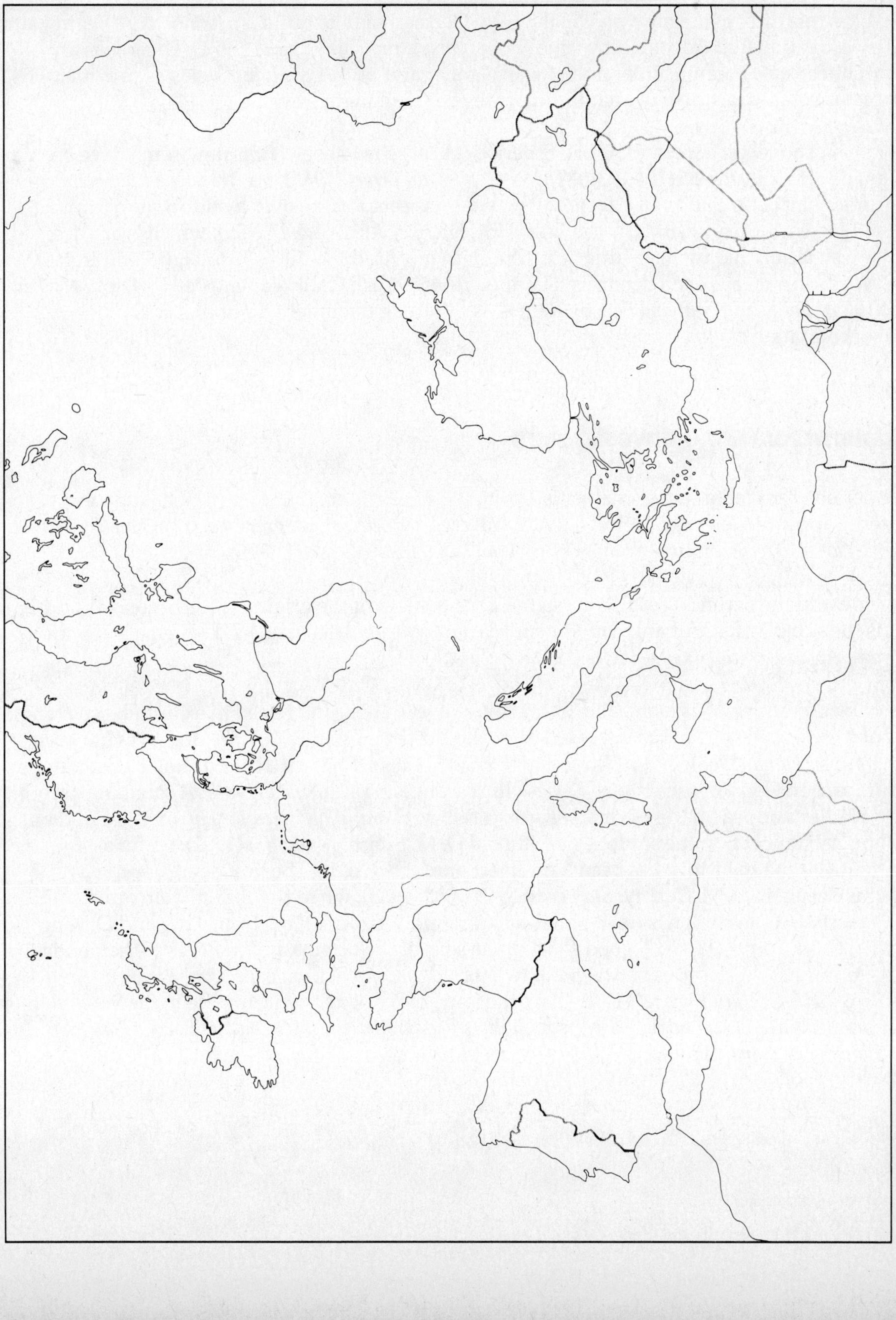

Outline Map 29.1

Understanding History Through the Arts

1. What role did architecture play in the Nazi German plan to build a new society? Begin your investigation into this subject with A. Speer, *Inside the Third Reich** (1971); Speer was an architect who became Hitler's chief war planner and one of the people closest to Hitler. His picture of Hitler's view of architecture is revealing in many ways.

2. What can we learn from films of the period? A large number of first-rank films have been made about Europe in the 1930s. *The Shop on Main Street* (1966) is a drama of a man living under Nazi occupation in Czechoslovakia who is sent to take over a button shop from an old Jewish woman. Similarly moving is *The Diary of Anne Frank* (1959), which is about a Jewish family hiding in an attic in Amsterdam in World War II. John Gielgud and Irene Worth narrate a French documentary about the Spanish Civil War entitled *To Die in Madrid* (1965). The film *Night and Fog*, by Renais, is a chilling documentary of the Nazi concentration camps.

Problems for Further Investigation

The period considered in this chapter is constantly undergoing reinterpretation, and new material appears each year. Helpful is A. Funk et al., *A Select Bibliography on Books on the Second World War** (1975), a bibliography of books published from 1966 to 1975.

1. How did the Second World War begin? The problem of the origins of the Second World War is the subject of K. Eubank, *The Origins of World War II* (1990), and W. L. Kleine-Ahlbrandt, ed., *Appeasement of the Dictators* (1970).

2. How did Hitler, Mussolini, and Stalin gain power? Those interested in examining the tangle of views on the life and motives of Hitler should begin with R. G. L. Waite, ed., *Hitler and Nazi Germany* (1965), and A. Bullock, *Hitler: A Study in Tyranny* (revised, 1962). For Hitler's impact on German society, see D. G. Williamson, *The Third Reich* (1984). A scholarly account of Hitler's appeal to the German people is R. Hamilton, *Who Voted for Hitler** (1982). About the Italian dictator, the student should read D. M. Smith, *Mussolini* (1982). Stalin's contribution to history has been the subject of much debate. The best overall summary of this debate is M. McCauley, *Stalin and Stalinism** (1983), while the chilling horrors of one aspect of Stalin's reign is dealt with (including photographs) in I. Deutscher and D. King, *The Great Purges* (1985). A good short discussion of the origins and motives of the political extremes of the decades between the two world wars is D. Smith, *Left and Right in Twentieth-Century Europe** (1970). And the issue of work and working life in the Soviet Union is dealt with in V. Andrle, *Workers in Stalin's Russia: Industrialization and Social Change in a Planned Economy* (1988).

---

*Available in paperback.

3. Few subjects in this period are as bloody and hate-filled as that of the civil war in Spain from 1936–1939. What happened and why? These and many other questions are examined in P. Preston, *The Spanish Civil War* (1986).

4. How can we begin to understand the Nazi treatment of the Jews? There has been a burst of literature on the Holocaust in recent years. One of the most readable books is L. S. Davidowicz, *The War Against the Jews, 1933–1945** (1975). Davidowicz writes about the German "final solution"—a chilling story, but one that needs to be told to every generation. The relationship between anti-Semitism and German fascism is further examined in Y. Bauer, *A History of the Holocaust** (1982), and the motives of a concentration camp commandant are evaluated in G. Sereny, *Into That Darkness** (1974, 1982). The least-known of the Nazi atrocities is dealt with in F. Rector, *The Nazi Extermination of Homosexuals* (1981).

5. What was the impact of totalitarian society on women? Did their position in society change in any significant ways? Was life for women in totalitarian Germany much different than for women in totalitarian Russia? Begin your investigation with two essays, R. Stites, "Women in the Revolutionary Process in Russia," and C. Koonz, "The Fascist Solution to the Women Question in Italy and Germany," in R. Bridenthal, C. Koonz, and S. Stuard, *Becoming Visible: Women in European History** (1987).

6. How did the Second World War affect civilian populations? What was it like to be a child in wartime Britain? See the interesting book *Children of the Blitz—Memories of Wartime Childhood** (1987), by R. Westall.

---

*Available in paperback.

Chapter 30
The Recovery of Europe and the Americas

Chapter Questions

After reading and studying this chapter you should be able to answer the following questions:

How did Europe recover from the Second World War? What were the causes of the cold war? How did economic nationalism transform Latin America? How and why did European empires collapse and Asian and African peoples gain political independence?

Chapter Summary

This chapter discusses the main political and economic trends in the Western world since the dark days of the Second World War. It shows how Europe, especially western Europe, recovered from the destruction of 1945, how the cold war split the Continent into communist and non-communist blocs, how European empires came to an end as the peoples of Africa and Asia achieved national independence, and how North and South America also revived and evolved in the postwar era.

The chapter begins by examining why the Grand Alliance of Britain, the Soviet Union, and the United States failed to hold together after they succeeded in defeating Nazi Germany. Military decisions, ideological differences, and disputes over eastern Europe were key factors in the origins of the cold war. By 1950, the Iron Curtain was in place, and western and eastern Europe were going their separate ways. Battered western Europe rebuilt quickly and successfully, helped by new leaders and attitudes, American aid, and the creation of the Common Market. Developments in East European countries closely followed those in Soviet Russia. Stalin reimposed a harsh dictatorship after the war, which Khrushchev relaxed but which Brezhnev tightened once again. An anticommunist popular revolt in Hungary failed, while material conditions in communist countries gradually improved and communist governments remained firmly in control.

European empires in Asia and Africa went out of business after the Second World War. India led the way to national independence right after the war, and other British, French, and Dutch territories followed. Most countries gained independence peacefully, but there were bitter colonial wars in Vietnam and Algeria. Western influence lives on in Asia and Africa, since most of the newly independent countries have retained Western nationalism and either communism or democracy as guiding ideas.

Study Outline

Use this outline to preview the chapter before you read a particular section in your textbook and then as a self-check to test your reading comprehension after you have read the chapter section.

I. The Cold War (1942–1953)
   A. The origins of the cold war
      1. The Allied decision to postpone political questions such as the makeup of postwar Europe strengthened the Soviets.
      2. The decision of the Big Three at Teheran (1943) to launch an American-British invasion of Hitler's empire via France meant that American-British and Russian troops would meet along a north-south line in Germany, and only Soviet Russia would liberate eastern Europe.
      3. At the Yalta Conference (1945) the Allies decided to divide Germany into occupation zones.
         a. It was agreed that Germany would pay heavy reparations to Russia.
         b. Stalin agreed to declare war on Japan after Germany was defeated and to join the United Nations.
      4. The Yalta Compromise over eastern Europe broke down almost immediately.
      5. At the Potsdam Conference (1945) Truman demanded free elections throughout eastern Europe, but Stalin refused.
         a. Stalin believed that only communist states could be loyal allies.
         b. He feared that free elections would result in possibly hostile governments on his western border.
      6. Short of war, the Western Allies could not really influence developments in eastern Europe.
   B. West versus East
      1. Truman cut off aid to Russia because of Stalin's insistence on having communist governments in eastern Europe.
      2. By 1947, many Americans believed that Stalin was trying to export communist revolution throughout Europe and the world.
      3. The Marshall Plan was established to help European economic recovery; the Truman Doctrine was meant to ward off communist subversion with military aid.
      4. The Soviet blockade of Berlin led to a successful Allied airlift.
      5. In 1949, the United States formed an anti-Soviet military alliance of Western governments, the North Atlantic Treaty Organization (NATO); in return, Stalin united his satellites in the Warsaw Pact.
      6. In 1949, Communists won in China.
      7. In 1950, when Communist North Korea invaded the south, American-led UN troops intervened.
      8. The Western attempt to check Stalin probably came too late and may have encouraged Russian aggression.

II. The western European renaissance
  A. The postwar challenge
    1. The war left Europe physically devastated and in a state of economic and moral crisis.
      a. Food rationing was necessary.
      b. Russia's border had been pushed west, as was Poland's; thus, many Germans were forced to resettle in a greatly reduced Germany.
      c. All the Allies treated Germany harshly.
    2. New leaders and new parties, especially the Catholic Christian Democrats, emerged in Italy, France, and Germany and provided effective leadership and needed reforms.
    3. In many countries, such as Britain, France, and Italy, Socialists and Communists emerged from the war with considerable power and a strong desire for social reform.
    4. The Marshall Plan aided in economic recovery and led to the Organization for European Economic Cooperation (OEEC); military protection was provided through NATO.
  B. Economic "miracles"
    1. Led by West Germany, a European economic miracle was underway by 1963.
      a. American aid helped get the process off to a fast start.
      b. European nations coordinated the distribution of American aid, so barriers to European trade and cooperation were quickly dropped.
    2. A free-market economy—with a social welfare network—brought rapid growth to Germany.
    3. Flexible planning and a mixed state and private economy brought rapid growth to France.
    4. A skilled labor pool, new markets for consumer products, and the Common Market stimulated economic development in western Europe.
  C. Toward European unity
    1. Democratic republics were re-established in France, West Germany, and Italy.
    2. The Christian Democrats were committed to a unified Europe, but economic unity proved to be more realistic than political unity.
    3. The six-nation Coal and Steel Community marked the beginning of a movement toward European unity and led to further technical and economic cooperation.
    4. The Treaty of Rome (1957) created the European Economic Community (EEC, or Common Market), whose immediate goal was to create a free-trade area by reducing tariffs.
    5. However, regenerated hopes for political union in Europe were frustrated by a resurgence of nationalism in the 1960s.
      a. De Gaulle, a romantic nationalist, wanted France to lead the Common Market.
      b. He withdrew from NATO and vetoed British attempts to join the Common Market.
  D. Decolonization of Asia and Africa
    1. The causes of imperial decline
      a. Nationalism brought demands for political self-determination in colonial areas after the First World War.

    b. The Second World War reduced European power and destroyed the Western sense of moral superiority.

  2. Nationalism in India and China

    a. Gandhi led the Indian nationalist movement, and India won limited self-government in 1937.

    b. Britain granted independence after the Second World War by creating a Hindu state of India and a Muslim state of Pakistan.

    c. After a bitter civil war, the Communists forced the Nationalists out of China to the island of Taiwan in 1949.

    d. Mao Tse-tung began building a Communist society along Soviet lines, with collectivization of the peasants and five-year plans concentrating on heavy industry.

    e. The French were defeated in Indochina by Ho Chi Minh, and Vietnam was divided into two zones pending unification on the basis of free elections.

  3. Arab nationalism and African independence

    a. Arab nationalism challenged imperial power and the new Jewish nation.

    b. A Jewish state was created out of part of British-controlled Palestine (1948) and was attacked by the Arab countries, who were defeated.

    c. Palestinian refugees refused to accept defeat and vowed to continue fighting to destroy the Jewish state of Israel.

    d. A successful nationalist revolution took place in Egypt (1952), and the new leader, Nasser, nationalized the Suez Canal.

    e. Arab nationalists in Algeria fought for and won independence from France in 1962.

    f. In most of the rest of Africa, independence was achieved without war, although many new African countries remained dependent on France and the Common Market.

III. Soviet Eastern Europe

  A. Stalin's last years

    1. The national unity of the war period ended in rigid dictatorship again.

    2. Stalin began a new series of purges and enforced cultural conformity.

      a. Soviet citizens living outside Russia were forced to return, and nearly a million of them, plus other Russians, died in labor camps.

      b. Culture, art, and the Jewish religion were attacked.

    3. Five-year plans were reintroduced; heavy and military industry were given top priority, while consumer goods, housing, and agriculture were neglected.

    4. Stalin's system was exported to eastern Europe.

      a. Only Tito in Yugoslavia was able to build an East European Communist state free from Stalinist control.

      b. Tito's success led Stalin to purge the Communist parties of eastern Europe in an attempt to increase their obedience to him.

  B. Reform and de-Stalinization

    1. Khrushchev and fellow reformers won the leadership of Russia over the conservatives, who wanted to make as few changes as possible in the Stalinist system.

    2. Khrushchev denounced Stalin at the Twentieth Party Congress in 1956 and began a policy of liberalization.

        a. The Soviet standard of living was improved, and greater intellectual freedom was allowed.

        b. Nevertheless, Pasternak was not allowed to accept the Nobel Prize in 1958 for *Doctor Zhivago*.

        c. Solzhenitsyn's book on life in a Stalinist camp, *One Day in the Life of Ivan Denisovich*, caused an uproar when it was published in Russia in 1962.

        d. Khrushchev pushed for "peaceful coexistence" with the West and a relaxation of cold war tensions.

    3. De-Stalinization caused revolution in eastern Europe in 1956.

        a. Poland under Gomulka won greater autonomy.

        b. Hungary expelled Soviet troops in 1956 and declared its neutrality but was invaded by Russia and defeated.

  C. The fall of Khrushchev

    1. Re-Stalinization began with Khrushchev's fall (1964).

        a. Khrushchev's policy of de-Stalinization was opposed by conservatives, who saw it as a threat to the whole communist system.

        b. Khrushchev's erratic foreign policy was also an issue—he was successful in building the Berlin wall but was forced to back down on the installation of missiles in Cuba.

    2. Brezhnev, who took over in 1964, stressed the ties with the Stalinist era and launched an arms buildup.

IV. The Western Hemisphere

  A. Postwar prosperity in the United States

    1. Conversion to a peacetime economy went smoothly, and the well-being of Americans increased dramatically.

    2. Until the 1960s, domestic politics consisted largely of consolidating the New Deal and maintaining the status quo.

        a. True innovations were rejected in the 1950s.

        b. In 1960, Kennedy was elected amid hopes he would revitalize the country.

  B. The civil rights revolution

    1. School segregation was declared unconstitutional by the Supreme Court in 1954.

    2. Blacks used militant nonviolence and growing political power to gain reforms in the 1960s.

        a. The Civil Rights Act of 1964 prohibited discrimination in public services and on the job.

        b. The Voting Rights Act of 1965 guaranteed all blacks the right to vote.

    3. The United States became more of a welfare state in the 1960s, as a surge of liberal social legislation was passed.

  C. Economic nationalism in Latin America

    1. Beginning with the Great Depression, more popularly based governments encouraged the development of national industry to reduce their dependence on raw-materials production and foreign markets.

    2. In Mexico the revolution of 1910 opened a new era of economic nationalism, social reform, and industrialization.

        a. President Cárdenas nationalized the petroleum industry in 1938.

        b. The Mexican state successfully promoted industrialization from the early 1940s to the late 1960s.

3. Under the strongman Vargas, Brazil also embraced economic nationalism and moderate social reform.
D. The Cuban Revolution
   1. Cuba was relatively rich but suffered from dictatorship, corruption, and a tradition of American intervention.
   2. The magnetic Fidel Castro led a successful revolution in 1958, which had major consequences.
      a. Castro repelled an American-supported invasion by Cuban exiles (the Bay of Pigs invasion), thereby winning great prestige.
      b. He established a typical communist dictatorship.
      c. The Cuban revolution brought the cold war to Latin America.
      d. In 1961, the United States helped create the Alliance for Progress to promote long-term economic development and social reform.

Review Questions

Check your understanding of this chapter by answering the following questions.

1. Describe the dispute between the United States and Russia at the end of the war. How and why did it escalate into a cold war?
2. Why were the Teheran and Yalta conferences important in shaping the map of postwar Europe?
3. What are the sources of the Soviet Union's paranoia about Germany and vice versa?
4. How did Europe accomplish economic recovery after the war? What factors contributed to its growth?
5. Which approach toward European unity was most successful, the political or the economic? Why?
6. Describe the steps taken toward European economic unity. What impact does this unity have on the European and world economy?
7. Was nationalism completely dead in postwar Europe? Who was Charles de Gaulle and what was his ambition?
8. What impact did the Second World War have on peoples' opinions about imperialism and European empires?
9. How did the development of nationalism in India compare with that in China.
10. Evaluate Stalin's postwar policy and actions. Why were many Russian nationalists disappointed in them? How would you judge Stalin's place in Soviet history?
11. Describe the circumstances surrounding Khrushchev's famous Twentieth Party Congress speech in 1956. What were the results of his policy?
12. What were the reasons for Khrushchev's fall from power and the beginning of the re-Stalinization of Russia in 1964?
13. Describe life in the Soviet Union after 1964. What were the positive and negative features of the Soviet state in the Brezhnev era?
14. "Postwar domestic politics in the United States consisted largely of making modest adjustments to the status quo." Why was this so?
15. What were the milestones in the civil rights revolution?

16. What are some of the key components of economic nationalism? How and why did it arise in Latin America?
17. How did Mexico and Brazil fare in the postwar period?
18. What were the causes and the consequences of the Cuban Revolution?

Study-Review Exercises

Define the following key concepts and terms.
European Steel and Coal Community

cold war

Truman Doctrine

de-Stalinization

decolonization

economic nationalism

Identify each of the following people and terms and explain their significance.
NATO

British Labour party

Indian Congress Party

Kuomintang

Alliance for Progress

Marshall Plan

Warsaw Pact

Organization of European Economic Cooperation

Common Market (EEC)

Taft-Hartley Act

Franklin D. Roosevelt

Josip Tito

Ho Chi Minh

Mahatma Gandhi

Nikita Khrushchev

Lázaro Cárdenas

Clement Atlee

Mao Tse-tung

Charles de Gaulle

Fidel Castro

Winston Churchill

Leonid Brezhnev

Chiang Kai-shek

Gamal Abdel Nasser

Getulio Vargas

Yevgeny Yevtushenko

Explain what happened at the following wartime conferences of the Big Three and what impact each one had on the postwar world.
Casablanca (January 1943)

Teheran (November 1943)

Yalta (February 1945)

Potsdam (July 1945)

Explain what the following events were, who participated in them, and why they were important.
The Berlin Airlift of 1948

Schuman Plan (1950)

Twentieth Party Congress of the Soviets (1956)

Chinese civil war (1945–1949)

partition of Palestine (1948)

Bay of Pigs invasion (1961)

Test your understanding of the chapter by providing the correct answers.

1. The successor to Sun Yat-sen and the leader of the revolutionary Kuomintang in China.

   _____

2. The American aid program that led to the establishment of the Organization for European

   Economic Cooperation. _____

3. The post–World War II military alliance of the Soviet bloc. _____

4. The resurgence of traditional nationalism in France was led, from 1958 to 1969, by President

   _____ .

Multiple-Choice Questions

1. French economic recovery following World War II centered on
   a. free-market capitalism alone.
   b. socialism.
   c. a mixed state and private economy.
   d. trade unionism.

2. Stalin's successor, Khrushchev
   a. denounced Stalinist policies and Stalin himself.
   b. carried on the Stalinist traditions.
   c. opposed reconciliation with the West.
   d. placed restrictions on cultural freedom.

3. The Soviet writer and poet who was forced by Khrushchev to refuse the Nobel Prize in 1958 was
   a. Pasternak.
   b. Solzhenitsyn.
   c. Gomulka.
   d. Beria.

4. The only eastern European communist leader to build an independent communist state free from Stalinist control was
   a. Nagy.
   b. Tito.
   c. Dubček.
   d. Schuman.

5. In Italy, the leading political party in the immediate postwar elections was the
   a. Communists.
   b. Catholic Center.
   c. Socialists.
   d. Christian Democrats.

6. American-Soviet conflict in the post–World War II era first centered on the problem of the future of
   a. France.
   b. East Germany.
   c. Yugoslavia.
   d. Poland.

7. In recent times, Latin American countries have demonstrated an increase in
   a. foreign control of industry.
   b. capital investment by foreign nations.
   c. economic nationalism.
   d. dependence on foreign markets and products.

8. Which of the following statements describes a policy of Stalin after the Second World War?
   a. He allowed Soviets abroad to remain in political asylum.
   b. He insisted on political conformity but allowed cultural freedom.
   c. He relaxed Soviet control of east European states.
   d. He revived forced-labor camps.

9. In Mexico, the Cárdenas presidency resulted in
   a. a counterrevolution that returned power to the landed elite.
   b. a return to the cultural connections between Mexico and Europe.
   c. the de-nationalization of the petroleum industry.
   d. the division of large estates among small farmers.

10. During and after World War Two, American leaders were most concerned that the East European countries would
    a. become American allies.
    b. be friendly toward Russia.
    c. have freely elected governments.
    d. reject German fascism.

11. The Frenchman who came to symbolize the resurgence of European nationalism was
    a. Jean Monnet.
    b. Charles de Gaulle.
    c. Robert Schuman.
    d. André Malraux.

12. Since the Second World War, Communist participation in West European governments has
    a. decreased.
    b. disappeared entirely.
    c. been outlawed in most countries.
    d. increased.

13. The only East European Communist country able to remain free of Stalin's control was
    a. Poland.
    b. Yugoslavia.
    c. East Germany.
    d. the Ukraine.

14. The country that blocked British entry into the Common Market and withdrew its forces from NATO was
    a. Belgium.
    b. West Germany.
    c. Italy.
    d. France.

15. Under Stalin, top priority in production in the Soviet Union was given to
    a. consumer goods.
    b. military goods.
    c. aid for rebuilding East Germany.
    d. building new housing.

16. After World War II, Stalin's chief policy goal was
    a. an extension of civil liberties.
    b. Russian domination of eastern Europe.
    c. his efforts to eliminate anti-Semitism in Russia.
    d. relaxing prohibitions against capitalism.

17. The Allied nations of the Second World War included all of the following *except*
    a. the Soviet Union.
    b. the United States.
    c. Austria.
    d. Britain.

18. Defeat by communist and nationalist leader Ho Chi Minh in 1954 marked the end of French control of
    a. Indochina.
    b. Algeria.
    c. South Sudan.
    d. Teheran.

19. Khruschev's de-Stalinization led to revolts in
    a. Italy and Turkey.
    b. Poland and Hungary.
    c. Volgograd and Leningrad.
    d. Yugoslavia.

20. All the following phrases characterize the views of the French government under Charles de Gaulle *except*
    a. Anti-British.
    b. Anti-American.
    c. willing to compromise French goals for European security.
    d. Anti-NATO and a reluctant participant in the Common Market.

21. Economic nationalism came to Brazil in 1930 with
    a. the establishment of a broad-based democracy.
    b. the Vargas dictatorship.
    c. the growth of regional centers of power.
    d. Kubitschek's "Fifty Years' Progress in Five" program.

22. The 1954 Supreme Court decision on segregation was based on the principle that
    a. separate but equal facilities are constitutional.
    b. separate educational facilities are unequal, hence unconstitutional.
    c. sit-ins and demonstrations are unconstitutional.
    d. the southern school system should remain unchanged.

23. The new leader of Poland in 1956 was
    a. Wladyslaw Gomulka.
    b. Nikita Khrushchev.
    c. Josip Tito.
    d. Boris Pasternak.

24. The six original members of the new coal and steel community, which eventually became the Common Market, were
    a. Britain, France, West Germany, Italy, Belgium, the Netherlands.
    b. Britain, France, West Germany, Italy, the Netherlands, Sweden.
    c. France, West Germany, Italy, Belgium, the Netherlands, Luxembourg.
    d. France, West Germany, Italy, Belgium, Luxembourg, Sweden.

25. Gamal Abdel Nasser is most famous for
    a. building the Suez canal.
    b. nationalizing the Suez Canal.
    c. reaching agreements with the European and Americans over foreign purchase of oil rights in Egypt.
    d. engineering a coup that restored the pro-Western king to power.

Major Political Ideas

1. Define the concept of European unity and trace its origins. Who belonged to this movement, what forms did it take, and why were people so willing to replace nationalism with a common Europe?

2. Define the term *economic nationalism*. Why did it emerge and what form did it take?

Issues for Essays and Discussion

With the defeat of Germany in 1945 there arose a new war, a cold war between the United States and the Soviet Union. What were the causes of this war? Could the United States have blocked the Soviet takeover of eastern Europe? Was the conflict a result more of Soviet strength or American weakness?

Interpretation of Visual Sources

Study the photograph entitled "The Berlin Air Lift" on page 963 of your textbook. What is taking place in this scene and what is the historical background? What features of this photo make it such a stirring reminder of the ideological battle of that time?

Geography

On Outline Map 30.2 provided, and using maps 30.1 and 30.2 in your textbook as references, mark the following: the location of the Iron Curtain that divided Europe after the Second World War, the territory lost by Germany after the Second World War (should East Germany be considered "lost" territory?), the territory gained by the Soviet Union after the Second World War (did Poland gain anything in return for its losses to the Soviet Union?), the original members of the Common Market, the countries that joined in later years, Berlin, Brussels, Paris, London, Warsaw, Rome, Belgrade, Moscow, Bonn, Prague.

Outline Map 30.2

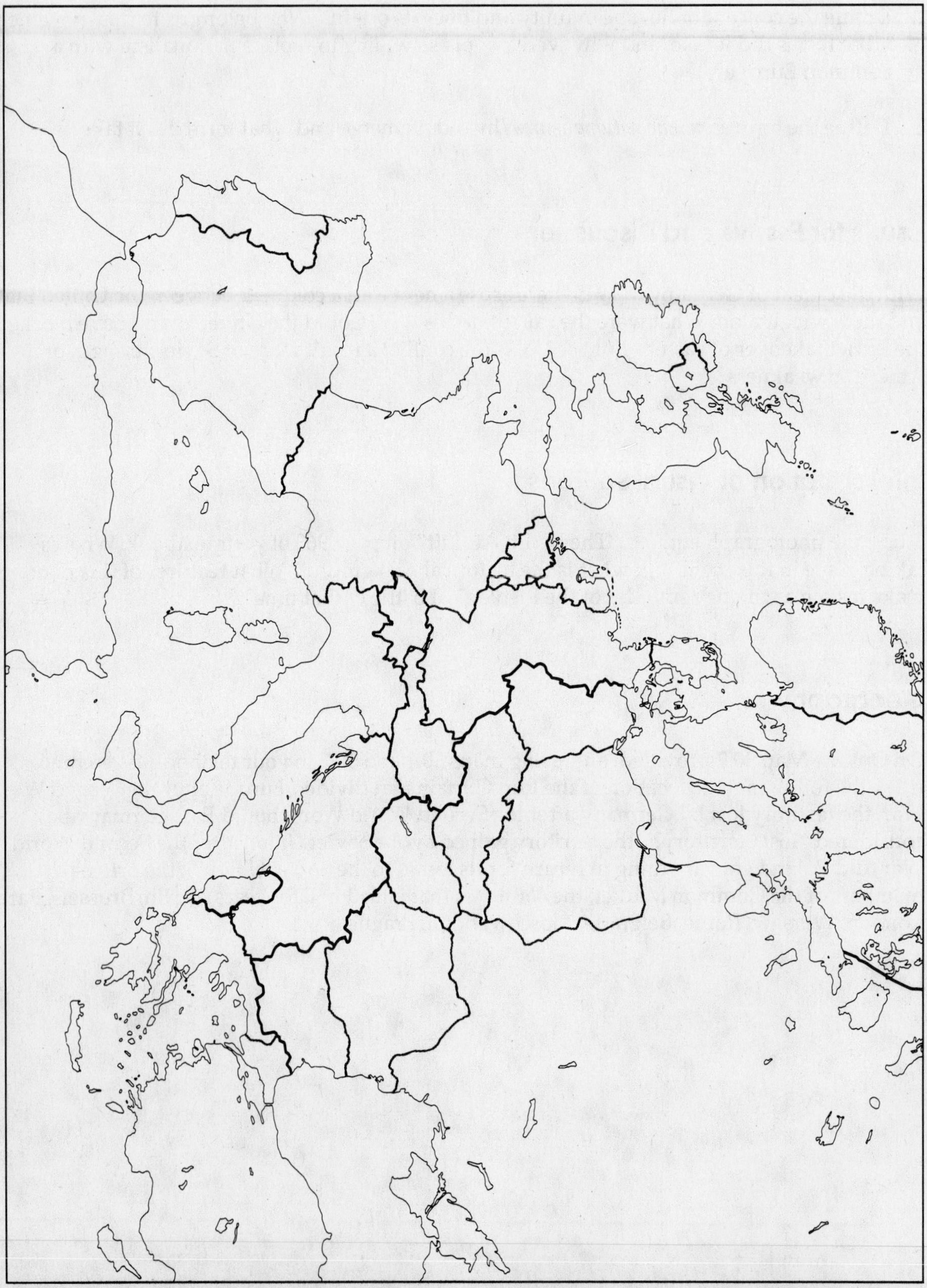

Understanding History Through the Arts

1. What literature did the cold war era produce? Alexander Solzhenitsyn's *One Day in the Life of Ivan Denisovich** is a powerful and moving story of one human being in a postwar prison camp in Stalinist Russia.

2. What do the songs of Edith Piaf tell us? The release from Nazi occupation gave an enormous boost to popular song throughout Europe. Nowhere were songwriters and young artists as inspired as in France, and no one was as loved by the French people as Edith Piaf. Piaf was a nightclub singer who sang *chansons réalistes*—songs about the joys, frustrations, and sorrows of the people of the streets. She made her first recording in 1936. Her first recording after the war, *Les Trois Cloches*, was described as "the folklore of the future." She died in 1963 after a full and sometimes tragic life. Many recordings of her performances are available.

3. How did the experiences of the Latin American nations mix with European influences to form a powerful and indigenous art? This is the subject of D. Ades, ed., *Art in Latin America* (1989).

Problems for Further Investigation

1. Who were the men who shaped the great postwar alliance between Europe, the United States, and Japan? What were the key events and ideas behind this alliance? Based on interviews, memoirs, and documents, the key figures of the postwar era—Eisenhower, De Gaulle, Kennedy, Schmidt, MacArthur, and others—come alive in R. Barnet, *The Alliance* (1983).

2. How did the cold war begin? Those interested in the military history of the Second World War and the postwar era will want to begin with P. Paret, *Makers of Modern Strategy, from Machavelli to the Nuclear Age** (1986). The origins of the cold war, according to its earliest interpreters, were rooted in the conflict between communist aggression and American benevolence. Preoccupied with the task of defeating the Axis powers, the United States misjudged the intentions of the Soviet Union and, unknowingly, opened the door to communist expansion. American policymakers then adopted policies designed to "contain" Russian aggression. For example, see G. F. Kennan, *American Diplomacy, 1900–1950* (1951). One of the best books on the cold war is L. Halle, *The Cold War as History* (1967). The turbulent sixties, which were characterized by a reappraisal of American truths, led some historians to re-examine the origins of the cold war. Revisionists such as W. A. Williams, *The Tragedy of American Diplomacy** (1959), and W. Lafeber, *America, Russia and the Cold War, 1945–1975** (1976), emphasized American economic expansion as a major reason for the confrontation between East and West. Armed with a monopoly of atomic weapons, the United States threatened Soviet security and thereby forced communist leaders to forge eastern Europe into a protective buffer under Soviet hegemony. For a good brief survey of

---

*Available in paperback.

cold war literature, see the pamphlet by B. Tierney et al., *The Cold War—Who Is to Blame?** (1967).

3. What do postwar Germans think of Hitler? This is the subject of D. Lang's interesting article, "Reporter in Germany: A Backward Look," *The New Yorker* (October 3, 1978): 47–107.

---

*Available in paperback.

Chapter 31
Life in the Postwar Era

Chapter Questions

After reading and studying this chapter you should be able to answer the following questions:

How has everyday life changed in the postwar era and why? What have these changes meant to people?

Chapter Summary

This chapter focuses on three of the most important areas of change in today's Western world: science, class structure, and women and the family.

Examining first science and technology, the chapter shows how the Second World War speeded up scientific achievement and gave rise to very large scientific projects involving great numbers of researchers and large government grants. This development has led to major changes in the lives of scientists and technicians, who have great influence in modern society. A second trend has been toward a more flexible and democratic class structure, where white-collar professionals and highly trained specialists provided the model for a new middle class. Reforms in education and expanded social security have strengthened the move toward social democracy. Although discontent like that which brought a student revolution in France in 1968 has not been eliminated, changes in education and new opportunities for men and women of talent has resulted in a more fluid and less antagonistic class structure. The family and the role of women also underwent well-publicized changes. The divorce rate went up while the marriage rate and birthrate fell. Married women were having fewer children and were ever more likely to work outside the home for wages. This trend reflects and encourages a growing spirit of independence among women. Women and the family experienced a truly revolutionary transformation.

Study Outline

Use this outline to preview the chapter before you read a particular section in your textbook and then as a self-check to test your reading comprehension after you have read the chapter section.

I. Science and technology
  A. The union of science and technology
    1. Generally, science and technology were joined together only occasionally until the 1930s.
    2. The Second World War focus on military problems brought them together.
    3. The results have been both good and bad.
       a. New industries were created, and rapid economic growth was achieved after 1945.
       b. The environment was adversely affected by technological change.
  B. The stimulus of the Second World War
    1. With the Second World War, pure science lost its independence as leading scientists worked for their governments to help fight the war.
    2. The war led to major technological breakthroughs, such as radar, improved jet engines, computers, and the atomic bomb.
       a. Einstein's letter to Roosevelt in 1939 about the theoretical possibility of the atomic bomb led to the Manhattan Project.
       b. The first atomic bomb was successfully tested in July 1945.
  C. The rise of Big Science
    1. Big Science could attack difficult problems by combining theoretical work with engineering techniques.
    2. Big Science needed a great deal of money, mostly for its complex equipment, which it received from government and large corporations.
       a. The European nations pooled their resources in CERN to build an accelerator.
       b. Astronomical and aeronautical research also became very costly.
    3. The United States took the lead in Big Science after World War Two.
       a. By 1965, most of the funds for scientific research came from the government.
       b. A large portion of scientific research was devoted to defense.
    4. Russia pioneered in the development of a space program by launching a satellite in 1957, but the United States put the first men on the moon, in 1969.
    5. European countries undertook financing of Big Science in order to stop the "brain drain" of their best scientists to the United States.
  D. The life of scientists and technologists
    1. There were many more scientists and much specialized knowledge.
    2. Specialization made teamwork, bureaucracy, and managers necessary.
    3. It became difficult to appraise an individual scientist's contribution to a team effort.
    4. Competition among scientists was often fierce.
II. Toward a new society
  A. The changing class structure in Europe
    1. After 1945 the traditional class distinctions became less clear-cut, and society became more mobile and democratic.
    2. Educational and employment opportunities made the middle class more open.

      a. Talent and expertise became more important to success than inherited property or family connections.

      b. The middle class grew greatly as entry became easier.

    3. The rural working class shrank in size due to the mass exodus from the country.

B. Social security reforms and rising affluence

    1. Social security reforms like health care and family allowances reduced class tensions.

    2. These reforms promoted greater social and economic equality.

    3. Lower food costs allowed for greater consumption of other goods.

      a. Greater consumption was accompanied by the problem of overeating, diet fads, and junk food.

      b. Automobile ownership increased; gadgets and household appliances, largely bought on credit, became necessities for most families.

    4. Leisure and recreation, especially travel, became big business.

C. Renewed discontent and the student revolt

    1. Many of the younger generation claimed that increasing materialism was harmful and that postwar society was repressive and flawed.

    2. The number of people entering European universities increased in the 1950s and 1960s.

      a. Overcrowding resulted, and a new "youth culture" emerged.

      b. Many students believed they were not getting the kind of education they needed.

    3. With help from workers, student revolts over these issues occurred in the late 1960s and early 1970s.

      a. In 1968, a general strike spread across France.

      b. De Gaulle moved troops toward Paris and called for new elections, which he won resoundingly.

    4. The student rebellion reflected a disillusionment with materialism, technological society, and the Vietnam War.

III. Women and the family

A. Women's emancipation

    1. Women became better educated and more independent.

    2. The changing position of women in society altered the modern family.

B. Marriage and motherhood

    1. Since the Second World War, the trend has been toward earlier marriage and greater birth control within marriage.

    2. The birthrate in Western countries declined in the 1960s and population growth slowed.

    3. Motherhood came to occupy a smaller portion of a woman's life than it used to.

      a. The average woman's life expectancy increased from fifty years to seventy-five years between 1900 and 1970.

      b. At the same time, most women were having their children when they were in their twenties and having fewer children.

    4. The age-old link between sexual intercourse and motherhood was severed by the development and use of birth-control methods.

C. Women at work

    1. Women entered the labor market as full-time wage earners.

2. Rising employment contributed to the growth of the women's liberation movement and the declining birthrate.
3. Women came to understand that interruption of their careers to care for small children led to lower wages.
4. The emotional aspects of marriage became more important as the nuclear family adapted to changing conditions.
5. The divorce rate rose partly because of increased female independence.

Review Questions

Check your understanding of this chapter by answering the following questions.

1. Why did science become Big Science in the postwar era? What is the purpose of Big Science?
2. For the first time in history, science and technology have been effectively joined on a massive scale. How did this happen and what are the implications?
3. How has the rise of Big Science altered the lives of modern scientists?
4. Cite the evidence supporting the claim that the standard of living improved in North America and Europe. Has the quality of life improved as well?
5. What changes have taken place in the European class structure since the war? Does greater or less mobility exist? Has the distribution of income remained the same?
6. What were the reasons and outcome of the European student rebellions of the late 1960s?
7. Why did the birthrate in Europe and the United States begin to fall in the 1950s?
8. What changes in lifestyle for women have occurred in the past thirty years? Have these changes been beneficial to both men and women? Explain.
9. What has happened to the fertility period of women to cause a greater need for birth control?

Study-Review Questions

Define each of the following key concepts and terms.

Big Science

scientific specialization

"brain drain"

managerial class

social welfare reforms

women's liberation movement

"consumer society"

Explain the significance of each of the following terms.
development of radar

microwave transmission

large-scale entry of women into the labor force

post–Second World War explosion in university education

student protests of the 1960s

changes in women's fertility

population decline in Europe and America

decline of the European peasant class

Test your understanding of the chapter by providing the correct answers.

1. Since 1945, the number of agricultural workers in western Europe has *increased/decreased*.

2. In the past twenty years, European society has witnessed a fairly significant *rise/fall* in the birthrate.

3. Since the Second World War, the percentage of women who are full-time wage earners has *increased/decreased* sharply.

4. The average European family today spends *more/less* of its income on food, as compared to a family living in the late nineteenth century.

5. Welfare-state reforms in Britain since the Second World War have resulted in *greater/lesser* economic equality in that country.

6. Sweden, where the rate of marriage has *risen/declined*, typifies the changing marriage patterns in Europe since 1945.

7. The trend since the 1940s has been *an increase/a decrease* in the cooperation between pure science and technology.

8. Since 1945, European society has moved toward a *more/less* rigid class structure.

9. It appears that the increase in economic independence among women has had *little/significant* effect on divorce and birthrates.

10. The trend in Europe and the United States since 1945 has been toward *greater/fewer* scientific bureaucracies.

Multiple-Choice Questions

1. The close and lasting cooperation of pure science and applied technology began
   a. during the depression.
   b. about 1900.
   c. during the Second World War.
   d. during World War I.

2. In eastern Europe today, most women
   a. seldom work out of the home.
   b. work until marriage.
   c. are usually employed until retirement.
   d. quit the work force after pregnancy.

3. Studies of marriage show that divorce in the postwar era is
   a. on the decline.
   b. more common among families in which women stay at home.
   c. more likely to occur in families in which the wife works.
   d. more likely to occur in southern Europe.

4. In the postwar era, the trend with regard to marriage and family size has been toward
   a. later marriage and a larger family.
   b. later marriage and a smaller family.
   c. earlier marriage and a larger family.
   d. earlier marriage and a smaller family.

5. Which of the following characterizes the European job market since World War II?
   a. A decline in farm labor
   b. An increase in industrial labor
   c. A decrease in white-collar and service jobs
   d. An increase in small businesses

6. Since the Second World War, science has been characterized by which one of the following?
   a. De-emphasis on weapons production
   b. A dramatic increase in private individual research
   c. A reliance on government research grants
   d. The divorce of science from technology

7. The welfare-state reforms of Europe have resulted in
   a. little if any redistribution of national income.
   b. slight redistribution of national income.
   c. considerable redistribution of national income.
   d. no changes in the standard of living.

8. As a result of Big Science, the control scientists have over their experimentation has
   a. increased.
   b. decreased.
   c. not changed since the prewar era.
   d. been taken over by universities.

9. Since about 1950 the number of European married women who work outside the home has
   a. considerably increased.
   b. considerably decreased.
   c. not changed from the prewar levels.
   d. decreased in the Soviet Union but increased elsewhere.

10. In the postwar era, women
    a. became more independent.
    b. married later.
    c. practiced less birth control.
    d. concentrated on becoming mothers and housewives.

11. The European "brain drain" refers to the
    a. loss of many scientists in the war.
    b. move of many scientists to the United States.
    c. lack of interest in science in society.
    d. control of science by the state.

12. The 1934 British Air Ministry's experiments on air defense led to the development of
    a. the atomic bomb.
    b. the double helix.
    c. jet aircraft.
    d. radar.

13. The famous 1939 letter to President Roosevelt that predicted the discovery of the atomic bomb was written by
    a. Albert Einstein.
    b. Ernest Rutherford.
    c. General Marshall.
    d. Winston Churchill.

14. The country that took the lead in Big Science was
    a. the Soviet Union.
    b. Germany.
    c. the United States.
    d. Britain.

15. All of the following statements about postwar scientists are true *except* that
    a. they have become more specialized.
    b. they have become subject to greater governmental influence.
    c. they increasingly work together in teams.
    d. they form a smaller but more diverse group.

16. The political party in Britain that took the lead in establishing a comprehensive national health system was the
    a. Liberal party.
    b. Conservative party.
    c. Workers' party.
    d. Labour party.

17. The 1968 revolt in France that threatened De Gaulle's government was started by
    a. industrial workers.
    b. the Communist party.
    c. university students.
    d. peasants.

18. The student revolt in France in the late 1960s was inspired in part by the
    a. Korean War.
    b. Vietnam War.
    c. Civil War.
    d. Second World War.

19. The welfare-state legislation in Britain since World War II has resulted in
    a. greater economic equality.
    b. government responsibility for all health and social needs.
    c. a dramatic rise in the birthrate.
    d. the disappearance of the aristocracy.

20. Since World War Two, the role of motherhood has occupied
    a. more of women's time.
    b. less of women's time.
    c. more time at a later period in life.
    d. about the same amount of time as in prewar society.

21. Prior to the postwar era in Europe, high school and university educations were
    a. pursued by most children of the upper class.
    b. undertaken by most men but few women.
    c. limited to a small elite.
    d. available only to those interested in applied training, such as business.

22. During the student revolts in France in 1968, the students received the support of
    a. President Charles De Gaulle.
    b. the university administration.
    c. the Paris police.
    d. the rank-and-file workers.

23. In the postwar society, the trend for women with regard to pregnancy was
    a. to control pregnancy with contraceptives and intrauterine devices.
    b. to rely more and more on their husbands in deciding about pregnancy.
    c. to avoid birth control because of psychological reasons.
    d. to have no need for birth control because the age of menarche had risen.

24. One of the changes in the lives of scientists after the Second World War is that scientific work became
    a. less influenced by the state.
    b. carried out on a more individual basis.
    c. much less competitive.
    d. highly collaborative.

25. In the postwar era, family expenditure in Western society changed significantly in that
    a. food and drink took up roughly two-thirds of the average family's income.
    b. consumption of staples like bread and potatoes increased.
    c. the average person ate more fish, meat, and dairy products.
    d. the average person became very nutrition wise and sought a balanced diet.

Major Political Ideas

1. Define Big Science. In what sense is this a political phenomenon? What are the political advantages and disadvantages to emerge from this development?

2. Some historians have argued that wars have actually promoted progress by speeding up technological change. Do you agree with this theory? Cite evidence from the Second World War and postwar era in support of your argument.

Issues for Essays and Discussion

How did Western society change in the postwar era? Discuss this by making reference to the role of science and government, the class structure of society, the discontent of the 1960s, and the position of women and the family.

Interpretation of Visual Sources

Study the graph labeled "The Decline of the Birthrate and the Increase of Working Wives in the United States, 1952–1979" on page 1004 of your textbook. What is the significance of these data? Are the explanations for these changes largely economic or social?

Understanding History Through the Arts

1. How has art reflected the ideals and trends of postwar society? The principal artists of the period and the origins of their works are considered in E. Lucie-Smith, *Movements in Art Since 1945** (1986), while the most noteworthy art trends of the 1960s are discussed in *Pop Art** (1985) by L. Lippard et al.

2. What effect has the threat of nuclear war had on postwar society? The danger of atomic war has fostered the production of a good number of films, including feature films such as *Dr. Strangelove, Fail-Safe*, and *Hiroshima, Mon Amour*, and documentary films such as *The War Games* and *To Die, To Live*. An analysis of these and other films about nuclear war is found in a book by J. Shaheen, *Nuclear War Films* (1978). A good recent (1982) documentary about the effects of atomic testing in the 1950s is *Nick Mazacco: Biography of an Atomic Vet*.

Problems for Further Investigation

1. What were the motives of the student radicals in 1968? Begin your study with D. Caute, *The Year of the Barricades, A Journey Through 1968* (1990).

2. How did the modern women's movement begin? In the 1960s, a number of women began writing about themselves and the institutions of marriage, childbearing, and work, contributing greatly to what became the women's movement of our day. Begin your investigation with S. De Beauvoir, *The Second Sex** (1953), and G. Greer, *Sex and Destiny** (1985). Those who wish to compare the recent women's movement with earlier movements should turn to K. Rogers, *Feminism in Eighteenth Century England* (1982). On another liberation issue, the emergence of gay and lesbian minorities in urban politics is the subject

---

*Available in paperback.

of the Academy Award–winning documentary film *The Times of Harvey Milk* (1985); it was a PBS television presentation and is available on videotape.

3. How have people of the postwar era viewed their society? One of the most readable of the futurist books is R. Heilbroner's *An Inquiry into the Human Prospect** (1974). A world future dictated by technology is discussed in J. J. Servan-Schreiber, *The World Challenge* (1981), while the search for ethics in the age of technology is the subject of H. Jonas, *The Imperative of Responsibility** (1984). R. Hardin et al., *Nuclear Deterrence** (1985), sketches out the positions of strategists and philosophers concerning a number of issues with regard to war and nuclear weapons. The problems and issues surrounding life in a British agricultural village in the 1960s are the subject of R. Blythe, *Akenfield** (1969).

4. What has happened to the European Jews since the end of the Second World War? This is the subject of H. Schar, *Diaspora: An Inquiry into the Contemporary Jewish World** (1990).

---

*Available in paperback.

Chapter 32
The Recent Past, 1968 to the Present

Chapter Questions

After reading and studying this chapter you should be able to answer the following questions:

Why did the world economy shift into reverse gear in the 1970s? What were the social consequences of this shift? What were the major political developments in Europe and the United States, and why did the United States enter into a time of troubles? How did these changes interact with the evolution of the Soviet bloc? Why did reform take place in Gorbachev's Soviet Union and then peaceful revolutions take place in eastern Europe beginning in 1989?

Chapter Summary

After about 1968 the self-confidence and social and economic stability that came to mark the postwar era evaporated. What followed were two decades of upheaval. First, in the early 1970s a combination of factors, including the collapse of the American-dominated world monetary order and a dramatic rise in energy prices, led to a worldwide recession that was to last well into the 1980s. Spurred on by war in the Middle East and revolution in Iran, oil prices skyrocketed, thereby setting into motion the worst world economic decline since the 1930s. The Western European countries, particularly hard hit, faced massive unemployment, economic stagflation, and a falling standard of living. All of this was accompanied by increased government spending on benefits for the unemployed and the needy and, correspondingly, by a buildup of huge national debts and inflation. By the late 1970s some leaders, like Thatcher and Reagan, perceived a need to eliminate huge deficits and cut spending, while a whole generation of young people became concerned about their job prospects. The student idealism of the 1960s was over.

One of the most significant developments of this era was the West German initiative, under Willy Brandt, to bring about reconciliation between eastern and western Europe, although downplaying the idea of German reunification. This policy of détente was furthered with East-West agreements at Helsinki. Meanwhile, the cold war reheated as the United States, in an effort to "roll back communism," carried on a long and unsuccessful war in Vietnam. In the end, the war brought down two American presidents and left the country divided and with diminished world prestige. In 1978 the Soviet Union became involved in a similar quagmire in Afghanistan, where the Russians used force to preserve their influence, and then, more successfully, put down a rebellion in Poland, where a powerful trade union movement had turned into a civil rights movement. In addition to repression in Poland, the Soviet leaders had earlier (1968) engaged themselves in successfully putting down a revolution in Czechoslovakia, which sought "socialism with a human face," and carried out at home a program of re-Stalinization that aimed at ending internal opposition and reasserting a unified national spirit.

Most revolutionary, since 1985 Mikhail Gorbachev has worked to democratize the Soviet Union, increase Soviet productivity, and end its control over eastern Europe. Gorbachev's realism was the spark that set off a series of largely peaceful revolutions (with the exception of Rumania) by the peoples of eastern Europe to cast out their Communist leaders, hold free elections, and start on the road to a free market economy.

The text concludes with some cautiously optimistic thoughts about the future of Western civilization—including a look at the prospects of war between the rich nations and the poor nations and the issue of nuclear proliferation. The Western ideals of individualism, representative government, and nationhood seem to be flourishing.

Study Outline

Use this outline to preview the chapter before you read a particular section in your textbook and then as a self-check to test your reading comprehension after you have read the chapter section.

I. The troubled economy
- A. Money and oil
    1. From 1944 (the Bretton Woods Agreement) to 1971 the world monetary system was based on the U.S. dollar.
        a. The U.S. guarantee that the dollar could be cashed in for gold at $35 an ounce encouraged growth and monetary stability.
        b. But U.S. shortage of gold by 1971 caused a panic as foreigners raced to exchange their dollars for gold.
        c. The price of gold soared on the world market, and the value of the dollar declined.
        d. The ensuing abandonment of fixed rates made for an uncertain future in international trade and finance.
    2. The era of cheap oil (which had stimulated Western economic growth) came to an end in 1973.
        a. Khadafy of Libya activated OPEC price increases.
        b. The Yom Kippur War (1973) and subsequent OPEC oil embargoes resulted in vast price rises.
- B. Inflation, debt, and unemployment
    1. The price revolution in energy sources plunged the world into its worst economic decline since the 1930s.
    2. Iran's Islamic revolution (1978–79) caused another oil shock.
    3. The crisis of unemployment and inflation (stagflation) hit western Europe harder than the United States.

4. International debt rose as both rich and poor states borrowed money to pay for oil and maintain social services.
5. Consumers borrowed as a hedge against inflation.

C. Some social consequences
1. Optimism gave way to pessimism.
2. Governments responded with extended benefits for the unemployed and the needy, thereby preserving political stability.
3. Increased government spending without increased taxation led to budget deficits, increased national debt, and inflation.
4. Thatcher and Reagan reacted against government spending and deficits by limiting the growth of social programs; Mitterrand first attempted a program of nationalization and public investment but, when this failed, was also compelled to impose austerity measures.
5. Funding for Big Science was cut, while many individuals adopted less indulgent lifestyles.
6. The age of marriage rose sharply, young people became more conservative and worried about jobs, and most women had to work.

II. The Atlantic alliance
A. Germany's eastern initiative
1. In 1970 West Germany's Chancellor Brandt sought reconciliation between eastern Europe and West Germany.
2. Since 1945 West Germany had rebuilt itself and had sought to undermine the East German government.
   a. West Germany became an invaluable member of NATO and the Common Market.
   b. Until the Berlin Wall was built (1961) it welcomed over 2 million East German refugees.
3. The election of Brandt as chancellor in 1969 brought the Social Democrats to power and illustrated that democracy was working in West Germany.
4. Brandt negotiated treaties with the Soviet Union, Poland, and Czechoslovakia and entered into direct relations with East Germany.
5. The establishment of more normal relations with the communist East contributed to a reduction in East-West tensions.

B. Political crisis in the United States
1. American involvement in Vietnam grew out of its efforts to contain communism.
2. The U.S. went along with South Vietnam's refusal to accept the verdict of elections and started providing military aid.
3. President Johnson vowed not to "lose" Vietnam and therefore carried out a massive military buildup and bombing, but without achieving victory.
4. Criticism of the war brought the defeat of Johnson and the 1968 election of President Nixon.
5. Nixon cut war costs and brought many troops home, but the war continued for another four years.
   a. Nixon journeyed to China in 1972 and reached a limited reconciliation with its communist government.
   b. A peace agreement with North Vietnam was signed in 1973, and the American forces completed their withdrawal.

6. Nixon's illegal activities led to the Watergate crisis and his resignation in 1974.
7. Vietnam became unified as a totalitarian state under communist rule, and the U.S. was left divided and uncertain.

C. Détente or cold war?
   1. The policy of détente (progressive relaxation of cold war tensions) resulted in an East-West agreement at Helsinki (1975) guaranteeing frontiers and human rights.
   2. Soviet involvement in Afghanistan and elsewhere convinced some that the Soviets were violating the spirit of détente.
      a. President Carter applied economic sanctions on the Soviets, but most European governments refused to join the sanctions.
      b. The U.S. arms buildup—to counter the perceived increase in Soviet military power—was accompanied by European governments allowing American cruise missiles with nuclear warheads on their soil.

III. The Soviet bloc
   A. The Soviet Union has shifted back and forth between a desire to reform itself and aggressive dictatorship.
      1. Then Gorbachev opened a new era of reform.
      2. The scope of reform and revolution in eastern Europe suggests that people have made a decisive breakthrough toward freedom and democracy.
   B. The Czechoslovak experiment
      1. Under the reformer Dubček, the Czech Communist party instituted reforms that stressed socialism with freedom and party democracy.
         a. The reforms were popular but frightened entrenched powers.
         b. The Soviets feared Czech neutralism or even a pro-Western policy.
      2. The Soviets responded in August 1968 by occupying Czechoslovakia.
         a. The Czech reforms were abandoned.
         b. The Brezhnev Doctrine was declared, giving Soviet Russia the right to intervene in any socialist country whenever it saw the need.
   C. The Soviet Union to 1985
      1. In the Soviet Union the Czech crisis caused a step backward toward re-Stalinization.
         a. However, the standard of living improved, particularly for the elite.
         b. Russian nationalism reinforced stability partly because the Great Russians feared demands for autonomy from East European and non-Russian nationalities.
         c. Nonconformity and protest were severely punished; Jews were persecuted, and some dissidents (such as Solzhenitsyn) were expelled.
      2. Nevertheless, a social revolution was in the making.
         a. The urban population grew to two-thirds of the total and become more sophisticated.
         b. A class of educated and self-confident experts grew.
         c. The public became more educated and political.
   D. Solidarity in Poland
      1. The Polish Communists dropped efforts to impose Soviet-style collectivization on the peasants and to break the Catholic church.
      2. The Polish economy suffered greatly because of poor leadership and the world depression of the 1970s.

3. The "Polish miracle" occurred when the economic crisis became a spiritual crisis as well.
    a. The new Pope, John Paul II, former archbishop of Cracow, called attention to the rights of all people.
    b. Strikes in August 1980 led to revolutionary demands, which were accepted by the government in the Gdansk Agreement.
    c. Lech Walesa led the new democratic trade union movement (Solidarity) in its demands for industrial, political, and economic rights.
    d. Solidarity had massive support and a sophisticated organization.
    e. It stopped short, however, of directly challenging the Communist monopoly of power.
4. When Solidarity lost its cohesiveness the Polish Communist leadership under Jaruzelski smashed the movement (1981) and imposed martial law.
    a. After 1981 Solidarity went underground and fought on with great popular support.
    b. Polish cultural and intellectual life remained vigorous despite the repression.

E. Reform in the Soviet Union
1. A new era of fundamental change began under Gorbachev in 1985.
    a. By 1982 economic decline was worsened by mass apathy and lack of personal initiative.
    b. Andropov tried to reinvigorate the system after Brezhnev's death, with little success.
    c. Gorbachev set forth a series of reforms to restructure the economy (*perestroika*) largely centering on a freer market economy, but the economy stalled midway between central planning and free-market mechanisms.
    d. He instituted *glastnost,* or openness in society and politics, leading to much more freedom of speech.
    e. Democratization of the Soviet state was begun; free elections were held in 1989 for the first time since 1917.
2. Democratization encouraged demands for autonomy by non-Russian minorities.
3. Gorbachev withdrew troops from Afghanistan and encouraged reform in eastern Europe, repudiating the Brezhnev Doctrine.

IV. The revolutions of 1989
A. In Poland, Solidarity was again legalized and won overwhelmingly in free elections.
B. Popular resistance and Communist liberalization in Hungary led to the end of one-party rule and free elections in 1990.
    1. A multiparty democracy was established.
    2. Borders between Hungary and East Germany were opened.
C. Growing economic dislocation brought revolution in East Berlin.
    1. The Berlin Wall was opened.
    2. Communist leaders were swept out of power.
    3. East and West Germany moved rapidly toward unification.
D. The people of Czechoslovakia ousted the Communist bosses.
E. Only in Rumania was the revolution violent and bloody.
    1. Ceauşescu was executed.
    2. Rumania's political prospects remained uncertain.

V. The future in perspective
  A. The ability to anticipate the future is aided by a knowledge of what has happened in the past.
  B. Many predictions for the future are pessimistic and foretell environmental disaster, atomic warfare, or class and race struggles.
     1. The prediction of a great North-South or "rich versus poor," world struggle is based on erroneous data.
        a. In reality there are five or six distinct categories of nations in terms of income level.
        b. Further, cultural, religious, and political differences among nations make the prospect of a global class war unlikely.
     2. The greatest problem is nuclear arms proliferation.
  C. All in all, Western ideals of individual rights, representative government, and nationhood are alive and well.

Review Questions

1. What were the causes of the worldwide economic crisis of the 1970s and 1980s. Could anything have been done to prevent it?
2. What were the social consequences of economic stagnation in the 1970s and 1980s?
3. What was Willy Brandt's policy of reconciliation and why was it important?
4. What is meant by the statement that Brandt's election victories marked West Germany's political coming of age?
5. Why did the United States become involved in a war in Vietnam? Why did the Vietcong win?
6. What were the consequences of the Watergate crisis?
7. Compare and contrast American presence in Vietnam to Soviet presence in Afghanistan. What are the differences and the similarities?
8. What was the reason for the installation of American nuclear warhead missiles on West European soil?
9. What were the motives of the Czechoslovakian Communist party reform movement of 1968 under Dubček? Why did the experiment fail? Why didn't western Europe give support to Czechoslovakia?
10. What is meant by the re-Stalinization of the Soviet bloc and the Soviet Union? Give examples.
11. Discuss the Solidarity movement in Poland in terms of origins, objectives, and outcome. What is meant by the claim that it was a "self-limiting" revolution?
12. What were the motives and the methods of Gorbachev? What impact has he had on Soviet society? On eastern Europe?
13. Describe the revolutions of 1989 in eastern Europe. Who were the participants and what were the results?
14. Discuss the often-presented argument that a global class war between "rich" and "poor" nations is inevitable. Is this a sound argument?

Study-Review Exercises

Define the following key concepts and terms.

Bretton Woods Agreement of 1944

OPEC

stagflation

two German states within one German nation

rich nations/poor nations

re-Stalinization

Brezhnev Doctrine

détente

Helsinki Conferences of 1973 and 1975

Geneva accords

Tet offensive

Vietcong

"socialism with a human face"

Solidarity

perestroika

glasnost

Identify the following people and explain their significance.
Willy Brandt

Lyndon Johnson

Alexander Dubček

Mikhail Gorbachev

Pope John Paul II

Lech Walesa

Nicolae Ceaușescu

Explain what the following events were, who participated in them, and why they were important.
1973 oil crisis

Yom Kippur War

Iranian revolution of 1978–79

Solidarity revolution

Afghanistan war

Vietnam War

Willy Brandt's electoral victory of 1969

eastern European revolutions of 1989

Test your understanding of the chapter by providing the correct answers.

1. The first time OPEC acted as a unified front and obtained a solid price increase.

   _____

2. The economic crisis of the 1970s and 1980s *did/did not* result in social and political instability comparable to that of the 1920s.

3. The German chancellor who sought reconciliation between West Germany and eastern

   Europe. _____

4. It is apparent that by the 1960s West Germany *had/had not* firmly adopted liberalism and democracy.

5. Events in the Soviet Union and Eastern Europe in 1989 and 1990 confirmed that the Brezhnev Doctrine *was/was not* the official policy of the Soviet leadership.

Multiple-Choice Questions

1. Between 1944 and 1971 the international monetary system was based on the
   a. price of silver.
   b. floating rates of exchange.
   c. American dollar.
   d. supply of gold.

2. All but which of the following led directly to oil price increases in the 1970s?
   a. The Yom Kippur War
   b. The Vietnam War
   c. OPEC embargoes
   d. Khadafy's pressure on oil prices

3. The "misery index" indicates that the people who suffered most from the economic crisis of the 1970s and 1980s lived in
   a. the United States.
   b. Japan.
   c. western Europe.
   d. eastern Europe.

4. United States involvement in Vietnam had its origin in
   a. fear of French imperialism.
   b. the U.S. attempt to impose free elections on the Vietnamese.
   c. an attempt to stop communism.
   d. U.S. economic interests in Asia.

5. The Czechoslovakia experiment of 1968 sought
   a. socialism with a human face.
   b. the end of communism.
   c. the expulsion of the Soviets.
   d. the adoption of a capitalist economy.

6. The trend in the Soviet Union under Brezhnev was toward
   a. re-Stalinization.
   b. de-Stalinization.
   c. democratization.
   d. greater cultural freedom.

7. The first initiative to bring about reconciliation between eastern and western Europe was undertaken by
   a. Jimmy Carter.
   b. Margaret Thatcher.
   c. Willy Brandt.
   d. Mikhail Gorbachev.

8. The attempt to undertake a revolution based on the idea of "socialism with a human face" took place in
   a. Poland.
   b. the Soviet Union.
   c. Czechoslovakia.
   d. East Germany.

9. Which of the following contributed to the economic crisis that began the early 1970s?
   a. Collapse of the world monetary system
   b. End of war in the Middle East
   c. Low birthrates in western Europe
   d. Decrease in oil prices

10. The American president who vowed not to lose Vietnam was
    a. Lyndon Johnson.
    b. Richard Nixon.
    c. John Kennedy.
    d. Dwight Eisenhower.

11. The American president who applied economic sanctions against the Soviet Union was
    a. Richard Nixon.
    b. Lyndon Johnson.
    c. John Kennedy.
    d. Jimmy Carter.

12. The Brezhnev Doctrine declared that the
    a. Soviets will go ahead with arms buildup.
    b. Chinese were not true socialists.
    c. party must reform itself.
    d. Soviets had the right to intervene in any socialist country.

13. Which of the following characterized Poland under Communist rule?
    a. A strong Catholic church
    b. Little private ownership of land
    c. Strong economic growth
    d. A weak trade union movement under government control

14. Which of the following phrases characterizes the effect of the Czechoslovakian reform movement on everyday life in the Soviet Union?
    a. Fall in the standard of living
    b. Decline in nationalist spirit
    c. Decline in bureaucratic influence
    d. Re-Stalinization

15. The leader of the Polish Solidarity movement is
    a. Walesa.
    b. Dubček.
    c. Brezhnev.
    d. Gomulka.

16. In 1971 the American dollar
    a. fell in value against most currencies.
    b. rose in value against most currencies.
    c. was placed on a fixed rate of exchange against other currencies.
    d. was made the basis of the international monetary system.

17. The Yom Kippur War began with
    a. the British takeover of the Suez Canal.
    b. the Israeli attack on Egypt.
    c. the Egyptian and Syrian attack on Israel.
    d. American military support of Israel.

18. OPEC is dominated by
    a. Israel.
    b. non-Arab oil-producing countries.
    c. Arab oil-producing countries.
    d. the Soviet Union.

19. With regard to free elections in Vietnam, the position of the United States was
    a. refusal to support elections.
    b. strong support of free elections.
    c. support of elections in North Vietnam only.
    d. support of the Geneva Accord.

20. The Helsinki agreements of 1975 centered on
    a. the guarantee of human rights and existing political frontiers.
    b. the reduction of military spending and arms production.
    c. an international ban on nuclear testing.
    d. tensions between Israel and Egypt.

21. During the Brezhnev era it appears that
    a. educated people increasingly debated political ideas.
    b. specialists and scientists adhered to the traditional party line.
    c. there was a decrease in political consciousness.
    d. the public was not interested in issues like the environment or urban transportation.

22. *Glasnost* is based on the notion of
    a. the expansion of the Soviet state.
    b. revival of Stalinist thought.
    c. openness of speech and expression.
    d. economic reform.

23. The eastern European country that experienced considerable bloodshed and violence during its 1989 revolution was
    a. Hungary.
    b. East Germany.
    c. Rumania.
    d. Czechoslovakia.

24. An initial/massive exodus of Germans from East Germany began as a result of
    a. the opening of the Berlin Wall.
    b. the fall of Brezhnev.
    c. the reunification of Germany.
    d. the fall of the iron curtain in Hungary.

25. Generally speaking, by early 1990 the result of Gorbachev's *perestroika* was
    a. a revolutionized economy.
    b. considerable economic progress.
    c. initial improvements but overall a stalled economy.
    d. Gorbachev's downfall.

Major Political Ideas

Define *glasnost*. Is this a new phenomenon in Russian history or does it have roots in the Russian past?

Issues for Essays and Discussion

Some of the most important developments in Western society in the past thirty years have taken place in eastern Europe. Describe these developments by discussing the policies and actions of Brezhnev and Gorbachev in the Soviet Union. What impact did their policies have on the Soviet people and the people of eastern Europe?

Interpretation of Visual Sources

Study the photograph entitled "Willy Brandt in Poland, 1970" on page 1018 of your textbook. Who are the participants? Why was this regarded a momentous event? In what way does this photograph illustrate the importance of photographers as journalists?

Problems for Further Investigation

1. What are Mikhail Gorbachev's criticisms of the past and his recommendations for the present? Begin with his own book, *Perestroika: New Thinking for Our Country and the World** (1990), and that by W. B. Miller, *Toward a More Civil Society? The USSR Under Mikhail Sergevich Gorbachev* (1990).

2. Could the United States have won the war in Vietnam? Why were Vietnamese peasants able to withstand the onslaught of American military technology? Did the war contribute to the Watergate scandal? These questions and many others are considered in two collections of documents: M. Gettleman, J. Franklin, M. Young, and B. Franklin, eds, *Vietnam and America, A Documentary History* (1985), and W. A. Williams, T. McCormick, L. Gardner, and W. LaFeber, *America in Vietnam, A Documentary History* (1975). Also useful are two books of

---

*Available in paperback.

readings: J. Kimball, *To Reason Why: The Debate about the Causes of U.S. Involvement in the Vietnam War* (1990), and R. J. McMahan, ed., *Major Problems in the History of the Vietnam War* (1990). Both narrative and interpretation are provided in G. M. Kahin, *Intervention: How America Became Involved in Vietnam* (1986), and in S. Karnow, *Vietnam, A History** (1983).

---

*Available in paperback.

Primary Sources
The Vietnam War

The Vietnam War was extremely complex and evolved over a long period of time. The historian thus faces the task of uncovering the motives of all sides involved, including the French, who dominated Vietnam from the late nineteenth century until their expulsion in 1954, the Vietnamese people and their leaders, and the American government. The following two documents represent conflicting views: that of Ho Chi Minh, the nationalist leader of Vietnam (who was a communist), and Dwight Eisenhower, the president of the United States, who sets forth here what was to become a very popular American view of the world and justification for American engagement in Vietnam.

How did each use the past to analyze the present and to shape his view of the future? How did each see the role of Vietnam in world events? What appears to be the motives of each? Keep in mind that between 1945, when Ho's *Declaration* was made, and 1954, when Eisenhower made his statement, China became a communist state (1949) and imperialist France was on the verge of losing its hold on Vietnam.

The Declaration of Independence of Vietnam, September 2, 1945*

"All men are created equal. They are endowed by their Creator with certain inalienable rights; among these are Life, Liberty, and the pursuit of Happiness."

This immortal statement was made in the Declaration of Independence of the United States of America in 1776. In a broader sense, this means: All the peoples on the earth are equal from birth, all the peoples have a right to live, to be happy and free.

The Declaration of the French Revolution made in 1791 on the Rights of Man and the Citizen also states: "All men are born free and with equal rights, and must always remain free and have equal rights."

Those are undeniable truths.

Nevertheless, for more than eighty years, the French imperialists, abusing the standard of Liberty, Equality, and Fraternity, have violated our Fatherland and oppressed our fellow-citizens. They have acted contrary to the ideals of humanity and justice.

---

*Source: Ho Chi Minh, *Selected Works*, 4 vols. (Hanoi: Foreign Languages Publishing House, 1960–1962), 17–21.

In the field of politics, they have deprived our people of very democratic liberty.

They have enforced inhuman laws; they have set up three distinct political regimes in the North, the Center and the South Vietnam in order to wreck our national unity and prevent our people from being united.

They have built more prisons than schools. They have mercilessly slain our patriots; they have drowned our uprising in rivers of blood.

They have fettered public opinion; they have practised obscurantism against our people.

To weaken our race they have forced us to use opium and alcohol.

In the field of economics, they have fleeced us to the backbone, impoverished our people, and devastated our land.

They have robbed us of our rice fields, our mines, our forests, and our raw materials. They have monopolized the issuing of bank-notes and the export trade.

They have invented numerous unjustifiable taxes and reduced our people, especially our peasantry, to a state of extreme poverty.

They have hampered the prospering of our national bourgeoisie; they have mercilessly exploited our workers.

In the autumn of 1940, when the Japanese Fascists violated Indochina's territory to establish new bases in their fight against the Allies, the French imperialists went down on their bended knees and handed over our country to them.

Thus, from that date, our people were subjected to the double yoke of the French and Japanese. Their sufferings and miseries increased. The result was that from the end of last year to the beginning of this year, from Quang Tri province to the North of Vietnam, more than two million of our fellow-citizens died from starvation. On March 9, the French troops were disarmed by the Japanese. The French colonialists either fled or surrendered showing that not only were they incapable of "protecting" us, but that, in the span of five years, they had twice sold our country to the Japanese.

On several occasions before March 9, the Vietminh League urged the French to ally themselves with it against the Japanese. Instead of agreeing to this proposal, the French colonialists so intensified their terrorist activities against the Vietminh members that before fleeing they massacred a great number of our political prisoners detained at Yen Bay and Caobang.

Notwithstanding all this, our fellow-citizens have always manifested toward the French a tolerant and humane attitude. Even after the Japanese putsch of March 1945, the Vietminh League helped many Frenchmen to cross the frontier, rescued some of them from Japanese jails, and protected French lives and property.

From the autumn of 1940, our country had in fact ceased to be a French colony and had become a Japanese possession.

After the Japanese had surrendered to the Allies, our whole people rose to regain our national sovereignty and to found the Democratic Republic of Vietnam.

The truth is that we have wrested our independence from the Japanese and not from the French.

The French have fled, the Japanese have capitulated, Emperor Bao Dai has abdicated. Our people have broken the chains which for nearly a century have fettered them and have won independence for the Fatherland. Our people at the same time have overthrown the monarchic regime that has reigned supreme for dozens of centuries. In its place has been established the present Democratic Republic.

For these reasons, we, members of the Democratic Provisional Government, representing the whole Vietnamese people, declare that from now on we break off all relations of a colonial character with France; we repeal all the international obligation that France has so far subscribed to on behalf of Vietnam and we abolish all the special rights the French have unlawfully acquired in our Fatherland.

The whole Vietnamese people, animated by a common purpose, are determined to fight to the bitter end against any attempt by the French colonialists to reconquer their country.

We are convinced that the Allied nations which at Tehran and San Francisco have acknowledged the principles of self-determination and equality of nations, will not refuse to acknowledge the independence of Vietnam.

A people who have courageously opposed French domination for more than eighty years, a people who have fought side by side with the Allies against the Fascists during these last years, such a people must be free and independent.

For these reasons, we, members of the Provisional Government of the Republic of Vietnam, solemnly declare to the world that Vietnam has the right to be a free and independent country—and in fact is so already. The entire Vietnamese people are determined to mobilize all their physical and mental strengths, to sacrifice their lives and property in order to safeguard their independence and liberty.

The American Domino Theory: President Eisenhower's Press Conference of April 7, 1954*

Q: Robert Richards, Copley Press: Mr. President, would you mind commenting on the strategic importance of Indochina to[†] to the free world? I think there has been, across the country, some lack of understanding of just what it means to us.

THE PRESIDENT: You have, of course, both the specific and the general when you talk about such things.

First of all, you have the specific value of a locality in its production of materials that the world needs.

Then you have the possibility that many human beings pass under a dictatorship that is inimical to the free world.

Finally, you have broader considerations that might follow what you would call the "falling domino" principle. You have a row of dominoes set up, you knock over the first one, and what will happen to the last one is the certainty that it will go over very quickly. So you could have a beginning of a disintegration that would have the most profound influences.

Now, with respect to the first one, two of the items from this particular area that the world uses are tin and tungsten. They are very important. There are others, of course, the rubber plantations and so on.

Then with respect to more people passing under this domination, Asia, after all, has already lost some 450 million of its peoples to the Communist dictatorship, and we simply can't afford greater losses.

---

*Source: Dwight D. Eisenhower, "The President's News Conference of April 7, 1954," No. 73, *Public Papers of Presidents of the United States: Dwight D. Eisenhower, 1954* (Washington, D.C., GPO, 1960), 83.
[†]Vietnam was a part of the old French colony of Indochina.

But when we come to the possible sequence of events, the loss of Indochina, of Burma, of Thailand, of the Peninsula, and Indonesia following, now you begin to talk about areas that not only multiply the disadvantages that you would suffer through loss of materials, sources of materials, but now you are talking really about millions and millions and millions of people.

Finally, the geographical position achieved thereby does many things. It turns the so-called island defensive chain of Japan, Formosa, of the Philippines and to the southward; it moves in to threaten Australia and New Zealand.

It takes away, in its economic aspects, that region that Japan must have as a trading area or Japan, in turn, will have only one place in the world to go—that is, toward the Communist areas in order to live.

So, the possible consequences of the loss are just incalculable to the free world. . . .

Appendixes: Answers to Objective Questions
Outline Maps

Chapter 12

Study-Review Exercises

Test your understanding.

1. did not
2. bad
3. England, France
4. Lollards
5. economic
6. decrease

Place the following events in chronological order.

1. 2
2. 7
3. 3
4. 5
5. 1
6. 6
7. 8
8. 4

Multiple-Choice Questions

1. d
2. d
3. a
4. c
5. b
6. a
7. c
8. b
9. b
10. d
11. b
12. c
13. a
14. c
15. b
16. b
17. b
18. a
19. b
20. c
21. c
22. d
23. b
24. d
25. a

Chapter 13

Study-Review Exercises

Test your understanding.

1. Niccolò Machiavelli
2. less
3. increased
4. Thomas More
5. declined
6. is not

Multiple-Choice Questions

1. a
2. d
3. d
4. b
5. b
6. b
7. c
8. d
9. a
10. d
11. d
12. d
13. c
14. b
15. b
16. b
17. b
18. b
19. a
20. d
21. a
22. b
23. d
24. d
25. a

Chapter 14

Study-Review Exercises

Test your understanding.

1. did
2. king
3. political
4. Martin Luther
5. Alexander VI
6. was
7. weaken
8. Protestant

Multiple-Choice Questions

1. c
2. d
3. b
4. a
5. b
6. b
7. c
8. c
9. a
10. b
11. a
12. c
13. a
14. d
15. c
16. b
17. b
18. c
19. a
20. c
21. c
22. a
23. d
24. b
25. c

Chapter 15

Study-Review Exercises

Test your understanding.

1. Thirty Years' War
2. Cortez
3. Edict of Nantes
4. sixteenth
5. Gustavus Adolphus
6. the United Provinces of the Netherlands
7. Amsterdam
8. Elizabeth I
9. skepticism
10. Charles V
11. Concordat of Bologna
12. Portugal

Multiple-Choice Questions

1. a
2. b
3. d
4. d
5. d
6. b
7. a
8. b
9. a
10. c
11. a
12. b
13. c
14. c
15. b
16. b
17. b
18. d
19. d
20. c
21. d
22. b
23. c
24. a
25. c

Chapter 16

Study-Review Exercises

Test your understanding.

1. stadholder
2. Colbert
3. entered
4. disaster
5. John Churchill
6. Laud
7. Calvin

Multiple-Choice Questions

1. b
2. d
3. a
4. d
5. d
6. a
7. d
8. b
9. a
10. d
11. c
12. d
13. d
14. b
15. c
16. b
17. a
18. a
19. c
20. c
21. a
22. a
23. d
24. b
25. a

Chapter 17

Study-Review Exercises

Test your understanding.

1. Peter the Great
2. increased
3. Suleiman the Magnificent
4. maintained
5. Frederick II (the Great)
6. weaker

Place the following events in chronological order.

1. 4
2. 1
3. 3
4. 2
5. 5
6. 6

Multiple-Choice Questions

1. d
2. c
3. d
4. a
5. c
6. a
7. d
8. b
9. a
10. b
11. b
12. c
13. b
14. b
15. c
16. c
17. b
18. a
19. a
20. b
21. c
22. a
23. a
24. a
25. a

Chapter 18

Study-Review Exercises

Test your understanding.

1. water, earth
2. did not
3. motion
4. universal gravitation
5. philosophy
6. Portugal
7. was not
8. did not
9. skeptic
10. Newton
11. failed

Place the following events in chronological order.

1. 4
2. 1
3. 5
4. 2
5. 3

Multiple-Choice Questions

1. a
2. b
3. c
4. d
5. d
6. c
7. b
8. d
9. d
10. b
11. a
12. a
13. a
14. b
15. a
16. c
17. b
18. d
19. c
20. d
21. a
22. a
23. c
24. c
25. a

Chapter 19

Study-Review Exercises

Fill in the blank line.

1. i	3. e	5. g	7. b
2. c	4. j	6. a	8. f

Multiple-Choice Questions

1. c	8. a	15. a	22. d
2. a	9. b	16. d	23. d
3. d	10. d	17. b	24. c
4. c	11. a	18. b	25. a
5. b	12. b	19. a	
6. a	13. a	20. b	
7. a	14. a	21. a	

Chapter 20

Study-Review Exercises

Test your understanding.

1. limited	3. did	5. longer	7. the common people
2. was not	4. potato	6. cowpox	8. Wesley

Multiple-Choice Questions

1. b	8. d	15. b	22. d
2. d	9. b	16. c	23. c
3. b	10. c	17. d	24. a
4. c	11. c	18. a	25. c
5. c	12. d	19. d	
6. b	13. a	20. b	
7. a	14. d	21. d	

Chapter 21

Study-Review Exercises

Test your understanding.

1. Trafalgar
2. an important
3. Thomas Paine
4. a great deal of
5. victory
6. a military ruler

Multiple-Choice Questions

1. c
2. d
3. d
4. a
5. d
6. c
7. c
8. a
9. d
10. c
11. d
12. d
13. a
14. c
15. a
16. a
17. a
18. b
19. b
20. d
21. d
22. a
23. d
24. d
25. b

Chapter 22

Study-Review Exercises

Test your understanding.

1. 1780/textile
2. increased
3. James Watt
4. iron
5. Liverpool-Manchester, *Rocket*
6. decrease
7. Crystal Palace
8. decreased
9. greater
10. Zollverein
11. decrased
12. Factory, decrease

Multiple-Choice Questions

1. d
2. a
3. d
4. a
5. a
6. b
7. b
8. b
9. b
10. d
11. b
12. a
13. b
14. a
15. a
16. c
17. a
18. d
19. d
20. a
21. c
22. a
23. d
24. b
25. d

Chapter 23

Study-Review Exercises

Test your understanding.

1. defeat
2. Louis Napoleon
3. Eugène Delacroix
4. should not
5. Austrian
6. Johann Herder
7. Louis Blanc
8. competition/victory

Multiple-Choice Questions

1. a
2. a
3. b
4. c
5. c
6. a
7. c
8. c
9. b
10. d
11. a
12. d
13. b
14. d
15. c
16. b
17. c
18. a
19. d
20. c
21. b
22. d
23. a
24. d
25. a

Chapter 24

Study-Review Exercises

Test your understanding.

1. decreased
2. Bentham
3. antiseptic
4. 1890
5. improved
6. no change
7. labor aristocracy
8. rose
9. music halls
10. love
11. stronger
12. more
13. decreased

Multiple-Choice Questions

1. a
2. b
3. a
4. c
5. a
6. d
7. a
8. d
9. c
10. b
11. a
12. c
13. a
14. c
15. d
16. c
17. d
18. c
19. b
20. b
21. c
22. b
23. a
24. b
25. a

Chapter 25

Study-Review Exercises

Test your understanding.

1. approved
2. middle class
3. defeat, freedom
4. opposed
5. fell
6. Protestant, against
7. France

Multiple-Choice Questions

1. b	8. c	15. a	22. d
2. b	9. c	16. b	23. a
3. c	10. b	17. d	24. d
4. d	11. c	18. b	25. c
5. b	12. b	19. b	
6. c	13. c	20. c	
7. a	14. d	21. a	

Chapter 26

Study-Review Exercises

Test your understanding.

1. Lord Kitchener
2. Khedive Ismail
3. H. M. Stanley
4. Evelyn Baring
5. Walter Bagehot
6. Commodore Perry
7. Sun Yat-sen
8. Tzu Hsi

Multiple-Choice Questions

1. c	8. d	15. a	22. a
2. d	9. b	16. b	23. c
3. b	10. a	17. c	24. c
4. a	11. a	18. a	25. d
5. b	12. b	19. a	
6. b	13. c	20. a	
7. c	14. b	21. d	

Chapter 27

Study-Review Exercises

Test your understanding.

1. Belgium
2. Vladimir Lenin
3. Georges Clemenceau
4. Leon Trotsky
5. Rasputin
6. Schleiffen
7. June 28, 1914
8. Alexander Kerensky
9. soviets
10. T. E. Lawrence
11. Brest-Litovsky
12. Bismarck
13. Black Hand
14. Russia
15. Duma

Place the following events in chronological order.

1. 1
2. 4
3. 3
4. 2
5. 5
6. 7
7. 6
8. 8

Multiple-Choice Questions

1. c
2. a
3. c
4. c
5. b
6. c
7. b
8. c
9. d
10. c
11. d
12. b
13. c
14. c
15. a
16. a
17. a
18. b
19. a
20. d
21. d
22. a
23. d
24. c
25. b

Chapter 28

Study-Review Exercises

Test your understanding.

1. were not
2. Germany, Britain, France, the United States
3. Paul Valéry
4. discard
5. challenge
6. J. M. Keynes

Multiple-Choice Questions

1. a
2. b
3. c
4. c
5. c
6. a
7. a
8. d
9. c
10. a
11. c
12. a
13. a
14. d
15. c
16. c
17. d
18. d
19. c
20. b
21. b
22. c
23. d
24. c
25. b

Chapter 29

Study-Review Exercises

Test your understanding.

1. favored
2. refused
3. victory/disaster
4. right
5. do not
6. Benito Mussolini
7. was
8. Adolf Hitler
9. declined
10. pro-German
11. did not

Multiple-Choice Questions

1.	d	8.	c	15.	d	22.	c
2.	d	9.	c	16.	d	23.	c
3.	d	10.	c	17.	c	24.	c
4.	a	11.	c	18.	a	25.	d
5.	a	12.	c	19.	b		
6.	d	13.	c	20.	b		
7.	c	14.	a	21.	c		

Chapter 30

Study-Review Exercises

Test your understanding.

1. Chiang Kai-shek
2. Marshall Plan
3. Warsaw Pact
4. Charles de Gaulle

Multiple-Choice Questions

1.	c	8.	d	15.	b	22.	b
2.	a	9.	d	16.	b	23.	a
3.	a	10.	b	17.	c	24.	c
4.	b	11.	b	18.	a	25.	b
5.	d	12.	d	19.	b		
6.	d	13.	b	20.	c		
7.	c	14.	d	21.	b		

Chapter 31

Study-Review Exercises

Test your understanding.

1. decreased	4. less	7. an increase	9. significant
2. fall	5. greater	8. less	10. greater
3. increased	6. declined		

Multiple-Choice Questions

1. c	8. b	15. d	22. d
2. c	9. a	16. d	23. a
3. c	10. a	17. c	24. d
4. d	11. b	18. b	25. c
5. a	12. d	19. a	
6. c	13. a	20. b	
7. c	14. c	21. c	

Chapter 32

Study-Review Exercises

Test your understanding.

1. 1971	3. Willy Brandt	5. was not
2. did not	4. had	

Multiple-Choice Questions

1. c	8. c	15. a	22. c
2. b	9. a	16. a	23. c
3. c	10. a	17. c	24. d
4. c	11. d	18. c	25. c
5. a	12. d	19. a	
6. a	13. a	20. a	
7. c	14. d	21. a	

Outline Map 13.1

Outline Map 14.1

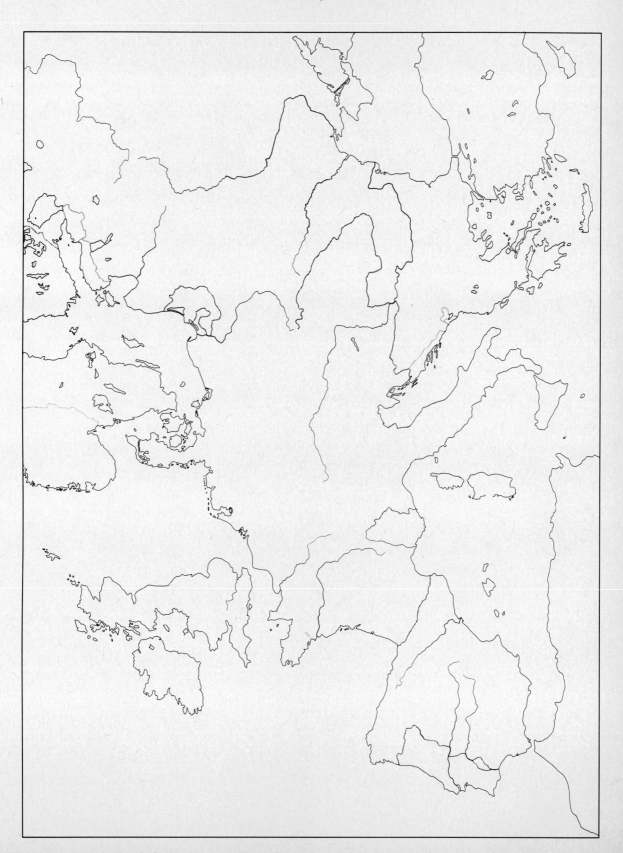

Outline Map 15.1

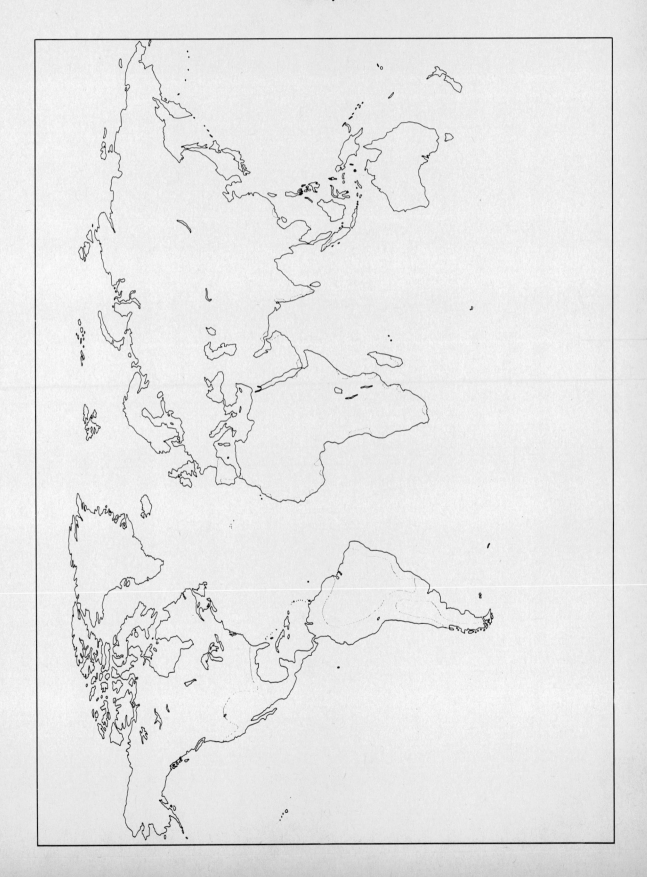

Outline Map 15.3

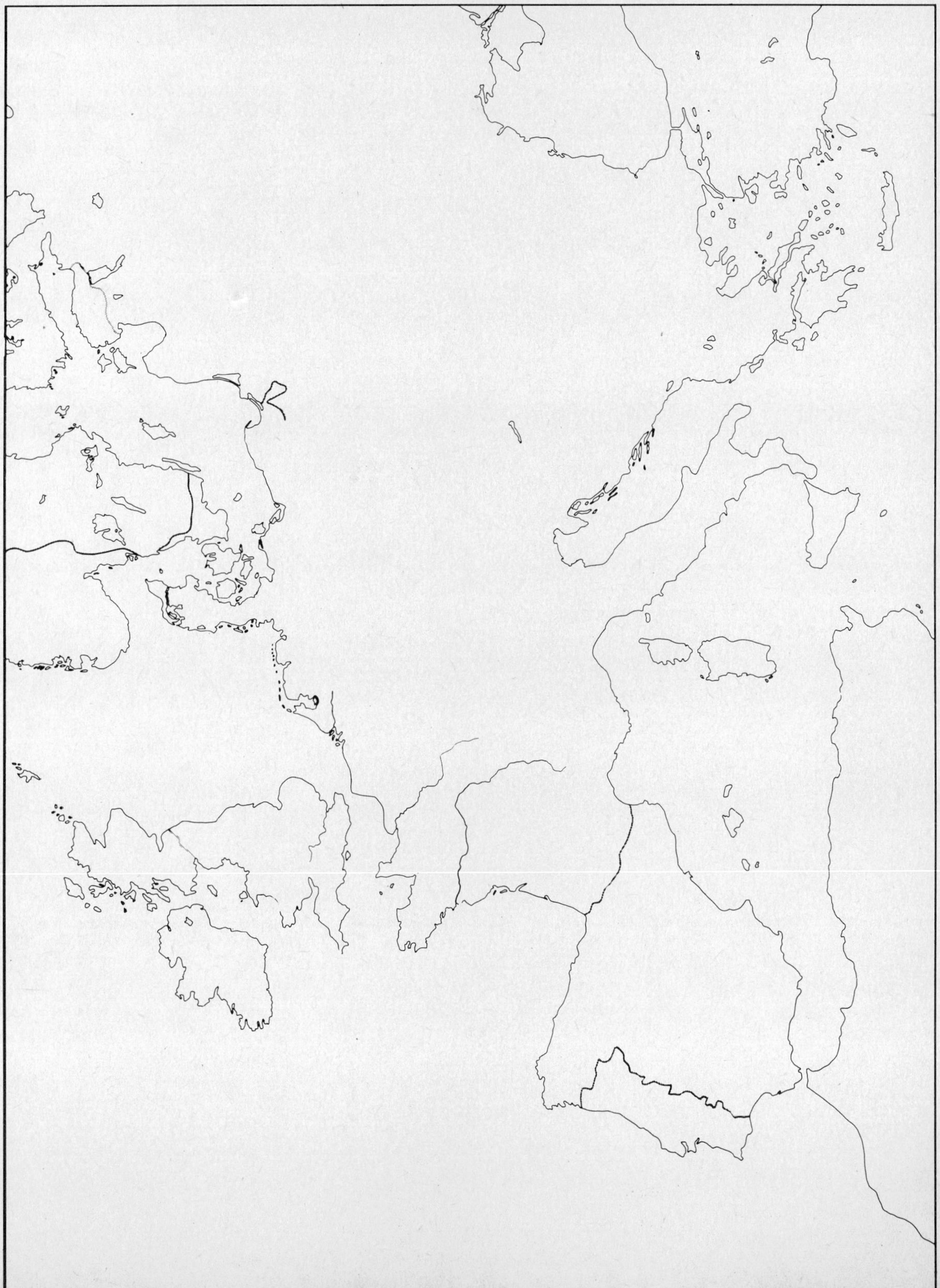

Outline Map 16.1

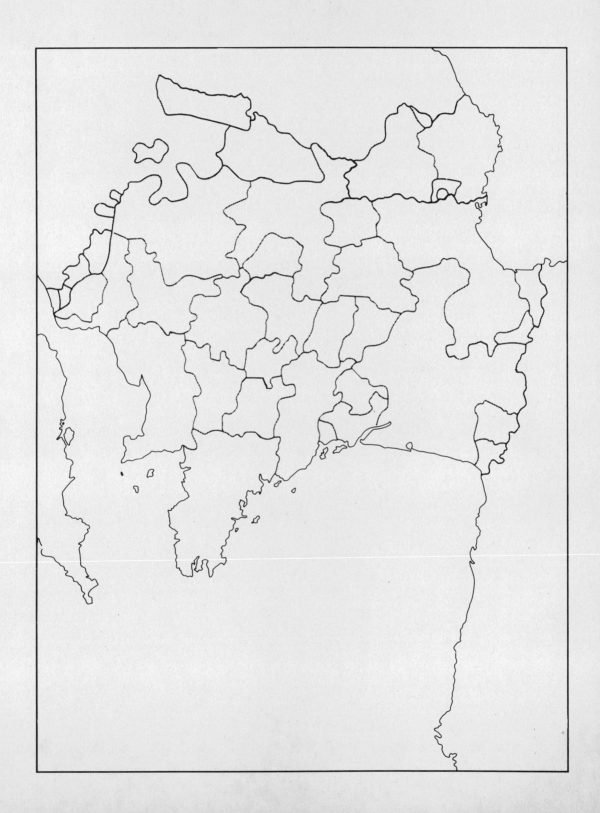

Outline Map 17.3

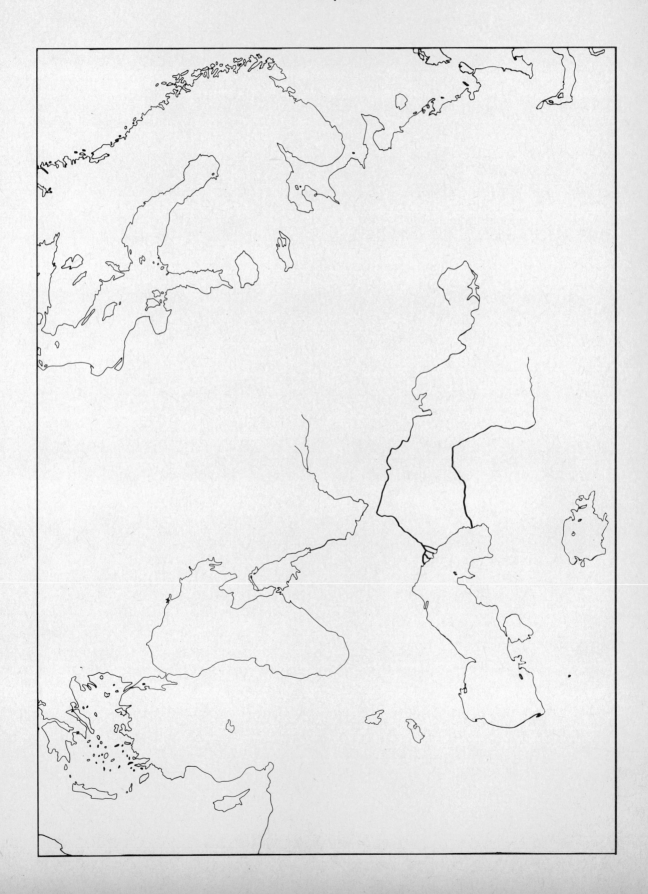

Outline Map 19.3

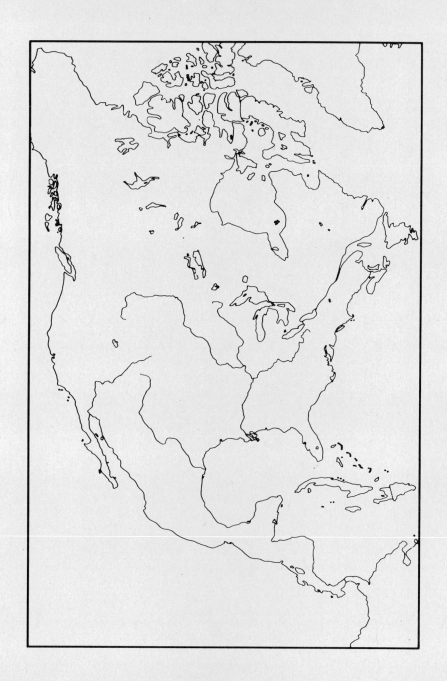

Outline Map 21.1

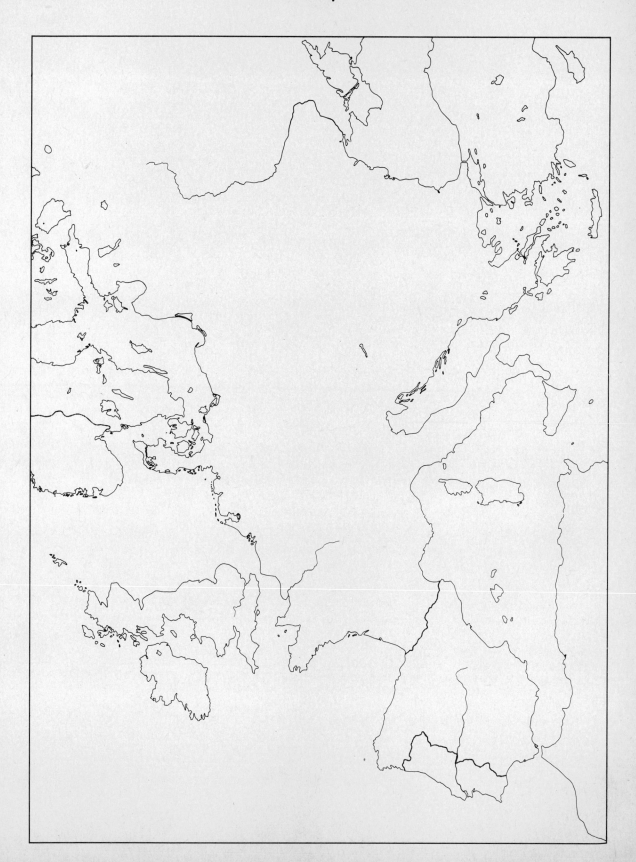

Outline Map 23.1

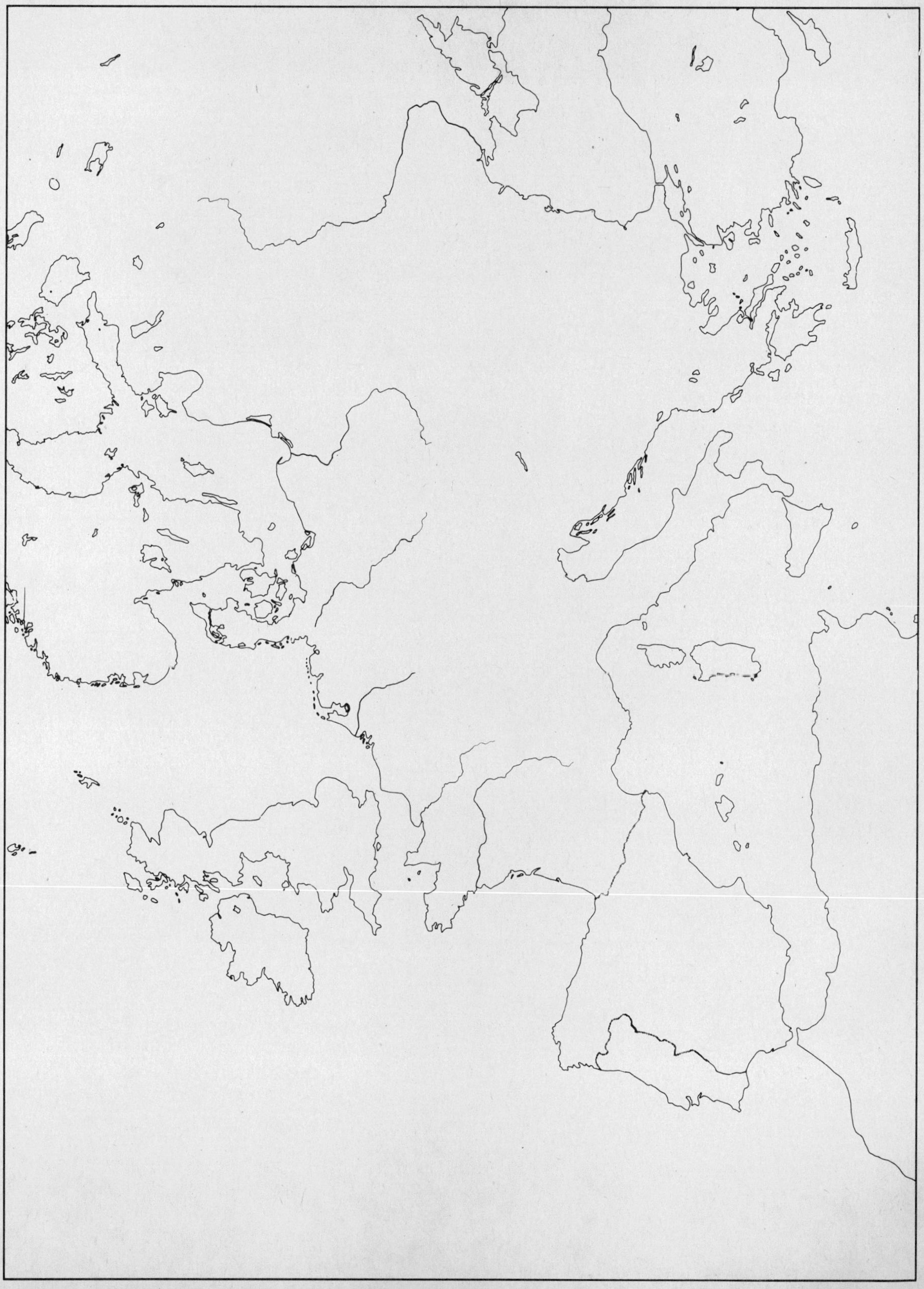

Outline Map 25.2

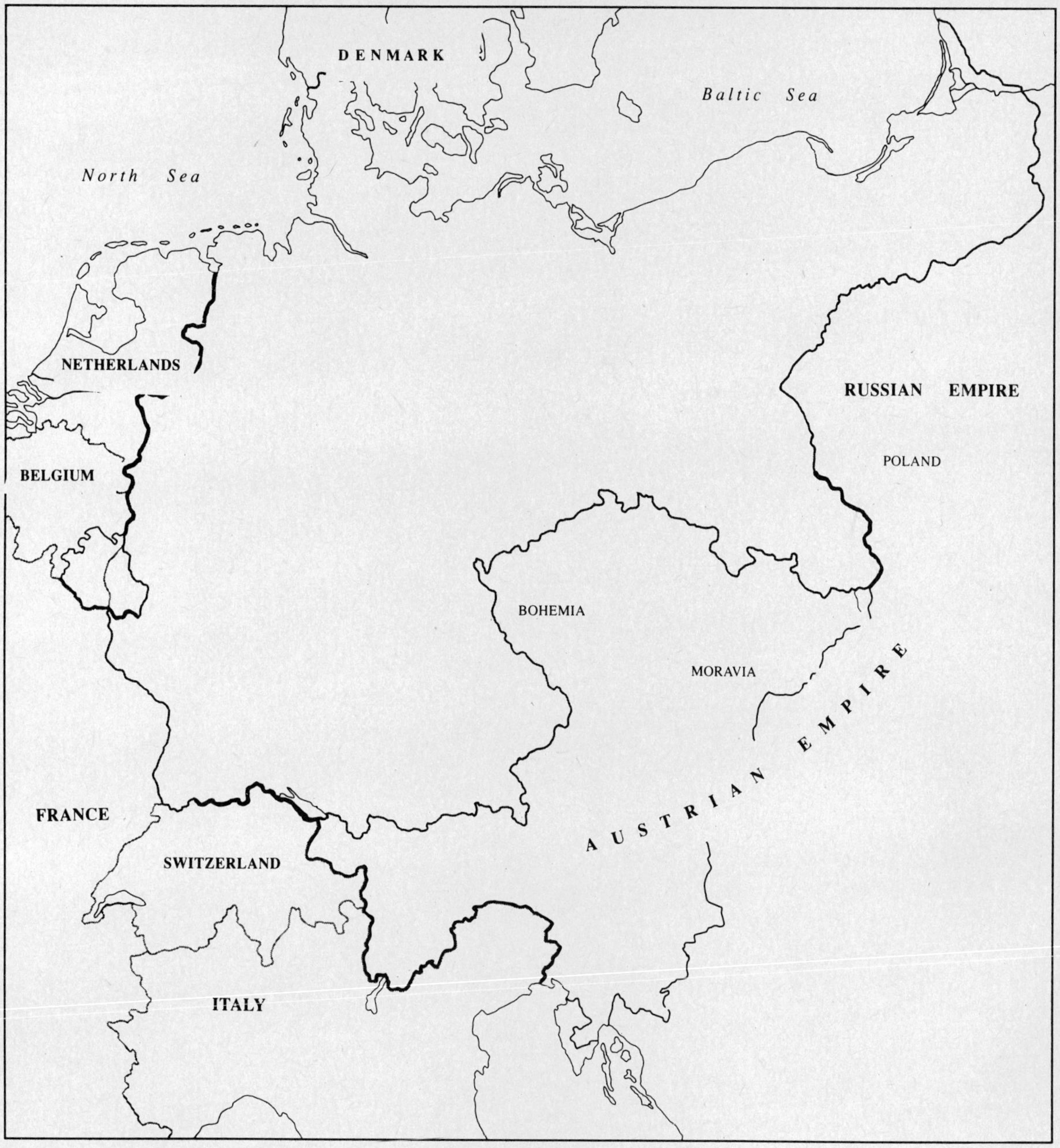
DENMARK
Baltic Sea
North Sea
NETHERLANDS
RUSSIAN EMPIRE
POLAND
BELGIUM
BOHEMIA
MORAVIA
AUSTRIAN EMPIRE
FRANCE
SWITZERLAND
ITALY

Outline Map 26.2

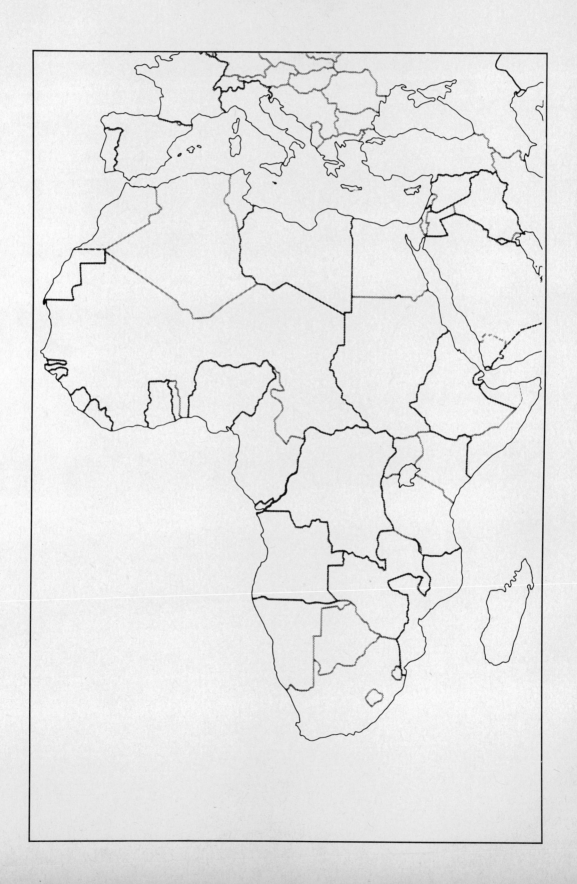

Outline Map 26.3

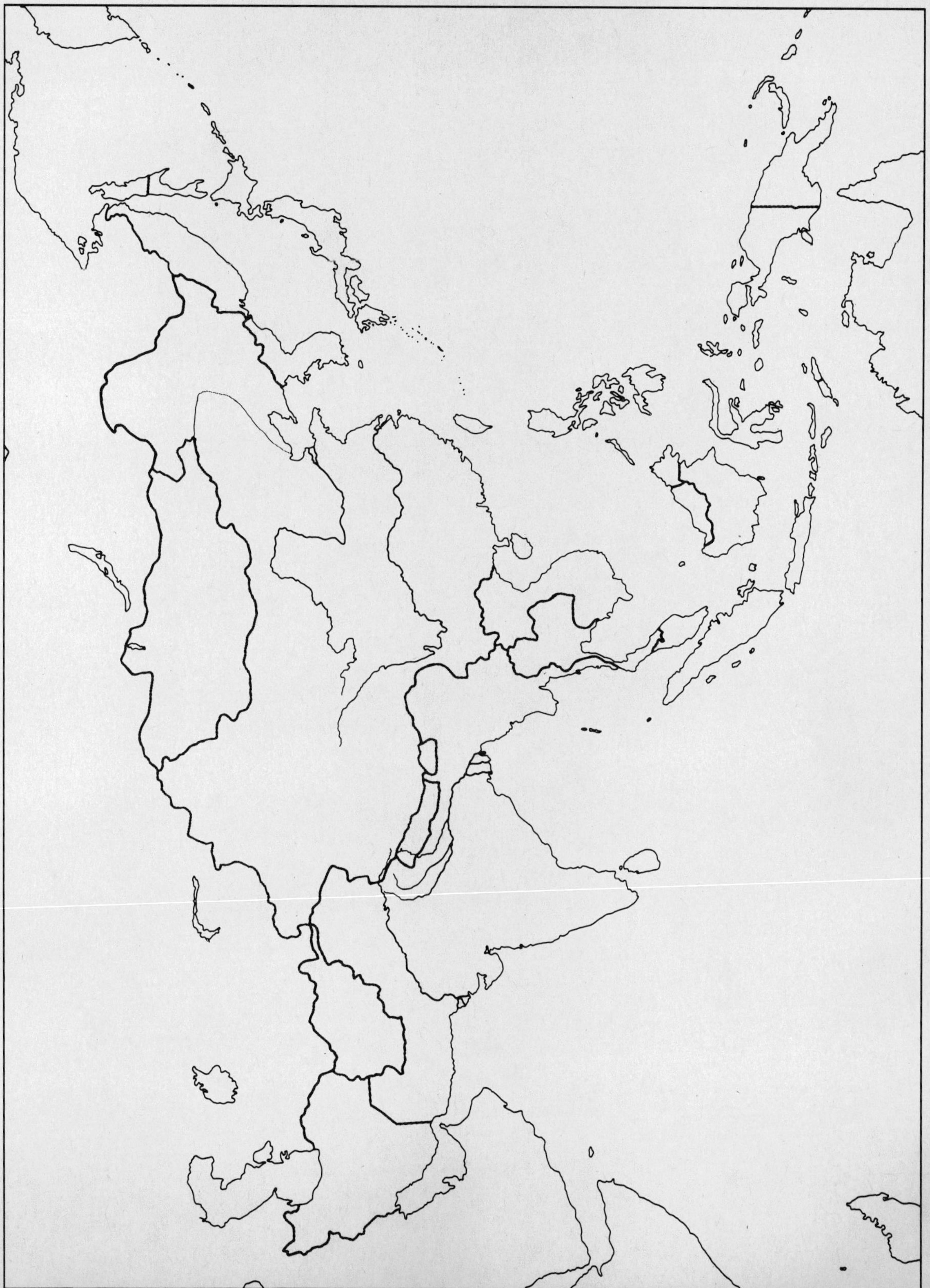

Outline Map 27.4

Outline Map 29.1

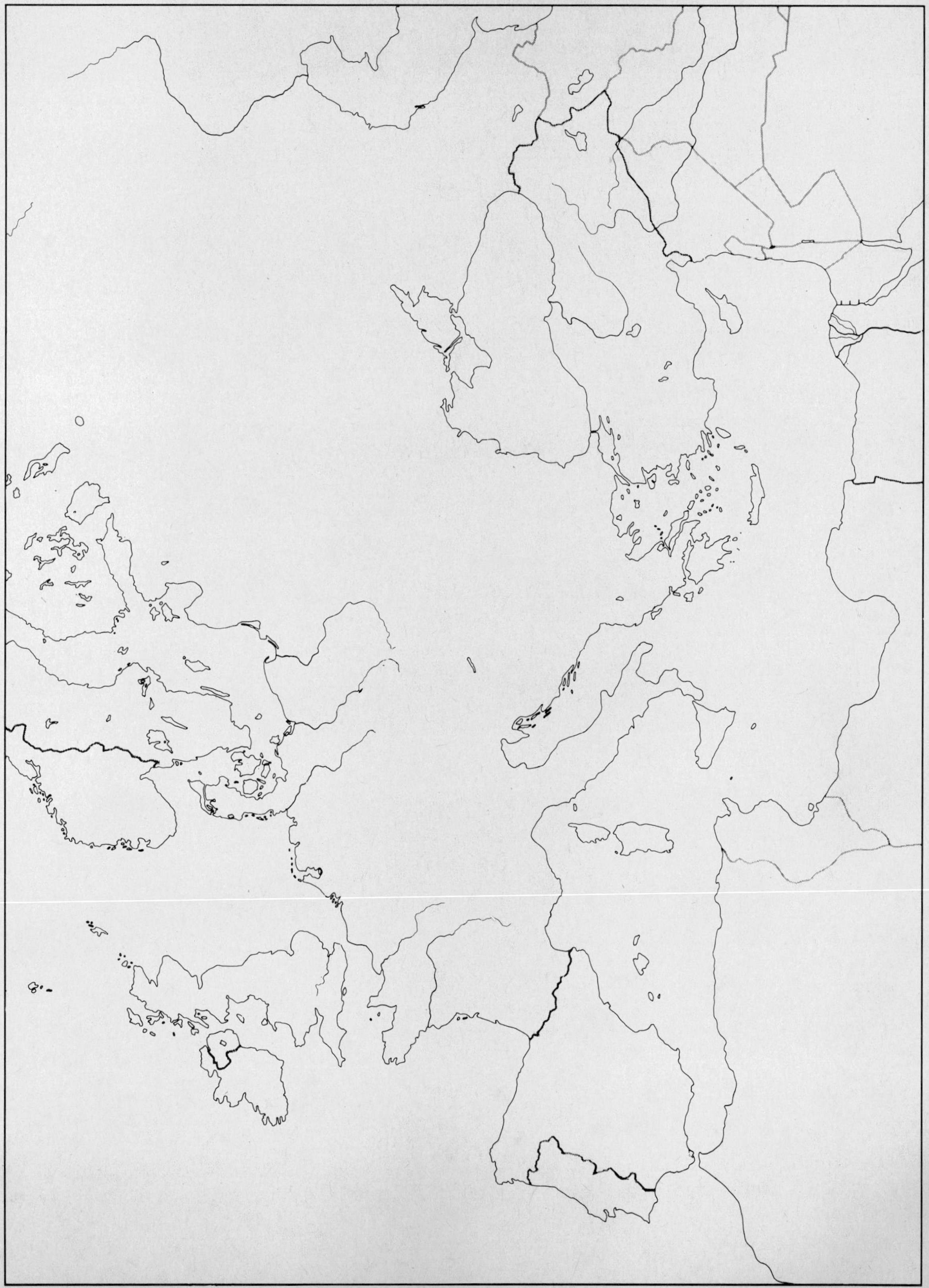

Outline Map 30.2

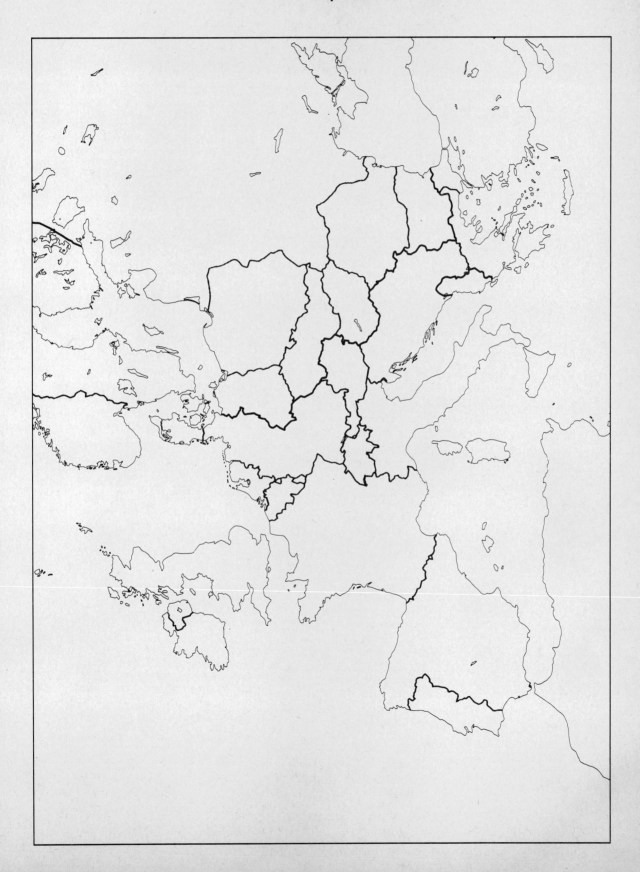